Nation-Building and Ethnic Integration in Post–Soviet Societies

Nation-Building and Ethnic Integration in Post–Soviet Societies

An Investigation of Latvia and Kazakstan

EDITED BY

Pål Kolstø

Westview Press
A Member of the Perseus Books Group

Copyright © 1999 by Westview Press, A Member of the Perseus Books Group

Published in 1999 in the United States of America by Westview Press, 5500 Central Avenue, Boulder, Colorado 80301-2877, and in the United Kingdom by Westview Press, 12 Hid's Copse Road, Cumnor Hill, Oxford OX2 9JJ

Find us on the World Wide Web at www.westviewpress.com

A CIP catalog record for this book is available from the Library of Congress.
ISBN 0-8133-3697-X

The paper used in this publication meets the requirements of the American National Standard for Permanence of Paper for Printed Library Materials Z39.48-1984.

10   9   8   7   6   5   4   3   2   1

Contents

Preface   vii
About the Contributors   viii
List of Tables and Figures   ix

1   **Aims and Aspirations,** *Pål Kolstø*   1
    Levels of Analysis, 8

2   **Bipolar Societies?** *Pål Kolstø*   15
    A Question of Identities, 15
    The Case for Fragmented Societies, 18
    Cross-Cutting Cleavages Among the Major Cultural
        Groups: The Case for Continuous Societies, 29
    Shared Experiences: The Case for
        Homogeneous Societies, 39
    Conclusion, 41

3   **Nation-Building and Social Integration Theory,** *Pål Kolstø*   44
    Nation-Building, 44
    Social Integration, 48
    The Applicability of Nation-building / Integration
        Theory to Non-Western Societies, 54
    Nations and Nation-Building in Eastern Europe, 56
    The Applicability of Nation-Building / Integration
        Theory to Post-Communist Realities, 59

4   **Nation-Building and Ethnic Integration in Latvia,**   63
    Aina Antane and Boris Tsilevich
    Background, 63
    Demographic Dynamics after the
        Restoration of Independence, 68
    Integration on the Political Level, 75
    The Political Rhetorics of Nation-Building, 81
    The Citizenship Issue, 85
    Political Representation and Participation, 99

The Language Situation, 108
Language in Education, 121
Ethnic "Division of Labour" and
    Socio-Economic Stratification, 132
Differences of Perceptions, 138
Russophone Organizations, 141
The Impact of the Russian Federation on Latvian
    Nation-Building and Ethnic Integration, 145
Conclusions, 149

5   **Political Integration in Kazakstan**, *Jørn Holm-Hansen*   153
    Civic vs. Ethnic Models of Integration, 153
    The Demographic Controversy, 157
    Nation-Building: Political Rethoric and Doctrines, 163
    Ethnicity and Legislation, 175
    Political Institutions and Integration, 191
    Non-State Organizations, 214
    Conclusions, 223

6   **Attitudinal and Linguistic Integration in Kazakstan
    and Latvia,**   227
    Irina Malkova, Pål Kolstø, and Hans O. Melberg
    Superordinate/Subordinate Relationships, 227
    Social Stratification, 232
    Political Identities and Allegiances, 236
    Cultural Identities and Forecasts, 240
    Ways and Means to Foster Ethnic Integration, 265
    Conclusions, 271
    Methodological Appendix, 275

7   **Comparisons and Conclusions,** *Pål Kolstø*   281
    Cultural Diversity, Stability and Democracy, 281
    Consociationalism, 284
    Stability through Domination, 288
    Stability through De-Bipolarization, 299
    What the Future Holds, 310
    Summing Up, 314

Bibliography   317
Index   335

Preface

This book is based on the research project "Integration and nation-building in bi-cultural post-Soviet societies, the cases of Latvia and Kazakstan," which was financed by The Norwegian Research Council, Programme for Eastern Europe, Project no. 110191/730. The team has consisted of two Norwegians, project coordinator Pål Kolstø, University of Oslo, and Jørn Holm-Hansen, the Norwegian Institute of Regional and Urban Research; two Latvians, Aina Antane, Institute of History, Latvian Academy of Sciences, and Boris Tsilevich from the independent research institute Baltic Insight; and one Kazakstanian, Irina Malkova from the Giller Institute in Almaty. At a later stage Hans O. Melberg was included in the team.

We present the report as a unified whole, not a collection of papers on related topics. The project was conceived in a fruitful dialogue among the research collaborators and we have all contributed with important inputs to the over-all scheme. The chapters are nevertheless signed by the person(s) who wrote them and we are responsible for each our own parts. The Latvian and Kazakstani contributions have been translated from Russian by the editor.

In compliance with the wishes of Kazakstan's political authorities we use the official spelling of the republic's name, i.e. *Kazakstan*, throughout the book (quotations excepted), rather than the more conventional "Kazakhstan." In line with this, we spell the attendant ethnonym thus: Kazak(s).

The book could never have been written without the invaluable support from our two outstanding project assistants, Solveig Rossebø and Hans Olav Melberg. We also would like to thank the following persons for having taken the time and effort to read and comment upon several chapters, sometimes even the entire book: Aadne Aasland, Shirin Akiner, Olga Brusina, Juris Dreifelds, David Laitin, Hans Olav Melberg, Aleksej Semenov, Graham Smith, Anton Steen and Øyvind Østerud. Many of the comments we received were extremely useful and helped us redo the original manuscript into a more coherent and, we believe, better book. Needless to say, the inconsistencies and shortcomings that remain are entirely our own responsibility.

Professor Pål Kolstø
Department of East European and Oriental Studies, University of Oslo
November 1998

About the Contributors

Aina Antane is head of department of educational and social projects at the Multinational Culture Center, Riga.

Jørn Holm-Hansen is a researcher (political science) at the Norwegian Institute for Urban and Regional Research, Oslo.

Pål Kolstø is professor of Russian and East European Area Studies at the University of Oslo.

Boris Tsilevich is a Research consultant at the Center for Educational and Social Research "Baltic Insight", and a member of the Saeima (Parliament) of the Republic of Latvia.

Irina Malkova is Director of the Research Group "Central Asian Project in Almaty."

Hans O. Melberg is a project assistant at the University of Oslo.

Tables and Figures

Tables

2.1	Language Shifts and Bilingualism in Kazakstan, Based on the 1989 Census.	31
2.2	Language Shifts and Bilingualism in Latvia, Based on the 1989 Census.	32
2.3	Marriages by Ethnicity in Kazakstan, 1978 and 1988	35
2.4	Marriages by Ethnicity in Kazakstan, 1978 and 1988	35
4.1	Ethnic Composition of Latvia's Population (1897–1989, Percentages)	64
4.2	Ethnic Changes in Latvia's Population since Independence	70
4.3	Age Structure of Ethnic Groups in Latvia (1989)	70
4.4	Ethnic Composition of Citizenry and Ethnicity of Non-Citizens (February 1996)	95
4.5	Representation of Ethnic Groups in the Parliaments of Latvia	101
4.6	Ethnic Composition of Citizens by Administrative Districts (1995)	104
4.7	Share of School-Age Children Attending Minority Schools, by Ethnic Groups (1995)	132
4.8	Who Should Have Priority For Employment in the Situation of Scarce Jobs?	137
4.9	Assessment of Main Threats to Peace and Security in Latvia	141
5.1	Migration of Russians and Kazaks (1991–1996)	160
5.2	Language of Executives in Kazakstanian Work-Places	180
5.3	Percentage Claiming That They Have Experienced Problems Carrying Out Their Profession Due to Lack of Knowledge in the "State Language"	181
5.4	Use of Language among Kazak Children	185
5.5	Number of Teaching Institutions Using Kazak as Language of Instruction Closed in 1996	185
5.6	Primary Schools and Language of Instruction (1996–97)	185

5.7   Students at institutions of Higher Learning in
       Kazakstan, 1995-96 School Year, by Language of
       Instruction   187
5.8   Ibid., by Nationality   187
5.9   Ethnic Composition of Leading Positions in Oblast
       Administration in 1992 and 1993 in Relation to Ethnic
       Composition of Oblast Population   197
5.10   Ethnic Composition of Leading Positions in Oblast
       Administration in 1992 and 1993. Percentage of Slavs   197
5.11   The Ethnic Composition of the Kazakstani Parliaments   203
5.12   Percentage Supporting President and Parliament   205
5.13   Which Institution Guarantees Inter-Ethnic Stability?   205
5.14   Type and Number of Administrative Units (1996)   207
5.15   The Relative Size of Maslikhat and Akimat in Three
       Localities   208
6.1   Time of Residence (% of total)   228
6.2   Do You Consider That You Belong to An Ethnic Minority?   229
6.3   Ibid.,—Ethnic Breakdown. Kazakstan   229
6.4   Ibid.,—Ethnic Breakdown. Latvia   229
6.5   Who Are Considered to Belong to a Minority Group?   231
6.6   Ibid.,—Ethnic Breakdown. Kazakstan   231
6.7   Ibid., Ethnic Breakdown. Latvia   231
6.8   Qualities Believed to Be Essential to Succeed in
       Kazakstan   233
6.9   Qualities Believed to Be Essential to Succeed in Latvia 233
6.10   In Which Ethnic Group Do We Find Most Rich People?   235
6.11   Ibid., Ethnic Breakdown. Kazakstan   235
6.12   Ibid., Ethnic Breakdown. Latvia   235
6.13   Are You Proud of Being a Kazakstanian?—Ethnic
       Breakdown   237
6.14   Are You Proud of Being a Latviets/Latvijas Iedzivotajs? 237
6.15   Which Country Do You Regard as Your Homeland?   239
6.16   Country Identification—Ethnic Breakdown Kazakstan   239
6.17   Country Identification—Ethnic Breakdown. Latvia   239
6.18   How Important Do You Think It Will Be to Master
       Kazak and Russian in Your Oblast Ten Years From
       Now?—Ethnic Breakdown   242
6.19   How Important Will Command of the Kazak Language
       Be in Your Oblast Ten Years From Now?   242
6.20   How Important Will Command of the Russian Language
       Be in Your Oblast Ten Years From Now?   242
6.21   How Important Do You Think It Will Be to Master
       Latvian in Your Region in 10 Years?   245

6.22   How Important Do You Think It Will Be to Master
        Russian in Your Region in 10 Years?   245
6.23   How Important Do You Think It Will Be to Master
        Latvian and Russian in Your Region in 10 Years?—Ethnic
        Breakdown   245
6.24   Parents' vs. Children's Language of Instruction in School,
        Kazakstan   247
6.25   Language of Instruction in School, Parent Generation—
        Ethnic Breakdown. Kazakstan   247
6.26   Parents vs. Children's Language of instruction in
        School—Ethnic Breakdown. Kazakstan   247
6.27   Parents vs. Children's Language of Instruction in School.
        Latvia   249
6.28   Parent vs. Children Language of Instruction in School—
        Ethnic Breakdown. Latvia   249
6.29   Cultural Self-Identification. Kazakstan   251
6.30   Coefficients of Cultural Self-Identification—Ethnic,
        Educational and Geographic Breakdown. Kazakstan   251
6.31   Which Culture Do You Consider Yourself as a
        Representative of? Latvia....   253
6.32   Cultural Self-Identification—Ethnic, Educational and
        Geographic Breakdown. Latvia   253
6.33   Do You Think That the Possibility of the Extinction of
        the Kazak Nation Exists?   255
6.34   Ibid., Breakdown by Oblast   255
6.35   Ibid., Ethnic Breakdown   255
6.36   What Will Happen to the Culture of the Russians in
        Kazakstan in the Future?   257
6.37   What Will Happen to the Future of the Culture of the
        Russians in Kazakstan?—Ethnic Breakdown Kazakstan   257
6.38   What Will Happen to the Future of the Culture of the
        Russians in Latvia?—Ethnic Breakdown   258
6.39   Do Russians in Kazakstan Differ From Russians in
        Russia?—Ethnic Breakdown   260
6.40   Do Russians in Kazakstan Differ From Russians in
        Russian?—Breakdown by Oblast   260
6.41   Do Russians in Latvia Differ From Russians in Russia?—
        Ethnic Breakdown   260
6.42   Ibid., Breakdown by Region   260
6.43   Perceived Peculiarities of Russian Culture. Kazakstan   262
6.44   Perceived Peculiarities of Russian Culture. Kazakstan—
        Average Coefficient, Ethnic Breakdown   263

6.45   Perceived Peculiarities of Russian Culture in Kazakstan.
       Kazak and Russian Ranking Lists   263
6.46   Perceived Peculiarities of Russian Culture. Latvia   263
6.47   Kazak Perceptions of How to Best Promote interethnic
       Consolidation   266
6.48   Latvian Perceptions of How to Best Promote Inter-Ethnic
       Consolidation   266
6.49   Nontitulars Perceptions on How to Contribute to the
       Improvement of interethnic Relations in Kazakstan   269
6.50   Nontitulars Perceptions on How to Contribute to the
       Improvement of interethnic Relations—Ethnic
       Breakdown. Kazakstan. Coefficients.   269
6.51   Non-Titulars' Perceptions on How to Contribute to Ethnic
       Integration in Latvia   270
6.52   Non-Titulars Perceptions on How to Contribute to the
       Improvement of Interethnic Relations—Ethnic
       Breakdown. Latvia   270
6.53   Distribution of Respondents by Oblasts. Kazakstan   275
6.54   Distribution of Respondents by Educational Levels.
       Kazakstan   276
6.55   Distribution of Respondents by Age. Kazakstan   276
6.56   The Ethnic Composition of the Kazakstani Sample   277
6.57   The Ethnic Composition of the Samples. Latvia   278
6.58   Samples by Educational Levels. Latvia   279
6.59   Age Distribution. Latvia   279

Figures

3.1   Congruent and Incongruent Orientations Towards
       Centripetal and Centrifugal Trends of Subordinates as
       Viewed by Themselves and Superordinates   53
4.1   Population of Latvia (1986-1996)   69
4.2   Ethnic Make-Up of the Largest Towns in Latvia   71
4.3   Natural Increase of Latvian and Non-Latvian Groups
       (1985–1995)   71
4.4   External Migration in Latvia (1989–1995)   73
4.5   Share of Citizens Within Main Ethnic Groups in Latvia
       (February 1996)   96
4.6   Results of Parliamentary Elections in Three Electoral
       Districts (1995)   106
4.7   Electoral Preferences of Latvians and Russian-Speakers
       (1995)   107

4.8	Knowledge of Languages by Ethnic Groups (1989)	109
4.9	Mother Tongue of Latvia's Residents	110
4.10	Results of the State Language Tests (1992)	116
4.11	Changes of Latvian Language Command by Ethnic Groups	119
4.12	Main Language of Communication in Family (1994)	120
4.13	Number of Pupils in Schools of Latvia by Their Instruction Language (Absolute Numbers)	122
4.14	Language of Instruction in Latvia´s Schools	128
4.15	Number of Schools in Latvia by Language of Instruction	128
4.16	Number of Students in Minority Schools (Classes) in Latvia	130
4.17	Whom Do You Consider to Belong to the New Rich in Latvia?	134
4.18	Ownership of Private Enterprise by Ethnicity, 1993	135
4.19	Ethnic Structure of Employed and Unemployed Residents of Latvia (1996)	135
4.20	Support of Latvia's Independence	139
4.21	Evaluation of the Threat of Extinction of the Latvian Nation	139
5.1	Map of Ethnic Kazaks in Kazakstan	154
5.2	Administrative Map of Kazakstan	155
6.1	Are You Proud of Being A Latviets/Kazakstanian?	236
6.2	How Important Do You Think It Will Be To Master Kazak and Russian in Your Oblast Ten Years From Now? (All Respondents)	241
6.3	How Important Do You Think It Will Be To Master Latvian and Russian in Your Oblast Ten Years From Now?	244
6.4	Do Russians in [Your Country] Differ From Russians in Russia?	259
7.1	Congruent and Incongruent Orientations Towards Centripetal and Centrifugal Trends of Subordinates as Viewed by Themselves and Superordinates	315

1

Aims and Aspirations

Pål Kolstø

Following the demise of Communism, fifteen new states were established in the former Soviet Union. A "state," however, in the full sense of the word, does not come about simply by political proclamation of independence, still not by international recognition. A modern state must have control of its frontiers, a monopoly of coercive powers on its territory, be able to collect levies and taxes, and so on. To carry out these tasks a modicum of administrative apparatus is needed, as well as a broad consensus in society concerning rules and routines for how the jobs shall be done.

In the fall of 1991 these preconditions were generally not fulfilled in any of the Soviet successor states. The armed forces on their territories and the levers of economic policy were beyond the control of the new state authorities. There were also no border defense systems, indeed, state borders were not even delineated in the terrain.

In this book, we will leave aside the economic and security problems of the new states and instead focus on some crucial political and cultural issues, "nation-building" as distinct from "state-building." In order to keep a state together in the modern world, it is essential that its population have a common identity and a shared feeling of common destiny. The citizens must be bound together by loyalty toward the same institutions, symbols, and values. This does not imply that all inhabitants of the state must partake in the same ethnic identity. National identity may, and in many cases must, be political rather than cultural.

The USSR prided itself on being a "multinational state," indeed, some hundred different ethnic groups were registered as living in its territory. In contrast, with the exception of Russia, all of the successor states have been proclaimed as "national states" or "nation-states." This basic concept can have (at least) two very different meanings. In the West, the dominant understanding is that of a political and civic entity, in which the nation is delineated on the basis of common territory, common government, and, to some extent, common political history. There exists, however, a rival concept of a nation as a cultural entity, based on common language, traditions, mores, and religion, in short: an *ethnic* nation.

In a civic nation-building project the authorities will try to secure the political loyalty of all inhabitants without encroaching upon their cultural distinctiveness. Political rights are extended to all inhabitants on an equal footing. Political traditions and symbols common to all ethnic groups are cultivated, or, if necessary, created from scratch. One of the shortcomings of this strategy is the weaker emotive power of supraethnic symbols. They may easily by dismissed as artefacts, which, of course, in a sense they are. Nevertheless, large population groups in multiethnic societies may develop a double set of identities: Politically, they are proud of being citizens of this or that particular state; culturally, they identify strongly with their own ethnic group.

In ethnic nation-building the symbols and traditions of the state are identified with the symbols and traditions of the titular nation. The state authorities try to bring about a maximum correspondence between the ethnic and political nation. The preferred methods are outmigration of the minorities and/or their exclusion from political decision-making. In principle, border revisions transferring minority-inhabited regions to neighboring countries could also lead to greater cultural homogeneity of the state, but few if any nation-builders will gladly countenance a truncation of the state territory.

From a demographic point of view all Soviet successor states, with the exception of Armenia, must be characterized as "multiethnic." In the cases of Latvia and Kazakstan, however, even this description is rather misleading. In these states we do not find one dominant titular nationality surrounded by numerous ethnic minorities but basically two cultures, both of which are held together by a common language of in-group communication: the culture of the indigenous ("titular") group, and the Russophone culture. In both Latvia and Kazakstan the "Russophones" comprise between forty and fifty percent of the total population – depending on the criteria used for definition.

Donald Horowitz distinguishes between two basic types of multiethnic states, centralized and dispersed. In dispersed systems, such as Tanzania, there are a number of major ethnic groups, none of which are able to dominate the others. Ethnic conflicts in such states usually take place in the periphery of the system, while the center may be able to pose as an impartial arbiter, elevated above particular group interests. Ethnic tensions in such societies may be severe, but they do not involve competition for control of the state or threaten its existence. "In such circumstances, the center usually has some flexibility. The demands of one group can sometimes be granted without injuring the interests of others."[1]

In centrally focused ethnic systems in Horowitz' typology, on the other hand, basically two cultural groups are confronting each other. Both of them may have a fair chance of securing control of the state apparatus. To the extent that politics are polarized along ethnic lines, pace Horowitz, such states are inherently unstable constructions:

> A centrally focused system possesses fewer cleavages than a dispersed system, but those it possesses run through the whole society and are of greater magnitude. When conflict occurs, the center has little latitude to placate some groups without antagonizing others. Conflict is not easily compartmentalized, and problems cannot be dealt with one at a time; they involve the whole state.

The degree to which a system is either dispersed or centralized is a function of group size to state size. For a centralized system, the ratio of 1:2 represents the extreme case.

Horowitz points out that when we determine the size of the various groups we should not be misled by objective indicators of ethnic group identity.

> Group size in many cases depends on the ability of subgroups to forge a common identity. This, in turn, depends heavily on perceived similarities among subgroups *vis-à-vis* other groups they confront. Given the dependence of group identity on felt distance from other groups, it is not surprising that states with large groups relative to state size have often experienced intensely hostile relations among the groups.

Classical examples of states where such an ethnodemographic structure has led to savage bloodshed and even to the total collapse of state order, are Rwanda, Burundi, and Sri Lanka.

The country which perhaps most closely fits Horowitz' typology is India. In fact, this subcontinent might be said to illustrate both of his ideal types in consecutive order, first as a highly volatile centralized system, second as a dispersed system in which ethnic violence has been on the whole containable. On the eve of independence the British crown colony of India was bitterly polarized along religio-cultural lines—Muslim vs. Hindu. The departure of the colonial power

---

[1] Horowitz 1985, 38.

unleashed communal violence of horrendous proportions. After 1949, on the other hand, "rump"-India has been a motley ethnolinguistic mosaic with numerous crosscutting cleavages. There are multiple potential and actual trouble spots, and, while blood has certainly been shed, the violence has never approached the dimensions of the partition turmoil, even remotely. Thus, the higher the number of trouble spots, the less trouble, or so it might seem.

In ethnodemographic, structural terms Latvia and Kazakstan fit Horowitz' definition of a centrally focused ethnic system. In these states, the Latvians, respectively the Kazaks, were an officially recognized category in the Soviet ethnic taxonomy, and continue to be so today. This is not the case with the other major cultural group in these countries, the Russophones. However, as I will argue in the next chapter, they fulfill Horowitz' criterion of a composite group with a high degree of perceived similarities among subgroups *vis-à-vis* other groups within the same territory.

As Timothy Sisk has pointed out, dire predictions of a steady slide into anarchy in multinational states have in many cases not been borne out. Since ethnic conflict does not always lead to violence Sisk suggests that we should try to identify the specific circumstances under which it is likely to happen. In particular, he points to three kinds of circumstances that are pertinent to our study. Firstly, he agrees with Horowitz that "dual societies," such as Rwanda or Sri Lanka, in which two ethnic groups compete for power in a zero-sum game, are especially intractable. Second, times of transition (both in the international system and in states) may be particularly perilous: In such periods ethnic relations "can deteriorate into intractable warfare at an unexpectedly precipitous rate."[2] Finally, "the expropriation of the symbols, power, and resources of the state to the exclusion of significant components of the population in multiethnic societies is a strong indicator of the likelihood of ethnic violence."[3]

If this analysis is correct these circumstances should lead us to expect a high level of ethnically motivated violence in both Latvia and Kazakstan. The rapid collapse of the Soviet state and communist system would seem to be the paradigmatic case of a transition period. Moreover, in both countries the titular group—the Latvians and the Kazaks—have, as we shall soon demonstrate, to a remarkable degree succeeded in appropriating political power for themselves and molding the symbols of the state around their own ethnic traditions and values.

---

[2] Sisk 1996/1997, 21.

[3] Ibid., 18.

Thus, it would not be amiss to expect a veritable carnage as the most likely outcome of transition politics in both Latvia and Kazakhstan.

Indeed, in both of these countries ethnic issues have played a very important role in politics since independence. At the same time, however, both states have so far, to a remarkably high degree, been spared the communal violence which has erupted in many other Soviet successor states. Unlike most other states with a centrally focused ethnic system and in contrast also to most other post-Communist countries of Eastern Europe, Latvia has faced no ethnic conflicts entailing violence since the very beginning of "Atmoda," the national revival during perestroika.

Similarly, in spite of the riots in Alma-Ata in December 1986, the leaders of Kazakstan have been able to portray their country as an oasis of stability in the otherwise very volatile Asian part of the former Soviet Union.[4] Official Kazakstani propaganda tries to foster a common supraethnic, civic Kazakstani identity among all citizens. Nevertheless, the tensions between the two major cultural–linguistic groups in both countries remain acute.

Stated very simply, the aim of this book is to explain the failure of "the Horowitz thesis," to name it thus for the sake of brevity, to be borne out—even under "Sisk circumstances" in Latvia and Kazakstan since independence. This failure—or perhaps it is only an apparent failure—may be explained in different ways: These countries may be the exceptions that prove the rule; they may not yet have reached the point where the dynamics required by the Horowitz thesis are set in motion; or the thesis, as summarized here, may indeed be in need of some modification.

Although we take Horowitz' seminal book as our starting point, we will not necessarily follow its multifaceted methodology in the execution of our task. Instead, we will draw on a wide variety of theoretical and methodological sources concerned with either nation-building and/or ethnic integration. Nation-building and ethnic integration we regard as two separate but interrelated and overlapping aspects of ethnic politics in new multiethnic states.

Rather than "centrally focused systems" we will use the term "bipolar societies" to designate the type of societal structures we find in Latvia and Kazakstan. This term is preferred also by certain other researchers who have analyzed ethnic politics in societies with a

---

[4] A detailed Western report recognizes that rivalry between Russians and Kazaks played some role in triggering "the December events," but generally downplays the ethnic aspect. See *Conflict in the Soviet Union*, 1990, 4.

similar demographic structure.[5] "Bipolar" societies, as we define this concept, is a subcategory, a narrower term than "bicultural," another term which may be encountered in the research literature. As used in this book "bipolar societies" have two basic characteristics: First, there are two, clearly distinguishable, major sociocultural groups in society, not more nor less; second, these two groups are demographically of roughly equal size.

The number of states in the world that fall into this category is relatively small. In our opinion, in the former Soviet Union only two states—Latvia and Kazakstan—qualify. Moldova and Estonia, for instance, where the titular nationality makes up approximately two-thirds of the total population, fall outside our purview.[6] By this narrowing down of criteria for "bipolar societies," we believe, we will be testing "the Horowitz thesis" at its strongest point.

To be sure, there are significant differences between Latvia and Kazakstan. While the former is a small country, the size of Ireland, with no more than 2.5 million inhabitants, the latter covers a territory as large as Western Europe, with a population of more than 18 million. In Latvia, the titular nation are Europeans who tend to see the Russians as bearers of a more Eastern, "Asian" culture than themselves. In Kazakstan, by contrast, the Russophones are regularly referred to as "the Europeans." The linguistic preconditions for interethnic intercourse are also very different in the two countries: Russians in Kazakstan are today learning Kazak almost from scratch—0.9 percent claiming fluency in the 1989 census—while in that same census as many as 22 percent of the Russians in Latvia claimed to be fluent in Latvian.[7]

Finally, since Latvia enjoyed political independence in the interwar period, nation-building in this country from the outset enjoys a source of legitimacy which Kazakstan is lacking. The recent statehood also means that in this state ethnic issues have to a large extent been commingled with the citizenship issue and with the need to redress the effects of the Soviet occupation in a way that has no parallel in Kazakstan. However, precisely this combination of important similarities and dissimilarities between the two cases makes, we believe, a comparison of Latvia and Kazakstan a potentially fruitful endeavor.

---

[5] In particular, Milne 1981.

[6] They are, however, the subject of a follow-up study to this book which has been ongoing throughout 1997 and 1998, involving two Estonian, two Moldovan and two Norwegian researchers. This new study is also comparative and focuses on the preconditions for ethnic conflict, or the absence thereof, in culturally heterogeneous countries.

[7] Data on bilingualism in the Soviet Union are subject to many problems of interpretation. The census-takers asked only about "fluency," (*svobodno*), while command of the local language on a more modest level was not recorded. See, e.g., Tishkov 1997, 85–98.

In both Latvia and Kazakstan "integration" is a key concept in the official state strategy to eliminate the bipolarization of society and to ease ethnic tensions.[8] This policy is regarded both as a safeguard of domestic stability and as a precondition for the democratic development of the state. However, the conceptual understanding of different varieties of integration—on the level of political leadership and among the populace at large—is far from transparent. The state authorities regularly complain that the Russians resist integration. It is frequently asserted that as members of a "great culture" the Russians consider it demeaning to them to be integrated into such a small culture as the Latvian or into such a young and undeveloped culture as that of the Kazaks. Many Russophones, however, insist that the absence, or slow speed, of integration is primarily due to the obstacles their integration efforts are met with from the side of the state authorities and from the members of the titular group.

Obviously, the key concept of "integration" is implicitly imbued with very different meanings by the protagonists. Vello Pettai has remarked that "For some, it may be a positive agenda for developing ethnic harmony and coexistence. For others it may seem a euphemism for assimilating a vulnerable minority population into a newly-dominant ethnopolitical order."[9] Generally speaking the idea of "integration" seems to be far less popular among the general populace than among the political elite. This is apparently true of titulars and nontitulars alike. An elderly Latvian woman quoted in *The Baltic Times* in May 1998 claimed that "Integration is a utopian idea," while a speaker at a Russophone rally in Riga in the same month accused the authorities of lying: "When they say integration, what they really mean is assimilation."[10]

Indeed, while the integration of national minorities in states with a clearly dominant culture would seem to be a feasible endeavor, in theory at least, it is far less clear what integration could or should mean in bipolar societies. Does it mean the integration of one culture into the other, or the mutual integration of both cultures? Does it imply cultural integration or primarily integration into social and political structures? To what extent will the Russophones in Latvia/Kazakstan have to distance themselves from the culture / the state of their "historical fatherland" (Russia, Ukraine, etc.) in order to be truly integrated into their present country of residence? Could it be true (as many of the minorities claim), that the retention of strong cultural links to the

---

[8] For Kazakstan, see, e.g., Nazarbaev 1994; Baitenova 1995a. For Latvia, see Pettai 1996.

[9] Pettai 1996, 49.

[10] *The Baltic Times*, 7–13 May 1998, p. 2; *The Baltic Times*, 21–27 May 1998, p. 5.

"historical fatherland" is a precondition for their successful political and social integration? These crucial issues are still covered under thick clouds of rhetoric and conceptual confusion in most of the former Soviet Union.

Anticipating the more detailed and technical discussion below,[11] I will here offer a brief outline of our own understanding of ethnic integration. Drawing upon a typology elaborated by R.A. Schermerhorn we see integration as a process involving, in principle, two actors: a superordinate and a subordinate group. Within the subordinate group some individuals may want to be accepted as full-fledged members of the superordinate (dominant) group and be totally immersed in it, while others may want to hold on to their separate identity, their separate social structure, and, in general, their own traditional way of life.

The sum of individual aspirations within a group Schermerhorn calls its "modal tendency." This tendency may be pointing toward the center of society, toward increased group involvement in the larger society, and/or a gradual eradication of cultural differences in the population. The modal tendency may also be centrifugal, pointing away from the center of society, toward autonomy (cultural and/or political), or, in extreme cases, full separation (secession).[12]

However, it takes two to dance a tango, and the goals of the subordinate group may be frustrated by the actions and attitudes of the dominant group. Integration is brought about when a centripetal modal tendency within the subordinate group is met by acceptance in the dominant group and is facilitated (or at least not impeded) by the nation-building and ethnic policies of the state authorities.

Levels of Analysis

The processes of integration and nation-building in Latvia and Kazakstan are in this book analyzed on two different levels (political integration and social integration), each of which is divided into various sublevels.

Political Integration

Level of Political Discourse. On this level we analyze official pronouncements outlining the attitudes of the authorities toward ethnic

---

[11] See p. 52–54.
[12] Schermerhorn 1970, 81ff.

integration and their understanding of this concept. We try to track down the usages of the word "integration" and related key concepts (such as "mono-communal state," *odnoobshchinnoe gosudarstvo*) among the various actors, including the academic community of nationality experts in each country.

Legislative Level. Here, we focus on the passing of legal and sublegal acts (laws, decrees, ordinances, regulations, statutes, etc.) defining and affecting the nontitular ethnic groups. Methodologically it is important to keep 1a and 1b apart since they may (though need not) conflict with each other. In some cases, harsh political rhetoric may be intended for "internal consumption," that is, to show that the authorities are not "soft on minorities," in order to make nationalists among the titular group more willing to accept a reasonably liberal minority legislation. Conversely, liberal political language may be used as a screen to cover a multitude of legislative and administrative misdeeds *vis-à-vis* the minorities.

Operationally, on this level we are concerned with content analysis of relevant political pronouncements and official texts, as well as with "context analysis" of the same, by examining law-implementation practices and the sociopolitical background of political statements. Our sources are the mass media in both countries (primarily printed media) in addition to official bulletins, parliamentary proceedings, and the like.

Participatory and Representative Levels. A good indicator of actual, as opposed to declared or intended, political integration is the number of representatives from minority groups in parliaments, elected offices, and state administrations. Such representation is the combined result of several factors. On the one hand, it is a product of the political activity/passivity of the minorities themselves. If they decide to remain aloof from politics and do not to make use of the ballot box and other vehicles to promote their candidates, they will most likely have few spokespersons in the corridors of power.

However, the levels of minority representation may also be actively influenced by the state authorities. Even in formally democratic states the authorities may be engaged in deliberate gerrymandering of minority involvement in politics. Such manipulation may in principle take two courses: it may be intended both to boost and to reduce the involvement of the minorities. Open and covert mechanisms may be set in motion to lower the political participation of the minorities, or to make it less effective. The electoral system may be designed in such a way that it deliberately reduces the representation of parties supporting minority interests. Or, as was the case in the Soviet Union, the ethnic minorities may be secured an almost mathematically exact representation in the putatively highest organs of state power, but these organs are effectively emasculated. The real loci of power are other institutions, over which members of the superordinate group have complete control.

However, the state authorities may instead conclude that it is in their own interest to have the leaders of the minority communities on the inside. They may open up various channels of information from these groups into the government by means of round tables, consultative minority councils, etc. Through cooption minority leaders may also become coresponsible for austerity programs and other unpopular policies.

At the same time, a high political visibility of persons with a minority background may simply be a matter of tokenism. Individuals who do not enjoy the support or even the respect of the ethnic communities they hail from, are hand-picked to unimportant positions at the top. This latter strategy may well be combined with schemes for the deliberate sidelining of popularly acknowledged minority leaders.

The legal preconditions for participatory and representative integration in Kazakstan and Latvia are very different. While Latvia after independence restricted the citizenship rights of post-World War II immigrants, Kazakstan adopted the so-called zero option of citizenship, according to which all permanent residents in the territory of the state were recognized as original citizens and officially given full political rights. Thus, the preconditions for political participation in this country, one would think, should be better than in Latvia.

However, the political representation of the non-titular population also in Kazakstan is considerably lower than their share of the total population.[13] Apparently, the Russians are either uninterested in politics, or they are deliberately and actively excluded from the political structures by informal mechanisms of exclusion. A combination of these two explanations is also possible.

Social Integration

Below the levels of legislation and political rhetoric, social processes of integration—or of increased bipolarization—are taking place. These processes are to some extent influenced by political developments, but may also operate by their own dynamics quite independent of them, and, in turn, determine the preconditions of the ethnopolitical discourse. These social processes are complex and sometimes contradictory. In our analysis we isolate two aspects and target them for particular scrutiny.

---

[13] See the sub-chapter on representative organs in chapter 5.

Attitudinal Integration. At this level we have tried to identify typical attitudes of the two cultural groups toward each other as well as their reciprocal stereotype perceptions (hetero-stereotypes). Do they see their relationship as one of dominance/subordination, or as nonhegemonial? What kind of characteristics and qualities do they ascribe to each other? Are the local Russians and other Russophones regarded as different from Russians in Russia, or are they all of the same kind? If the local Russians are considered to possess any characteristic traits, what are these traits?

Furthermore, we tried to find out to what degree the various groups feel emotionally attached to their country of residence. Do they identity with its titular culture? Have they developed any sense of pride in or patriotism toward this new—or newly restored—political creation? Or do they perhaps regard another country as their motherland? In the latter case, their political orientation must be characterized as strongly centrifugal.

We engaged a public opinion research institute in each country to carry out surveys among a large number of respondents. The responses we received indicated that on some issues there are significant and sometimes unexpected (to our team at least) differences in attitudes and stereotype ethnic perceptions between the two countries as well as among the various respective population groups in each of them.

Linguistic Integration. Our respondents were questioned not only about their attitudes and opinions but also about their actual life stories. In particular, we were interested to find out if there were any signs of a shift in school choices in the two countries, from Russian schools to schools offering education in the titular language. In order to detect intergenerational shifts we asked first what kind of school the parents had been educated at and then what kind of schools the children were sent to.

In the communist period, Russian was the preferred medium of instruction in the Soviet Union, but during perestroika the language of the titular ethnic group was proclaimed the state language in all Soviet republics. To various degrees this has raised the social prestige of the language. Ambitious students, we expect, will gravitate toward schools offering education in the language that will best promote their career chances.

At the outset, we assumed that a high degree of mutual bilingualism would foster increased integration. Indeed, this is also the official rationale behind the strong pressures put on the Russophones in both countries to learn Latvian/Kazak. Nevertheless, in spite of growing willingness on the side of the minorities to learn Latvian, Russophones have found it hard to gain entrance into Latvian-language schools.

Officially, this is said to be due to financial problems ("these schools are already overcrowded"), but it also seems to reflect widespread fears among Latvians that ethnically mixed schools will sharpen ethnic tensions among the youth. This, it is asserted, was often the result of mixed schooling in the Soviet period. At other times it is claimed that if large numbers of Russian kids are let into Latvian classes, the cultural integration will go in the "wrong" direction: the Latvian pupils will adapt more to the lifestyle of their Russian classmates than the other way around.[14]

In Kazakstan, so far, the only group which has shown any inclination to switch from education in Russian to the titular language is the linguistically Russified ethnic Kazaks, and even in this group, as will be shown below, the tendency is weak. To the degree that this tendency will be enhanced in the future and no other groups follow suit, an increase in Kazak-language education will, paradoxically, lead to increased linguistic bipolarization rather than to the creation, or strengthening, of a common cultural space in this country.

In the concluding chapter of the book Latvia and Kazakstan are compared with each other with regard to the nation-building policies pursued by their respective governments and with regard to the effects these policies have on the population. The course of ethnic politics in these countries is also measured against various conceptual frameworks for analysis of ethnic and civic nation-building. Two of the most common models to be identified by sociologists and political scientists are "consociationalism" and "ethnic democracy." Both of these models are briefly outlined and their applicability to Kazakstan and Latvia is discussed.

Ethnopolitical relations in Latvia and Kazakstan are very much in a state of flux. Their resemblance to this or that theoretical model may therefore be of a transient nature. In our study we have tried not to analyze these relations as a fixed and rigid system, but rather isolate and determine important factors influencing the direction in which these relations are developing.

Also, our two cases are compared with ethnopolitical strategies in bipolar states in other parts of the world. In 1981 R.S. Milne published a comparative study of politics in three ethnically bipolar states— Guyana, Malaysia, and Fiji.[15] In each of these countries there are basically two ethnocultural groups confronting each other, Africans vs. Indians in Guyana, Malays vs. Chinese in Malaysia, and Fijis vs. Indians in Fiji. Of these, the Malays and the Fijis are autochtonous while all

---

[14] Author's interviews in Riga, May 1995.

[15] Milne 1981.

the rest are immigrant communities. However, in Guyana the Africans immigrated (or rather, were moved there) earlier than the Indians, and are considered somehow more "settled." In each state the indigenous ethnic group (or in the Guyanian case, the oldest immigrant group) has been able to establish what amounts to a relatively stable political hegemony, in spite of the fact that, at the time when Milne was writing, none of them constituted a numerical majority.

Milne agrees with Horowitz that "in general, ethnically bipolar situations may be likely to produce cleavages which will lead to more intense ethnic competition and result in more undesirable political consequences than those arising from ethnic divisions which are not bipolar, *unless appropriate action is taken by political leaders to prevent this.*"[16] The latter part of the sentence is emphasized in the original and is, of course, an important qualification. As a matter of fact, while both Guyana and Malaysia experienced ethnic violence in the 1960s, and, to a smaller extent in the 1970s, it is generally fair to say that, in all of these three countries, the danger of ethnic turmoil has been contained. Hence, neither do these states offer strong support for the Horowitz thesis.

The typologies of both Horowitz and Schermerhorn are basically structuralist, focusing on demographic and social structures. Such structures are undeniably important and are indeed subjected to detailed analysis also in this book. However, it is important to point out that while such structures place definite constraints on the freedom of action of the elites, structures by themselves do not predetermine actions or political outcomes.

It would be foolhardy to make predictions on the future of stability and democracy in multiethnic states on the basis of their degree of bipolarity alone. William J. Foltz supports the thesis that "in general terms there seems no reason to disagree with the assumption that open conflict between only two parties rigidly divided along multiple lines of cleavage, including the ethnic, is the most likely to be violent, to evoke total emotional commitment, and to produce radical structural change..."[17] However, Foltz also points out that a purely structural analysis will tend to use the same arguments to explain instability as it would do to explain the persistence of stability during the period before the instability broke out.

Thus, an analysis of cultural cleavages can serve only as a starting point. Of crucial importance are the political strategies that the state authorities design to cope with these cultural patterns and how the

---

[16] Ibid., 7-8.
[17] Foltz 1974, 108.

population reacts to these policies. Two major chapters in the book give
a comprehensive presentation and analysis of the ethnopolitical development in Latvia and Kazakstan since independence.

We certainly do not believe that our book has "settled" or "solved"
the issues of nation-building and integration in either Latvia or Kazakstan. Nevertheless, we think that it may contribute to a long-needed
clarification of these crucial questions which may also be of immediate
benefit to the members of these societies. On the theoretical level we
believe that our findings may contribute to a better understanding of
ethnosocial processes in bipolar societies in general.

2

Bipolar Societies?

Pål Kolstø

A Question of Identities

Cultural relations revolve around the question of identities. On the individual level, identity means that a person is distinguishable from others in the immediate surroundings. Thus, it carries with it an element of uniqueness. However, identity formation is a result of socialization into a given society, and is therefore culture-specific. Human communities differ from each other in important respects, and individuals brought up in the same communities inevitably have a large number of common traits which distinguish them in turn from members of other communities. There are, therefore, definite limits to the possible uniqueness of each of us. This has led some scholars to talk of the "collective identities" of human communities.[1] Peter L. Berger and Thomas Luckmann shy away from that concept since in their view it may lead to false and reifying hypostatization. Instead, they prefer the term "identity types," which to a larger degree allows for individual variation and deviation from the common denominator of the group.[2] In addition, this concept more flexibly allows for temporal change.

The Soviet Union was founded on a class ideology and class identity was extolled above all others. Officially, the Soviet state was antinationalist, vigorously combating all expressions of ethnic self-aggrandizement. At the same time, ethnic identity (or "nationality," as it was called) was recognized as real and legitimate, and recorded in

---

[1] For instance the leading culturalist theoretician of nationalism today, Anthony D. Smith. Smith 1991.

[2] Berger and Luckmann 1966/76, 194–197.

the fifth point of the passports. Indeed, when the passport entry indicating class membership was abolished in 1974, the fifth point was retained.[3]

When the Soviet passport regime was introduced in 1932, every passport holder was free to state which nationality s/he belonged to. At this time his or her subjective perception was not challenged by the authorities. Later, the element of choice was abandoned. If anyone had second thoughts about the identity, it was extremely hard, often next to impossible, to have the official nationality legally changed. (Though with handsome bribes much could still be accomplished.) When a child reached the age of maturity at 16 and was given its first passport, s/he inherited the ethnicity of the parents, whether or not s/he identified with it.[4] If the parents were of different ethnic extraction, their children could—and had to—choose an ethnic identity. Their choice, however, was restricted to the nationality of one of the parents. In contrast to Yugoslavia, where the citizens were allowed to choose "Yugoslav" as their national identity, in the Soviet Union mixed, dual identity and new identities were not among the options. Thus, for instance, a son or a daughter of a Jewish father and a Tatar mother living in Moscow, practicing no religion and speaking only Russian, was normally not allowed to list himself/herself as "Russian" in the passport. In such cases the fifth point often functioned as a kind of stigmatization. It also had the effect of conserving the ethnocultural fragmentation of society.

According to the Soviet researcher Olga Komarova the children of mixed background usually chose the nationality of their father or mother depending on the "prestige" of a given nationality in a certain environment. "For instance, children from families of Russian women and Ukrainian men prefer their mother's nationality and consider themselves to be Russians in the Russian Federation, [while] in the Ukraine children from such families usually regard themselves as Ukrainians."[5] Data collected by other Soviet researchers indicate that this may, perhaps, not have been equally true of all Ukrainian cities: Thus, for instance, in the 1960s 56.3 percent of all children in mixed Ukrainian–Russian families in Kiev chose Russian as their nationality.[6] However, Komarova's general description is supported by the available material from the Baltic republics and Central Asia: Thus,

---

[3] Zaslavsky and Luryi 1979.

[4] Zaslavsky 1982, 94–96.

[5] Komarova 1980, 33; see also Zaslavsky 1982, 97.

[6] L.N. Terenteva, "Forming of ethnic self-consciousness in nationally mixed families in the USSR," cited by Karklins 1986/1989, 38. A majority of the children in mixed titular-Russian families chose Russian as their nationality also in the Moldovan and Belarusian capitals.

for instance, in Riga 57 percent of the children in Latvian–Russian families registered themselves as Latvians.

Soviet census practices were more liberal than the passport system, at least on the surface. The census-takers were not allowed to copy the information recorded in the passports directly onto their files. Instead, they were required to ask the respondents which nationality they subjectively felt that they belonged to. The censuses, therefore, reflected ethnic change more accurately and flexibly than did the passport system and are regarded by most experts on Soviet nationalities as fairly reliable sources of information.[7] At the same time, there is every reason to believe that the ethnic self-awareness of most Soviet citizens was strongly influenced by the official nationality ascribed to them. The passport regime retarded the process of ethnic reidentification of the population.[8]

Official registration, or ascription, of ethnicity in the Soviet Union has far-reaching consequences today. While ideologized class identification has been discredited together with the Soviet system, this is not the case with ethnicity.[9] On the contrary, in many places it has assumed a position as *the* paramount identity. Many people in the post-Soviet world identify both themselves and others first and foremost according to their ethnicity, and their ethnic categories are still strongly influenced by the official registration system in the Soviet passports.

One can only speculate as to the reasons why the ethnic component of the Soviet passport system was introduced in the first place, but the desire to keep a maximum degree of control over the citizenry and its movements was clearly one of them. Today, the Soviet experience has taught the political leaders in the successor states that ethnicity can be politically regulated and manipulated. The passport regulations of the new states do vary, however. Some have retained the Soviet system more or less unaltered, while others have decided to do away with it altogether. In between these two extremes some former Soviet republics have decided to keep a nationality point, but to make entry into the passport optional.[10]

Even in those former Soviet republics that have decided to do away with the official registration of ethnicity, the Soviet ascriptive system may have a strong and lasting impact, both as regards identity

---

[7] Kaiser 1994b, 233.

[8] Anderson and Silver 1983.

[9] Slezkine 1994.

[10] See the sub-chapters on passport policies in in Latvia and Kazakstan in chapter four and five.

formation on the individual level, and as regards public discourse on cultural and ethnic policies. In the discussion below I will frequently refer to the official Soviet nationality data but at the same time I will also try to demonstrate that these ethnic categories are not the only cultural identity options available to the residents of the post-Soviet states. Other foci of identification, such as tribes, regions, language communities, are resurfacing, or being recreated. Of these, I believe, the language communities are the most important and corresponding most closely to the cultural communication patterns in contemporary Latvia and Kazakstan.

The Case for Fragmented Societies

The main proposition of this book rests on the premise that both Latvia and Kazakstan may be described as bipolar societies. To what extent is this really the case? This question must be addressed before the analysis can commence. The discussion below will at the same time serve the purpose of outlining the sociocultural landscape of Latvia and Kazakstan in some detail.

Our proposition may be challenged in three ways. First, the critic can seek out cleavages and rifts *within* each of the two main groups. If these cleavages are not only numerous, but also deep and significant, Latvian and Kazakstani societies ought to be described as *highly fragmented* rather than bipolar.[11]

Second, one can attempt to show that a large number of overarching cultural and socioeconomic traits are common to both dominating groups in society, mitigating and even nullifying the dichotomy of the bipolar model. If this attempt is successful, these societies will appear as basically *homogeneous*.

Third, the bipolar model will also be undermined if there is a plenitude of intermediate stages between the two main categories in society. Certain members of society may borrow cultural traits and traditions from both poles. A large number of such in-between, culturally mixed individuals will create a society which more appropriately should be described as a *continuum*. Like the bipolar society the continuous culture may be bicultural, but in contradistinction to it there are no major fault lines between the two poles. Rather, the ethnic pictures resemble a seamless web in which one culture almost imperceptibly shades into the other.

---

[11] This definition of fragmentation follows Rabushka and Shepsle 1972, 177.

The four rival descriptions of Latvian and Kazakstani societies delineated here—bipolar, homogeneous, continual, and fragmented—are all ideal types in the Weberian sense. Actually existing societies may only approximate them more or less imperfectly.

The cleavages and the cultural links and ties in Latvian and Kazakstani societies may be of various kinds—religious, linguistic, tribal, historical, territorial, and socioeconomic. Below, I will act as my own devil's advocate and expose our premise to the evidence which may be mustered against it along these various parameters.

Religious Fragmentation

The ethnic Latvians are religiously divided between a dominant Protestant (Lutheran) group and a Catholic minority, the latter of which comprises roughly one-third of the total. This is the most important in-group religious cleavage in our material. Russians and other Slavs in Latvia and Kazakstan are predominantly Orthodox Christians, while practically all Kazaks are Muslims of the Sunni faith of the Hanafi school.[12]

Also, several minority faiths have active congregations in both Latvia and Kazakstan. A part of the Russian community in Eastern and Central Latvia consists of Old Believers who escaped from religious persecution in Russia in the seventeenth and eighteenth centuries. Traditionally they have kept to themselves and only recently have they begun to merge with the Russian settler community. New Protestant denominations such as the Baptists, the Methodists, and the Pentecostalists cut across ethnic divides, but have generally more adherents among the nontitulars than among the Latvians and the Kazaks.[13]

At the same time it is important to bear in mind that both Latvian and Kazakstani societies have been exposed to heavy doses of secularization. While few people in neither country will declare themselves to be committed atheists, indifferentism is widespread. The Kazaks were Islamized in the seventeenth century but the Muslim faith never struck as deep roots among the nomadic Kazaks as among the sedentary populations around the oases in Uzbekistan and Tajikistan.[14] Many Latvians, for their part, tend to regard Lutheranism as the faith of their

---

[12] Since the Russophone group in both societies includes also Russified Tatars, Russified Bashkirs, Azeris, etc., one may also encounter Muslims among them, but they are so few in number as to be statistically negligible.

[13] Goeckel 1995, 206; *Uroven ` religioznosti* 1996.

[14] Bennigsen and Wimbush 1985; Ro'i 1990.

one-time masters, the Germans. Thus, Protestantism bears the imprint of something alien, imposed upon them from without.[15]

In various surveys over the last decade 50–80 percent of the Latvian population have stated that they are "believers." In Kazakstan, the figures are usually somewhat lower, in the range of 40 percent. "Believer," however, may mean many different things, and in both countries only a minority of those who profess a religious faith actually practice it. In 1993 David Laitin found that 18 percent of the Russians in Latvia and 10 percent in Kazakstan described themselves as "practicing believers."[16] Another survey found 10–11 percent to be the typical level of religious activity among all ethnic groups in Kazakstan. Only the Uzbek minority was significantly more fervent in their devotion.[17]

Still, compared to the Soviet period these figures testify to a certain religious revival in both Latvia and Kazakstan. Such revivals may presumably lead to heightened antagonism between believers on the one hand and non-believers on the other. In the neighboring states of Lithuania and Uzbekistan, respectively, tensions within the titular nations along the religious–secular divide are strong. However, in Latvia and Kazakstan there are few signs that religion is becoming a divisive issue within the respective ethnic communities. On the contrary, among the secularized sections of the Latvian, Russian, and Kazak publics there is a high degree of tolerance and respect, at times, even enthusiasm, for the religious faith of their devout ethnic brethren. Many modern Latvians, Russians, and Kazaks perceive of the churches and the mosques as guardians of the "unique national character" which they themselves, while not personally able to embrace the religious expression of it, are also eager to resuscitate.

In sum, the importance of religion as identity marker among the inhabitants of Latvia and Kazakstan is limited. To the extent that religion nevertheless does play a role in Latvia and Kazakstan, it tends to reinforce the bipolarization of society in the sense that faith is seen as an aspect of the ethnolinguistic cultures along which the main bifurcation runs. Even in a very secular setting it is not the same to be "a former Christian" as to be a "former Muslim."[18] Religion leaves behind an important cultural imprint on a community, also when people no longer believe in it. In this respect, the gap between a once-Muslim community

---

[15] Goeckel 1995, 202.

[16] Laitin 1998, 319. This was not very high but nevertheless higher than the figures for Russians in Russia (9.7 percent) and in Estonia (7.9 percent).

[17] *Uroven' religioznosti* 1996, 8 and 13.

[18] Gellner 1990, 69–70.

and a once-Christian community is considerable larger than between formerly Protestant, Catholic, and Orthodox communities. The latter may be regarded as three varieties of the same invariant type.

Linguistic, Regional, Historical, and Tribal Fragmentation

Among the Latvian-speakers, the South-Eastern Latgalians have their own dialect which is occasionally used as a literary and liturgical language. This is one aspect of the peculiar Latgalian identity which also draws strength from territorial, historical, and religious factors. Latgale has historically been under the sway of the Poles, not of the Germans and the Swedes as was the fate of the other major Latvian regions, Kurzeme and Vidzeme. While the latter were incorporated into the Russian empire at the very beginning of the eighteenth century, Latgale remained Polish until the end of that century. In tsarist Russia Latgale was administratively not a part of the Baltic provinces, but was apportioned and appended to two of the "inner" guberniias.

The predominant religion among the Latvian-speakers in Latgale is Catholicism, and Latgalians tend to take their religion somewhat more seriously than their Lutheran compatriots. There is also a certain element of apprehensiveness among Latgalians toward what is being perceived as the centralizing and homogenizing proclivities of Riga-based politicians. Conversely, among Latvians in other parts of Latvia, certain condescending attitudes toward their poorer, more rustic, and allegedly less cultured coethnics in Latgale, may be encountered.

The Kazaks are divided into three subgroups that are alternately referred to as "hordes," "supertribes," and "superclans." The Kazak name for this is "zhuz", a term which gradually seems to be supplanting the other, less precise terms in academic literature. The largest zhuz, as the name indicates, is the Great (*Ulu*) zhuz in the south around the cities of Almaty, Zhambul, and Shymkent. The Little or *Kishi* zhuz is located in the Northwest while the Middle (*Orta*) zhuz resides in the Northeast.

Unlike Latvian regionalism, the zhuz divisions do not draw strength from religious or linguistic cleavages among the groups. The southern Kazaks in the Zhambul and Shymkent regions are historically influenced by the nearby Uzbeks and may be somewhat more fervent in their Islam devotion than are the Northern Kazaks, but for reasons elucidated above, these differences are of minor importance. Linguistically, there are slight dialectal variations among the Kazak speakers, but there is only one literary standard based on the Middle zhuz dialect.

Deep down, the basis of the zhuz is the tribal structure of the extended families. Many Kazaks know their pedigree seven generations removed, and awareness of these ancestral links is often of great importance to them. Within this seven-generations kinship, exogamy is practiced. At the same time, most Kazaks marry within their own zhuz. The zhuz as such is a tribal federation which, above the tribal level, is nevertheless held together by bonds other than those of consanguinity.

In addition to its genetical basis, the zhuz structure is reinforced by territorial and historical factors. The zhuzes do not only inhabit separate territories, but these territories are wide apart. While it takes only a couple of hours on the train to go from Latgale to Riga, a journey from Almaty to the heartland of Little zhuz and Middle zhuz is both expensive and time-consuming. Added to this, the core areas of the three zhuzes are separated by vast areas of sparsely populated desert, semi-desert, and steppes. There is no strong demographic center to bind them together. However, a growing migration among the various regions in Kazakstan in the Soviet period has blurred somewhat the close zhuz–territory correspondence.

The three zhuzes submitted to Russian suzerainty at different points in time—the Little and Middle zhuz in 1731 and 1740, respectively, and the Great zhuz a century later.[19] This means that the northern zhuzes have been somewhat more exposed to Russian culture and civilization for historical reasons. The Russian influence on these groups is also reinforced by the factors of territorial proximity to Russia and of the Russian demographic preponderance in the regions where they live, particularly in the case of the Middle zhuz.

Members of the same clans and zhuzes often feel a strong obligation to support each other and to promote each other's interests. A Kazak who is lucky enough to climb a good way up a career ladder, will do what he can to pull his kith and kin up after him. This is how strong family networks are created in various ministries, departments, and state firms.[20]

Historians have long been aware of the significance of zhuzes, and lately it has been maintained that they have a strong impact also on contemporary Kazakstani politics.[21] The character and degree of this impact, however, is a matter of great uncertainty and controversy. To many researchers—Kazak, Russian, and Western alike—the zhuz

---

[19] Olcott 1995.

[20] Akiner 1995, 53.

[21] Rotar et al. 1994.

divisions do indeed represent strong and politically relevant cleavages within the Kazak nation.[22] The zhuz identity is older and seems to be more consolidated than the Kazak identity which, in may ways, is rather brittle and insecure. Analyses of the zhuz affiliations of top executives in the political elite, it is believed, may reveal important political constellations and power relations in Kazakstani politics.

Some other experts are far more skeptical about the political relevance of zhuz affiliations. Shirin Akiner believes that those who speak and write about the zhuzes in Kazakstan today often have ulterior, nonacademic reasons for doing so: ultranationalists hark back to a "golden past"; persons who feel excluded from power blame their misfortune on zhuz rivalry; Russians and Russified Kazaks who see Kazak society as primitive attribute this to its "tribal" character. Finally, some authors write about zhuzes for purely pecuniary reasons: Zhuz analyses are what Western grant-allocating institutions are willing to pay for.[23] The zhuzes may well be a less divisive factor within the Kazak community than many observers have been led to believe. While the actual strength of these loyalties remains a matter of controversy, it seems safe to conclude that zhuz rivalries do not take the edge off the Kazak–Russophone bipolarity in Kazakstani society.

Among the Russophones in both Latvia and Kazakstan there are several cultural subdivisions worth pointing out. Most obvious is the ethnic diversity. It is an important part of official Kazakstani ideology that Kazakstan is a highly multinational national state. The figure of 131 ethnic groups living in the country is frequently cited.[24] However, this figure is strongly misleading. The vast majority of these 131 groups are too small to be statistically significant. Of the remainder, a large number consists of groups whose members usually are so Russified that ethnicity plays only a minute role in their identity formation.

The term "Russophones" covers all those members of society who regard Russian as their mother tongue or who use Russian as their daily language of communication, privately and professionally. A person will usually be included in the group also when the language s/he is most familiar with is a minority language—such as Moldovan or Georgian—if s/he prefers Russian to the titular language as his/her language of second choice.

Into this Russophone group, then, in both Latvia and Kazakstan, fall the vast majority of the local Ukrainians and Belarusians, in addition

---

[22] Melvin 1993, 210; Kobets 1993; Masanov 1996a.

[23] Akiner 1995, 75–77; and Akiner in personal communication with the author.

[24] See e.g. *O demograficheskoi* 1996, 48; *Kazakhstanskaia pravda* 2 March 1996.

to an array of minor ethnic groups. In fact, the only nontitular groups that are likely to be excluded are those which have "historic roots" in the same region. In Latvia, this region will be the Baltics; in Kazakstan, Central Asia. This means that in Latvia, Estonians, Lithuanians, Livs, and most Poles and Roma as a rule are not included among "the Russophones." The Jewish group is divided, but most will regard themselves—and be regarded by others—as Russophones. Intriguingly, the few Kazaks living in Latvia will almost invariably be seen as "Russophones."

Conversely, in Kazakstan not only all Ukrainians and Belarusians, but also the chance Latvian living there will most likely be included among the Russophones. In fact, the term is elastic enough to encompass even the significant group of Koreans which was forcibly resettled there by Stalin in the early 1930s. In local parlance all these groups are often indiscriminately lumped together as "the Russians." Statements such as "in our class there are three Russians: Volodia, Vania, and Kim" may sound strange to a foreigner who has understood that Kim is an ethnic Korean, but makes perfect sense to everybody else in Almaty.[25] Linguistic identity clearly prevails over ethnic and even racial identity. In Kazakstan, and to a slightly smaller extent also in the Baltics, a common Russophone identity is crystallizing.[26]

Most ethnic groups indigenous to Central Asia—such as Uzbeks, Kyrgyzs, Karakalpaks, and Uighurs—have a Turkic mother tongue which is related to Kazak and comprehensible to most educated Kazaks.[27] At the same time, these minorities are usually not assimilated into the Kazak nation but retain their separate identities.

A Kazakstani researcher, A.T. Peruashev, has suggested that a trichotomy rather than a dichotomy most aptly fits the ethnic map of Kazakstan: the titular nation; the Slavs; and a residual category, the group of "small numbers."[28] This model has much to commend it. However, with regard to demographic strength these groups are far from equal. According to Peruashev's own figures, the Slavs are the largest group (43.4 percent), the runner-up Kazak group stands at 42.8 percent, and the rest add up to only 13.7 percent. However, if we substitute "the Russophones" for "the Slavs," which in my view makes more sense, this group increases to above 47 percent and the residual group of "small

---

[25] Vasil'eva 1991.

[26] Laitin 1995.

[27] In some other cases, such as the Dungans (Muslim Chinese) and Tajiks, whose mother tongue is not Turkic, their proficiency in Kazak is generally not particularly superior to the proficiency of the European groups (2–5 percent). See *Natsional'nyi sostav* 1991, 102–03.

[28] Peruashev 1994, 5.

numbers" is correspondingly reduced. While not dismissing this "third force" as a trifle, I nevertheless contend that it is not important enough to invalidate our dichotomous model.

To be sure, the question of who belongs to the minorities and who does not may not be settled by reference to demographics alone; it is also a matter of self-perceptions and politics.[29] For reasons laid out above, national leaders who perceive a bipolar cultural structure in their country as inherently destabilizing very much hope that the nontitular population will not coalesce into one, compact, monolithic group. Instead, they would clearly prefer to see it fragment into smaller, politically less powerful and more manageable components. The Latvian–American political scientist Rasma Karklins, has opined that

> among the non-citizens, we must distinguish between the various ethnic groups. I believe that it is not profitable (*nevygodno*) to accept the term "Russophones". This is a vague concept. We should emphasize that they are Ukrainians, Belarusians, and peoples of other extractions.[30]

To what extent, then, are these ethnic divisions within the Russophone communities actually operative? In Latvia, as well as in Kazakstan, a certain tendency toward ethnic revival within the Russophone diaspora communities is discernible. Ukrainian, German, Jewish, and other cultural centers have been established in an attempt to rekindle the various ethnic cultures which were Russified in the Soviet period. Additionally, new schools are being opened in which the Russified non-Russians may study their national traditions and perhaps refind their long lost ethnic identities.[31] This tendency seems to be somewhat stronger in Latvia than in Kazakstan, but may be observed even there.[32] Moreover, among the ethnic Russians it is possible to encounter people who resent the term "Russophones."[33] They want to cultivate an "undiluted,"—even "uncontaminated,"—Russian culture in the ethnic sense. However, while counter to the process of Russophone consolidation, this tendency is certainly not prevailing. As one Kazakstani researcher admits, "Today, there is often no other difference between a Ukrainian, a Belarusian, a Pole, and a Russian in Kazakstan than the nationality entry in their passports."[34]

---

[29] For self-perceptions, see "A nation of minorities" in Chapter six.

[30] *Diena*, 9 June 1993. For a similar statement from the President of Kazakstan, N. Nazarbaev, see p. 167.

[31] *Natsional'nye i etnicheskie* 1996; Fleishman 1995; and pp. 131–132 and p. 186 below.

[32] Janabel 1996, 18.

[33] *Russkoiazychnye* 1991; Aasland 1994, 244.

[34] Peruashev 1994, 4; see also Melvin 1995, 116.

Arguably, more important than the ethnic differences among the Russophones is the distinction between old-timers (*starozhily*) and newcomers. The former groups usually have a better understanding of the local culture and (in Latvia but not in Kazakstan) a better command of the local language. Some of them can trace their ancestry back to local Russian settler communities three and even four generations back and have an acute sense of living on ancestral soil. Newcomers who are born outside Latvia/Kazakstan are more likely to identify with the Russian core group in the Russian Federation.[35]

In 1989, the ratio of native-borns to immigrants within the Russian communities was 41.6 to 58.8 in Latvia and 46.8 to 53.2 in Kazakstan.[36] Thus, in both countries immigrants were somewhat more numerous, but the trend is clearly toward greater permanent settlement.[37] Since more Russians and other Russophones are leaving from than arriving in both countries, the immigrants' share of the communities are continuing to decline, rendering the Russophone groups gradually more homogeneous and local.

A final subgroup among the Russophones in Kazakstan are the Cossacks. They are sometimes regarded as a spearhead of the Russophone group, promoting all-Russian causes; at other times they are represented as a separate community, pursuing an agenda of their own. Like Cossacks in other parts of the former Soviet Union, most of them both identify with, and distinguish themselves from, "ordinary Russians" at the same time.[38]

Contemporary Cossack societies are recruited from two sources, those who sympathize with the Cossack cause and those who are run of Cossack stock. In many places the latter makes up only a very small share of the total. For instance, among the three thousand members of the Ural Cossack *voisko* in 1991–92 only about 200 had Cossack forbears.[39] The others had joined for ideological reasons.

Socioeconomic Fragmentation

Within both the Latvian and Kazak ethnic communities, the most significant socioeconomic dividing lines run between the rural population and the urbanites. Until recently, the titular groups in both

---

[35] Abyzov 1992; Kolstø 1996b, 618.

[36] Arutiunian 1992, 52.

[37] See p. 228.

[38] Elagin 1993, 3.

[39] Averin 1995, 165.

countries were predominantly rural and it is only in this century that they have they begun to move into the cities. Before World War I the urban centers were dominated by Germans, Jews, and Russians in Latvia, and by Russians and other Slavs in Kazakstan. After World War II, Russians took over the role of the Germans and the Jews as the dominant population in Latvian cities. As recently as in 1989, only 36.5 percent of the population of Riga was ethnically Latvian.[40] In that same year, 38 percent of the inhabitants of the capital of Kazakstan belonged to the titular nationality.

Urban dwellers tend to develop tastes and attitudes which set them apart from their rural cousins. Neither has this global tendency bypassed the Latvians or the Kazaks. Since city air in their countries has such a strong Russian redolence, it also means that they have been more exposed to Russian impulses of various kinds. These cultural encounters may yield very different results. Either the new migrants to the cities may become more Russified, or they may react with repulsion against the alien, nontitular culture they meet there and develop strong nationalist sympathies.[41]

Recent election results in Latvia and Kazakstan indicate that the rural–urban divide within the titular nation is politically relevant in both countries and ought to be taken into consideration.[42] Nevertheless, this distinction should not be overdramatized. In Latvia, life in the countryside is not radically different from city life. Most of the benefits of civilization that are available in the city are accessible also to the rural population, if by no other means than a swift trip to the nearest city.

In Kazakstan, by comparison, the cultural gap between the countryside and the city is much more pronounced. Sometimes a traveler may be left with the feeling of crossing a time barrier from one century to another. Even so, this situation has not created an unbridgeable chasm between rural and most urban Kazaks. Since Kazak migration to the cities started only recently, the majority of the Kazak city dwellers have never cut the ties to the village from which they hail. They stand, as it were, with one foot in rural culture and the other in the city.[43] The cultural split, therefore, runs not so much *between* two groups of Kazaks, as *within* the individual Kazak urbanite, who, as a member of two cultural milieus, may be uncertain as to where he "really"

---

[40] *Russkie v Latvii* 1992, 63.

[41] Or, as Ernest Gellner pointed out, they may react in both ways at the same time. See Gellner 1990.

[42] Kolstø and Tsilevich 1997, 52–54; Masanov 1996a.

[43] Amrekulov 1995, 68–69.

belongs. In the estimate of one researcher, the thoroughly urbanized Kazak population makes up hardly more than 5 percent of the total Kazak group.[44]

To sum up this section: within the Latvian group I detected one important subgroup, the Latgalians. The numerical and emotional strength of this identity type is difficult to ascertain, since it does not show up in any statistics. Probably, most Latvians living in the counties of Latgale—Daugavpils, Rezekne, Kraslava, and Ludza—will identify themselves primarily as Latvians, and only secondarily as Latgalians with only a minority reversing this priority. Some will not have any Latgalian identity whatsoever. No one, to our knowledge, will claim that s/he is only a Latgalian, plain and simple, and not a Latvian. Latgalianism, in other words, is a case of cultural regionalism, not of nationalism.

Within the Kazak ethnic group, there are identity cleavages among the three zhuzes although their political relevance is a matter of dispute. In any case, to most Kazaks their zhuz identity and their ethnic identity do not compete with each other. They relate to different "levels" of social reality and are played out in different competition games. If the issue at stake is related to the Kazak–Russophone rivalry, they effortlessly don their all-Kazak identity.

The ethnic differences within the Russophone group in both Latvia and Kazakstan are, in my view, considerably less important than they are often made out to be. More important is the distinction between old-timers and newcomers. In Latvia, the criterion for being judged an old-timer is not so much to be born in the country as to have ancestral roots in interwar Latvia. This distinction has been reinforced by the politics of the Latvian state. Descendants of interwar citizens are granted automatic citizenship rights irrespective of ethnicity while postwar immigrants are not. 30–40 percent of the Russophones in Latvia can be classified as belonging to the old-timers' group in this sense.

In Kazakstan, the distinction between newcomers and old-timers is less sharply drawn. Russian immigration has proceeded in waves, with peaks around the Stolypin reforms, the first five-year plans in the 1930s, and Khrushchev's virgin-soil program in the late 1950s.[45] However, there has been a constant replenishment of the Russian communities also between these high-water marks. There are no obvious cut-off points for a dichotomization based on arrival times.

A probably more significant cleavage within the Russophone community in Kazakstan follows the geographical distinction between

[44] Masanov 1995, 122.

[45] Brusina 1996, 5.

north and south. Russophones in the south have been forced by the necessities of life to be more adaptable and to acquire at least a rudimentary knowledge of the Kazak lifestyle. In the compactly Russian communities in the north such knowledge has until quite recently been less necessary.

Crosscutting Cleavages Among the Major Cultural Groups: The Case for Continuous Societies

Linguistic Crosscutting Cleavages

To a large extent the category of ethnicity in the Soviet Union followed the linguistic criterion: a Latvian speaks Latvian, a Russian speaks Russian, and a Kazak speaks Kazak. But ethnicity and linguistic affiliations, while basically overlapping, were not identical. Language change did not necessarily lead to ethnic reidentification. Linguistic "anomalies" and intermediate groups could, and did, arise.

In principle, linguistic dichotomization between cultural communities can be softened in two ways: a part of the groups switches to the language of the other group and/or some members of one or both groups become bilingual. All of these occurrences took place in the Soviet Union, but to vastly different degrees.

The number of nontitulars in Latvia and Kazakstan who in 1989 claimed the titular language as their mother tongue was very small (see Table 2.1 and 2.2 on pp. 31–32). In Latvia, this amounted to 10,000 Russians, 3,000 Belarusians, and some 800 Ukrainians.[46] In percentages of the total groups, in each case this was less than 0.2 percent. In Kazakstan, the corresponding figures were absolutely negligible: 699 Germans, 580 Russians, 189 Ukrainians, and 46 Belarusians listed Kazak as their first language. By contrast, in Lithuania the figures were much higher: 3.5 percent of the Russians and 5 percent of the Poles regarded Lithuanian as their mother tongue in the 1989 census.

Somewhat larger groups of the *titular nations* in these two republics in 1989 claimed Russian as their mother tongue: 35 thousand (2.5 percent) in Latvia and 88 thousand (1.3 percent) in Kazakstan. Very possibly these official figures are too low in that Soviet census data were based on the self-evaluation of the citizens. This means that a subjective factor would come into play. People understand identical words

---

[46] For reasons explained above, ethnic groups with historical roots in the Baltics—Estonians, Lithuanians—have not been counted.

and questions differently. The Russian equivalent of "mother tongue" *(rodnoi iazyk)* can be translated as "the language of birth" or "the language of my kin" *(rod)*. Some Kazaks who spoke exclusively or predominantly Russian at home seem to have stated "Kazak" as their *rodnoi iazyk* as the language of their "kin." Some evidently felt it to be shameful to have abandoned the tongue of their forebears. For these reasons the number of 98.5 percent Kazaks in Kazakstan claiming Kazak as their *rodnoi iazyk* in 1989 is most likely grossly inflated.[47] Analysts who based their interpretations solely on these official data were clearly led astray.[48] Modern estimates put the Kazak literacy among ethnic Kazaks to somewhere in the range of 60–72 percent.[49]

Who, then, are these linguistically Russified Latvians and Kazaks? Could they serve as bridge-builders between the main ethnic groups in the country? In my view, the answer is no. In the Soviet era, these groups were disproportionately well represented in the corridors of power. Today, they are regarded not only as Russified, but also as inordinately Sovietized. Strong social mechanisms of ostracization have been let loose in both countries because they were seen as traitors to their own nations or ethnic groups. In Latvia, a high percentage of them are made up of so-called *Russian Latvians*, descendants of Latvians who migrated to Russia under the tsars in search of work and who spent the interwar years in the USSR. Some of them returned to Latvia "riding on the top of tanks" and were given prestigious jobs in the Soviet Latvian administration. They are decidedly not the group that can facilitate ethnic bridge-building in Latvia today.

In Kazakstan, the occupation syndrome is absent, but the mechanisms of ostracism are not. Drawing on a novel by the Kyrgyz author Chingiz Aitmatov, Kazak nationalists denounce their Russified coethnics as *"mankurts"*, meaning persons who have lost their identity. Many of the most well-educated intelligentsia are included in this group.[50]

Bilingualism, on the other hand, is quite a different matter. While language shifts among many non-Russian groups in the former Soviet Union were regarded as a disgrace, bilingualism was not. It was both much more acceptable and more widespread. In 1989, 68 percent of the Latvians in Latvia claimed fluency in Russian while the correspondent figure for Kazaks in Kazakstan was 64 percent (including those who

---

[47] Kaidarov 1992.

[48] Pipes 1975, 459–61.

[49] Dave 1996a. Saulesh Esenova claims that 30 percent of the Kazaks speak only Russian. See Esenova 1996, 692.

[50] See e.g. Baibazar Erbakyuly, activist in the Kazak tili movement in *Ana tili*, as quoted in *Kazakhstanskaia pravda* 27 March 1996.

TABLE 2.1 Language Shifts and Bilingualism in Kazakstan Based on the 1989 Census (in percentages of the total ethnic group)

	Absolute numbers, thousands	Regard as mother tongue			Fluency in another language			
		Nationality language	Kazak	Russian	Nationality language	Kazak	Russian	Other
Kazaks	6535	98.6	-	1.4	0.2	-	62.8	0.2
Russians	6228	99.9	0	-	0	0.9	-	0.7
Germans	958	54.4	0.1	45.4	-	0.6	50.6	0.7
Ukrainians	896	36.6	>0.1	63.3	5.8	0.6	32.3	0.7
Belarusians	183	34.5	>0.1	65.3	6.0	0.4	31.8	1.4
Koreans	103	51.7	0.3	48.0	-	1.0	47.0	1.9
Poles	60	12.2	>0.1	76.4	-	0.4	19.8	50.0
sum Russophones	8423							
Uzbeks	332	95.6	1.3	2.8	0.3	4.6	52.1	0.3
Tatars	327	68.9	3.4	27.3	3.2	3.2	64.3	0.7
Uighurs	185	95.1	1.5	3.1	-	9.1	62.0	0.5
Azeris	90	87.1	0.5	10.4	0.9	5.7	64.7	1.5
sum, Turkic groups	934							

TABLE 2.2 Language Shifts and Bilingualism in Latvia Based on the 1989 Census (in percentages of the total ethnic group)

	Absolute numbers, thousands	Regard as mother tongue			Fluency in another language			
		Nationality language	Latvian	Russian	Nationality language	Latvian	Russian	Other
Latvians	1388	97.4	-	2.6	1.3	-	65.7	0.4
Russians	906	98.8	1.1	-	0.7	21.1	-	1.8
Belarusians	120	32.2	2.5	64.8	11.6	15.6	29.7	1.6
Ukrainians	92	49.5	0.9	49.4	14.7	8.9	43.8	1.2
Poles	60	27.3	14.7	54.2	0	22.8	33.8	15.2
Jews	23	22.5	2.0	74.9	4.4	27.0	17.5	28.5
Tatars	5	46.7	0.6	51.6	11.3	6.6	44.6	5.7
Germans	4	34.0	12.4	53.0	-	16.4	36.1	3.9
sum Russophones	1120							
Lithuanians	35	63.9	23.8	11.9	9.6	40.3	36.0	0.3
Roma	7	84.7	10.2	4.8	3.4	52.3	28.6	0.8
Estonians	3	50.3	25.1	24.2	12.2	28.7	40.1	1.7
Livs	>1	37.0	62.2	-	17.0	27.4	31.1	4.0
sum Baltic minorities	45							

regarded Russian as their mother tongue). Here, again, the subjective factor comes into play. People use very different yardsticks when they estimate their own proficiency in foreign languages. And indeed, how much is required before it is reasonable to talk about fluency (*svobodno vladeet*)? Circumstantial evidence suggests that many Kazaks regard fluency as being able get the main message across somehow, while Latvians are more demanding of themselves. If this is a correct observation, the census data in Kazakstan for titular bilingualism have been inflated while the corresponding figures for the Latvians are on the low side.[51]

What is the level of fluency in the state language among the Russophones? In both states, it leaves much to be desired, although in Latvia it is in fact not all that bad. In 1989, 22 percent of the Russians regarded themselves as fluent in Latvian. (There was probably a high degree of overlapping with the 20 percent Russians who descend from interwar Latvian citizens.) Figures for some other nationalities were lower: Belarusians, 18 percent, Ukrainians, 9.8 percent[52] (see Table 2.1). This is not very surprising. Many members of the Russified minorities will try to keep up their skills also in their native language. To these people, Latvian will be not a second but a third language. The number of Russians and other Russophones in Latvia who know the titular language at a subfluency level is difficult to estimate, but it is probably quite large, and growing. The prospects for reciprocate bilingualism in Latvia is therefore not altogether bleak.[53]

The situation in Kazakstan is different. The Russians in this country have the dubious distinction of being less versed in the titular language than any other Russian diaspora group in the former Soviet republics: in 1989, only 0.9 percent of them claimed fluency in Kazak. Part of the reason for this dismal achievement may be the greater difficulty for Slavs to learn a Turkic language compared to Latvian, which is more similar to Russian in syntax and grammatical structure. However, the lower prestige of the Asian languages in the Soviet linguistic hierarchy clearly also played a part.[54]

---

[51] There were, however, some exceptions. The number of Estonians who claimed fluency in Russian dropped from 45.2 percent in 1970 to 39.9 percent in 1979. Most researchers regard these startling figures as evidence of a mute protest against increased pressure of Russification in the republic. Some fluent Russian-speakers among the Estonians would not admit to knowing Russian since it was the language of the "occupiers." See, e.g., Kaiser 1994a, 289.

[52] However, for Jews it was higher, 27 percent. This probably reflected the inclusion of "indigenous," Baltic Jews in this group.

[53] G. Smith 1996, 200; Rose and Maley 1994, 52. See also chapters 4 and 6.

[54] Aasland 1996, 483.

By 1992, the Kazak fluency figure for Russians had increased to approximately 2 percent.[55] However, as pointed out above, fluency may be an unreasonably stringent criterion. A survey conducted in 1995 showed that, in addition to these 2 percent of fluency speakers, 10 percent of the Russophones were able to read a Kazak text with the help of a dictionary. Roughly 25 percent claimed that they could understand oral Kazak although not speak it themselves.[56] However, even with these clarifications, it is clear that, linguistically, Kazakstan is a far more bipolar society than is Latvia.

Mixed Marriages

As in the case of bilingualism, ethnically mixed marriages create a group of people receiving impulses from two cultures. A high number of such marriages in a country will presumably raise the level of cultural homogeneity. However, not only the numbers but also the structure of such interethnic marriages are important. If the scions of a given nationality frequently fall in love with members of certain ethnic groups only, while shunning others, this will create new cleavages in society.

Soviet ethnographers used to claim that an increasing number of mixed marriages in the Soviet Union facilitated rapprochement among the ethnic groups, creating greater contact and understanding in the most intimate social arena, the family.[57] Data published in 1989 showed that, among all the Soviet republics, Latvia had the lowest proportion of marriages in which both spouses were of the titular nationality (37.8 percent). Next followed Kazakstan, with 40.9 percent. These figures, however, reflect the low share of the titular nation in these two republics and not a high propensity for interethnic marriages among Latvians and Kazaks.

When the aggregate figures in each republic are broken down by ethnic groups, a variegated picture emerges (Table 2.3 and 2.4). Certain groups intermarry far more frequently than others. Of all ethnic Latvians in Latvia who married in 1988, 19.9 percent chose a non-Latvian spouse, (down 0.6 percent percentage points from 1978). In the same year as many as 37.4 percent of all Russians in Latvia who entered into matrimony had found a partner from another ethnic background. The same was true with 84.8 percent of all Ukrainians and the same number of

---

[55] *Sovety Kazakhstana*, 22 April 1992.

[56] Arenov and Kalmykov 1995a.

[57] Kozlov 1982, 262; Borzykh 1972–73.

TABLE 2.3 Marriages by Ethnicity in Latvia, 1978 and 1988

Ethnic group	Year	Mono-ethnic	Male mixed	Female mixed	Total people	Percent mixed
Latvians	1978	9,282	2,321	2,473	23,358	20.5
	1988	9,561	2,339	2,400	23,681	19.9
Russians	1978	6,236	3,329	3,376	19,177	35.0
	1988	5,747	3,396	3,467	18,357	37.4
Ukrainians	1978	132	977	688	1,929	86.3
	1988	178	1,049	935	2,340	84.8
Belarusians	1978	236	1,050	1,268	2,790	83.1
	1988	197	1,058	1,139	2,591	84.8

Source: "Data on Ethnic Intermarriages" 1990. *Journal of Soviet Nationalities*, 1 (Summer) pp. 160–174.

TABLE 2.4 Marriages by Ethnicity in Kazakstan, 1978 and 1988

Ethnic group	Year	Mono-ethnic	Male mixed	Female mixed	Total people	Percent mixed
Kazaks	1978	45,733	2,837	1,573	95,876	4.6
	1988	66,570	2,975	2,422	138,537	3.9
Russians	1978	50,171	14,346	16,177	130,865	23.3
	1988	42,768	13,692	15,893	115,121	25.7
Ukrainians	1978	2,490	7,740	7,615	20,335	75.5
	1988	1,757	7,482	7,383	18,379	80.9
Belarusians	1978	317	1,612	1,830	4,076	84.4
	1988	107	1,851	1,712	3,777	94,3
Uzbeks	1978	2,389	409	275	5,462	12.5
	1988	3,249	526	419	7,443	12.7
Tatars	1978	1,180	1,701	1,896	5,957	60.4
	1988	984	2,183	2,332	6,483	69.6

Source: "Data on Ethnic Intermarriages" 1990. *Journal of Soviet Nationalities*, 1 (Summer) pp. 160–174.

Belarusians in Latvia. In the case of Russians and Belarusians, this meant an increase of 2.4 and 1.7 percentage points over the last ten years.[58] Clearly, the Latvians were considerably more endogamous than the Slavs. The data also showed that Russians and Latvians tended to marry culturally kindred groups more often than each other. The Latvians were particularly attracted to Lithuanians, the Russians to Ukrainians and Belarusians.[59]

---

[58] *Naselenie SSSR* 1989; *Data on ethnic intermarriage* 1990.
[59] Komarova 1980, 33.

These same tendencies could be discerned in Kazakstan. Here, 25.7 percent of all Russians, 80.9 percent of all Ukrainians, and no less than 94.3 percent of all Belarusians who married in 1988 did so with a partner from another ethnic background. This represented increases of 2.4, 5.4, and 9.9 percentage points, respectively, over the last ten years. By contrast, only 3.9 percent of all Kazaks living in their home republic who married in 1988 chose a non-Kazak spouse. This was down from 4.6 percent ten years earlier. Thus the already very strong Kazak tendency toward endogamy was increasing. And even among the very few Kazaks who chose a non-Kazak spouse, the likelihood that he or she would tie the knot with a Slav was so small as to be statistically negligible. Religious differences seemed to serve as a strong barrier against marriage.[60] The Kazak that does not marry a person of his or her own group has traditionally preferred to wed an Uzbek, a Karakalpak, or (preferably) a Kyrgyz.[61] Also among the Uzbeks in Kazakstan endogamy is very strong; only 12 percent Uzbeks who married in 1988, chose a non-Uzbek partner. This was far less than among the Russophones.

Also for the Slavs religion and other cultural factors appear to be important. While nourishing few prejudices against mixed marriages in general, they clearly prefer to get spliced with other Orthodox and other Slavs. A.A. Susokolov:

> In the Central Asian republics, in Transcaucasia (with the exception of Armenia), in Kazakstan as well as in Estonia and Latvia, the Russian population is more endogamous in relation to the indigenous population than in [Ukraine, Belarus, Moldova, and Lithuania]. This must first of all be explained by the higher ethnocultural difference between Russians and the indigenous population in the former group of republics. The contingent of ethnically mixed marriages there is made up mainly of marriages between Russians and Ukrainians, Belarusians, Jews, and Tatars who migrated to these republics in the same years as did the Russians.[62]

Mixed marriages, then, do indeed soften the cultural *fragmentation* in Latvia and Kazakstan though, significantly, the phenomenon does not for that reason lead to all-encompassing cultural *homogeneity*. Rather, the homogenizing processes are contained within two separate vessels, the titular culture and the Russophone culture, respectively. The net effect is a *strengthening* rather than an easing of societal bipolarization.

---

[60] Silver 1978.

[61] See Borzykh 1972–73, 395–96 for admittedly rather old data on this.

[62] Susokolov 1992, 195.

Social anthropologists have often observed that exogamy is more frequent among large ethnic groups than in smaller ones. The former are apparently less afraid of being submerged or dissolved by the larger cultural environment, thus losing their distinctiveness. This observation may account to some extent for the great willingness of Russians in Latvia and Kazakstan to marry outside their own group, but it does not explain the even *stronger* enthusiasm for such marriages among Belarusians and Ukrainians in these countries. Outside Belarus and Ukraine, Belarusian and Ukrainian cultures are indeed endangered species,[63] but this does not seem to unleash any protective mechanisms within the ethnic groups such as seems to be the case with, for instance, the Uzbek minority in Kazakstan.[64]

The Belarusian and Russian figures are not readily comparable due the vast size differences. The likelihood that a Belarusian in Pavlodar or Rezekne will run across a potential marriage partner of his or her own nationality is much smaller. Nevertheless, we must be allowed to draw the conclusion that the majority of the non-Russian Slavs in Latvia and Kazakstan do not see a need to preserve their ethnic cultures through endogamy. Rather, they are prone to regard themselves as members of a common Russophone culture and intermix freely within that group. This tendency is particularly strong in Kazakstan and seems to be related to the factor "cultural distance to the dominant culture." As Donald Horowitz has observed, when this distance is very large, it may lead to greater amalgamation among kindred national minorities within the state.[65]

Interethnic Regional Cooperation

Viewed in a center–periphery perspective, people who inhabit the same periphery territory, irrespective of cultural background, may have common interests *vis-à-vis* the central authorities. A merger of local interests among heterogeneous groups may contribute to a softening of ethno-cultural-political polarization in society. In Latvia, I identified one group of Latvians who live in a predominantly Russophone-populated area, the Latgalians. In Kazakstan, the Middle zhuz, living as an ethnic minority in the northeast, finds itself in a similar position.

---

[63] In the Belarusian case, perhaps even within the Belarusian republic.

[64] An additional reason why the Uzbeks in Kazakstan manage to maintain a high degree of endogamy is that many of them live in concentrated rural settlements near the Uzbek border.

[65] Horowitz 1985, 40.

At least one researcher claims to have detected instances of joint Kazak–Russian cooperation in the north directed against national authorities in the center. When an ethnic Russian in the spring of 1993 was ousted as head of the Pavlodar television company in favor of a "politically correct" Kazak replacement from the Great Horde, Kazaks and non-Kazaks alike banded together in his defense.[66] A similar case involving the demotion of a liberal Kazak from Karaganda has also been reported. However, such incidences seem to be exceptions rather than the rule as regards interethnic solidarity in the Kazakstani north. The scope for local politics in Kazakstan, as will be demonstrated below, is also rather limited as the present national authorities are clearly set on establishing a unitary and centralized state and employing the necessary means to achieve this goal.[67] The decision to move the capital from the southern border to Astana in the north has been interpreted as an indication of this determination.[68]

Living together with a large number of Russophones, many Latgalians have adopted a number of characteristics typical of the surrounding Slavic cultures in the region (Polish as well as Russian). One might therefore surmise that a common ground for joint action against the center may be found. So far, however, the political leaders of the Latgalian community have chosen confrontation rather than cooperation toward the local Russophones. In 1991, central Latvian authorities dissolved the city councils of the major towns of Latgale—Daugavpils and Rezekne—on charges of alleged complicity with the plotters in the August coup in Moscow. In both of these cities, Russians and other Slavs predominate demographically. In the political vacuum created by these dissolutions Latgalian activists were installed in the municipal governments in what amounted to a local minority rule. As a lasting result of this episode the climate for Latgalian–Russophone cooperation in Latgale was severely impaired.

To sum up this subchapter, the case for a cultural continuum seems to be stronger in Latvia than in Kazakstani society. The cultural distance between the two main cultural groups is smaller and the number of crosscutting cleavages between them is higher. These circumstances clearly mitigate societal bipolarization. However, compared to a genuinely continuous society such as the Ukraine—where the Russophone culture of the east almost imperceptibly fades into the "pure" Ukrainian culture of the west—the Latvian scene remains basically a society of a

---

[66] Melvin 1993, 210.

[67] See chapter 5.

[68] Bremmer and Welt 1996, 185.

bipolar type, or at least moderately so. In the case of Kazakstan the case for a continuous culture falls flat to the ground.

Shared Experiences:
The Case for Homogeneous Societies

All former citizens of the Soviet Union have been exposed to large doses of Soviet culture and none of them have remained immune against it. Thus, while the Soviet Man touted by the Communist *agitprops* never materialized, a large reservoir of shared experiences—triumphs and tragedies—does exist.

Nevertheless, the common historical baggage of the past does not necessarily bring the inhabitants of the new states of Eurasia closer together. On the contrary, in most respects the Soviet legacy appears to be a divisive factor. Nationalist activists in Latvia and Kazakstan— as well as in all other former Soviet republics—see their nation as particularly hard hit by the Stalinist terror. While all Soviet nationalities certainly suffered under the repression, they believe that *their* pain exceeds that of the others.

Even more important, the Russians are often regarded not as covictims, but as perpetrators of the heinous crimes committed against their nation. Kazak nationalists often point out the Slavic names of Stalin's henchmen in their republic—Goloshchekin, Ponomarenko, and Brezhnev.[69] In Latvia, the Soviet occupation is regularly referred to as "the Russian occupation" and the local Russians as "occupants." Thus, the common character of the ordeals which the long-suffering Soviet peoples have undergone is emphatically denied.

However, there are certain aspects of the common past which may bring the inhabitants of Latvia and Kazakstan closer together. This is not what they have learned from their Soviet masters, but what they have learned from each other. Already one hundred years ago a leading Muslim intellectual of the Russian empire, Ismail Gaspirali, was of the opinion that Russians had a remarkable capacity for adapting to the culture of other peoples with whom they lived together. "They adopted their language—without, of course, abandoning their own—as

---

[69] Russian activists in Almaty retaliate by pointing out the Jewish nationality of Goloshchekin. They want to shift the blame for the Kazak holocaust on to the Jews. (See *Russkii vestnik*, the organ of the Russian cultural center in Almaty, 1992 no. 1, pp. 2–3.) However, this is to miss the point no less fundamentally than the Kazak nationalists. Whatever his nationality Goloshchekin was first and foremost a Communist *apparatchik* and acted in that capacity.

well as some customs, popular beliefs and dresses."[70] In recent years a number of researchers have concluded that the high degree of cultural cross-fertilization between the Russians and the local peoples on the outskirts of the Russian state over the centuries has lead to the creation of separate Russian communities on the periphery that are clearly distinguishable from the core group.[71]

Indeed, most spokespersons of the Russophone communities see themselves as somehow different from "Russia-Russians." In Kazakstan, many Russophones will claim that they are less prone to drink and more given to marital fidelity than their coethnics in the Russian Federation. These advantages they attribute in no small degree to the wholesome influence of the basically Muslim environment in their republic.[72]

In Latvia, the divorce rate among ethnic Latvians is very high, but few Russians would put the blame for their own incapacity to adhere to the marriage oath on the Latvians. Instead, many of them will insist that by living in the Baltics, they have acquired a capacity for punctuality and hard work that sets them apart from the Russian core group in the Russian Federation. These qualities they attribute to their exposure to "the Baltic way of life." What is important here is not only the perception of cross-cultural influences, but also the positive values associated with them. It seems, however, that in Latvia at least, this feeling of cultural fertilization is mostly a one-way affair. Few local Latvians would, in a similar manner, admit that they have adjusted to—and certainly not improved—their manner of life under the influence of the local Russians.

In Kazakstan, there seems to be a greater readiness to distinguish between Russian political penetration (which is regarded as traditional imperialism and has few, if any, mitigating features), on the one hand, and Russian cultural penetration on the other. Both at the official level and among the Kazak population at large, a positive evaluation of Russian culture may often be heard. President Nazarbaev has asserted that

> it is no secret that we Kazaks study Russian culture and literature with alacrity. Conversely, the spirit of our steppes penetrates deeply into everyone who lives in this republic and is attached to Kazakstan in his heart.

---

[70] Gasprinskii 1993, 38.

[71] Pavlovich 1980; Laitin 1995; Kolstø 1996b.

[72] Impressions based on interviews in Almaty, Shymkent, Semipalatinsk and Ust-Kamenogorsk in May 1993 and September 1996, see also chapter 6.

Therefore, we may talk about a common self-identification among all citizens in our country.[73]

There is certainly some truth in the first parts of this quotation. Modern Kazak culture—particularly in the cities, but not only—is saturated with Russian impulses, far more than the cultures of other post-Soviet Central Asian states, and probably also more than the indigenous Baltic cultures. However, Nazarbaev's conclusion is clearly overstated. The cultural cross-fertilization in Kazakstan may have influenced the self-identification of both major groups, but it has not merged them.[74]

The case for a homogeneous society in Latvia and Kazakstan seems to be weak. It should be noted that even to the extent that the Russophone diaspora communities acquire new character traits under the impact of the surrounding milieu, they do not shed their self-understanding as being Slavs/post-Soviets (in Latvia) and Europeans/Russians (in Kazakstan). Both in their own eyes and in the eyes of the disinterested observer they retain their own identity. The development of a unique diaspora culture is primarily a matter of dissociation from the Russian (Ukrainian, Belarusian, etc.) core group, not of amalgamation with or assimilation to the local groups.

Conclusion

This survey of the cultural landscape in Latvia and Kazakstan has, inevitably, taken the official Soviet census data as its starting point. These data, as we have seen, are marred by certain methodological problems and must be used with caution. The inaccuracies and distortions are partly a result of Soviet state policies, partly unintended effects of how the questionnaires were formulated and people responded to them.

Most importantly, the Soviet approach to the nationality question had the effect of elevating ethnicity to the position as *the* paramount cultural marker. In this chapter I have tried to detect and assess other criteria and characteristics which may affect the reidentification and realignment of the population—religion, territory, historical experiences, social environment, etc. In most cases I have found that these additional perspectives add to rather than retract from the impression that Latvia and Kazakstan are bipolar societies. Two of the most

---

[73] Nazarbaev 1994, 18.

[74] See e.g. Akiner 1997, 382.

important parameters—religion and language—have the double effect of drawing the majority of the non-titular population closer together in a new diaspora identity and, at the same time, erecting a reinforced divide between them and the titular nation. While some other parameters may again blur this bicultural picture, I find that bipolarization—rather than continuum, fragmentation and homogeneity—most aptly describes contemporary Latvian and Kazakstani society.

In a well-informed article, Federica Moroni describes Kazakstan as "an extremely fragmented country."[75] In support of this conclusion, she adduces arguments of ethnic and religious diversity as well as evidence of intra-ethnic tensions within the titular ethnos caused by clan and urban–rural rivalry. While her discussion of Kazakstani society is perceptive, the characteristics she is pointing out I believe, do not necessarily add up to an extremely fragmented country.

However, also Moroni indirectly acknowledges that the European–Kazak dichotomy is the most important feature in the cultural mosaic of Kazakstan. She makes the interesting remark that the three basic elements of Kazak identity—Turkishness, Islam, and nomadism—have crystallized largely in contrast to Russia and to the Russians who, in a sense, represent their "constituting other." Thus, in negative terms, the Kazaks see themselves as "a non-Russian, non-Orthodox, non-sedentary people."[76] This is a description of a cultural landscape characterized by binary oppositions.

Some final caveats, however, must be added. First, while Kazakstan must be recognized as strongly bipolar, Latvia in our view is only moderately so. Second, the cultural cleavages between these communities are not cut in stone. There are certain overlappings at the edges and certain splits within each community that may widen if they are exploited for political purposes. And indeed, as we shall see in chapters 4, 5, and 7, efforts to restructure the cultural landscape—fragment some groups and amalgamate others—is indeed an important element of nation-building and ethnic policies in both Latvia and Kazakstan.

I present bipolarization only as a description, not as a prescription and make no claim that continued bipolarization is either inevitable or necessarily desirable. The collapse of the Soviet Union has opened up a

---

[75] Moroni 1994, 34.

[76] Moroni 1994, 35. For a general discussion of identity formation through contrast to "the constituting other," see Neumann 1993.

whole new game of ethnopolitics. The future cultural relations and social alignments in Latvia and Kazakstan will depend on both the policies pursued by the state authorities regarding nation-building and social integration and on the responses and initiatives of the population itself.

3

Nation-Building and Social Integration Theory

Pål Kolstø

Nation-building

The term "nation-building" came into vogue among historically oriented political scientists in the 1950s and 1960s. Its main proponents
included such captains of the American academic community as Karl
Deutsch, Charles Tilly, and Reinhard Bendix. Nation-building theory
was primarily used to describe the processes of national integration and
consolidation that led up to the establishment of the modern nation-
state—as distinct from various form of traditional states, such as feu-
dal and dynastic states, church states, empires, etc. "Nation-building"
is an architectural metaphor which, strictly speaking, implies the
existence of consciously acting agents such as architects, engineers, car-
penters, and the like. However, as used by political scientists, the term
covers not only conscious strategies initiated by state leaders but also
unplanned societal change.[1] In the apt phrase of Øyvind Østerud, the
concept of "nation-building" became for political science what
"industrialization" was to social economy: an indispensable tool for
detecting, describing and analyzing the macrohistorical and sociological dynamics that have produced the modern state.[2]

The traditional, premodern state was made up of isolated communities with parochial cultures at the "bottom" of society and a distant, and aloof, state structure at "the top," largely content with col-
lecting taxes and keeping order. Through nation-building these two

---

[1] Friedrich 1963, 28; Tilly et al. 1975.
[2] Østerud 1978, 117ff.

spheres were brought into more intimate contact with each other. Members of the local communities were drawn upwards into the larger society through education and political participation. The state authorities, in turn, expanded their demands and obligations toward the members of society by offering a wide array of services and integrative social networks. The *subjects* of the monarch were gradually and imperceptibly turned into *citizens* of the nation-state. Substate cultures and loyalties either vanished or lost their political importance, superseded by loyalties toward the larger entity, the *state*.

Stein Rokkan's model saw nation-building as consisting of four analytically distinct aspects.[3] In Western Europe these aspects had usually followed one upon the other in more or less the same order. Thus, they could be regarded not only as aspects but also as *phases* of nation-building.

The first phase resulted in economic and cultural unification at the elite level. The second phase brought ever-larger sectors of the masses into the system through conscription into the army, enrollment in compulsory schools, etc. The burgeoning mass media created channels for direct contact between the central elites and periphery populations and generated widespread feelings of identity with the political system at large.

In the third phase, the subject masses were brought into active participation in the workings of the territorial political system. Finally, in the last stage the administrative apparatus of the state expanded. Public welfare services were established and nationwide policies for the equalization of economic conditions were designed.

In the oldest nation-states of Europe, those along the Atlantic rim, the earliest stage of these processes commenced in the Middle Ages and lasted until the French Revolution. While it is impossible to pinpoint exactly when the entire nation-building process was completed, it certainly went on for several centuries. In the ideal variant, each consecutive phase set in only after the previous one had run its course. This ensured the lowest possible level of social upheavals and disruptions, Rokkan believed.

In the mid-1970s, discussions on nation-building took a new turn. In a seminal article pointedly titled "Nation-building or Nation-destroying?" Walker Connor launched a blistering attack on the school of thought associated with Karl Deutsch and his students.[4] Connor noted that the nation-building literature was preoccupied with social cleavages of various kinds—between burghers and peasants, nobles and

---

[3] Rokkan 1975, 570ff.

[4] Reprinted in Connor 1994, 28-66.

commoners, elites and masses—but virtually or totally ignored *ethnic diversity*. This Connor regarded as an inexcusable sin of omission, since, according to his computation, only 9 percent of the states of the world could be regarded as ethnically homogeneous.

Since "nation-building" in the Deutschian tradition meant assimilation into the larger society and the eradication of ethnic peculiarities, Connor believed that, in world history, it had produced more nation-*destruction* than nation-*building*. However, the efficiency of active engineering in nation-building, he held, had generally been greatly exaggerated. Very often it was counterproductive, regularly producing a backlash of ethnic revivalism. Complete assimilation of ethnic minorities had largely failed all over the world, even in that alleged stronghold of consummate nation-building, Western Europe.

Another cause of the fundamental flaws of nation-building theory Connor found in the terminological confusion caused by the diverse usages of the word "nation." As he pointed out, this term is sometimes used with reference to cultural groups and peoples, while, at other times, it describes political entities (states), i.e., expressions such as "United Nations" and "international politics." Even more misleading, he felt, was the tendency to use the term "nation" to describe the total population of a particular state without regard for its ethnic composition.

While reserving the term "nation" for ethnic groups only, Connor discarded all objective cultural markers as valid identity demarcations for these units. Neither common language, common religion, nor any other shared cultural reservoir within a group qualified as a genuine sign of nationhood. Any such attempt to objectivize the nation was to mistake the cultural manifestations of a nation for its essence. The true nature of the ethnos was in all and every case the sense of common ancestry shared by its members, Connor asserted. The nation is the ultimate extended family. To be sure, hardly ever could a common origin of the members of a nation be proven. In fact, very often it can be established that a nation stems from diverse ethnic sources. The belief in a common genetic origin can therefore usually be shown to be pure myth. Nonetheless, adherence to this myth has remained a *sine qua non* for every nation, Connor maintained.[5]

Later theoreticians developed Connor's understanding in two different directions. The "modernists"—such as Benedict Anderson, Tom Nairn, Ernest Gellner and Eric Hobsbawm – strongly underlined the myth aspect of the nation. In a celebrated book title, Benedict Anderson coined the expression "imagined communities" to describe modern

---

[5] Connor 1994, 92–94 (Reprint from 1978).

nations. The nation is a product of imagination in the sense that the members of the community do not know each other personally and can only imagine themselves to be in communion with each other. However, Anderson distanced himself from Gellner and Hobsbawm who took the "imagination" metaphor one step further, interpreting it in the direction of "invention" and "fabrication." The nation should not be defined as "false consciousness" Anderson insisted. Definitions like that would imply that there are such things as "true communities" which can be juxtaposed to "artificial" nations. "In fact, all communities larger than primordial villages of face-to-face contact (and perhaps even these) are imagined."[6]

At the same time, Anthony Smith, Rasma Karklins and others developed Connor's themes in another direction, strongly emphasizing the ethnic aspect of the nation. While agreeing with the modernists that "nations" as we know them are recent phenomena, Smith insisted that they have a long prehistory, evolving out of ethnic cores. Of the conglomerate of ethnic groups existing in earlier ages, some developed into would-be nations aspiring for nationhood and a state of their own, with a few eventually acquiring it. Why do some groups succeed while others fail? Often this must be explained as a result of historical contingencies, a confluence of felicitous circumstances—but it may also be due to the active efforts of determined nationalists, the nation-builders.[7]

Smith and his disciples retained but reemployed the term "nation-building" introduced by the earlier, modernist school of thought. In accordance with their "neoprimordialist" understanding of all modern nations as products of age-old ethnic building material they heavily underlined the cultural, symbolic, ethnic and myth-making aspects of nation-building:

> Even for the most recently created states, ethnic homogeneity and cultural unity are paramount considerations. Even where their societies are genuinely "plural" and there is an ideological commitment to pluralism and cultural toleration, the elites of the new states find themselves compelled, by their own ideals and the logic of the ethnic situation, to forge new myths and symbols of their emergent nations and a new "political culture" of anti-colonialism and the post-colonial (African or Asian) state.[8]

---

[6] Anderson 1983/1994, 6.

[7] A. Smith 1992, 74.

[8] A. Smith 1986, 147.

Social Integration

In the liberal tradition of the nineteenth century we may identify two somewhat divergent views on national integration. One dominant line of thought regarded the cultural and linguistic dissolution of the minorities into "high cultures" as not only historically inevitable but also as indisputably beneficial to the minorities themselves. This process was often labelled "assimilation," "acculturation" or "amalgamation" rather than "integration," but no clear distinctions were made among these concepts. It goes without saying that an individual fully assimilated into the national culture also would be successfully integrated into the larger society.

A classic expression of the assimilationist view may be found in John Stuart Mill's *Considerations on Representative Government*:

> Experience proves that it is possible for one nationality to merge and be absorbed in another: and when it was originally an inferior and more backward portion of the human race the absorption is greatly to its advantage. Nobody can suppose that it is not more beneficial to a Breton, or a Basque of French Navarre, to be brought into the current of the ideas and feelings of a highly civilised and cultivated people—to be a member of the French nationality, admitted on equal terms to all the privileges of French citizenship, sharing the advantages of French protection, and the dignity of French power—than to sulk on his own rocks...[9]

A somewhat different view was taken by Lord Acton. He was more inclined to see cultural diversity as a blessing for the members of society and a safeguard against tyranny:

> The presence of different nations under the same sovereignty [...] provides against the servility which flourishes under the shadow of a single authority, by balancing interests, multiplying associations, and giving the subject the restraint and support of a combined opinion.[10]

Not unity and uniformity, but diversity and harmony ought to reign in society, was Acton's view. However, by no means did he regard all cultures as equal or equally worthy of preservation. On the contrary, one of the main reasons why people from different cultures ought to be included in the same state was that "inferior races" could thereby be raised, by learning from intellectually superior nationalities:

---

[9] Mill 1861/1946, 294–95.
[10] Acton 1862/1967, 149.

> Exhausted and decaying nations are revived by the contact of a younger vitality. Nations in which the elements of organisation and the capacity for government have been lost [...] are restored and educated anew under the discipline of a stronger and less corrupted race.[11]

In fact, Acton was prepared to use such phrases as "the cauldron of the State" in which a "fusion" takes place through which the vigor, the knowledge, and the capacity of one portion of mankind may be communicated to another. Thus, his arguments for a multicultural state lead us toward a surprising result: under the tutelage of a superior nationality, members of the less advanced cultures in the state will shed many of their distinctive traits and learn true civilization. Exactly how much will remain of their peculiar identities (to use a modern word which Acton does not employ) remains unclear,[12] but his vision of social integration was not as far removed from John Stuart Mill's as many observers have been led to believe.

Most of what was written on nation-building and integration in the 1960s and 1970s stood in the combined tradition of Mill and Acton. To Karl Deutsch and his disciples, nation-building and national integration were but two sides of the same coin, indeed, simply two ways of describing the same process. A major object of nation-building was to weld the disparate elements of the populace into a congruent whole by forging new loyalties and identities at the national (= state) level at the expense of localism and particularistic identification. Deutsch specified four stages by which he expected this process to take place: Open or latent resistance to political amalgamation into a common national state; minimal integration to the point of passive compliance with the orders of such an amalgamated government; deeper political integration to the point of active support for such a common state but with continuing ethnic or cultural group cohesion and diversity, and, finally, the coincidence of political amalgamation and integration with the assimilation of all groups to a common language and culture.[13]

The modernists saw successful assimilation as a prerequisite for upward social mobilization for members of minority cultures. Only those individuals who mastered the language and the cultural code of the dominant group could aspire for achievement. In most of his writings,

---

[11] Ibid., 150.

[12] On the one hand, he saw the multinational character of Austria as one of the assets of this state. In the Habsburg domains no single nation was so predominant as to be able to overcome and absorb the others. One the other hand, Acton accepted the idea that, in the course of time, "a State may produce a nationality." Acton 1862/1967, 152 and 156.

[13] Deutsch 1963, 7–8.

Deutsch also saw the creation of the homogeneous society, with equal opportunities for all groups, as fully attainable.[14]

Walker Connor took issue with the assimilation theory of the modernizationists on two accounts. He did not believe that the eradication of cultural differences in society was necessarily a good thing.[15] Also, he questioned the one-to-one relationship between modernization and cultural homogenization.

> The continuous spread of modern communication and transportation facilities, as well as statewide social institutions such as public school systems, can have a great influence upon programs of assimilation. But can the nature of that influence be predicted? It is a truism that centralized communications and increased contacts help to dissolve regional cultural distinctions within a state such as the United States. Yet, if one is dealing not with minor variations of the same culture, but with two distinct and self-differentiating cultures, are not increased contacts between the two apt to increase antagonism?[16]

In later articles Connor dropped the question mark and more and more forcefully insisted that this was indeed the case. Advances in communication and transportation tend to increase cultural awareness among minorities by making their members more conscious of the distinctions that set their own community apart from other groups. The individual comes to identify more and more closely with his own in-group, contrasting himself to the immediate surroundings.[17]

This view was accepted and even somewhat sharpened by Arend Lijphart, another pioneer of the new trend in integration theory. Lijphart distinguished between essentially homogeneous societies, where increased contacts are likely to lead to an increase in mutual understanding and further homogenization, on the one hand, and "plural societies," where close contacts are likely to produce strain and hostility, on the other. In societies of the latter type, segregation among the dominant cultural groups would be preferable to integration, he maintained. "Clear boundaries between the segments of a plural society have the advantage of limiting mutual contacts and consequently of

---

[14] Connor pointed out that there existed some vacillations and inner inconsistencies in Deutsch's writings on the subject. Connor 1994, 30–35 (Reprint from 1972). Deutsch' basic optimism was at times interrupted by fits of pessimism. The upbeat mood prevailed, however, and resonated in a number of scholarly works on ethnic integration in the 1970s, often written by assimilated non-European members of the American scholarly community. See, e.g., Shibutani and Kwan 1965.

[15] He described it as "succumbing to foreign cultural inroads." Connor 1994, 139 (Reprint from 1969).

[16] Connor 1994, 21 (Reprint from 1966).

[17] Connor 1994, 37 (Reprint from 1972); see also Connor 1994, 171 (Reprint from 1979).

limiting the chances of ever-present potential antagonisms to erupt into actual hostility."[18]

The writings of Lijphart and Connor produced "a minor revolution" in the thinking about processes of national integration, as Anthony Birch put it.[19] It would certainly be wrong to see this as a switch from the assimilationist vision of Mill to the more pluralist vision of Acton: their "revolution" was far more radical than that. Whereas Acton remained a firm believer in the blessings of cross-cultural intercourse, and for that very reason extolled the multinational state as an unqualified good, Connor, and especially Lijphart, on the contrary not only accepted but relished the abundance of plural states. They were skeptical not only to the possibility but indeed also to the desirability of assimilation.

On the issue of assimilation, Ernest Gellner took a stance in-between the two positions sketched above. Himself a Central European thoroughly integrated into British academe, he shared the conviction of the early liberals and modernizationists that full assimilation of cultural minorities was highly desirable, but he was somewhat more pessimistic about its feasibility. Gellner identified what he called "entropy resistance" as a major obstacle to successful assimilation, and, by the same token, to the social mobilization of minorities. By "entropy" Gellner meant the inherent tendency of modern industrial society to erase social and regional barriers, creating a homogeneous, equalized society. The territorial and work units of industrial societies are basically *ad hoc*, he pointed out: "Membership is fluid, has a great turnover, and does not generally engage or commit the loyalty and identity of members. In brief, the old structures are dissipated and largely replaced by an internally random and fluid totality, within which there is not much (certainly when compared with the preceding agrarian society) by way of genuine sub-structures."[20]

However, some group attributes, Gellner maintained, have a marked tendency not to become evenly dispersed throughout society over time. Very often these entropy-resistant, ineradicable traits are of a physical/physiological nature, such as black skin (or, to stick to Gellner's more surrealistic variant: blue pigmentation). Whenever a high number of persons of blue (black) complexion are located near the bottom of the social ladder, color may become an easily detectable identity marker checking the upward social drift of all blue people. A convenient tool

---

[18] Lijphart 1977, 88.

[19] Birch 1989, 70.

[20] Gellner 1983/1990, 63.

for social stigmatization and oppression of the have-nots has thus been found.

So far, it would seem that Gellner's theory of entropy resistance would belong to the research of racial discrimination rather than to the study of ethnocultural integration. However, Gellner goes on to claim that "some deeply engrained religious–cultural habits possess a vigor and tenacity which can virtually equal those which are rooted in our genetic constitution.... [A]n identification with one of two rival local cultures [may be] so firm as to be comparable to some physical characteristic."[21] Thus, while Connor and those who agree with him see the impediments to smooth cultural assimilation as stemming from the very logic of modernization itself, Gellner located these hindrances in traits and characteristics which are usually borne only by some members in society.

A sophisticated theory of ethnic integration which avoids the one-sidedness of both the assimilationist and the segregationist schools, has been presented by R.A. Schermerhorn.[22] Schermerhorn primarily tries to identify conditions under which contact between two ethnic groups will lead to integration and when it will lead to conflict.[23] He starts from the premise that all relationships between ethnic groups are unequal. "[T]he probability is overwhelming that when two groups with different cultural histories establish contacts that are regular rather than occasional or intermittent, one of the two groups will typically assume dominance over the other."[24] Schermerhorn's argument in support of this assumption is logical rather than empirical: "complete equality of power is the least probable condition—a kind of limiting case."

Of crucial importance for the development of an ethnic relationship is the compatibility of group goals. The various possible goals which a subordinate group can strive toward Schermerhorn divides into two opposite tendencies—centripetal and centrifugal. Under the first tendency fall all strivings for (cultural) assimilation and (structural) incorporation, under the latter, calls for autonomy, separation, federation, and secession.

Both among the superordinate and the subordinate group each of these two orientations may be prevailing. If there is a congruency of

---

[21] Ibid., 71.

[22] Schermerhorn 1970.

[23] By focusing on binary relationships only, Schermerhorn does not want to limit his theory to ethnically bipolar societies only. He reduces the number to two simply in order to be able to concentrate on other variables than numbers; this analytical limitation, however, makes his framework particularly suitable to our purposes.

[24] Schermerhorn, 1970, 68.

goals, this will lead to integration, Schermerhorn asserts, but if the goals are incompatible, conflict will arise. If a majority in the subordinate group want to be assimilated, and this ambition is resisted by the superordinate group, this will inevitably lead to tension. The opposite combination may also frequently arise: The superordinate group insists on assimilation while the subordinates want to retain their separate identity, and, for that reason, demand cultural autonomy, etc.

Schermerhorn concludes that if we look at both upper and lower groups in reciprocal interaction we get the outcomes matrix depicted in Figure 3.1. Whenever there is an incongruency of goal orientations—the centripetal or centrifugal trends of the subordinate group being opposed and frustrated by the superordinate group—conflict will be endemic or intermittent. Whenever both groups favor a centripetal policy, this will facilitate integration. And "if both groups favor a centripetal policy, this too will foster integration, though of a different kind (such as "live and let live")."[25]

The lasting value of Schermerhorn's theoretical framework is its strong emphasis on perceptions and objectives rather than on policy options alone. No policy can be deemed as conflict-producing *per se* unless we know what the involved groups actually want. The only problem with his analysis, as I see it, is the very wide definition of "integration" which is too far removed from everyday language. In my

FIGURE 3.1 Congruent and Incongruent Orientations Toward Centripetal and Centrifugal Trends of Subordinates as Viewed by Themselves and Superordinates

Tending towards integration

	A	B
Superordinates	Cp	Cf
Subordinates	Cp	Cf
	Assimilation Incorporation	Cultural pluralism Autonomy

Tending towards conflict

	C	D
Superordinates	Cf	Cp
Subordinates	Cp	Cf
	Forced segregation with resistance	Forced assimilation with resistance

Cp = centripetal trends, Cf= centrifugal trends

[25] Ibid., 82–83.

opinion, a live-and-let-live society may well be peaceful and harmonious, but it should not be described as "integrated." Rather, I will reserve the term "integration" for cell A in Schermerhorn's figure. This means that, in Schermerhorn's terminology, a sentence such as "also non-integrated societies may avoid ethnic conflict" will be a contradiction in terms. As the term "integration" will be used in the following sections of this book, however, the sentence makes perfect logical sense. This will be the case if the group relations conform to the constellation in cell B in Schermerhorn's framework.

I would also emphasize, perhaps more strongly than Schermerhorn does, that the modal tendencies in his typology must be treated as dynamic and susceptible to constant change. The predominant orientation within a cultural community may be redirected as a result of generational shifts or of other internal developments, or as a result of exogenous influences. In particular, a reorientation of the goals of the superior group will inevitably impinge upon the goals of the subordinate group, and vice versa.

Finally, the "modal tendency" sums up not only the orientations of a high number of individuals but also of goal orientations in many different social arenas: language preferences, political loyalties, cultural attachments, etc. Goal orientations sometimes come in bundles, but not always. A member of a nontitular group in Latvia may feel strongly attached to his/her "historical homeland," Russia, but nevertheless want to participate in Latvian political life and/or send his/her children to Latvian-language schools. Other combinations of orientations are also quite possible. Below, we will often isolate one particular arena and identify one aspect of the modal tendency at a time.

Is Nation-Building / Integration Theory
Applicable to Non-Western Societies?

The classical theory of nation-building was an endeavor to understand the evolution of Western states. Inevitably, it reflected Western realities. Nevertheless, its proponents maintained that the theory was applicable also to the study of non-Western societies. This belief was based in part on a linear perception of history which was not always made explicit: all societies were, by the inner logic of human development, bound to pass through the same stages. In addition, most nation-building theorists believed that Western society was really a better society to live in. If they were not compelled by the forces of history to emulate the West, the leaders of non-Western states ought to do so—for their own sake and the sake of their population.

In fact, contrast with the outside world was, from the very beginning, part and parcel of the endeavor. It was certainly not fortuitous that this theory developed in the 1960s. The increased interest in the genesis of states came as a response to the flurry of new state-making in the wake of decolonization in Africa. Nation-building theorists wanted to underline that "states" could mean very many different things in different settings, and that one should not too readily equate these new, hastily created political contraptions with the sturdy, time-tested nation-states of old.[26] At the very most, these new members of the international community should be viewed as nation-states in the making only. A fair number of the contemporary nation-building projects, it was assumed, would never succeed.[27] Such unfortunates would either sink back into non-existence, or remain internationally recognized states devoid of any national character.

Rokkan remarked that the one distinguishing factor that set nation-building in the new states off from the "old" processes was the time factor. Developments which in Western Europe had lasted for centuries, now had to be telescoped into decades. Under such circumstances the various phases could hardly be kept apart, but would overlap or even run parallel. This, in his opinion, would produce "fundamentally different conditions." The risks of wrong turns and discontinuities would multiply. Likewise, the element of conscious social engineering in the nation-building process would increase. Nevertheless, Rokkan felt that the new states could learn from European experience, "more from the smaller countries than from the large, more from the multiculturally consociational polities than from the homogeneous dynastic states, more from the European latecomers than from the old established nations."[28]

The assumptions which informed the nation-building debate in the post-colonial era of the 1960s and 1970s also have a bearing on the debate on nation-building in the post-Communist world of the 1990s. Once again we see the state authorities and scholars in today's newly independent countries employing the categories and terminology of Western political science to describe—and prescribe—social processes in their own countries, while their Western colleagues hasten to remind them that similarities in terminology easily may obscure significant differences in substance.

---

[26] Friedrich 1963, 32.

[27] Strayer 1963, 25.

[28] Rokkan 1975, 600.

Nations and Nation-Building in Eastern Europe

As pointed out in Chapter 1, the key term "nation" may have two very different meanings: as a community of a state and as a community of culture—the civic nation vs. the ethnic nation. In the former case, the nation will be coterminous with the population of a (nation)-state; in the latter case, it may be both larger and smaller than the population in the state in which it resides.

In Eastern Europe—east of the Elbe—the ethnic understanding of the nation has deep roots, whereas the civic concept has tended to have very few adherents.[29] There are probably two important, interrelated reasons for this. First, in the West the bourgeoisie was the main motor behind the civic nation-state and civic national consciousness, while in Eastern Europe the national bourgeoisie has traditionally been conspicuously absent.[30] Trade and commerce were regarded as not very prestigious occupations, often relegated to outsiders. As a result, the thin stratum of bourgeoisie that could be found was very often of foreign stock—diaspora groups of Jews, Armenians, Germans, and Greeks. Such groups were frequently vilified as unnational leeches on the national body.

In addition, the imperial, dynastic state held its ground much longer in Eastern Europe than along the Atlantic rim. Both the Habsburg and the Romanov empires collapsed only as a result of the cataclysm that was World War I. The appellation and identity of these two states were in principle unrelated to the nations which were politically dominant, the Germans and the Russians. Both states represented cultural and ethnic patchworks—in the Habsburg domains, Germans made up less than 25 percent of the total population in the nineteenth century.[31] In the Russian census of 1897, 146 nationalities were listed; the largest of them, the Russians, constituted only 45 percent.[32] In the Habsburg as well as the Romanov empires, local privilege and customary law held sway in many regions to the very end.

The cultural and territorial heterogeneity of the East European empires was not a result of their size alone. It also reflected the fact that their rulers were far less energetic and systematic nation-builders than were their Western counterparts.[33] As long as internal peace was

---

[29] Kohn 1946; Liebich 1995.

[30] Sugar 1969/1994; Pipes 1974/1979, 191–221.

[31] Pearson 1983.

[32] Shanin 1985/1986, 58.

[33] Kappeler 1992; Kommisrud 1996.

retained and taxes paid, they were basically uninterested in the inner life of the various linguistic and religious groups of the state. Left to their own devices, these communities could over time develop strong national identities based on their cultural particularities. As long as the state was imperial, the nation could remain cultural and non-state.

In Russia, the ethnic understanding of the nation was reinforced rather than weakened after the Bolshevik takeover.[34] As early as in 1903, Lenin's party declared the right of all nations to self-determination, "nations" here being unequivocally identified with the (major) ethnic groups of the empire. However, as soon as Communist power had been consolidated, the promised right to secede from the state became so heavily circumscribed as to be rendered totally unattainable. Instead, national homelands in the form of Union republics and autonomous republics were instituted as a kind of substitute nation-states. These territorial units were given the name and, up to a point, the cultural imprint of the dominant ethnic group, the so-called "titular nations."

The 1920s and early 1930s saw a vigorous policy of promoting (often this meant creating) new elites among these groups.[35] This is usually referred to as the policy of *korenizatsiya* or "nativization," but one leading Western expert on Soviet nationality policies prefers to call it the Soviet policy of "nation-building."[36]

In most respects, the USSR was a strictly unitary state in which the powers of the center were formidable. Throughout most of Soviet history, the federal element in the state structure was largely dismissed as a mere sham. However, in the final years of the Brezhnev period, the ethnically based federation became imbued with a certain degree of real content. Although this trend fell short of a complete return to the *korenizatsiya* period, federalism did become an important fact of Soviet life.[37]

The Union republics of the Soviet Union were strange halfway houses between civic and ethnic units. In the dual-layer Union legislature they were represented in the Chamber of Nationalities. Deputies to this chamber were chosen not solely among the titular nationalities, but among all residents of the republic. In some cases only a minority of the deputies from a certain autonomous formation actually belonged to

[34] Slezkine 1994; Suny 1993; Kolstø 1993b, 9–11.

[35] Carrère d'Encausse 1992.

[36] Simon 1986/1991. By this term, Gerhard Simon was referring on the one hand to the purposeful policy of the party and the state to consolidate or create nations and, on the other, to the internal processes of change that convert an ethnic community into a nation.

[37] Zaslavsky 1982/1994, 91–129; Gleason 1990; Zaslavsky 1992.

the titular group. As far as these deputies had any political clout at all, they were expected to represent the interests of the territorial unit, not of the titular ethnic group.

To the other chamber of the Supreme Soviet, the Chamber of the Union, delegates were chosen according to the territorial principle, and ethnicity played no role. The real organs of power—the Politburo, the Secretariat of the Central Committee, the KGB and the Armed Forces—were also formally ethnically neutral, but in reality, ethnic Russians (and, to some extent, other East Slavs) were clearly overrepresented.[38]

Thus, not only the Union republics, but also the very Union itself was a curious hybrid of an ethnic and a civic state: on the one hand, it was a multinational state based on a nonethnic ideology (Soviet Marxism), on the other—an ethnic empire based on the power dominance of the largest nation, the Russians. This duality gave rise to a perennial debate on the nature of Soviet nationality policy—"internationalism or Russification?"[39]

Russian culture, and especially the Russian language, certainly enjoyed a privileged position and was forced on the non-Russians as well. Nonetheless, it should be borne in mind that the autonomous formations did in fact give the various titular groups some special rights within their respective territories. Indeed, whatever privileges and protection the non-Russians enjoyed in the Soviet Union (primarily in the fields of culture, education and language policy), they enjoyed *only* within "their" republics. Members of a nationality living in other parts of the Union had no special rights, even if they happened to dwell in a compact ethnic community. Such diaspora groups were more exposed to assimilation than the core group. The important lesson which the Soviet nationalities elites drew from this arrangement was that protection of minority rights "necessarily" takes the form of territorial arrangements. Nonterritorial schemes of minority protection was something they had no experience of. The Austro-Marxist idea of cultural (nonterritorial) autonomy had been rejected by the future People's Commissar of Nationalities, Joseph Stalin, as early as 1913, and remained a dead issue.[40]

At the same time, Soviet authorities did nothing to create ethnically pure Union republics in the demographic sense. The many ethnic groups had for centuries been living heavily intermingled with each other, and considerable interrepublican migration in the Soviet period

---

[38] Carrère d'Encausse 1979.

[39] See e.g. Nahaylo and Swoboda 1990.

[40] Stalin 1913/1946, 320-332.

further complicated the ethnic map.[41] This is the dual legacy which the new states of Eurasia have to come to grips with today as they embark upon their various nation-building projects: on the one hand, an exclusionary nation concept which equates the nation with the ethnic group. On the other hand, a medley of disparate ethnic groups living on the territory of the state.

Is Nation-Building / Integration Theory Applicable to Post-Communist Realities?

Throughout the former Soviet Union the new leaders have proclaimed their states as national states or "nation-states." As Rogers Brubaker has suggested, they might perhaps more appropriately be called "nationalizing states." They are ethnically heterogeneous, "yet conceived as nation-states, whose dominant elites promote (to varying degrees) the language, culture, demographic position, economic flourishing, or political hegemony of the nominally state-bearing nation."[42]

The distinction between nation-states and "nationalizing states" is analytically useful, but is one of stages and degrees rather than of qualitative differences. As Anthony Smith has argued, even the oldest nation-states in Western Europe, such as France, seem to have evolved out of ethnic cores.[43] Moreover, the forging of a national identity is, in a sense, a never-ending process: thus, all "nation-states" are also "nationalizing states." In Ernest Renan's celebrated expression, the nation is constituted and reconstituted in "a daily referendum."[44] Like a house which has to be kept up and repaired continuously once the construction period is over, nation-building in "nationalizing states" gradually shades into what we might call "nation-maintenance."

Even so, nation-building in newly independent states does not necessarily have to repeat the experiences of Western Europe or end up with the same architectural solutions. While there is hardly any question of *whether* the leaders of the post-Soviet states will pursue a policy of nation-building (they have repeatedly said that they will), we will need to find out *what kind* of nation-building this is supposed to be.

Rogers Brubaker has suggested a tripartite typology of alternative nation-building models in the nationalizing states in the new Europe:

---

[41] Lewis et al. 1976; Titma and Tuma 1992.

[42] Brubaker 1996b, 57.

[43] A. Smith 1986.

[44] Renan 1882/1992.

1. The model of the civic state, the state of and for its citizens, irrespective of ethnicity.
2. The model of the bi- or multinational state, as the state of and for two or more ethnocultural core nations.
3. The hybrid model of minority rights in which the state is understood as a national, but not a nationalizing state. Members of minority groups are guaranteed not only equal rights as citizens and thus protected, in principle, against differentialist nationalizing practices, but also certain specific minority rights, notably in the domain of language and education and are thus protected, in principle, against assimilationist nationalizing practices.[45]

In the civic state, ethnicity and ethnic nationality have no place, while in the bi- or multinational state, they have major public significance. In the former case, the constituent units of the polity are individuals, in the latter—ethnonational groups. The third model draws on elements from both.

Another typology, overlapping Brubaker's, has been suggested by Alexander Motyl.[46] Although his typology is particularly geared toward the Ukrainian situation, in principle it is applicable to all post-Soviet states. Motyl contrasts two types of ethnic nation-building—exclusive and inclusive—with a political/territorial model which, for all practical purposes, is identical to Brubaker's civic model. The exclusive variant, which is based on the linguistic, religious, and cultural traditions of the titular nation only, has relatively few adherents in the Former Soviet Union, Motyl notes with relief. Its disruptive potential may therefore easily be exaggerated. The real temptation for contemporary post-Soviet nation-builders, he believes, is the inclusive model. This model is not necessarily inconsistent with a state-based national idea, but it nevertheless views the ethnically defined titular nation as the cornerstone of state-building. What Motyl strongly advocates is the political, non-ethnic model of nation-building.

Jack Snyder has remarked that civic nationalism normally appears in well-institutionalized democracies.[47] Ethnic nationalism, in contrast, appears in an institutional vacuum. Therefore, it predominates when institutions collapse, when existing institutions are not fulfilling people's basic needs, and when satisfactory alternative structures are not readily available. This, Snyder believes, is the main reason why

---

[45] Brubaker 1996a, 432.

[46] Motyl 1993, 80.

[47] Snyder 1993, 12.

ethnic nationalism has been so prominent after the collapse of the Soviet state.

Certainly, in the new states of Eurasia strong, smoothly-functioning state organs are a scarce commodity. The establishment of such institutions will inevitably be a protracted process. Nevertheless, they are slowly coming into existence. According to Snyder, then, the time factor should work in favor of civic nationalism. Gradually, the new state leaders will feel that they have the necessary tools and the political security they need to implement a color-blind and culturally neutral variety of nation-building. Brubaker, however, disagrees. He recognizes that since the civic model has a certain international legitimacy, civic principles have been incorporated into some constitutional texts and are being evoked in some public declarations:

> But these civic principles remain external. It is hard to imagine a civic understanding coming to prevail given the pervasively institutionalized understanding of nationality as fundamentally ethnocultural rather than political, as sharply distinct from citizenship, and as grounding claims to "ownership" of polities—(which, after all, were expressly constructed of and for their eponymous ethnocultural nations).[48]

It is not difficult to find evidence in support of Brubaker's conclusion. What follows below is a random selection of quotations from post-Soviet academics.

In April 1994, a Kazak law professor tried to define the difference between "national" (*natsional'nyi*) sovereignty and "popular" (*narodnyi*) sovereignty. He concluded that "in character" Kazakstan is a national state of the Kazak nation, but "in content" it is a democratic, law-governed state. These two aspects, in his view, do not contradict each other:

> To my mind, a national state stems from the fulfilment of a nation's right to self-determination. In our case, this means the Kazak nation, as the indigenous nation which has an historical and unalienable right to fulfil its right to self-determination on its own territory.[49]

The ethnic understanding of the nation is here unmistakable.

In 1997 a Latvian professor of sociology reminded his readers that a national state is not the same as a monoethnic state—that, in fact, an absolute monoethnic society does not exist anywhere. Therefore, he believed, also Latvia can become a national state. "The idea of the

---

[48] Brubaker 1996a, 432.
[49] Sabikenov 1994, 9.

national state is that it ensures the security of the ethnic nation in the long run," he concluded.[50]

The ethnocentrism of the statements quoted above are perhaps not representative of the whole spectrum of the nation-building debate in their respective countries. However, it should be pointed out that this kind of thinking may also be found among post-Soviet scholars who represent liberal traditions clearly oriented toward the West and Western values. The prominent Estonian scholar and former Estonian minister of nationalities, Klara Hallik, asks: "Is it possible to combine the idea of a nation-state with the integration of the non-citizens and democratic perspectives of the state?"[51] Hallik's question is based on an ethnic understanding of "the nation." She explicitly states that "restored national statehood must guarantee the ethnic security of the Estonian nation." "The Estonian nation" here is equated with the ethnic Estonians.

In her question Hallik links the concept of the nation-state directly to the issue of integration, as did the pioneers of classical nation-building theory. However, the way she poses this question would probably made little sense to them. The early nation-building theorists, as we have seen, *defined* nation-building as the inclusion of parochial, culturally anomalous groups into the greater polity. Reinhard Bendix, for one, saw the extension of citizenship to members of ever-larger groups as the very hallmark of successful nation-building.[52] Clearly, the key concepts of the debate have undergone significant transmutations since their first formulation. These transmutations we must keep in mind as we now turn to the actual nation-building strategies in Latvia and Kazakstan.

---

[50] Vebers 1997, 158.
[51] Hallik 1994, 9–10.
[52] Bendix 1977.

4

Nation-Building and Ethnic Integration in Latvia

Aina Antane and Boris Tsilevich

Background

Statehood

In the thirteenth century the forbears of the contemporary Latvians were conquered by the Teutonic knights. At that time, the Latvian tribes had not yet coalesced into a coherent nationality. The Teutonic state formation on the territory of contemporary Latvia and contemporary Estonia existed until 1561. On its disintegration, the easternmost part of Latvia—Latgale—passed to Poland remaining under Polish rule until 1772, when it was ceded to Russia. Between 1629 and 1721 the territory of Vidzeme (northwestern Latvia) was ruled by the kingdom of Sweden. It was conquered by Russia during the Great Nordic war. The Duchy of Kurland, covering the regions of Kurzeme and Zemgale (western and southern Latvia), existed between 1651 and 1795. In the latter year its territories were incorporated into the Russian empire.

In tsarist Russia the territories of contemporary Latvia were divided among three *guberniias*: Kurland, Lifland, and Vitebsk. The *guberniia* of Vitebsk, to which a part of Latgale belonged, was not administratively a part of the Baltic provinces, but belonged to the "inner" guberniias.

In November 1918, after the collapse of the Russian empire, Latvia proclaimed its independence and in 1920 a peace treaty was signed by

TABLE 4.1 Ethnic Composition of Latvia's Population (1897–1989, in percent)

	1897	1920	1935	1959	1989
Latvians	68.3	72.6	75.5	62.0	52.0
Russians	12.0	5.7	10.6	26.6	34.0
Belarusians	-	4.1	1.4	2.9	4.5
Ukrainians	-	0.0	0.1	1.4	3.5
Germans	6.2	3.6	3.2	0.1	0.1
Jews	7.4	5.0	4.8	1.7	0.9
Poles	3.4	3.3	2.5	2.9	2.3
Lithuanians	1.4	1.6	1.2	1.5	1.3
Other	1.3	4.0	0.9	0.9	1.4

Sources: *Pervaia vseobshchaia perepis'* 1905; *Narodnoe khoziaistvo* 1990, 14; Mezgalis and Zvidrins 1973, 82.

Latvia and Soviet Russia. In the early 1920s Latvia gained official recognition from the leading states of the world and became a member of the League of Nations. The fact that Latvia existed as an independent nation-state in the interwar period has a direct and strong impact on the political development of post-Communist Latvia. Thus, after the collapse of the Soviet regime, Latvia did not establish independence, but restored it, and was in a position to draw upon the entire legal and constitutional corpus of the predecessor state in its nation-building efforts.

In 1940, as a result of the so-called Ribbentrop–Molotov pact, Latvia was annexed by the Soviet Union. This act was not internationally recognized. In June 1941, the country was overrun by the German army, but 1944–45 saw the return of the Soviets and the interrupted process of Sovietization continued.

During the period of perestroika the Popular Front became the dominant political force in Latvia. It won the majority of the votes in the 1990 elections to the republican Supreme Soviet. On 4 May 1990, this assembly passed a Declaration of Independence, reestablishing *de jure* the sovereign Latvian Republic of the interwar years. Central USSR authorities recognized the independence of Latvia only in September 1991. From that date Latvia was also *de facto* independent.

Development of the Ethnodemographic Situation

In 1897, the total population of Latvia was 1,929,400 persons, the majority of whom were Latvians (68 percent). The largest minorities were the Russians (read: East Slavs), 12 percent; Jews, 7.4 percent; Germans, 6.2 percent; and Poles, 3.4 percent (Table 4.1).

Unfortunately, there are no accurate data on the Latvian population at the time of the outbreak of World War I. Most experts believe, however, that in 1914 there were approximately 2,493,000 people within the confines of present-day Latvia, or 2,552,000 if we include the district of Abrene—presently a part of the Pskov oblast in Russia.[1] The ethnic Latvians made up slightly more than 60 percent, the remaining 40 percent belonged to broad variety of other nationalities.[2] The significant ethnodemographic changes that had taken place since 1897 were apparently linked, among other things, to the rapid industrialization which had taken place in the meantime. This industrialization had required an influx of large numbers of migrants from other parts of the Russian empire. The lower percentage of Latvians did not reflect a decrease in the absolute number of Latvians. On the contrary, it seems that, in the immediate prewar years, the Latvian population reached an all-time high of 1.5 million.[3]

World War I was a demographic catastrophe for so small country as Latvia. By 1920, as a combined result of military actions, flight, and evacuation to remote regions of the Russian empire, the population of Latvia tumbled to two-thirds of its prewar level.[4] By 1919, only 1,480,000 inhabitants remained in Latvia.[5]

The ethnic composition of the population had also been significantly altered. As a part of the war effort large industrial plants in Riga and other Latvian cities were dismantled and shipped eastward into the interior of Russia. Along with them, the workforces of the plants were also evacuated. These workers were mainly non-Latvians. Ethnic Latvians were less affected by these measures since they, to a large extent, lived in the countryside. Thus, while the total population of Latvia decreased radically, the share of the Latvians noticeably increased (see Table 4.1).

In the 1920s, some of the refugees and evacuees returned to Latvia. Among these groups, ethnic Latvians predominated. According to one source, 236,000 persons returned to Latvia from Soviet Russia between 1920 and 1928.[6] Nevertheless, neither the return migration nor the

---

[1] *Pervaia vseobshchaia perepis'* 1905; *Narodnoe khoziaistvo* 1990, 14; Mezgalis and Zvidrins 1973, 82.

[2] Skujenieks 1930, 132–33.

[3] *Cina* 8 March 1990; Mezs 1995, 31.

[4] *Latvijas statistika* 1921, 8–12.

[5] *Latvija citu* 1939, 79.

[6] *Sovetskaia Latviia* 1985, 117.

natural increase of the population sufficed to reestablish the prewar population, which in 1940 was 25 percent below the 1914 level.[7]

The first census conducted in the independent Latvian Republic, in 1920, showed that the share of the titular nation comprised 73 percent. Three subsequent censuses—in 1925, 1930, and 1935—gave witness to a gradual rise in the proportion of Latvians. Two of the main causes were their higher than average birthrates and the assimilation of non-Latvians, particularly in Latgale. In 1935, the Latvians comprised 75.5 percent of the total population of Latvia.[8] Thus, the ethnic composition of Latvia at this time was relatively homogeneous. Among the minorities, no particular ethnic group predominated. Here, the Russians made up the largest group (8.8 percent in 1935), but also the Germans (3.3 percent) and the Jews (4.9 percent) were very influential, particularly in certain fields of the economy and culture. In the state administration, on the other hand, the ethnic Latvian dominance was very pronounced. The overwhelming majority of the bureaucrats were Latvians.

All large and medium-sized minorities had their own schools which were financed by the state. Added to this, there were a ramified networks of social and cultural organizations serving the ethnic minorities. In the 1920s, Latvia and Estonia were regarded as two of the most democratic states in Europe with regard to minority policy. However, after Karl Ulmanis' *coup d'état* in May 1934 the cultural autonomy rights were severely circumscribed. Nevertheless, a part of the minority school system continued to function right up to the beginning of World War II.

New dramatic changes in the numbers and proportions of Latvia's population took place during the war years. In 1939, practically all Baltic Germans, totaling approximately 60 thousand persons, were "repatriated" to Germany on Hitler's insistence.[9] Two years later, the Stalinist regime conducted its first wave of repressions and deportations in Latvia. Latvian researchers usually cite the figure of 15–16,000 deportees.[10] The deportees were selected not on the basis of nationality but social background—in particular, state officials, military personnel and wealthy people—and represented no particular ethnic group. Naturally, ethnic Latvians predominated among them since they were the most numerous group in the population at large.

---

[7] *Narodnoe khoziaistvo* 1989; *Statisticheskii ezhegodnik* 1990, 14; Mezgailis and Zvidrins 1973, 52.

[8] *Ceturta* 1936–39.

[9] Dreifelds 1984; Rutkis 1960, 449.

[10] Mezs 1995; *Cina* 31 January 1989.

During the German occupation, which started in 1941–42, almost the entire Jewish population of Latvia was exterminated. (In German documents one can find references to Jews living in Latvia in 1943–44. These Jews, however, were exiled to Latvia from Western Europe at a later stage, to be interned in the Riga ghetto.)[11] Together with the Jews, also the majority of the Latvian gypsies were liquidated. The number of people sent to forced labor in Germany was 32–33,000.[12] In 1944 more than 100,000 inhabitants of Latvia fled to the West in order to escape the approaching Soviet Army. And finally, thousands died in combat, fighting on both sides of the front.

When the war was over, Latvia had for the second time in thirty years lost a third of its total population. According to Latvian and Western researchers, no more than 1.3–1.4 million persons remained on Latvian soil in 1945.[13] After the war, arrests and deportations continued, culminating in 1949, when approximately 45,000 persons were deported at the same time.

Latvia has traditionally had a low natural population increase and these enormous losses could hardly be recouped simply by procreation. However, an influx of migrants from other Soviet republics raised the population again. As at the beginning of the century, this immigration was facilitated by an extensive development of the Latvian economy which created a great demand for more workers. The growth of the Latvian industrial sector led to the establishment of non-Latvian enclaves around the major new plants (Ogre, Olaine, Ventspils, etc.) Also, a significant number of the new immigrants consisted of employees of Soviet Army units deployed on Latvian territory, as well as their dependents. A great many Soviet officers and NCOs, who had completed their service in Latvia, decided to stay on in the country after demobilization. In fact, Riga become one of the most popular and prestigious residential areas in the entire Soviet Union for retired Soviet officers. One reason for this was the limited opportunity these people had to gain a residence permit for Moscow, Leningrad, or along the Black Sea coast.

In this way, immigration became the most important factor behind both the Latvian population increase and the concomitant change in its ethnic composition in the Soviet period. In the 1970s and '80s, Latvia had the highest levels of immigration of all Union republics. The fairly advanced economy, the relatively high quality of the cultural and recreational facilities (by Soviet standards), plus Riga's

---

[11] Rutkis 1960, 432.

[12] *Sovetskaia Latviia* 1985, 229; Rutkis 1960, 437.

[13] Misiunas and Taagepera 1983, 274–75; Dreifelds 1984; Mezgalis 1985, 57.

long-standing reputation as a "European" city, combined to persuade many people from other parts of the USSR to move to Latvia. Naturally, this situation left an imprint on the economic and social situation of the indigenous (first and foremost, the titular) nation, as well as on their psychology and world view.

Demographic Dynamics
After the Restoration of Independence

Numerical Changes of the Population

As already mentioned, the growth of the Latvian population in the Soviet period was primarily brought about by a massive influx of people from other regions of the USSR. In 1988, the Latvian government introduced a number of measures to check this influx (limiting the possibility of acquiring residence permits [*propiska*], changing the procedures for housing distribution, etc.) Importantly, also the attitudes toward the new settlers among ordinary Latvians changed. Hostile sentiments which for a long time had been relatively widespread among large sections of the ethnically Latvian population, were now vented openly. Thanks to the new policy of glasnost, these feelings could also be expressed at public meetings and in the mass media. As a result of all this, the migration balance became negative in 1990 for the first time in many years, remaining so thereafter. In the 1990s, Latvia experienced a persistent and stable population decrease (see Figure 4.1).[14] Between 1991 and 1996 the population decreased by 165,000, that is, by more than 6.5 percent.

Latvia has achieved the position as the European country with the sharpest population decrease, surpassing both Estonia and Lithuania.[15] In the first half of 1996 there were 4.1 births per thousand inhabitants, as against 4.5 the year before. The mortality rate in the same period was 7.2 per 1000, as against 8.2 in the first half of 1995.[16]

The most important factor influencing the demographic balance in Latvia in 1991–93 was the negative migration balance. However, this balance, while still negative, is gradually leveling out, and the relative importance of the negative natural population increase is growing.

---

[14] *Latvija skaitļos* 1996, 21.

[15] *Biznes and Baltija*, 21 August 1995.

[16] *Diena* 9 September 1996.

FIGURE 4.1 Population of Latvia (1986–1996)

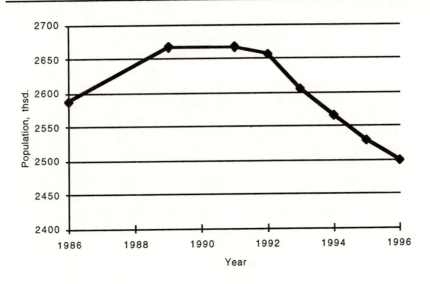

Source: Latvija skaitlos 1996, 21.

In 1994 the population losses caused by these two factors where approximately of the same size, but in 1995 the natural population decrease began to play a more decisive role than did the migration balance.

Ethnic Composition

By February 1996, the share of the titular nation—the ethnic Latvians—of the total population of Latvia had reached 56.49 percent. Russians comprised 30.38 percent; Belarusians, 4.29 percent; Ukrainians, 2.79 percent; Poles, 2.55 percent; Lithuanians, 1.42 percent; and Jews, 0.58 percent.[17] Then followed Gypsies, Germans, and Estonians, in descending order. The autochtonous Livian group numbered only 199 individuals.

As before, the ethnic composition of the urban population was very different from that of the rural population. In 1995, ethnic Latvians made up less than half of the population in all major cities of Latvia.[18]

---

[17] *Natsional'nye i etnicheskie gruppy* 1996, appendix.

[18] 'Par Latvijas Republikas cilvekiem', *Latvijas vestnesis*, 22 March 1995.

In the early 1990s the relative share of ethnic Latvians in the total population of Latvia started to rise, slowly but surely (Table 4.2). This came about both as a result of outmigration[19] and of the different levels of natural population increase among the various ethnic groups in the country. In 1985, the natural population increase among ethnic Latvians had been negative while it was positive among the nontitular population. However, between 1986 and 1989 the Latvians witnessed a positive natural population increase. Among the non-Latvians, the natural population increase continued to rise until 1987 but began to fall drastically from 1988. While both groups at present are experiencing negative growth, the decrease in the Latvian population is progressing more slowly (Figure 4.2).

In 1994, only one of the larger ethnic groups of Latvia, the Roma, experienced a positive population growth. Of the others, the Ukrainians had the least negative growth, followed by the Latvians. The most drastic decrease could be registered among the Jews. Since the late 1980s, the relative proportion of Latvians among newborn babies (recorded by nationality of the mother) has been steadily growing and

TABLE 4.2 Ethnic Changes in Latvia's Population since Independence

	1989	*1992*	*1994*	*1996*
Latvians	52.7	53.1	54.8	57.2
Russians	34.4	34.3	33.4	30.7
Belarusians	4.5	4.5	4.1	4.3
Ukrainians	3.5	3.4	3.1	2.8
Poles	2.3	2.3	2.2	2.6
Lithuanians	1.3	1.3	1.3	1.4
Other	1.1	1.1	1.0	0.9

Sources: *Natsional'nye i etnicheskie gruppy* 1996, appendix. *Etnosituacija Latvija* 1994, 4; *Diena* 15 February 1995.

TABLE 4.3 Age Structure of Ethnic Groups in Latvia (1989)

	0-14	*15-19*	*20-24*	*25-29*	*30-34*	*35-39*	*40-44*	*45-49*	*50-54*	*55-59*	*60+*
Latvians	22	7	6	7	6	5	5	7	6	6	19
Russians	23	7	7	8	8	8	6	5	6	5	14
Belarusians	12	5	7	10	9	9	6	8	8	7	16
Ukrainians	15	6	10	11	10	9	7	6	6	4	12
Poles	15	5	6	7	7	7	8	8	7	7	25
Jews	12	4	3	5	7	7	8	5	7	7	32

Source: *Etnosituacija Latvija* 1994, 7.

---

[19] Cf. section on migration below.

FIGURE 4.2 Ethnic Make-Up of the Largest Towns in Latvia

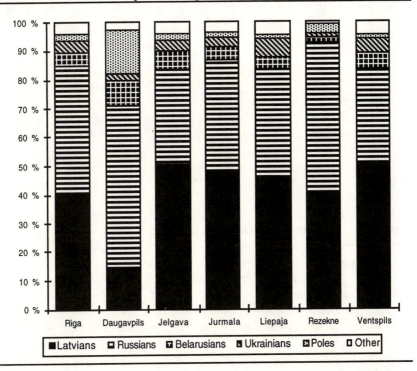

FIGURE 4.3 Natural Increase of Latvian and Non-Latvian Groups (1985–1995)

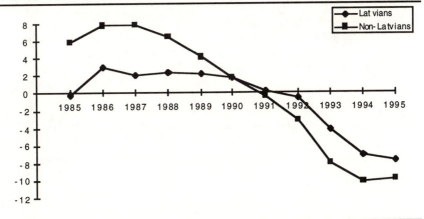

Sources: Latvijas demografijas 1995, 48; *Latvijas demografijas* 1996; Mezs 1994, 22; *LR Valsts statistikas komiteja* 1996, 47.

in 1994 reached 62.5 percent. In that year, the share of Latvians among the newborns was considerably higher (10 percent) than in the population at large. In all other ethnic groups, except the Lithuanians, this relationship was reversed.

Migration

As a result of the role played by migratory processes in the Soviet period in altering the demographic picture in Latvia, the question of migration became the subject of intense discussion in the 1990s. From the very beginning of the national renaissance, under perestroika, the migration issue—along with the language issue—were subjected to heated disputes. The very word "migrant" became loaded with a negative, pejorative content.

Various political groups in Latvia began to contemplate the possibility of redressing the ethnic balance established during the Soviet period by means of mass emigration or, as it was called, "repatriation" of non-Latvians who had arrived in the country post-World War II. A number of political parties promoted the "scientifically proven" thesis that, in order to secure the survival of the Latvian people, ethnic Latvians had to make up no less than 75 percent of the total number of citizens in Latvia. This idea was retained in the party programs of several parties (in particular the Movement for National Independence and the Farmers' Union of Latvia)[20] right up to the 1993 election campaign. In 1993, the future prime minister V. Birkavs wrote on various possible approaches to the "Russian question." He pointed out that

> among the national radicals, in particular among the national extremists, the idea of exiling the non-Latvians (or the "occupants" and "colonists," as they prefer to call them) dominate the discourse. The rationale behind this idea is to bring about a ratio of 75:25 of Latvians to non-Latvians in Latvia, as a minimum.[21]

For his own part, Birkavs, who is one of the leaders of the liberal-national party "Latvian way," has suggested that the optimal solution to this problem has to be found in a "very careful policy of naturalization" combined with an active support for "voluntary repatriation" and "free emigration to third countries."[22]

---

[20] *Diena*, 9 February 1993.

[21] *Diena*, 11 March 1993.

[22] *SM-segodnia*, 30 December 1993.

Frequently, spokesmen of the executive powers have also expressed an opinion on the issue. For instance, in 1993 the press secretary of the Department of Citizenship and Immigration said with regard to the postwar immigrants and their children, most of whom have been born in Latvia: "At all times the Department has emphasized and we want to reiterate that sooner or later all of these 700,000 inhabitants will have to leave Latvia."[23]

Since 1989 the migration balance has been negative. The number of immigrants has gradually decreased, and in 1995 only 2,800 persons entered the country.[24] This situation is linked to the extremely stringent criteria for immigration which have been set out by the Latvian legislators. For all practical purposes, the only three ways to acquire a permanent residence permit are 1) family reunification (with a spouse or a minor whom the citizen or the permanent resident of Latvia is providing for); 2) to invest no less than 1 million U.S. dollars in the Latvian economy[25]; or 3) in order to be repatriated.

Emigration peaked in 1992 when more than 53,000 persons left Latvia, for varying reasons: As a result of the recession in the Soviet-type industry high numbers of workers were being laid off. In order to find a

FIGURE 4.4 External Migration in Latvia (1989–1995)

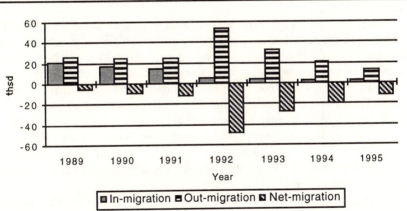

Sources: Latvija skaitlos 1996, 28; *Diena*, 2 April 96, *Iedzivotaju* 1996, 1; *Latvijas demografijas* 1996, 134.

---

[23] *Labrit*, 17 February 1993.

[24] *Latvija skaitlos* 1996, 28.

[25] Zakon LP "O v"ezde i prebyvanii," *VS-SM* (supplement to *Diena*) 31 July 1992.

new job, they had to pass a language exam to demonstrate their command of the Latvian language. In addition, all residents had to be registered in the Registry of Residents, and, at that time, many people who were living in dormitories (in addition to several other categories of people) were denied such registration. At the same time, a number of factory dormitories were closed down, and people who were out of work, having no place to live, even temporarily, and poor chances of finding a new job, had nothing that kept them in Latvia any longer.

At the same time, the redeployment of the former Soviet army units which were now under Russian jurisdiction, also intensified. Finally, on 1 January 1992 a new law on privatization of cooperative flats entered into force.[26] This law allowed those who wanted to leave the country to sell their privatized flats legally.

However, since 1993 emigration from Latvia has gradually slowed down. Thus, the predictions of the sociologists who said that the overall majority of the Russian-speaking inhabitants of Latvia had no intention of returning to their ethnic homeland, have been borne out.[27]

As before, the country of destination for the largest group of emigrants is Russia. In 1994, 77 percent of those who left Latvia headed for Russia, in 1995, 70 percent. The next most popular destinations were Belarus and Ukraine (5 and 7 percent, respectively). Only 2 to 3 percent left for U.S.A, Germany, or Israel.[28] Emigration to other countries was insignificant.

Generally speaking, these migrational processes have contributed to an aging of the remaining Latvian population. Naturally, elderly people have fewer real chances of achieving their goal if they should want to leave. Young people are everywhere more mobile. Among the emigrants there have been disproportionate numbers of individuals in their Thirties and Forties while the relative weight of persons over sixty years of age is only half their share of the population at large.

As regards the age group 16–29 years, they tend not to emigrate as much as the 30–50 year olds. One researcher, V. Volkov, has surmised that this reflects their greater hopes for successful adaptation to new life conditions in independent Latvia.[29]

Among the emigrants married people with children are overrepresented, as are persons with higher and medium levels of education.[30]

---

[26] Zakon LP "O privatizatsii ...," *VS-SM* (supplement to *Diena*) 24 December 1991.

[27] For instance, in December 1990 only 3 percent of the non-Latvians responded that they would leave the country if the Bill on Citizenship then under discussion became law. See Zepa. 1995, 32. Other surveys elicited identical or similar responses.

[28] *Iedzivotaju* 1995, 3.

[29] Volkovs 1995, 161.

[30] *Biznes un Baltija*, 18 March 1994.

These people may more easily find employment elsewhere than persons with low or no education.

Integration on the Political Level

Constitutional Provisions

The 1922 constitution—the Satversme—which was reenacted in 1991 without any significant changes, does not contain any specific references to human rights or minority rights. In 1996 the Saeima (the Latvian Parliament) started deliberations on a draft for a new second part of the Constitution which will be exclusively devoted to human rights in general and to certain guarantees of minority rights in particular.[31] However, by the end of 1996 the draft had not yet passed even its first reading.

A Constitutional Law on the Rights and Obligations of Individuals and Citizens, which was adopted in December 1991, compensates for this lacuna to a certain extent.[32] Thus, for instance, Article 12 of this Act proclaims that all persons are equal before the law, irrespective of race, nationality, and language.

The Law on Cultural Autonomy

In March 1991, the Latvian Supreme Soviet adopted legislation on the free development of national and ethnic groups in Latvia and on their right to cultural autonomy.[33] This law guarantees all ethnic groups in Latvia the right to cultural autonomy and self-rule in matters concerning their own ethnic culture. They have the right to observe their traditions, to use their own symbols, and celebrate their national holidays. Article 5 gives all ethnic groups the right to establish national cultural societies and associations, and these organizations are guaranteed the right to address the public through government-controlled mass media as well as the right to set up their own printed media. According to Article 14, such cultural societies also have the right to engage in commercial activities and to enjoy tax privileges. Article 10 states that state organs of the Latvian Republic shall extend

---

[31] *Diena*, 28 February 1996.

[32] *Constitutional law* 1995, 19.

[33] *Likums par Latvijas nacionalo*, 1995, 38.

material support to the development of the language, culture, and educational facilities of the national and ethnic groups living in Latvia and allocate financial means for these purposes over the state budget.

The national societies shall have the right to establish and run their own educational institutions. For their part, the national-cultural organizations are obliged to observe the laws of the Latvian Republic and to respect its sovereignty and territorial integrity (Article 6).

In the fall of 1993 the radical nationalistic Saeima faction "Fatherland and Freedom" presented a draft for an amended version of the Law on Cultural Autonomy. In their new version, the right to cultural autonomy should be extended to citizens of Latvia only. However, this amendment was rejected by the parliamentary majority.[34] A law adopted in April 1995—called the Act on the Status of Former Citizens of the USSR Who Do not Have Citizenship in Latvia or Any Other State (shortened below to Act on the Status of Former Citizens)—guarantees all permanent residents in Latvia, also non-citizens, the right to "preserve their native language and culture within the rights of national cultural autonomy and within their traditions, as long as these traditions do not conflict with Latvian laws" (art. 2, p.(2) 4).[35]

Implicitly, the law on cultural autonomy operates with a certain hierarchy of ethnic groups in Latvia. The preamble declares that "in the Latvian Republic lives the Latvian nation and the ancient indigenous nationality of the Livs, as well national and ethnic groups." No official documents define the distinction between "national" and "ethnic" groups. Off the record the architects of the law will say that, by "national," they had in mind groups which have their own statehood outside Latvia, such as, for instance, the Ukrainians, while the expression "ethnic" groups refers to those who have no statehood anywhere, such as, for instance, the Roma. Article 4 of the Act underlines the special responsibility of the state to preserve the national identity and the cultural and historical environment of the ancient indigenous nationality, the Livs.

In the Latvian political and public discourse frequent calls have been made for a further elaboration of this ethnic classification system. "Who, in fact, in scientific terminology, belongs to a national group, to an ethnic group, and to a historical minority, and which groups in Latvia may not be included among the autochtonous minorities?"[36] Appeals

[34] *Diena* 12 November 1993; *Panorama Latvii*, 13 November 1993.

[35] *SM-segodnia*, 4 May 1995.

[36] *Diena* 11 June 1996.

for such categorization are met with fierce resistance from those minorities that are not regarded as "historical" in Latvia, the Ukrainians in particular. However, Latvian legislation currently in force does not distinguish among the minorities according to these "categories."

The Law on Cultural Autonomy was one of the first of its kind in the post-Communist states and was highly regarded by the representatives of various international organizations who studied it. Its main shortcoming is its purely declaratory character. The Law contains no mechanisms for the implementation of its declared principles. No legal regulations or instructions that could have compensated for this flaw exist. Therefore, to this day, there is no clear understanding in the Latvian legislation as to which organizations qualify for the appellation "national-cultural society." As a result, the actual implementation of the rights for which the law provides hinges on the economic situation in the country and on the good will of the bureaucrats in the executive organs of power.

Official Ethnicity Registration in Latvian Passports

As stipulated in normative acts enacted by the Latvian Republic,[37] Latvian passports record not only the citizenship of the passport holders, but also their "nationality" (read: ethnicity). Thus, Latvia has retained the Soviet practice of official, mandatory ascription of ethnic extraction in personal IDs. The nationality point is retained also in the new passports which are conferred on the non-citizens in conformity with the provisions in the Act on the Status of Former Citizens. Also in the Registry of Residents the nationality of the inhabitants, including newborn babies, is recorded.[38] In cases of mixed marriages the nationality of one of the parents will be ascribed to the child.

Article 2 in the Act on Cultural Autonomy from 1991 laid down that the permanent residents should have the right to choose their nationality freely in accordance with their ethnic self-understanding. However, departmental instructions issued by the Ministry of Internal Affairs allow for changes in the official registration of nationality only in cases when a passport holder of ethnically mixed parentage

---

[37] *Noteikumi par Latvijas,* 1995, 5.
[38] *LR Likums* "Par ledzivotaju. registru," 17 December 1991, 6 and 8.

wants to adopt the nationality of the other parent or of one of the grandparents. After prolonged legal disputes a new law was finally adopted in June 1994 which sets forth procedures for changes of first names, last names, and nationality.[39] For all practical purposes, this law legalizes changes of nationality by "blood" only, not according to self-identification. A person who wants to have the nationality entry in his or her passport changed to "Latvian" must not only produce evidence that one of his or her parents is/was Latvian, but also "present a school certificate or another document showing the he has a command of the state language corresponding to the third (highest) level."[40] The provisions of the law on cultural autonomy were subsequently amended to correspond to this new law.[41]

In 1996, the Saeima adopted some amendments to the law on changes of first names, last names, and nationality. The language requirements were lowered for certain categories of applicants who wanted to be registered as "Latvians": disabled persons of Group 1 whose invalidity was permanent; disabled persons of Group 2 with a speech or hearing impediment, as well as persons over 75 years of age. These groups were now required to have a command of the Latvian language equal to the second (medium) level only.[42]

At the same time the regulations for registering as a "Liv" were also amended: In cases in which the applicant is unable to produce evidence of his Livian extraction, a resolution from the Organization of Livs testifying to the ethnic origin of the applicant may be attached to the application. This resolution must be certified by the Cabinet of Ministers.

How many nationality entries have actually been altered according to these procedures we do not know, as there are no exact data available about the practical implementation of this law. However, circumstantial evidence allows us to draw certain conclusions. Thus, in 1995 12,200 Jews were registered in Latvia;[43] a year later this group had increased to 14,200.[44] This change could hardly have been brought about by natural increase, not least because the Jews have the lowest natural growth of all the ethnic groups in Latvia. The only possible explanation behind this expansion of the Jewish community must therefore be sought in adjustments in the nationality entry in the passports. In a similar

---

[39] LR *Likums* "Par varda, uzvarda un tautibas ieraksta mainu," 15 June 1994.

[40] Concerning the requirements for command of the state language, cf. section on the language situation below.

[41] The amendment was adopted on 30 June 1994. See *Diena*, 19 July 1994.

[42] *Diena*, 12 June 1996.

[43] *Latvjia skaitlos* 1996, 25.

[44] *Natsional'nye i etnicheskie gruppy*, 1996, supplement.

manner, the numbers of Latvians, Poles, and Germans are growing. Obviously, these processes reflect a changing cultural identity among certain Russified groups, but some cases also bear the unmistakable imprint of very mundane considerations (especially among the "new" Jews and Germans, who thus gain the opportunity to emigrate to Israel or Germany).

To sum up: while the Latvian legislation prohibits ethnic discrimination on principle it does contain certain provisions which single out certain groups for special treatment. In practical terms, however, the only such provision that has really significant consequences is the stipulation in the Citizenship Law providing for citizenship on an ethnic principle.[45]

Consultative Institutions

In January 1991, the Latvian Supreme Council adopted a statute on the establishment of a Consultative Council of Nationalities to be attached to the Supreme Council of the Latvian Republic. The main purpose of this council would be to "provide for the participation of representatives of all national and ethnic groups in the legislative process in order to secure their equal rights in economic, social, political and cultural matters."[46] The statute of the Supreme Council stipulated that each ethnic group should delegate three representatives to this Consultative Council. The Council should have the right to present draft laws (enjoy the right of legal initiative). Resolutions passed by the council should be regarded as a recommendation to the Supreme Council. Also the Law on Cultural Autonomy from March 1991 (discussed above) refers to the establishment of a consultative council. However, neither the law nor the statute laid down rules for the nomination or election of members to the Council, the only stipulation being that its final composition must be confirmed by the Parliament. When the activists of the various cultural societies finally, after prolonged efforts, managed to present a list of council members to the Supreme Council the majority of the MPs voted against the proposal. The consultative council was therefore never able to commence its work.

In the spring of 1993 the newly elected president of the Latvian Republic, Guntis Ulmanis, declared his intention to establish a consultative council on minority question to be attached to the president's office. The model for Ulmanis' scheme was the Round Table for minority

---

[46] *Ofitsial'naia informatsiia press-tsentra Verkhovnogo Soveta LR*, 11 February 1991.

problems which had been created by the president's office in Estonia the same year. It took approximately three years to implement President Ulmanis' idea. The Presidential Consultative Council of Latvia did not meet for its first session until mid-July 1996.[47] The Association of National Cultural Societies of Latvia had been asked to appoint six members to this council, while some others were personally invited by the president to participate.

In the summer of 1991 the Latvian Council of Ministers established a Department of Nationalities. The task of this department was to assist in the resolution of problems related to national minorities and their organizations. Initially, the Department was independent and not subordinated to any particular ministry. It employed more than ten officials. However, as a result of several reshufflings in early 1995 the Department was turned into a section under the Ministry of Justice and its staff complement was reduced to three. At the same time the prerogatives of the office were curbed. It was now restricted for all practical purposes to assist the national societies in conducting their cultural activities.

In 1990 a new Section of Minority Schools was created within the Ministry of Education. Staffed with four officials, this section was assigned the task of promoting the establishment of minority schools and handling issues related to Russian-language educational institutions. However, very soon the Section was reorganized into an office with only two employees and subsequently even this office was scrapped. Matters concerning schools with a non-Latvian language of instruction were entrusted to a single expert in the Ministry.[48] Finally, this position was eliminated too.[49]

In the fall of 1988, when the country was in the grips of a national revival, a Forum for the Peoples of Latvia was convened. This was a major event, and, in many respects, defined the future course of the official ethnic policy for some years to come.[50] In spite of the fact that plans were made to convene new forums with regular intervals, this first forum was fated to be the last one as well. In succeeding years neither the Parliament nor the Government took any initiative for its convocation.

---

[47] *Panorama Latvii*, 20 July 1996.

[48] See, for instance, the interview with one of the members of the Committee on Human Rights and Nationality Affairs in the Latvian Supreme Soviet, E. Aboltins, *SM-segodnia*, 23 April 1993.

[49] *SM-segodnia*, 21 April 1994.

[50] *Latvijas PRS Tautu* 1989.

The Political Rhetorics
of Nation-Building

From the very outset, all the political forces that were engaged in the drive for the reestablishment of Latvian independence devoted much attention to questions related to nation-formation in an independent Latvian state. Their ideologies and strategies revolved around such issues as ethnopolitical strategies, the role of the ethnic factor, and the role of the various ethnic groups in state-building and nation-building.

Nationalist Latvian organizations set forth the principle of ethnocentricity for the independent Latvian state. Thus, already in the summer of 1990, the vice-chairman of the Movement for the National Independence of Latvia, Mirdza Vitola, was declaring: "The main objective of our program is a create a Latvia in which the Latvian people will be masters on their own soil."[51] To a large extent this statement characterized the position of many other influential Latvian social movements as well. For instance, the chairman of the Popular Front of Latvia (PFL), Romualdas Razukas, forecasted that the membership of the Front would gradually become more and more ethnically homogeneous: "The time has passed when more non-Latvians can become members of the PFL. [...] Perhaps other democratic organizations will be created for the non-Latvians, labor unions, for instance."[52] These and similar utterances reflected quite graphically the dominant way of thinking among most ethnic Latvians regarding the role and place of the non-Latvians in public life in an independent Latvia.

Many leaders of the PFL and other prominent organizations emphasized that the idea of democracy alone could not provide for a stable social development of an independent Latvian state. The idea of the priority of the Latvian ethnonation had to be introduced as a supplementary conceptual basis of Latvian statehood.[53] The leaders of the nationalistic organizations reacted very strongly against all attempts to protect the interests of the minorities.

> I regard the Law on the Free Development of National and Ethnic Groups in Latvia and on their Right to Cultural Autonomy as a spit in the face. [...] First and foremost the rights of the indigenous nation must be secured. Only then may the indigenous nation decide on the question of the national minorities in a democratic manner.

---

[51] *Sovetskaia Molodezh'*, 4 July 1990.

[52] *Atmoda*, 25 September 1990.

[53] See, e.g., the article by Ia. Freimanis in *Atmoda*, 15 January 1991.

wrote Olgerts Dzenitis, the leader of the Latvian branch of the "Organization of Unrepresented peoples."[54]

Also Latvian scholars contributed to the discussion on ethnonational statehood, giving this idea an academic basis for "the wider public" to build on. One of the leading Latvian ethnologists, Leo Dribins, wrote in a popular article that,

> when a people is deprived of a national purpose it is reduced to a conglom-
> erate of individuals existing on a certain territory, a formless grey popula-
> tion, exasperated by everyday, prosaic disorders, and living by a pecuniary
> hope of succeeding in their private lives. The national purpose unites and
> elevates the people. Also a national state must serve this goal.[55]

In this way the idea of an ethnic statehood was presented as a lofty moral ideal. It was addressed from an ethical viewpoint, not from a perspective of rational and democratic social structures.

Another ethnologist, Elmars Vebers, insisted that the issue of the rights of the Latvian ethnonation needed a more detailed, legal elabo-ration. These rights he linked to the idea of "ethical Latvian-ness" by which he meant "the synthesis of ethnic and ethical values." In Ve-bers' opinion, an implementation of this approach would turn Latvia into a "state of national justice, that is, into an (ethnically) Latvian country."[56]

The assertion that ethnic rights ought to have paramount value was opposed by the inner core of PFL leaders. Usually, they formulated their positions in terms of culture, but in their rhetoric also considera-tions of political strategy may be easily detected. For instance, one of the main architects behind the Popular Front, the poet, philosopher and man of letter Viktors Avotins, wrote: "I am in favor of a normal and principled solution to the painful problems which Stalinism has cre-ated for my people's statehood and constitutional rights. But I will *actively* go against any kind of discrimination."[57] This position was supported by those members of the non-Latvian intelligentsia who took active part in the movement for the restoration of Latvian independ-ence. As formulated by the Director of the Department of nationalities, Vladimir Steshenko:

> I believe that the starting point on the road toward Latvian independence
> must be a recognition of the fact that we are people of different nationalities.

---

[54] *Jurmala*, 12 September 1991.

[55] *SM-segodnia*, 6 February 1992.

[56] *Literatura un maksla*, 7 February 1992.

[57] *Sovetskaia molodezh'*, 2 July 1988. Emphasis in the original.

> We have ended up in this country for very different reasons, but all of us regard her as our Motherland and want her to be free and to prosper. Therefore, we are the people of Latvia [...].[58]

Vladlen Dozortsev, a deputy to the Latvian Supreme Soviet, formulated this position even more trenchantly: "It is hardly a sign of health in a community if the people are doing their utmost to attain national uniformity."[59] It should be pointed out that the attitudes of Steshenko and Dozortsev were reflected in the vast majority of official documents produced by the Popular Front. The Baltic Assembly, for instance—a joint conference of leaders from the Popular Fronts of Estonia and Latvia as well as from the Lithuanian movement of Sajudis—in 1989 pledged "to secure the civic rights of all national and ethnic groups who live on the territories of our states, as well as to concede them the right to cultural self-rule."[60]

Thus, in the following years, two concepts for nation-formation—one ethnic and one civic and political—became bones of strong contention in the struggle for social paradigms at the level of Latvian political rhetoric and *belle-lettres*.

Toward the end of 1992, the concept of a "single community state" (*odnoobshchinnoe gosudarstvo*) came into vogue as a description of the desired evolution of the nation-building process. For instance, one of the leaders of the Movement for the National Independence of Latvia, Einars Cilinskis, claimed that if the so-called "zero option" of citizenship was accepted (which would grant all permanent residents of Latvia full citizenship rights),

> Latvia will be turned into a two-community state with two political groups and two representative bodies. [...] World experience has shown that such two-community states are very brittle. [...] We are in favor of decolonization and deoccupation. All those who entered Latvia along with the occupation army should leave the country together with it. [...] There is also the option of emigration, to be repatriated. Most importantly, the political power must be in the hands of the [ethnic] Latvians. That is the only way to secure that Latvia will become a national state.[61]

Thus, the national radicals understood the term "one-community state" first and foremost as an instrument to "squeeze out" of Latvia as many non-Latvians as possible and to deny those who stay behind any participation in the wielding of political power. More moderate

---

[58] *Jurmala*, 12 September 1991.

[59] *Daugava* 1992, 4, 112.

[60] *Baltiiskaia assambleia* 1989, 5.

[61] *SM-segodnia*, 28 November 1992.

Latvian politicians, for their part, regarded the notion of one-community rather as an instrument of assimilation, albeit a more or less harsh instrument. As expressed by the political commentator Valdis Egle, "the centrists would like to see a [national] unification on the basis of Latvian culture."[62]

In 1995 the term "political nation" cropped up in the political and publicistic debate. Apparently, the introduction of this concept reflected the increased contacts with Western political and scholarly milieux, which greatly intensified when Latvia became a member of the Council of Europe. Initially, to most people, the idea of a "political nation" was regarded as identical to the "one-community state," and this view is still widespread. However, most authors today who apply the concept of a "political nation" to Latvia, think somewhat differently.

One of the founders of the Latvian Popular Front, currently Latvian ambassador to Russia, Janis Peters, writes:

> The only solution is to create a single nation in the Latvian state. At present, we don't have such a nation, we have only nationalities, one of which is the Latvians. A state in which the population does not have a shared sense of belonging to one nation, will find it hard to defend its interests, since the ethnic interests are not identified with the national interests of the state. In a state, the concept of "national" is a transethnic concept.[63]

This opinion is seconded, albeit somewhat ambiguously, by Leo Dribins: "The political nation is a community of people which is united by political objectives and interests. [...] Ethnic nationalism loses its positive power if it is not able to rally all nationalities around its national state, that is, if it is not able to create a political nation."[64] The journalist Ainars Dimants, who enjoys a reputation as a strong and inflexible supporter of liberalism, lends his support for the idea: "we should by all means strive toward the creation of a democratic state with a socially responsible market economy, and should not stress ethnic values only."[65]

Saeima member Janis Urbanovish emphasized that it is imperative to integrate the Russian-speakers into Latvian society. Without such integration a political nation may not be achieved: "the apprehensions of the Russians have persisted for five years, and will not subside until

---

[62] *Latvijas Vestnesis*, 8 May 1993.

[63] *Diena*, 28 December 1995.

[64] *Diena*, 14 March 1996.

[65] *Diena*, 21 October 1996.

an answer has been found to the question: what will the political nation of Latvia look like, in which common goals and mutual trust reign?"[66]

At the same time, also other versions of the political nation, based on older, ethnocentric ideas, are actively circulated on the level of political rhetoric. For instance, the philosopher Vilnis Zarins writes: "when all citizens of Latvia can read and write in good, literate Latvian, only then will any talk of a political nation have a real basis."[67] Latvian-language newspapers frequently publish letters from readers who protest against the very idea of a political nation: "Russians, Ukrainians, and Belarusians who live in Latvia may not be regarded as national minorities, since all these people have their own ethnic territories somewhere else in the world. If they want to live in the territory of Latvia, they must, without any reservations, accept all the laws, the social structure, the mentality, language, and culture of the Latvians, in short, everything that characterizes the life of the Latvian people."[68]

To conclude: toward the end of 1997 the concept of "ethnic statehood" continued to dominate the discourse at the level of political rhetoric and collective consciousness, although a number of other interpretations also had been introduced into the debate.

The Citizenship Issue

Restored Citizenship

Among the new states of the former Soviet Union the solution to the citizenship problem in Latvia and Estonia was unique and, to large extent, defined the specific character of the ethnopolitical conflict. As will be recalled, these two Baltic states were the only post-Soviet states which did not adopt the "zero option" of citizenship after the restoration of independence. Only those individuals who were citizens of Latvia before 1940 and their descendants were recognized as citizens of the reestablished states. This solution was based on formal-legal considerations—the concept of legal restoration.

When Latvia was annexed by the Soviet Union in 1940, all citizens of Latvia were granted Soviet citizenship through a decree of the Supreme Soviet of the USSR and their Latvian citizenship was annulled.

---

[66] *Diena*, 26 October 1996.

[67] *Diena*, 8 November 1996.

[68] *Netkariga Rita Avize*, 11 April 1996.

Many democratic states refused to recognize the legality of this annexation, although the nature of this refusal was more political than legal.

In the elections to the Latvian Supreme Soviet in the spring of 1990 all inhabitants of Latvia could participate, including Soviet military personnel. The Popular Front of Latvia won a resounding victory at the polls. A significant number of non-Latvians voters also supported this alternative. The PFL election program contained what, for all practical purposes, amounted to support of the "zero option" citizenship alternative,[69] and this plank in the Front's platform was decisive in securing the support of many Russian-speaking voters. The "zero option" was also publicly endorsed in the speeches and statements of many PFL leaders. Andrej Pantelejevs, for one—who was elected to the Saeima and became the leader of the Latvian Way caucus in the 5th and 6th Saeimas—declared in March 1990 that, "I believe that anyone who regards himself as a patriot of Latvia may become a Latvian citizen. The definition and the criteria for the acquisition of citizenship ought to be each Latvian inhabitant's personal, voluntary, and conscious expression of will."[70] Later, Pantelejevs explained why the Popular Front retreated from this position:

> I will say this very candidly and somewhat cynically. Theoretically, the ethnic Latvians could have fought for their independence with honest means. That would have led to confrontations with weapons in hand. The alternative course, therefore, looked much more sensible: To penetrate by legal means the power structures which existed at that time. In order to do that we needed votes, and, as you know, at that time all inhabitants of Latvia had the right to vote. So, we fully consciously said that our goal was the so-called zero option. Yes, this was a conscious lie in order to avoid human casualties.[71]

This pragmatic approach was common to quite a few members of the relatively narrow new political elite which was in the process of being formed at the time.

---

[69] *Atmoda*, 12 February 1990.

[70] *Atmoda*, 16 March 1990.

[71] *Latviia ——ch"ia ona rodina?* 1994, 105.

Perceptions of the Citizenship Issue
Among Different Ethnic Groups

Among the Latvian population at large the restrictive approach to the citizenship problem was often based on ethnic considerations: more effectively than any other solution this approach secured the goal of making the ethnic Latvians "masters on their own soil."[72] A restrictive citizenship legislation would secure their control of the levers of the state apparatus, and such control was in turn regarded as indispensable in order to prevent the physical disappearance of the Latvian people.[73]

Very soon after the achievement of independence the idea of restricted access to citizenship gained prominence among ethnic Latvians. Of course, part of the reason for this turn was the active propaganda of the nationalist organizations, but one should not exaggerate their importance. A survey conducted in 1991 at the request of the Danish newspaper *Weekendavisen*, showed that 41percent of the ethnic Latvians were in favor of a "stern" attitude in the citizenship question, while only 8 percent supported the liberal "zero option."[74] Another survey conducted in 1993 by Richard Rose and William Maley indicated that half of all ethnic Latvians were in favor of extending citizenship to citizens of prewar Latvians and their descendants only.[75]

At the same time, the overwhelming majority of the ethnic Latvians conceded that post-1940 emigrants to Latvia ought to be allowed to be naturalized on specific, more or less stringent conditions. Thus, in a third survey conducted in August 1993 by the Baltic Research Centre, with financial support from the Central European University and the Latvian Scientific Council, 39 percent of the interviewed Latvians thought that citizenship ought to be granted on a quota basis in order to secure that the share of ethnic Latvians among the citizens did not fall below 75 percent. In the same group, 53 percent believed that "citizenship ought to be open to all persons who have lived for a certain period of time in this country, who know the Latvian language, and are loyal toward the Latvian Republic." Only three percent supported the zero option.[76] In this opinion poll, the attitudes of the non-Latvians differed very markedly from those of the Latvians: the three options outlined above were supported by 3 percent, 31 percent and 61 percent,

---

[72] See, e.g., *Atmoda*, 25 September 90. Ibid., 2 October 1990; passim.

[73] See, e.g., the resolution from the conference "The chances of the Latvian nation," in *Latviesu nacijas izredzes* 1990, 142.

[74] Poulsen 1994, 26.

[75] Rose and Maley 1994.

[76] *Diena*, 7 October 1993.

respectively. Thus, the question of citizenship is one the issues which most clearly divides the attitudes of the Russophones from those of ethnic Latvians.

The survey conducted by the Baltic Research Centre showed that despite the negative attitude toward the restrictive citizenship options which predominated among the non-citizens, a large number of them intended to do everything which was required of them by the laws in order to achieve Latvian citizenship. However, if as much as 67 percent thought so in January 1993, this percentage had dropped drastically by August of the same year when only 41 percent adhered to this view. Obviously, in January very many people did not grasp how complicated the naturalization procedure would become. In August, on the other hand, the Parliament had begun to discuss various draft laws for citizenship. These discussions were reported in the press, and many noncitizens realized that they would be unable to fulfill the stringent criteria or even fall within the categories that could apply for citizenship in the foreseeable future. From January to August 1993 the percentage of non-citizens who intended to "stay on in Latvia without citizenship" rose from 7 percent to 28 percent. The numbers who planned to "move to another country," on the other hand, remained relatively constant (3 percent in January, 4 percent in August).

The evolution of the responses in this two-stage survey may be regarded as short-term changes brought about by the greater clarity surrounding the likely naturalization procedures. The long-term tendencies, on the other hand, went in the other direction. In particular, research conducted by the Baltic Data House between 1989 and 1994 showed that an increasing number of non-citizens wanted to become citizens of Latvia.[77] In 1990, approximately 40 percent of the non-Latvians expressed a desire to receive Latvian citizenship; by 1994 this figure had risen to three-quarters of the Russians and two-thirds of the non-Russian non-citizens. In the latter year, only 10 percent of the non-Latvians either did not want to become a citizen of Latvia, or had not made up their mind.[78]

By the time the citizenship law was adopted, the majority of the ethnic Latvians apparently regarded the issue as exhausted. For the non-citizens, on the contrary, the question had become even more acute. Evidence of these divided attitudes may found in a survey conducted in December 1994 by the Institute of Market and Social Research "Latvijas fakti": the non-citizens regarded the problem of citizenship as a question which the Latvian Parliament and government ought to give

---

[77] Zepa 1995, 31–44.
[78] Ibid.

priority over all other issues. (34.6 percent of the non-citizens adhered to this view while 32.5 percent indicated unemployment as the most important problem. 26.6 percent ticked off for the need to reestablish local industry, and 24.8 percent regarded crime prevention as the most urgent task of the legislators.) Citizens of Latvia, on the other hand, did not list the problem of citizenship among the top ten important questions of contemporary Latvian society at all.[79]

Citizenship and Human Rights:
The Attitudes of the International Community

The problem of citizenship in Latvia provoked lively debates among international human rights experts. Since there was no precedence for legal state restoration after such a long period of foreign annexation, the opinions of the experts differed significantly.[80] In the early 1990s, numerous studies devoted to this issue were published in the West as well as in Latvia. Some of the experts inclined toward a restorationist concept of citizenship,[81] while others concluded that the principle of "citizenship restoration" conflicted with the norms of basic human rights documents.[82] A third group of analysts insisted that there was no contradiction between the Latvian citizenship principles on the one hand and internationally accepted human rights on the other.[83]

One of the most incisive analyses of these problems was provided by Rogers Brubaker. He distinguished between three models, i.e., new states, restored states, and compromise models. The task of a new state is to define an initial body of citizens: this is usually done in a territorially inclusive fashion. The task of a restored state is to confirm the status of an already existing citizenry and to restore citizenship and statehood to real effectiveness. In the compromise models the existing citizenry is confirmed but it is not considered as a sufficiently inclusive body for the restored state.[84] With few reservations, Brubaker's approach to the citizenship issue was accepted by most international organizations, and the principle of "restored citizenship" as such became ever-more rarely the topic of questioning from a human rights point of view. At the same time, the international organizations continued to

---

[79] *Labrit*, 11 January 1995.

[80] For a detailed analysis of the conclusions of the various experts and fact-finding missions, see Birckenbach 1997.

[81] See, e.g., Bojars 1992, 331.

[82] In particular, Eide 1992.

[83] For instance, Fehervary 1993, 392.

[84] Brubaker 1992, 269.

monitor closely the process of citizenship legislation in Latvia and the implementation of the citizenship law. Particularly important in this respect was the CSCE/OSCE Mission to Latvia, which was mandated, first and foremost, to observe on the citizenship situation.[85]

As Vello Pettai has remarked, the policy of nonrecognition of the Soviet annexation of the Baltic states, which most Western countries had adopted during the Cold War, led them to "objectivize" the eth-nonationalism of the Baltic peoples by treating it in the terms of international law. For that reason, the first parliamentary elections to be held in Latvia and Estonia after the restoration of independence were declared "free and fair" despite the fact that a large part of the permanent residents were barred from participating in them. Rather than bringing pressure to bear on the Baltic countries the West chose to integrate them into European political structures in the expectation that the "Baltic trauma" would eventually pass and that the influence of ethnonationalism in the state policies of these countries would gradually diminish.[86]

The Adoption of the Citizenship Law

When Latvia adopted its declaration of independence in May 1990 what amounted to a situation of "dual power" existed for a while in Latvia.[87] The extreme lack of clarity which this situation engendered was aggravated by strong disagreements within the Latvian political elite and by the ambiguous signals emanating from the international community. As a combined result, for a long time after the formal restoration of independence no legal acts were passed on the citizenship issue.

In the midst of the January crisis in 1991, during which Soviet OMON units fought against police units that were loyal to Riga authorities, a bilateral treaty between the Republic of Latvia and the Russian Federation was hastily signed (on 13 January) and equally hastily ratified by the Latvian Supreme Council (on 15 January). One of the articles in this agreement granted all individuals who were permanent residents of Latvia at the time of the restoration of Latvian

---

[85] On the activities of the OSCE mission to Latvia, see Lange 1994; Tsilevich 1995.

[86] Pettai 1993.

[87] Between May 1990 and August 1991 there existed in Latvia both a police corps which was loyal to the government and Soviet OMON forces which did not take orders from Latvian authorities. Similarly, the were two parallel Attorney Generals' offices, etc.

independence (May 1990) the right to choose freely between Latvian and Russian citizenship. However, this agreement was never ratified by the Russian Parliament and therefore did not enter legal force.

The Latvian Supreme Council returned to the question of citizenship legislation only after the coup attempt in Moscow in August 1991 had collapsed and the international community had recognized Latvian independence. The nationalist faction in the parliament asserted that since this organ had been elected by the entire corpus of Latvian residents, it did not have the right to decide on the question of citizenship, only to restore citizenship rights to the prewar body of citizens. A law regulating the principles of naturalization could, they maintained, be adopted only by a Saeima elected exclusively by citizens. The Supreme Council acceded to this point of view. Thus, on 15 October 1991, it adopted a Resolution on the Restoration of the Body of Citizens and on the Main Principles of Naturalization.[88] Based on this resolution a registry of persons who held Latvian citizenship before 1940 and their descendants was compiled. Those who entered this registry were allowed to participate in the parliamentary elections of 1993. Only in the fall of 1993 did the new parliament, the Saeima, begin to discuss the citizenship law anew.

The protracted and stormy Saeima debates on this issue focused primarily on the dilemma of "providing guarantees for the survival of the Latvian nation," on the one hand, and the need to adopt a law which was in accordance with European standards, on the other.[89] In the upshot, the Saeima adopted a draft law in its first reading. The main peculiarity of this draft was the introduction of the principle of yearly quotas for naturalization, to be fixed annually by the Cabinet of Ministers and confirmed by the Saeima. These quotas, it was stated, should be "based on the demographic and economic situation of the state, and geared toward the development of Latvia as a national, one-community state."[90]

However, the Council of Europe and the CSCE objected strongly against this principle.[91] The discussions in the Latvian Parliament continued for some months, in the course of which a number of basic principles in the draft law underwent essential changes. Finally, on 21 June 1994 the Law on Citizenship was passed in a third reading. Also in this

---

[88] An English translation of the Resolution has been published in the documents of the seminar *Citizenship and Language Legislation* 1993.

[89] The minutes of the plenary session of the Saeima were published in *Latvijas vestnesis*, 2 December 1993.

[90] *Latvijas vestnesis*, 30 November 1993.

[91] See van der Stoel, 'Comments on the Draft citizenship law' 1994,' *SM-segodnia* 24-26 February 1994.

definitive edition the law contained certain clauses which ran against
the recommendations of the European organizations (in particular, the
quota system, although in this version it was limited to fewer
categories).

As a result of the parliament's handling of the citizenship issue Latvia ran the risk of being denied membership in the Council of Europe.
President Ulmanis therefore made use of his constitutional right to
reject the law and returned it to the Parliament for renewed examination. On 22 July 1994, the Saeima debated the draft law once again and
introduced some more amendments based on the recommendations of
European experts. When this had been done the president promulgated
the law.

In the final version of the citizenship law the quota system was replaced by a "timetable" or by "windows" of naturalization. Only persons who belonged to certain privileged categories could begin to apply
for citizenship immediately after the law entered into legal force.
These were ethnic Latvians; Livs; spouses of citizens who had been married for at least ten years; persons who had had legal residence in Latvia before 1940; graduates from Latvian-language schools, and former
citizens of Lithuania and Estonia, as well as certain other groups.

The second category, which included individuals who were born in
Latvia and aged between 16 and 20 years old, could begin to apply for
citizenship on 1 January 1996. Next, from 1 January 1997 individuals
under 25 years of age could begin to apply, etc. Persons born outside Latvia may begin to apply for citizenship in 2001 if they entered Latvia as
minors, in the year 2002 if they were 30 years or younger on arrival, and
all others after 2003.[92]

In all categories the applicants must fulfill the same criteria of naturalization: five years of residence in Latvia; a command of the Latvian
language; familiarity with the fundamental aspects of the Latvian
constitution, of the Constitutional law, of the text of the national anthem, and of the history of Latvia. They must also document that they
have a legal source of income in Latvia, and renounce their previous
citizenship (expatriation). Persons belonging to some categories may
never apply for citizenship. Among these are, *in casu*, persons who have
chosen Latvia as their country of permanent abode after being demobi-
lized from the Soviet Army.

---

[92] The law text is printed in Latvian, Russian, and English in *Latvijas vestnesis*, 11 August
1994.

Naturalization

The first months after the adoption of the citizenship law were used to draw up and pass the necessary legal implementation documents to go with it, as well as to hire personnel to staff the Naturalization Authority. Thus, the actual naturalization process was able to start up only on 1 February 1995. It soon transpired that there was no stampede to become Latvian citizens: by the end of July 1996, the Cabinet of Ministers had granted citizenship rights to no more than 2,459 persons while 4,474 cases remained under examination in the various regional offices of the Authority.[93] By 31 January 1997 altogether 4,161 new citizenships had been granted and, by March of the same year, 4,644.[94] Much bigger groups were eligible for naturalization: in 1995, approximately 60,000 persons (those having the right to preferential treatment); in 1996, an additional 33,000 (Latvian-born young people in the age groups 16–20); and in 1997 another 31,000 (Latvian-born people younger than 25). Thus, as pointed out by the director of the Naturalization Board, E. Aldermane, by June 1997 124,000 individuals were eligible for naturalization.[95]

The low volume of naturalization came as a surprise to all involved parties. All surveys (referred to above) indicated that a majority of the non-citizens wanted Latvian citizenship. Different attempts have been mad to explain the low number of applications: A survey conducted by the Naturalization Board of Latvia suggested the following main reasons for the evident disinclination of the non-citizens to apply for citizenship:[96] Insufficient command of the Latvian language (26 percent); insufficient familiarity with Latvian laws and history (26 percent); lack of necessary information (14 percent); and too heavy naturalization fee (11 percent).[97] Among other reasons given were a reluctance to serve in the Latvian army; unwillingness to lose an opportunity to travel to Russia without a visa, and general passivity among the non-citizen population.

The non-citizens themselves, as well as representatives of the political opposition, often question these conclusions.[98] They argue that also girls who are not subject to conscription into the army fail to apply for

---

[93] *Naturalizacijas process Latvija. Galvenie raditaji.* 13 August 1996.

[94] Information sheet of the Latvian Naturalization Board, 10 February 1997; information from the Latvian Ministry of Foreign Affairs, 4 April 1997.

[95] *SM-segodnia,* 9 June 1997.

[96] *On naturalization* 1997, 30–31.

[97] 30 Lats, the equivalent of 60 U.S. dollars.

[98] See, e.g., *SM-segodnia,* 23 April 1997, and many similar comments.

citizenship. Also, the USSR passports on the basis of which the non-citizens can travel visa-free to Russia, will soon be invalid. Finally, school children and university students enjoy a fifty-percent discount on the naturalization fee, and money in itself is hardly a crucial factor.

The main obstacle to fast naturalization, it is argued, is to be found in the far too stringent tests. The OSCE High Commissioner on National Minorities Max van der Stoel, has claimed that most citizens of the Netherlands would fail a test consisting of similar questions about Dutch history and law.[99] What may be even more important is the non-citizens' growing sense of alienation from the state. Many non-citizens consider the conditions for receiving citizenship as unjust and degrading. Also, they do not trust that the state will "play fair" and abide by its own rules. The authorities have already deceived them once, by reneging on the promise of the "zero option." Thus, there are good reasons to believe that the causes behind the unexpectedly low volume of naturalization applications should be sought, first of all, in the state policies which effectively discouraged non-citizens and undermine their initial enthusiasm about naturalization.

A survey conducted in November 1996 showed that only 19 percent of the non-citizens were strongly determined to apply for citizenship while 24 percent were thinking about doing so.[100] In a similar survey conducted one-and-a-half years earlier by the same research team, twice as many—38 percent—had been determined to apply.

Ethnic Aspects of Citizenship

Some of the naturalized citizens received their new status as a result of amendments to the citizenship law that were adopted in March 1995. These amendments gave ethnic Latvians and graduates from schools with instruction in the Latvian language the right to become citizens without any more ado, simply by registering as such.[101] As a result, many people were now faced with the problem of proving their Latvian origin. When the registration deadline expired (on 1 March 1996), it transpired that approximately 17,000 persons living permanently in Latvia and claiming to be ethnic Latvians, did not have but wanted to gain Latvian citizenship.[102] Some of these were people who had themselves lived in Russia in the interwar period, or their parents had.

---

[99] RFE/RL Newsline, 8 April 1997.

[100] Rose 1997a, 59.

[101] *Latvijas Republikas Pamatlikumi* 1995, 25.

[102] *Natsional'nye i etnicheskie* 1996.

The March amendments created for the first time a direct linkage between Latvian citizenship and ethnicity. To be sure, also before these amendments were adopted the "ethnic dimension" of the citizenship legislation was rather transparent. Although the resolution adopted by the Supreme Council of the Latvian Republic in 1991 on the restoration of the body of Latvian citizens did not contain any overt ethnic criteria it nevertheless automatically turned the vast majority of ethnic Latvians into citizens while the majority of the Russian-speaking residents in Latvia were categorized as citizens of USSR who, when the Soviet Union collapsed shortly afterwards, became *de facto* stateless persons.

Table 4.4 shows the ethnic composition of the body of citizens and non-citizens in Latvia as of February 1996. Among the citizens, ethnic Latvians make up 78.5 percent while their share of the population in general is around 56 percent. For the Russians, the figures are 16 and 30 percent, respectively.

By February 1996, 99 percent of all ethnic Latvians in Latvia had acquired Latvian citizenship, while only some 38 percent of the Russians, 19 percent of the Belarusians, and 6 percent of the Ukrainians had (see Figure 4.5). Among the so-called "historical minorities," such as Roma and Poles, the percentages of people acquiring citizenship were significantly higher.

TABLE 4.4 Ethnic Composition of Citizenry and Ethnicity of Non-Citizens (February 1996)

	percent of citizens	*percent of non-citizens*
Latvians	78.6	2.5
Russians	16.3	65.1
Belarusians	1.2	12.0
Ukrainians	0.2	9.0
Poles	2.2	3.4
Lithuanians	0.5	3.8
Jews	0.4	1.1
Roma	0.4	0.1
Germans	0.1	0.4
other	0.2	2.7

Source: Natsional'nye i etnicheskie 1996.

FIGURE 4.5 Share of Citizens Within Main Ethnic Groups in Latvia (February 1996)

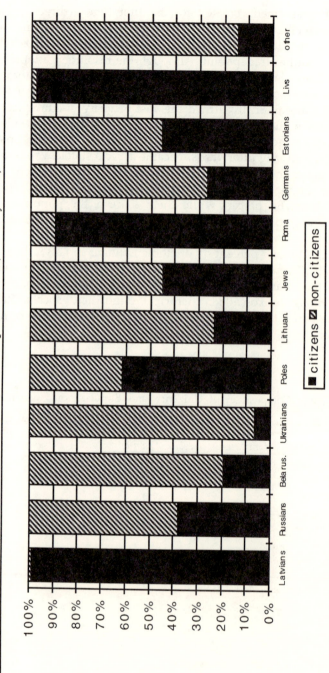

Source: Natsional'nye i etnicheskie 1996.

Latvian Residents Who Are Citizens of Another State

In addition to applying for Latvian citizenship Russian-speaking non-citizens of Latvia have the option of applying for citizenship in another state. Every former Soviet citizen could become a citizen of Russia through a process of formal registration. Belarusian citizenship law is also very liberal in this respect. Ukrainian citizenship law contains somewhat stricter limitations, but the current version of this law gives emigrants from the Ukraine the right to become Ukrainian citizens without physically moving to the Ukraine.

There are no exact data available on the numbers of permanent residents of Latvia who have taken up citizenship in another state. From time to time fragmentary information is published in the media. For instance, the following figures have been cited in the press with reference to sources in the Russian embassy in Riga: by April 1993, the number of persons who had received Russian citizenship through Russian consulary offices in Latvia was given as 12,000,[103] as of July 1993, 17,000,[104] and by February 1997 approximately 65,000.[105] By the summer of 1994 around 20,000 persons had become Belarusian citizens.[106] The number of Estonian, Lithuanian, and Ukrainian citizens was estimated to be considerably lower.

It is difficult to ascertain the veracity of these data. As it happens, many people apply for Russian citizenship immediately before their departure for Russia, and the Russian consulate does not know how many of the "new" Russian citizens stay on in Latvia and how many leave.

The first official Latvian statistics to shed some light on this issue were published in the demographic yearbook of 1996.[107] Referring to information taken from the Registry of Residents, the compilers of the yearbook could tell that by the beginning of 1996 citizens of the Russian Federation made up 0.15 percent of the total population of Latvia. In absolute figures, this amounted to 3,750 persons. 1,250 persons were citizens of Lithuania, and 500 were Ukrainian citizens. Another 0.04 percent of the residents of Latvia (1,000 individuals all told) were citizens of other countries. These data, however, can hardly be regarded as complete or accurate.

---

103 *SM-segodnia*, 27 April 1993.

104 *Diena*, 8 July 1993.

105 *SM-segodnia*, 18 February 1997, quoting the Russian ambassador to Latvia, A. Udaltsov.

106 *Russkii put'*, 2 July 1994.

107 *Latvijas demografijas* 1996, 38.

In any case, it seems clear that only a minute proportion of the non-citizens in Latvia are electing to take the citizenship of another country. In this respect, the Latvian situation contrasts sharply with the situation in Estonia. While the total number of Russophone non-citizens in Estonia is only half of what it is in Latvia, as many as 83,000 of them had taken Russian citizenship by February 1996. Another 1,000 had taken Latvian citizenship, 750 Lithuanian, and 400 Ukrainian.[108] By October 1996 the number of Russian citizens in Estonia had reached 116,000.[109] Thus, the Russophone non-citizens of Estonia prefer to take citizenship in another state considerably more often that do the non-citizens of Latvia.

The Status of the Non-Citizens

Until April 1995, the legal status of permanent residents of Latvia who have not been recognized as citizens remained undefined. Prior to that time a number of laws, regulations, and administrative decisions were adopted which limited the social and economic rights of non-citizens: property rights, the right to work in certain professions, the right to receive social benefits, the right of self-defense, freedom of conscience, and a number of others.[110]

The prolonged legal vacuum in Latvia led to a situation in which radically minded officials and local administrators in the municipalities could act arbitrarily. Systematic administrative violations were perpetrated by officials in the Department of Citizenship and Immigration which was entrusted with the task of compiling the Register of Residents. Any person denied registration in this register was barred from legal employment, social benefits, marriage registration, etc. This situation attracted the attention of several international human rights organizations.[111]

The radical nationalist parties continued their active campaign for the "decolonization" of Latvia. According to their notion, non-citizens should be regarded as "illegal immigrants" and "colonists."[112] In April

---

[108] *Estonia today.* http://www.vm.ee. 21 February 1996.

[109] This figure was cited by member of the Estonian Parliament, S. Isakov, in his presentation at the symposium "Russian minorities in the Baltic countries. National identity and state loyalty," Lübeck–Travemünde, 25–27 October 1996.

[110] For a more detailed examination of the different rights enjoyed by citizens and non-citizens in Latvia, see Tsilevich and Ruchkovsky 1994, 13; and Opalski, Tsilevich, and Dutkiewicz 1994 (appendix).

[111] *Violations* 1993.

[112] *Diena*, 8 January 1993; ibid., 30 September 1993; *passim*.

1995, however, a law was adopted on "the status of former citizens of the USSR who are not citizens of Latvia or another state."[113] This law legalized the continued residence of the non-citizens in the country, guaranteed their right to leave and reenter Latvia freely, and granted them a (somewhat circumscribed) right of family reunion. It also confirmed the non-citizens' right of cultural autonomy. In effect, this law introduced a new legal status: the former citizens of the USSR were regarded neither as citizens of Latvia, nor as foreigners (that is, they are not citizens of another state), but they are not treated as stateless persons, either.

While the adoption of this law greatly clarified the situation, its implementation was hampered by serious problems. The promised "non-citizens' passports," which will give these people an actual chance to realize their freedom of movement, were issued in April 1997, two years after the adoption of the law. Also, no amendments had been made in the laws regulating immigration procedures which could put flesh on the declared right of family reunion. As before, the border guards continued to demand "reentry guarantees" or "return visas" whenever a non-citizen left the country even for shorter journeys. Nevertheless it must be concluded that the situation of the non-citizens has clearly been stabilized.

Political Representation and Participation

Representation in Governmental Institutions

The opportunities for nontitular ethnic groups to gain representation in Latvian bodies of power are first and foremost regulated by the citizenship law. Naturally, the significant discrepancy between the ethnic composition of the population at large, on the one hand, and the ethnic composition of the citizenry, on the other, has guaranteed the titular ethnic group a solid dominance in all elected bodies. However, the strong tendency toward Latvian overrepresentation in the parliament and Russian underrepresentation (and, to a somewhat less extent, the underrepresentation of other ethnic groups as well) did not start with the citizens-only elections to the 5th and 6th Saeima. It was clearly observable in the Supreme Soviet of the Latvian SSR which was elected in 1990 by all inhabitants of Latvia.

---

[113] The complete text of this law was published in Russian in *SM-segodnia*, 4 May 1995.

In spite of this, we believe that the mechanisms that created these disproportions in 1990 were different from the dynamics at work in 1993 and 1995. In 1990, many Russophones voted for candidates of the Popular Front, disregarding the fact that the majority of them were ethnic Latvians. These candidates were considered as proponents not of ethnic, but democratic ideas and values in general, and as clearly preferable to the conservative candidates of the Communist Party.[114] The outcome of the parliamentary elections in 1993 and 1995, on the other hand, resulted largely from a very low level of ethnic mobilization among the nontitular population (or more correctly, among those nontitulars who had been granted Latvian citizenship).[115] It should also be noted that Latvian election legislation does not give every citizen an automatic right to run for office, but only those who can document a mastery of the Latvian language at the third (highest) level.[116] This provision affects almost exclusively non-Latvian citizens.

As regards non-Latvian representation in local government, it should be noted that, in contrast to the situation in Estonia, non-citizens who are permanent residents in Latvia enjoy neither passive electoral rights (the right to run for office) or active rights (the right to vote) in local elections. In addition, the law on local elections requires all runners for a seat on the municipal councils to be fluent in Latvian both oral and written. Combined with the factors referred to above this stipulation has secured an absolute dominance of ethnic Latvians in the bodies of local (municipal) power. Thus, while the Latvians make up only approximately 40 percent of the total population in Riga, the Riga municipal council elected in 1994 had only three Russian deputies, all other representatives were ethnic Latvians.[117] In Daugavpils, where Latvians make up some 14 percent of the population, seven Latvians were elected to the city council, which consists of fifteen seats all told.[118] In a number of major Latvian cities—Jelgava, Jurmala, Lijepaja, Ventspils, etc., no non-Latvians were elected to the city council at all.[119] However, after the March 1997 local elections, the situation in

---

[114] For different viewpoints on the character of the national movement in Latvia and the attitude of the Russians in Latvia to this movement, see Ustinova 1991; Apine 1994, and Tsilevich 1994.

[115] We discuss some psychosocial causes for this lack of mobilization on p. 141–142.

[116] The text of the election law has been published in *Latvjias Respublikas 6. Saeimas* 1996, 10–16.

[117] *Latvjias Respublikas pasvaldibu* 1994, 9–10.

[118] Ibid., 10–11.

[119] Ibid., 12–16.

TABLE 4.5 Representation of Ethnic Groups in the Parliaments of Latvia (in percent)

		Latvians	*Russians*	*Other*
LSSR SC	Electorate	52.0	34.0	14.0
1990	Deputies	69.5	22.5	8.0
5 Saeima,	Electorate	78.6	16.3	5.1
1993	Deputies	88.0	6.0	6.0
6 Saeima,	Electorate	79.3	15.9	4.8
1995	Deputies	90.0	6.0	4.0

Sources: Latvijas Republikas Augstaka 1991, 20–80; Latvijas Republikas 5. Saeimas 1993; Latvijas Republikas 6. Saeimas 1996, 779–783.

some municipalities improved. For instance, in the new Riga municipal council seven Russians, two Jews, one Lithuanian and one Liv took seats.

The representation of the various ethnic groups may be regarded as an indicator of their respective ethnic mobilization. The ethnic representation in the organs of the executive, on the other hand, reflects first and foremost the personnel policy of the state. A number of researchers believe that in the Soviet period Latvia diverged from the standard pattern of cadre indigenization which prevailed in most Union republics. Not Latvians, but Russians and other Slavic groups were disproportionately well represented within the republican political elite. Cadre policy in Latvia discriminated against ethnic Latvians.[120] This view has frequently been challenged, however. Its opponents usually point to the disproportionately high numbers of deputies in the Latvian Supreme Soviet who belonged to the titular nation, as well as the many Latvian ministers, supervisors in the city and district party cells, etc.[121] It is a well-established fact that, in the Soviet period, appointments to the organs of state power were conducted according to a list of criteria compiled "at the top," which included, inter alia, regulations of the ethnic compositions of the government, supreme soviets, etc.

It is not necessary for our purposes to solve this dispute on the cadre policy of Soviet Latvia. We observe, nonetheless, that whether or not the Russians and the other nontitular ethnic groups were over- or

---

[120] Muiznieks 1995, 114; Karklins 1987; Levits 1987.

[121] See, e.g., Hodnett 1979; and the article by Oleg Shchiptsov, a former member of the Latvian Supreme Soviet, in *Panorama Latvii*, 8 March 1994.

underrepresented prior to 1991, for all practical purposes they were completely squeezed out of the political elite after the reestablishment of Latvian independence. As Anton Steen has remarked, "Russians are almost non-existent in top state bureaucracy and in the judiciary. [...] The inclusion of Russians into the elite structure is seen by the elites as a real threat to national culture and independence."[122]

As mentioned above, the changes in the bureaucratic elites were largely predetermined by the citizenship law: non-citizens were barred from top jobs in the bodies of state power, the judiciary, etc. Another hurdle was put in place by the language legislation. An applicant to any state job had to be fluent in the state language. Nevertheless, these legal restriction by themselves do not seem to sufficiently explain the low percentages of non-Latvians among the contemporary political elite in Latvia. Other informal sanctions and screening mechanisms must also have come into play.

Although almost no statistical data on the ethnic composition of the bodies of state power in Latvia exist, certain indirect evidence seems to corroborate this conclusion. Thus, for instance, persons who have received their education in the Latvian language are exempted from the language-certification requirement when they apply for a job.[123] As a rule, these applicants will be ethnic Latvians. We know that in 1992 only two person had to obtain a language certification in all institutions and offices attached to the Latvian Ministry of Foreign Affairs. The figure for the Ministry of Economic Reform was seven persons.[124] In the same year tens of thousands of applicants for jobs in the structures of the Ministry of Transport and the Ministry of Internal Affairs had to undergo attestation, of whom most were bus drivers and policemen, etc., and very few white-collar bureaucrats. These inconsistencies give some idea of the informal systems of "ethnic stratification" and "ethnic division of labor" at work.

In early 1994 the entire Latvian government was made up of ethnic Latvians,[125] and since the reestablishment of independence not one ethnic Russian has served as a minister in Latvia. As of January 1994, 152 judges were employed by the Latvian courts. Of these, 142 were Latvians, nine Russians, and one a Pole.[126] The official release of this information is a rare exception to the rule that data on the ethnic composition of the bureaucratic elites are hardly ever published.

---

[122] Steen 1997b, 48 and 54.

[123] See p. 113–116 below.

[124] Muiznieks 1993b.

[125] Muiznieks 1995, 115.

[126] *Latvijas vestnesis*, 29 January 1994.

Political Behavior and Electoral Preferences

Generally speaking, the political behavior of the ethnic Latvians differs significantly from the behavior of the Russophone citizens of Latvia. The vast majority of political parties in Latvia (including parties with relatively liberal ethnopolitical programs), have practically no Russophones as active members. Among the ten or so parties represented in the 6th Saeima there are only three exceptions to this rule: the Popular Concord Party (in which two out of four deputies were non-Latvians in the fall of 1996); the bloc of Socialist parties (three non-Latvians of three elected); and the For Equal Rights Party (one out of two). All Russian deputies in the Saeima were elected from these lists.

Certain evidence suggests that ethnic Latvians participate more actively in elections than do non-Latvians. According to a survey conducted by the polling institute "Prognoz" on the eve of the parliamentary elections in September 1995, 70.2 percent of the Latvian respondents had definitely made up their mind to vote, while only 10.1 percent in this group were certain that they would not be turning out. Among the non-Latvian citizens, on the other hand, the corresponding figures were 56.8 and 19.1 percent.[127] This information was corroborated by the official data on the actual behavior of the voters. In electoral districts with high numbers of non-Latvians among the registered voters the turnout was generally below average.

One should note that any analysis of electoral preferences based on a formal classification of Latvian political parties may be more confusing than clarifying. The multiparty system in the country in still in flux, and neither the names of the parties, nor their images—created partly by themselves and partly by the press—give an adequate idea of their political profile according to conventional customs of classification (conservative, liberal, social democratic etc.). It is therefore more or less inevitable that any categorization of the party system in Latvia will have to be approximate and inaccurate and, as such, could hardly serve as a starting point for analysis.[128]

It should also be noted that, in contrast to a number of other states in Eastern and Central Europe where ethnic minorities make up significant parts of the population (Slovakia, Rumania and Estonia), Latvia has no influential minority parties organized on the basis of ethnicity. To be sure, among the groups contesting the Saeima seats in 1993 and 1995

---

[127] *SM-segodnia*, 29 September 1995.
[128] This is true, for instance, of the party description in Nørgaard et al., 1996, 98–105.

there were lists which contained the word "Russian" in the party designation. In 1993 this list was organized jointly by the Centre of Democratic Initiatives and the Baltic Constitutional Party.[129] In the 1995
elections this list did not participate but the Party of Russian Citizens
of Latvia did. This party was an offshoot of the Abrene society, an organization with Latvian nationalist leanings. An important plank in
this party's platform was its demand for compensation to former property owners in the district of Abrene, a region which had been annexed
by the Russian Federation after World War II.[130] In both 1993 and 1995
the "Russian" list garnered slightly above one percent of the total
vote[131] and did not even approach the electoral hurdle, which in 1993
was 4 percent, but increased to five percent in 1995.

As non-Latvians make up approximately 20 percent of the electorate
it seems clear that, so far, no more than 5 percent of them have been
ready to support a "Russian" list. Moreover, since this alternative in
the two elections was represented by very different parties, in terms
both of programs and personalities, it seems that this conclusion holds
true irrespective of the actual profile of the Russian party. This conclusion seems to support our thesis that the political mobilization of the
Russians in Latvia on ethnic programs is very low.

Due to the secrecy of the ballot there are no exact data on the electoral preferences of the non-Latvian voters. However, we may draw
certain conclusions on the basis of various sociological surveys in combination with an analysis of the voting results broken down by electoral
districts.

The Latvian electoral law divides the country into five electoral
districts in which the candidates are elected by a proportional system.
The districts are coterminous with the traditional, historical regions of

TABLE 4.6 Ethnic Composition of Citizens by Administrative District, 1995

	Riga	Vidzeme	Latgale	Kurzeme	Zemgale
Latvians	70.4	89.5	53.4	94.5	90.0
Russians	23.1	8.3	35.8	3.2	6.9
Others	6.5	2.2	10.8	2.4	3.1

Source: *Latvijas vestnesis*, 22–23 March 1995.

---

[129] *Diena*, 6 May 1993; *SM-segodnia*, 20 May 1995.

[130] For more information on PRCL, see its party organ *Zemliaki*, as well as *SM-segodnia*, 29
December 1994.

[131] *Latvijas republikas 5. Saeimas velesanas; 1993; Latvijas republikas 6. Saeimas velesanas. 1995.*

Latvia, and their ethnic composition varies therefore considerably (Table 4.6). The "most Latvian" district is Kurzeme in the westernmost part of Latvia. Here, ethnic Latvians make up almost 95 percent of the voters. In the easternmost district of Latgale, on the other hand, the percentage is slightly above 50.

Figure 4.6 shows the number of votes attained by some important electoral lists in three districts. Without going into details on the political profile of these parties, the particulars of the programs, or motivations of the electorate,[132] we will only note here certain characteristics of the electoral results on the basis of which we may draw some conclusions about the electoral preferences of the various ethnic groups.

The radical-nationalistic parties—MNIL and Fatherland and Freedom—attracted an insignificant number of votes in the "least Latvian" district, Latgale. At the same time the results of the these parties were considerably better in ethnically heterogeneous Riga than in the "most Latvian" district of Kurzeme. Thus it seems that the average Latvian voter in the cities inclined more toward nationalist positions than the average Latvian voter in the countryside. In Riga, Latvians have much more frequent intercourse with Russians than in compactly Latvian rayons. It follows therefore that there will be a greater incidence of everyday conflicts and fiercer competition for the most prestigious jobs in the former than in the latter.

On the other hand, the Popular Concord Party and the Socialist Party managed to surpass the electoral threshold solely due to the votes they received in the "most Russian" districts, Latgale and Riga. Their respective results in the "most Latvian" districts fluctuated around one percent.

The results of the more centrist, moderate parties with liberal nationalist orientations (Latvian Way and DP Saimnieks) were much more evenly distributed and much less dependent on the ethnic composition of the electorate.

These data allow us to draw the following conclusion: While the Latvian voters divide they sympathies between the radical-nationalist and moderate parties, the Russophone voters give their support to these same moderate parties plus the "anti-nationalist" parties—Popular Concord and the leftist Socialist Party.

---

[132] For a more thorough analysis of the relationship between the electoral results of the various parties and ethnic composition of the electoral districts and a general discussion of the ethnic factor in Latvian parliamentary elections, see Kolstø and Tsilevich 1997.

FIGURE 4.6 Results of Parliamentary Elections in Three Electoral Districts (1995)

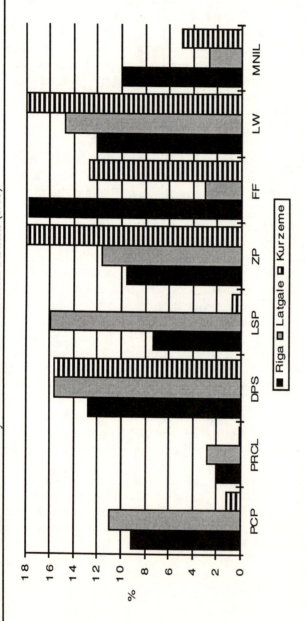

Source: Latvijas respublikas 6. Saeimas velesanas 1995.
Legend of party names: PCP – Popular Concord Party; PRCL – the Party of Russian Citizens in Latvia; DPS – the Democratic Party "Saimnieks" ("Master"); LSP – the joint list of the Latvian Socialist Party and the Equal Rights Movement; ZP – the popular movement Latvia: Zigerist's Party; FF, the Fatherland and Freedom Party; LW, the "Latvian Way" Party; MNIL – the Movement for the National Independence of Latvia.

FIGURE 4.7 Electoral Preferences of Latvians and Russian-Speakers (1995)

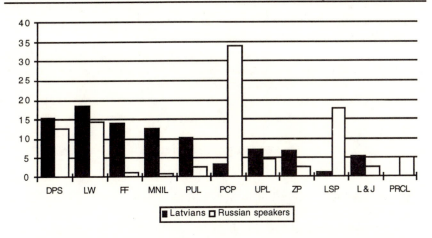

Source: SM-segodnia 29 September 1995. Legend of party names (not already listed in Figure 4.6 above): PUL—the Peasant Union of Latvia; UPL—the Unity Party of Latvia; L&J—the coalition "Labor and Justice." The latter list represented a coalition of the Social Democrats and the Party of Deceived Investors "Tainsiba" ("Justice")

These clear differences in the electoral preferences of the Latvian and Russophone voters are also vividly brought out by the sociological surveys. Figure 4.7 reproduces the results of an opinion poll conducted on the eve of the elections to the 6th Saeima by the Prognoz polling institute. The results bear witness to significant differences in the electoral preferences of the ethnic Latvians on the one hand and the Russophones on the other.

Another survey was carried out by the Baltic Data House immediately after the elections to the 6th Saeima (the poll was limited to those parties that made it over the five-percent electoral threshold). The results of this survey corroborate the conclusions we drew above based on the electoral results in the various districts: The non-Latvians make up the vast majority of the supporters of the Popular Concord Party and the Socialist Party. As regards the moderate Democratic Party—"Saimnieks"—and the extreme populist Zigerist's Party, the share of non-Latvians voters is slightly below the share of the non-Latvians in the population at large. For the liberal-nationalist party the Latvian Way this ratio was as high as 1:2. The radical nationalistic parties such as Fatherland and Freedom and the Movement for the National Independence of Latvia had practically no Russophone voters. Approximately 45 percent of the Russophone voters supported either the centrist Popular Concord Party or the leftist Socialist Party, both of which favor a liberal minority policy, a speedy naturalization of the non-citizens, and revocation of limitations on property rights, labor rights, and social security rights of non-citizens. Between 10 and 15 percent of the non-Latvians voted for moderate Latvian parties.

The Language Situation

Linguistic Conditions in the Soviet Period

In the rural areas of Latvia, Latvian continued to dominate the language situation in the postwar period. Latgale presented the only significant exception to this rule. In the cities, however, the social spheres in which the Latvian language could be freely used, became increasingly narrower. In the state administration and in material production the language of work was almost exclusively Russian. To a somewhat greater extent Latvian stood its ground in cultural life, in the agricultural sector, and, significantly, in the realm of science and education.

In the Soviet period, there were no legal documents requiring Latvian residents to master the Latvian language. Most people who moved to Latvia with the intention of settling there permanently had no incentives to learn the local language. As a result, in the 1989 census only 22.3 percent of the Russians who lived in the Latvian SSR claimed to be fluent in Latvian. The figures for other East Slavic groups were even lower: 18 percent of the Belarusians and 9.8 percent of the Ukrainians claimed to have a good command of Latvian (Figure 4.8). Of the total population 62 percent were fluent in Latvian, as against 81 percent who were fluent in Russian.

Generally speaking, Russian was the preferred language in ethnically mixed families. As the 1989 census data showed, in most ethnic groups in Latvia a majority regarded Russian as their "mother tongue" (*rodnoi iazyk*) (see Figure 4.9). The only exceptions were the Latvians, the Lithuanians, and the Roma. To most Latvians the resulting language situation was very disconcerting and the language problem became one of the main factors behind the ethnic Latvian mobilization during perestroika and "Atmoda" (the national revival).

FIGURE 4.8 Command of Language by Ethnic Group (1989)

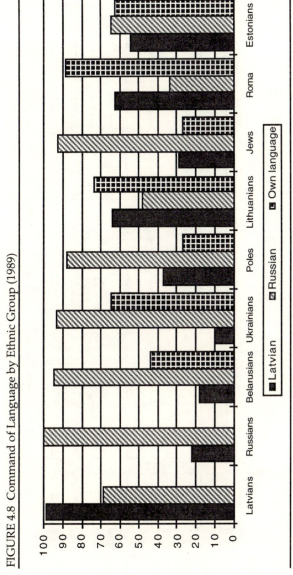

Source: Mezs 1994, 25.

FIGURE 4.9 Mother Tongue of Inhabitants of Latvia

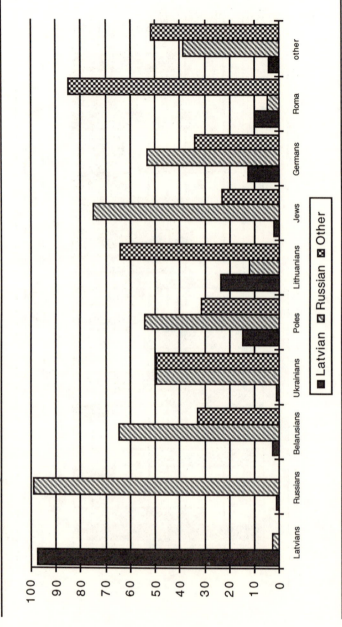

■ Latvian ⊠ Russian ⊠ Other

Source: Etnosituacija Latvija 1992, 10.

Legislation

One of the first legal acts to be carried out on the road to the restoration of Latvian independence was the Latvian Supreme Soviet resolution of 6 October 1988, conferring on Latvian the official status as "state language" in the Latvian Soviet Republic. In December that year, the Latvian Council of Ministers passed another resolution outlining a plan of action to introduce Latvian as the state language.[133] Characteristically for that time, the program also contained certain sections on ways and means to improve the study of the Russian language; it was still necessary to keep a certain "political balance". A Language Commission consisting of 18 persons was formed and attached to the Supreme Soviet.

The Act on the Languages of the Latvian Republic was adopted on 5 May 1989.[134] Latvian was proclaimed the sole state language and all official business should henceforth be conducted in Latvian. Alongside this basic principle, however, the 1989 law also contained certain guarantees for the continued use of Russian. In particular, in correspondence and oral communication between a resident and state bodies, the resident, though not the official, was entitled to select the language of communication.

The language law's period of implementation was stipulated to three years. However, in March 1992, two months before the law was about to enter legal force, the Latvian Parliament passed a number of significant amendments to it which, in reality, changed its very essence.[135] As a result, Russian, for all practical purposes, became a foreign language in Latvia, to be treated on a par with any other non-Latvian language. The Russian language is mentioned only once in the law, in Article 8: "The bodies of state power are obliged to accept and examine documents from the residents of Latvia which are written in either Latvian, English, German, or Russian." At the same time, Articles 8 and 9 stipulated that all documents in which a state body—that is, any institution, enterprise or organization belonging to the state—addresses the citizens, including written responses to letters and complaints, shall be written in the state language. It is true that Article 9 permitted responses to be written in the same language as that used by the citizen in the first place, but from now on, the choice of language in cases such as this was left to the discretion of the official.

---

[133] *Latvijas PSR Ministru* 1989, 184–188.

[134] Guboglo 1994, 36–39.

[135] The text of the law in Latvian, English and Russian translations is published in *Valsts Valoda* 1992.

All official administrative tasks, and all meetings and conferences in state bodies are to be conducted in the state language (Article 6). Another language may be used as well, but in such circumstances the organizers of the meeting must provide for translation into Latvian if one of the participants so requires. Also all other enterprises, institutions, and organizations operating within the borders of the Latvian Republic, are required to employ Latvian in all official business as well as in all domestic correspondence (Article 7).

At congresses, conferences, meetings, and rallies there is a free choice of language. However, if a meeting is open to the public, the organizers must provide for translation into the state language (Article 5).

Perhaps the most important article of the Act was Article 4, which stated that all employees in bodies of state power, that is, all institutions, enterprises, and organizations belonging to the state, had to have a command of and employ the state language, as well as other languages, to the extent required by the person's professional duties. This prerequisite was extended to cover the private sphere as well. On the basis of this particular legal norm large-scale attestations of Latvian language proficiency were carried out (see below). No regulations or proficiency tests with relevance to the other languages were mentioned in this article.

The adoption of the Language Act was followed by a number of ordinances and other sublegal acts which together regulated the usages of the various languages in Latvia. Thus, for instance, on 1 July 1992 an appendix to the Administrative code was adopted, establishing a system of punishment for violations of the Language Act.[136]

The Regulations on the Use of the State Language in Appellations and Information, adopted 4 November 1992,[137] authorized the use of non-state languages in public information only in the following instances: for security reasons; at events organized by national cultural societies: at international seminars and conferences; and when such information is intended for foreign tourists. In the latter case, special permission must be obtained by the State Language Center. In addition to this limited number of cases, information on the tax system was also exempted from the general prohibition against the use of non-state languages in public documents.[138] Whenever a non-state language is used in these excepted instances, the same information must also be provided in the state language, and "the text written in the state language must be

---

[136] Published for the first time in Russian in *VS i SM* (supplement to *Diena*), 24 July 1992.

[137] Published for the first time in Russian in *VS i SM* (supplement to *Diena*), 11 December 1992.

[138] *Grozijumi Nolikuma* 1995.

more conspicuous" (Article 5.2). In all other instances public information must be given in Latvian only.

Latvian electoral law states that only citizens of Latvia who have a command of the state language at the third level (= highest level) may be registered as candidates for the Saeima and for local elected bodies. Candidates whose education took place in a non-Latvian language are required to present a certificate of language proficiency at the third level on registering.[139]

The Language Inspectorate

On 22 July 1992, a State Language Inspectorate was established in order to secure compliance with the Language Act as well as with all ordinances and other sublegal acts which regulate the language situation.[140] One of the chief objectives of this office was to maintain act as a watchdog *vis-à-vis* the official language of administration and business in enterprises and institutions; ascertain which languages were employed for public information purposes; ascertain that the tests of proficiency in the state language were carried out in accordance with the rules, and so forth.

The Inspectorate employed 16 inspectors, each of whom had the right to impose fines for violations of the language law amounting to as much as 75 *lats*, the equivalent of 150 U.S.D. The head of the inspectorate could impose fines not exceeding 150 lats. In addition, the ordinance on the State Language Inspectorate allowed for private citizens to work as volunteer language inspectors. In the fall of 1994, 211 persons were attached to the Inspectorate in this capacity.[141] In a number of cities and districts local authorities have organized their own municipal language inspections.

Since they commenced their work in 1992 through 30 June 1994, the language inspectors filed more than one thousand administrative protocols on violations of the language legislation. The total sum of the fines which have been imposed, amount to 21,425 lats (more than 40 thousand U.S.D).[142] The activities of the language inspectorate have stirred up strong emotions among the public, and been subjected to attacks from very different quarters. Many Russophones, as well as many Latvians, were very upset when the inspectorate attempted to annull the

---

[139] The text of the law is published, inter alia, in *Latvijas Respublikas 6. Saeimas*, 10–16.

[140] *VS i SM*, (supplement to *Diena*,) 18 September 1992.

[141] Kamenska 1994, 21.

[142] Ibid., 22.

mandates of a number of elected deputies on the Daugavpils City Council on the grounds that they allegedly lacked a sufficient command of the state language.[143] At the same time, reports in the Latvian-language press about a volunteer inspector who was attacked when dutifully carrying out his job,[144] sparked off a highly charged debate, although it was never established whether the attack was a reaction against his work for the language inspectorate.

Language Tests

The Council of Ministers Resolution no. 189, adopted on 25 May 1992, approved the establishment of a system of language attestations and the procedures for such attestations.[145] The Resolution introduced three levels of proficiency in the state language: the first and lowest indicates an elementary understanding of, and ability to speak, Latvian; the second and intermediate, the ability to speak and write well enough to carry out one's professional duties at the workplace ; and finally, the third and highest level, the ability to speak and write Latvian.

On the basis of this resolution several networks of attestation commissions were established. The main network consisted of commissions attached to ministries, institutions, and enterprises. The various workplaces were instructed to compile lists of positions and professions which were subject to attestation, indicating what level of proficiency was required in each case. Persons who had received their education in the Latvian language were exempt from attestation. In practice, employees in all kinds of professions except manual workers, but including, for instance, cleaning assistants and guards, had to undergo attestation procedures.

An employee who had passed the attestation assessment required of him received a certificate confirming his language capabilities. In accordance with amendments to the Labor Code,[146] a person who lacked the correct certificate for a particular job could not be employed in it. These amendments also made it possible to sack employees lacking the necessary certificate, on grounds of "professional incompetence." In practice, no mass dismissals on such a basis were carried out. No

---

[143] *Dinaburg*, 9 June 1994.

[144] *Diena*, 29 November 1995.

[145] The text of this resolution was published in *VS i SM*, (supplement to *Diena*), 12 June 1992.

[146] Published in *AP MP* (supplement to *Diena*), 28 August 1992.

research is available to account for the causes for this. We assume, however, that in most cases some of the following social dynamics may have played a role: first, people who felt incapable—or were unwilling—to learn Latvian looked for another job in advance, preferring to leave voluntarily in order to avoid a record of dismissal due to lack of professional abilities. Second, people prepared themselves for the test and passed—but afterwards quickly forgot what they had learned. Third, an employer might prefer to keep on his payroll people who had failed the test: since he was entitled to fire them at any time, they could be expected to work harder and make fewer complaints. Nonetheless, the press has reported instances of entire groups of employees being dismissed. This has happened, for instance, to a number of teachers a t the Daugavpils Musical College[147] as well as to employees at Polyclinical Hospital no. 3 in Riga.[148]

The affected institutions and public offices operated with very different levels of language demands. Despite the fact that the State Language Center had published detailed lists of sample questions to be used during the attestation procedures,[149] as well as methodological guidelines for the commissions,[150] all efforts to standardize the language requirements failed.[151] As a result, the chances of passing the attestation in a particular locality depended in no small part on the good will—or caprice—of the members of the commission.

In the testing period which lasted from 15 June 1992 to 15 December 1993 300,000 employees were supposed to undergo language attestation. On the expiry of the deadline, however, only a half, or 154,000, had actually been tested.[152] The results of the tests which were carried out in 1992 are reproduced in figure 4.10.[153] A number of ministries and departments in which a very large proportion of the workforce consisted of non-Latvians, *in casu*, in the Ministry of Internal Affairs, as well as railway workers, were given an extended deadline for language attestations.

Also after the completion of the test period permanent attestation commissions continued to function. Every Latvian resident might at any time sign up for a language test, but now he or she would have to pay for

---

[147] *Latgales Laiks*, 31 August 1995.

[148] *SM-segodnia*, 23 December 1992.

[149] *Saeima un Ministru Kabineta*, 2 June 1992.

[150] *VS i SM*, (supplement to *Diena*), 13 November 1992.

[151] Kamenska 1994, 19.

[152] Ibid., 1994, 13.

[153] The data are from Kamenska 1994, 13.

FIGURE 4.10 Results of the State Language Tests, 1992 (level, failures, absent)

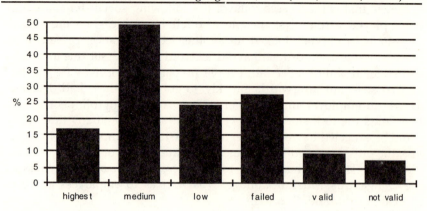

it. In the fall of 1994 the fee for employed persons was six lats and for unemployed three lats.[154] According to expert estimates, about 250,000 persons had gone through language attestation by the end of 1995.[155]

Regional Regulations

In contrast to the situation in Lithuania and Estonia Latvia has not adopted any special rules for the use of the non-Latvian languages in areas where the Russophones or other minorities make up compact majorities. This situation creates special problems, first and foremost for Daugavpils, the second largest city of Latvia, where ethnic Latvians make up less than 14 percent of the population.

Dzintars Abikis, the chairperson of the parliamentary commission on education, science, and culture, believes that uniformity is one of the basic principles of Latvian language policy. There may be certain regional variations with the regard to the timetables for the introduction of the language legislation, but, he says, not with the regard to the lasting language regimes to be introduced.[156]

---

[154] Kamenska 1994, 17.

[155] Druviete 1996, 25.

[156] Abikis' presentation at the seminar on Interethnic Relations, Ethnopolitics, and Social Integration in the Baltic states, Jurmala, 13–15 September 1996.

New Draft Language Law

In November 1995, the Latvian Cabinet of Ministers approved a new draft law on the state language referring it to the Parliament for further discussion.[157] In this draft the language regulations were even tighter than in the existing legislation. In particular, the new draft permitted communication with state bodies and local government bodies in the state language only. An address written in another language had to be accompanied by a correct translation attested by an authorized notary. Thus, even the formal requirement that state and local officials "have a sufficient command of other languages to carry out their professional duties" was removed. In addition, the draft law stipulated that the working language at all meetings in firms and enterprises, public organizations, and religious societies should be Latvian. The draft also contained a number of other restrictions on the usage of all other languages than the state language.

One of the architects behind the draft, the leader of the State Language Center, Dzintra Hirscha, claimed that "the draft bill on the state language marks a definitely new level in the development of our language policy. It protects the linguistic rights and human rights of the titular nation, without encroaching, of course, upon the rights of the minorities."[158] On another occasion she maintained that "unlike other laws, the language law is a process. It indicates the goals toward which we may slowly draw near in the future."[159]

The new draft law was strongly criticized by the State Bureau on Human Rights as well as by some international organizations. The Commissioner on Democratic Institutions and Human Rights in the Council of Baltic Sea States, Ole Espersen, discussed the draft law in his Annual Report in 1996. He had been informed by the chairperson of the Latvian parliamentary commission on education, science, and culture that the draft had been returned to its architects for further improvement.[160] This piece of information, however, has not been confirmed by any Latvian sources.

---

[157] *Latvijas vestnesis*, 1995, 28 November 1995.
[158] Ibid.
[159] *Diena*, 29 November 1995.
[160] *Council of Baltic Sea States 1996*, 73.

The National Program
for Latvian Language Training

In the fall of 1995, the Latvian Cabinet of Ministers approved a National Program for Training in the State Language. The UN Development Programme Office in Latvia participated actively in the elaboration of this program.[161] The program envisages the training of highly qualified teachers to teach Latvian to 150,000 pupils in schools where the language of instruction is non-Latvian, as well as to 150,000 adults. The program budget was approximately 23.9 million U.S.D and was to be footed by a group of foreign donor countries. Sweden would contribute with 5.3m Swedish kronor, and Norway, Finland, the Netherlands, as well as some other countries were also meant to participate.[162] After some delay an agreement on the release of the first tranche of 3.2m U.S.D was signed on 6 December 1996.[163] A special State Language Training Unit has been set up. This unit has been training teachers who, in turn, will be teaching other teachers. Latvian-language courses for teachers at Russian schools have been conducted. The idea behind these courses is to give the teachers the competency to teach their subjects in Latvian, thus removing the main obstacle in the way of turning Russian schools into Latvian-language schools, i.e., the lack of suitably qualified teachers.

Changes in the Language Situation in the 1990s

Few data are available on the dynamics of the language situation in Latvia since the restoration of independence. It seems clear that in many cases the language tests did not lead to a permanent change in the languages people used at their workplaces. Having passed the test they continued to employ a non-state language in everyday discourse. This is particularly true in non-Latvian work collectives where there is no incentive to use Latvian.[164] At the same time, independent researchers have drawn the conclusion that "Russians in the Baltics are beginning to recognize the success of the nationalizing programs, and have made substantial efforts to develop facility in the titular language."[165]

---

[161] *Latvia. Human Development Report,* 1996, 73.

[162] *Diena,* 17 February 1996.

[163] *Diena,* 3 December 1996.

[164] Kamenska 1994, 20.

[165] Laitin 1996a, 23.

FIGURE 4.11 Changes in Command of Latvian Language by Ethnic Group

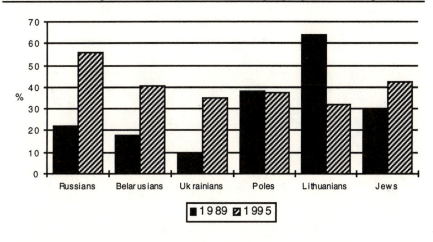

Sources: 1989 Census data, and Druviete 1995, 23.

Figure 4.11 shows the results of a survey conducted in 1995 in some Latvian cities. When juxtaposed with the 1989 census data this survey indicates a radical increase in the Russians' proficiency in the Latvian language (55.8 percent, up from 22.3 percent). Admittedly, data from surveys and censuses are not directly comparable, but the same marked change is corroborated also by other sources. Thus, the National Media Survey, for instance, indicates a 60 percent proficiency among the Russians for the same year, while the Rose 1995 survey gives as high a figure as 62 percent.[166] These increased figures probably reflect changes in the self-perception of those who were interviewed. Under the new circumstances in independent Latvia, when the Russophones are forced to speak some Latvian, at least occasionally, they upgrade the assessment of their own language capabilities. Some other psychological factors may also be at work.[167]

More reliable data are provided by the Department of Immigration and Citizenship (Figure 4.12). When residents enroll in the Register of Residents they are questioned as to the preferred language of

---

[166] *Baltic Media Book* 1996, 14; Rose 1995, 45.

[167] We are much more skeptical about data indicating that the proficiency in the Latvian language has decreased drastically among certain other minorities, for example, among the Lithuanians. The Lithuanian figures are hampered by a serious problem of representativity. The absolute numbers in the survey are very small, and, in addition, this poll was conducted in the cities only, while the majority of the Lithuanians live in compact rural settlements in the southern part of the country, along the Lithuanian border.

FIGURE 4.12 Main Language of Communication in Family (1994)

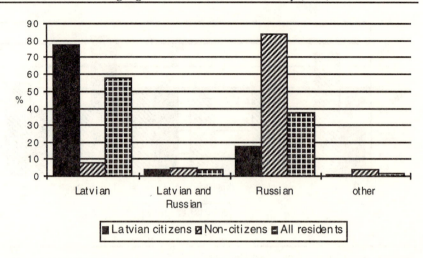

Source: Kamenska 1994, 53.

communication in the family. These data show that few changes have occurred in the language practices of ethnically mixed families. On the whole, they indicate that, on the family level, the qualitative language situation which dominated in the late 1980s remains basically unaltered. As before, the language preferences of Latvian citizens differ sharply from the language habits of non-citizens.

A survey conducted by the Baltic Data House in May 1994 gives some idea about the languages of communication in state bodies and in the service industry.[168] Those interviewed were asked how often a question posed in Latvian received an answer in Russian at their workplace. Fifteen percent of the Latvians said that this happened "often"; 48 percent answered "sometimes," while 34 percent said it never happened. Conversely, 10 percent of the Russians claimed that they often received an answer in Latvian when they addressed someone in Russian. 39 percent had experienced this sometimes, while 48 percent had always been answered in Russian. This means that the subjective feeling of language comfort was, in fact, still somewhat higher among Russians than among Latvians.

---

[168] Zepa 1995, 42.

Language in Education

Historical Overview

In independent Latvia in the interwar period, a complex system of minority language education was in existence.[169] The 1919 Act on Education declared that the pupils ought to receive their mandatory education in their "family language" (Article 39).[170] The parents themselves determined which language they regarded as their family language (Article 40).[171] The state and local governments were obliged to provide schools for the minorities to the extent that this was necessary to fulfill their needs. In order to start an entire class in a minority language a minimum of 30 pupils was required (Article 41).

A special Law on Minority Schools laid down the norms and procedures for the financing of such schools: of the total sum allotted by the state and the municipalities for educational purposes the minority school should receive a share commensurate with their fraction of the total population in a given territory (Article 2). At the Ministry of Education a special department dealt with matters concerning minority schools. This department was divided into special sections for each minority. The heads of these sections were appointed on the basis of nominations by the minorities themselves. These officials represented their respective minority groups in all cultural matters and also had the right to be present and to speak at the sessions of the Cabinet of Ministers. They had consultative status in all matters concerning the cultural life of the minorities (Articles 6 and 7).

In the 1933/34 school year there were 1,502 Latvian language schools in operation in Latvia, among them, 55 high schools. In addition, there were 555 minority schools, including 41 high schools. Broken down by language groups, 88 schools were Russian (including 10 high schools); 88 (9) were German; 100 (14) were Jewish; 35 (3) were Polish; 23 (1) Belarusian; 13 (1) Lithuanian; and 4 (0) Estonian.[172] It is estimated that approximately 80 percent of all pupils coming from minority families received their education in minority schools that year. After the coup d'état in 1934 the number of minority schools was drastically reduced, but part of the minority school system continued to exist.

---

[169] Antane 1991.

[170] *Likums par Latvijas* 1919.

[171] *Likums par mazakuma* 1919.

[172] *Natsional'nye* 1996, 12.

FIGURE 4.13 Number of Pupils in Latvian Schools of Latvia by Language of
Instruction (Absolute numbers)

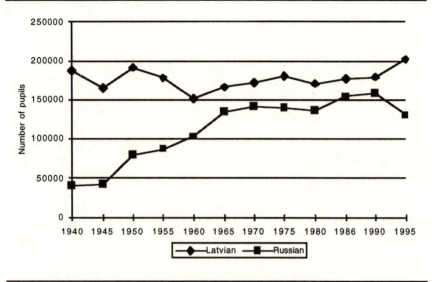

Source: Latvian State Archive, data collected by Ilmars Mezs.

In the Soviet period, education in Latvia at all levels was offered in
Latvian and Russian only. The dynamics of the language preferences of
the pupils in Soviet Latvia are shown in figure 4.13.[173]

Legislation

The current Law on Education was adopted in June 1991.[174] It guarantees the right to be educated in the state language at all levels (Article
5). Representatives of nontitular ethnic groups are granted "the right
and the guarantee" to receive education in their native language "in
accordance with the Law on Languages." The law states furthermore
that the Latvian state will provide the necessary means to ensure the
enjoyment of this right.

---

[173] Mezs 1997, data compiled from the Latvian State archive.
[174] "Latvijas respublikas Izgitibas likums," *Diena*, 26 July 1991.

All pupils who attend an educational institution at any level which is subject to the jurisdiction of the Latvian Republic, are obliged to study the Latvian language. This is the case irrespective of the language of instruction in the actual school and irrespective by whom the school is run. Graduate students from medium-level schools (high schools and technical colleges) have to pass an exam proving their proficiency in Latvian. In all higher institutions of learning which are financed by the state, Latvian is the basic language of instruction for all students, starting from the second school year.

Thus, the Latvian Education Law assumes the existence of non-Latvian schools, but neither the Act itself nor any other legal Acts spell out the conditions under which such schools may be opened. This is very different from the detailed regulations regarding Latvian-language schools. According to the law such schools must be opened on the insistence of the parents of no less than ten pupils at the first level, and of the parents of no less than 25 pupils at the medium level. Questions relating to the opening and closure of minority schools are delegated to the municipal administrations which frequently make willful decisions on the matter.

Since the Law on Education was adopted in 1991 it has been subject to numerous amendments. For instance, new regulations introduced in the 1996/97 school year established that in elementary schools (from the first through the ninth grade) with a non-state language of education no less than two subjects must be taught in Latvian. On the high school level (tenth through twelfth grade) this requirement was expanded to include no less than three subjects.

According to Article 62 in the current version of the law, up to 80 percent of the budget of licensed private schools may be covered by the exchequer. However, in May 1994 the Cabinet of Ministers decided that such financing shall be extended only to private schools in which the language of instruction is Latvian.[175] This new system was retained in the new Rules for State Financing of Private Schools which were adopted in July 1996. (True, state subvention could be granted "in exceptional circumstances" also to elementary minority schools, but not to medium and higher educational institutions.)[176]

A new draft law on education was adopted on its first reading in the Saeima in the fall of 1996.[177] This law introduced an innovation which had been on the cards for some time already: By 2005, all medium-level educational institutions will have to have switched to Latvian as their

---

[175] *Latvijas vestnesis*, 9 June 1994.

[176] *LR Ministru kabineta noteikumi* 1996.

[177] The draft law was published in *Izglibita un kultura*, 4 January 1996.

sole language of instruction. The draft permitted education in Russian and "other non-state languages" in elementary schools only. The law also gave a new conceptual definition of minority schools: these are schools in which the instruction is given "in Latvian and in the language of the minority." In effect, the draft leaves it to the Ministry of Education to decide at its own discretion which subjects may be taught in the minority language and which will require instruction in the state language.

The draft provoked serious concern and protests from the Russian-speaking public. On the initiative of the Latvian Committee for Human Rights and the Equal Rights Movement more than 50,000 signatures were amassed in a very short time protesting the elimination of medium-level Russian education.[178] Also many experts on educational organizations strongly criticized the draft.[179] After its first reading 709 suggestions for amendments of the law were submitted, that is, seven amendment proposals on average for every article. This huge number of proposals made it practically impossible to continue the work on the draft law in the Saeima. As a result, by the fall of 1997 the basic principles for minority language education had still not been decided on.

Main Controversies

The main problem for the non-Latvians as regards educational policy is the uncertainty of the future of Russian-language education. In spite of the guarantees for education in minority languages which are contained in the current version of the Law on Education, many Latvian politicians and official spokespersons of the Latvian Republic already in the early 1990s began to talk about the necessity of eliminating instruction in "non-state" languages above high school level and even above the elementary level. This, it was claimed, was necessary in order to facilitate the integration of Latvian society.

In 1993, the Minister of Education, Janis Vaivads, expressed the following:

> I don't think that we ought to have two different school concepts in Latvia, [one for state-language schools and one for Russian schools]. When the state becomes mononational, it will be impossible to countenance different educational systems . Still, it is true that the process of rolling back the Russian school will be very long-winded and gradual.[180]

---

[178] *SM-segodnia*, 12 April 1996.

[179] For instance, *SM-segodnia*, 12 March 1996.

[180] *Panorama Latvii*, 31 August 1993, as quoted in *Diena*, 12 October 1993.

Another scenario was advanced with relative frequency: the Russian schools had to be reformed in order to make sure that the next generation of non-Latvians obtained a complete grasp of the state language. In 1996 an advisor to the Minister of Education, Baiba Petersone, backed this idea at a meeting with teachers from Russian schools: "we cannot accept that the educated younger generation be fettered in any way for want of language proficiency."[181] The ministry adhered to the view that it is impossible to gain full mastery in a language by studying it as a second language alone. Complete command can only be obtained in the language that is used as the medium of instruction in the schools, not in the languages taught as one of several subjects, the Ministry insisted. The leader of the State Language Center, Dzintra Hirscha, rounded off with the following sweeping statement: "The reform is necessary, since knowledge of the Latvian language in and of itself does not signify loyalty toward the state or integration into society. Only the curriculum and the overall methods of instruction may create the preconditions for such integration."[182] In this statement, the political motive behind the language legislation was apparent for all to see.

This strategy provoked strong cries of resentment from the Russophone public and from Russophone cultural organizations. The vice-chairperson of the Latvian society of Russian culture, Tatiana Arshavskaia, objected that education in a language other than one's native tongue, that is, in a language in which the pupils have not yet gained full proficiency, inevitably will lower the achievement levels of Russian school kids. Further complicating the situation is the acute lack of qualified teachers who are fluent in both Latvian and Russian, in addition to being well versed in the subject they are teaching. It is very likely that the Russian pupils would acheive a good command of the Latvian language if the teaching standards of Latvian as a second language were improved, Arshavskaia believed. This option, however, has not been given much consideration in the Ministry. On the contrary, the training of Latvian-language teachers for Russian schools has to all intents and purposes ceased.[183]

The quality of Latvian-language education in Russian schools is frequently subjected to harsh criticism in the Russian-language media in Latvia.[184] This criticism, it seems, reflects a widespread feeling among the non-Latvian population. For instance, in a survey conducted in 1993 by the American political scientist David Laitin, 95.2 percent of the

---

[181] *SM-segodnia,* 26 March 1996.

[182] *Diena,* 1 June 1996.

[183] *SM-segodnia,* 6 June 1996.

[184] See, for instance, *SM-segodnia* 13 May 1996.

Russians in Latvia believe that Latvian ought to be a mandatory subject
in all schools in Latvia.[185]

Another survey which was organized by Ina Druviete in 1995,[186]
showed that 90.9 percent of the Russians wanted their children to be
fluent in Latvian. The corresponding figures for the Belarusians and
Ukrainians were 87.7 percent and 88.9 percent, respectively. 64.1 percent
of the Russians, 62.8 percent of the Belarusians, and 67.6 percent of the
Ukrainians expressed dissatisfaction with the quality of instruction in
Latvian given to their children.

In the Druviete poll, furthermore, the persons interviewed were
asked about their preferred model for Russian-language schools. 43.5
percent of the Russians and 43.9 percent of the respondents of other non-
Latvian nationalities said that "education ought to be given in Russian
while Latvian ought to be taught as a second language." 28.6 percent of
the Russians and 25 percent of the "others" thought that "most of the
teaching ought to be conducted in Russian, but some subjects ought to be
taught in Latvian." 17.2 and 11.7 percent, respectively, supported the
view that "all education ought to be in Russian," while 9.7 percent of
the Russians and 15.3 percent of the "others" believed that "most of the
education ought to be in Latvian while some subjects (such as Russian
and literature) ought to be given in Russian." Finally, only 1 percent of
the Russians and 4.1 percent of the non-Russian minorities wanted all
education to be conducted in Latvian.

Thus, there is a radical discrepancy between the reform in the Russian schools contemplated by the political leadership in Latvia, on the
one hand, and the preferences of the national minorities themselves, on
the other.

In this situation, the Latvian Society of Russian Culture and the
Latvian Association of Russian-Language Teachers put forward a constructive "Alternative Concept for language policy in Latvian national
minority education."[187] The main ideas here included beginning the
teaching of the state language to Russian-speaking children at an early
stage; achieving a proper balance between Latvian and mother tongues
in required reading texts ; broadening the opening for students to choose
optional courses in Latvian in accordance with their preferences and
future educational plans; and establishing special centers for the re-
training of teachers for Russian and minority schools.

Most likely, in the final outcome the future system of education for
the nontitular population in Latvia will be decided upon through a

---

[185] Laitin 1996a, 7.

[186] Druviete 1995.

[187] The Concept was published in *Diena* (supplement), 29 May 1996.

complex give-and-take process which will involve not only the Latvian political elite and the cultural organizations of the Russophones, but also the participation of international organizations and even Russia.

Linguistic Shifts in the Latvian Educational System

From 1988 to 1997 the share of pupils in Latvian schools who studied in Latvian rose from 51.1 to 61.9 percent. In the same period, the proportion of students choosing Russian-language schools fell from 48.5 to less than 39 percent. This tendency was particularly marked in the lowest grades. In the elementary schools (first through fourth grade) as many as 66 percent of the children attended Latvian-language classes in the 1995/96 school year.[188] The number of schools that are offering Russian language education is slowly, but surely, getting smaller and smaller. At the same time the number of Latvian schools is on the increase (see Figure 4.15).

The government insists that these changes in the school structure are a consequence of the altered demographic composition of the population. In particular, when the Russian army was withdrawn in August 1994, a number of Russian schools attached to the military garrisons were closed. Moreover, official spokespersons will explain, there is a growing tendency among Russophone parents to send their children to Latvian-language schools. Hence, the increasing closure of Russians schools is both natural and democratic.[189] Most Russophones nevertheless perceive the ever-more limited chances to be educated in Russian as discriminatory. They believe that the quality of the education offered to Russian children is purposely and systematically lowered. As a corollary, their competitiveness at university entry and in the labor market is weakening. Their most vocal reactions the Russophone parents have reserved for the local municipalities that, in a number of cases, have closed down solid, prestigious Russian schools through arbitrary decisions. One such incidence was the closure of the 26th School in Riga in June 1994 which caused protracted protests: hunger strikes, pickets, petitions, etc.[190]

---

[188] *Diena*, 23 March 1996.

[189] See, e.g., *Diena*, 23 March 1996; and the reply of the Minister for Education and Science, Maris Grinblats, to an official inquiry from a Saeima deputy, Parliamentary Doc. no. 1–2--102 of 5 June 1996.

[190] *SM-segodnia*, 28 June 1994, as well as numerous other publications on this theme in the same paper.

FIGURE 4.14 Language of Instruction in Latvia´s Schools

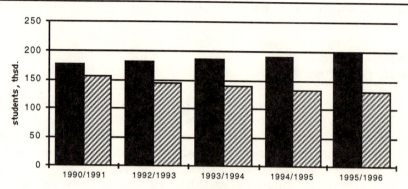

Sources: Latvija skaitlos 1996, 55; *Ethnosituacija Latvija* 1994, 16. The "other" category does not show up in the figure since it amounts to less than one percent.

FIGURE 4.15 Number of Schools in Latvia by Language of Instruction

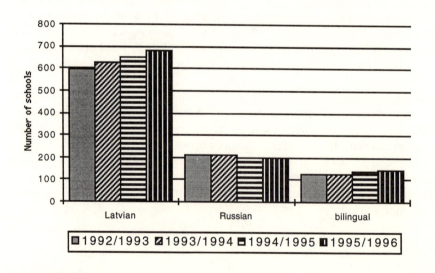

Sources: Izglitibas iestades 1996, 46; Tomasuns 1994.

In order to give as objective an assessment as possible of the arguments of both parties in this dispute we would need exact data on the number of non-Latvians pupils who are attending Latvian schools. Unfortunately, no such official statistics are available. All we have been able to obtain are data on the ethnic composition of the student mass in ten primary schools in the Vidzeme district of Riga. They show that, for about 20 percent of the students in grades 1 through 4 in Latvian-language schools, Latvian was not the main language of communication in their family. This figure had remained fairly stable for the last four years.

Very often when significant numbers of Russian children try to get entrance into Latvian-language schools, the parents of the Latvian kids file protests. They fear that the Russian kids will influence the language, culture, and behavior of their Latvian school mates more than the other way around. In a reply to concerned Latvian parents the Minister of Education, Maris Grinblats, declared in June 1996 that "under no circumstances will we [...] accept a mechanical mixture of Latvian children and children of other nationalities in the same school or in the same class."[191] Against the backdrop of such declarations it is not quite clear how one should understand the official concept for a reform of the non-Latvian education, according to which most Russophone youngsters should receive their medium-level education in Latvian. It appears that, as the Russian high schools are closed down, new "Latvian-language schools for Russian-language children" will have to be constructed, to exist alongside the regular Latvian schools. How this will foster increased ethnic integration in society, is far from clear. Ever more often the somber prediction is heard that as a result of the school reform the Russian children will choose not to take any medium-level education at all. Education above the elementary level is not mandatory in Latvia.[192]

The number of pupils in the Russian schools is on average far higher than in the Latvian schools. To a certain extent this can be explained by the fact that the majority of the non-Latvian population is concentrated in the cities, while the small country schools are mostly Latvian. As regards specialized high schools and technical schools, all of them are losing students, irrespective of language of instruction. However, the students are deserting the Russian schools faster than they are deserting the Latvian ones.

In 1994, the Russian language was continuing to fulfill its functions as a *lingua franca* in Latvia. While ethnic Latvians in that year made up

---

[191] *Latvijas vestnesis,* 13 June 1996.
[192] *Minority Rights and Mechanisms* 1996, 6.

FIGURE 4.16 Number of Students in Minority Schools (Classes) in Latvia

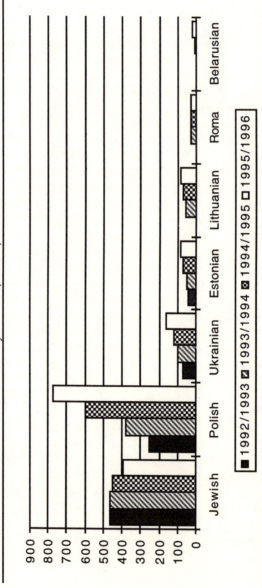

■ 1992/1993 ▨ 1993/1994 ⊠ 1994/1995 ☐ 1995/1996

Source: Izglītības iestādes, 1995/96, 1996, 46; Tomasuns 1994; and unpublished material from the Information Center of the Ministry of Education and Science.

approximately 97 percent of the pupils in Latvian language schools, ethnic Russians made up slightly more than 70 percent of the total student mass in Russian-language schools. Remarkably, in these schools the share of ethnic Latvians continued to be above 10 percent. To some degree, this seems to be a legacy from the Soviet period when children from ethnically mixed families usually went to Russian schools. Also, these figures probably reveal a mismatch between the formal ethnicity and the actual mother tongue and self-awareness of some pupils. In spite of being listed in the census data as Latvians they felt themselves to be Russians.

Minority Schools

In the late 1980s a process of reestablishing national minority schools started in Latvia. In 1989, the Riga Jewish high school was opened. At that time, this was the only Jewish school throughout the whole of the USSR.[193] Over the next years two Polish, one Ukrainian, one Estonian, and one Lithuanian school were opened in Riga. Classes were available in Belarusian. Polish schools were opened in Daugavpils, Rezekne, Jekabpils and Kraslava; Lithuanian classes in Liepaja, and Roma classes in Ventspils. In the 1995/1996 school year the number of students increased in practically all minority schools except the Jewish ones, though no new schools or classes were opened (see Figure 4.16). In some cases financial support from the "ethnic homeland" (in particular, Poland and Israel) plays an important role in the upkeep of these schools.

It should be pointed out that the minority language is not always used as the language of instruction in the "national" schools. Thus, in the Jewish and Ukrainian schools[194] most subjects are taught in Russian, and in Latvian in the Estonian school. What makes these schools "national" is the inclusion of several additional subjects in the curriculum, such as courses in the national language, national history, and national culture.

The pupils who study in minority schools in Latvia make up less than one percent of the total student body. However, among the pupils at the lowest level (grades 1 through 4) the percentage is slightly higher.[195] Jews tend to be attracted to national schools more than other

---

[193] *Natsional'nye i etnicheskie* 1996, 36.

[194] *SM-segodnia*, 20 March 1996.

[195] Data from the Information Center of the Ministry of Education and Science.

TABLE 4.7 Share of School-Age Children Attending Minority Schools by Ethnic Groups, 1995

Ethnic group	Percentage
Belarusians	0.5
Poles	11.4
Lithuanians	3.2
Jews	30.6
Estonians	6.7
Roma	3.8

Source: Information Center of the Ministry of Education and Science.

minorities, apparently in preparation for emigration to Israel. Among all other groups the percentages are considerably lower (see Table 4.7).

Ethnic "Division of Labor" and Socioeconomic Stratification

The restoration of Latvian independence brought about significant changes in the social structure of the Latvian and the Russophone communities. For one thing, as a corollary of the establishment of a number of new state institutions a multitude of new jobs were created in the organs of government. The vast majority of the officials who filled these positions were ethnic Latvians.

Representatives of the Russophone population tend to be employed more often than Latvians in the crisis-ridden Latvian industry, not least in the mastodon plants which used to be oriented toward the all-Union Soviet economic structure. A significant part of the non-Latvian population of working age was/is made up of blue collar workers and young specialists who worked at these plants as well as at research institutes and engineering design agencies.

Russians have also traditionally dominated in the middle and higher administrative levels of the national economy. In these areas, ethnic Latvians made up only 31.5 percent of the workforce in the mid-1980s. Finally, Russophones were also clearly overrepresented in jobs with very low pay and prestige such as transport, construction and unskilled industrial work.[196] In contrast, ethnic Latvians have

---

[196] Muiznieks 1995, 115.

traditionally dominated in agriculture (71.9 percent) as well as in culture and the arts (69.2 percent).[197] In these sectors the crisis set in only some years after the depression had hit the heavy industry.

Specifically, two main factors contributed to the new ethnic stratification of the Latvian job market: the introduction of new market principles in the economy, on the one hand, and the titular nationality's near total control over the levers of political power on the other. To some considerable degree these two factors run at cross-purposes. While a market economy in principle is ruled by an "invisible hand," the monopolization of political power in the hands of one group meant that it is able to decide "the rules of the game."

Conventional wisdom insists that private business in Latvia is mostly controlled by Russophone tycoons. For instance, at a meeting of the Council of Europe in Strasbourg in 1993, the Latvian Minister of Foreign Affairs, Georgs Andrejevs, asserted that "80 percent of the finance capital of Latvia is in the hands of non-Latvians."[198] In an interview with the Russian weekly *Golos* the ambassador of Latvia to Russia Janis Peteris in 1992 claimed that "82 percent of the Latvian capital belongs to non-Latvians."[199]

According to our data, more than 40 percent of the ethnic Latvians believe that the *nouveaux riches* in Latvia are Russians, while only slightly more than 5 percent believe that Latvians predominate in this social segment. The corresponding figures for Russians are 12 percent and 6 percent (see Figure 4.17). One might say that, on the level of stereotypes, the Russians now occupy the position traditionally reserved for the Jews.

No objective data exist to either substantiate or disprove these opinions. Nonetheless, the leading Latvian political scientist Nils Muiznieks is of the opinion that the prevalent idea about the dominance of non-Latvians in Latvian business life has some element of truth: Non-Latvian managers in the industry and in the transport sectors have traditionally had good contacts in Russia and have been better placed for a launch into private business than Latvians who have been engaged in agriculture or in the cultural sphere.[200]

An important factor behind the emerging ethno-professional structure is also the exclusion of non-Latvians from public administration.

---

[197] Mezgailis and Katkovska 1992, 68.

[198] *Diena*, 4 February 1993.

[199] Quoted in *SM-segodnia*, 10 November 1992.

[200] Muiznieks 1994.

134

FIGURE 4.17 Whom Do You Consider to Belong to the New Rich in Latvia?

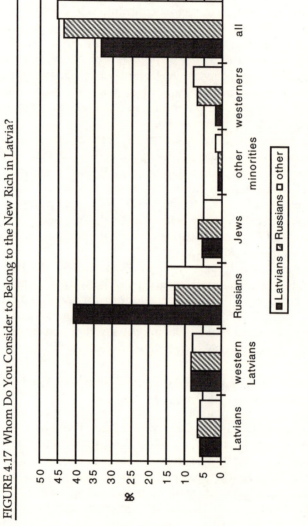

FIGURE 4.18 Ownership of Private Enterprises by Ethnicity (1993)

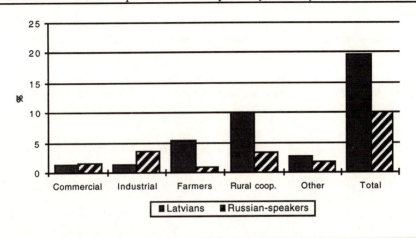

Source: Dreifelds 1996, 160–61.

FIGURE 4.19 Ethnic Structure of Employed and Unemployed Residents of Latvia (1996)

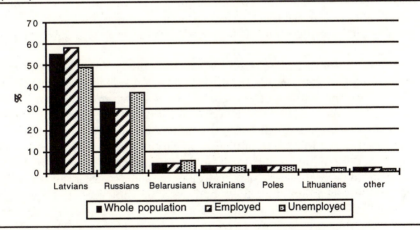

Source: Darbaspeks 1996, 29 and 64; *Par bezdarbu valtsti* 1996, 4.

The president of the major Latvian bank Pareks, Valerii Kargin, has opined that

> business in this country is controlled more by Jews and Russians than by Latvians. This fact makes the Latvians angry, although to some extent it is their own fault. Russians and Jews were squeezed out from positions in government institutions and to compensate they started their own business, just like kids who are learning to swim by being thrown into the water. Thus, the following situation has emerged: Latvians dominate in public administration and non-Latvians in the national economy.[201]

The data reproduced in Figure 4.18 give some idea about the relative shares of the various ethnic groups among Latvian property owners (although they tell us nothing about the distribution of capital among ethnic groups). The data were commissioned by the Canadian researcher Juris Dreifelds and collected by the Latvian Centre of Social Research in 1993. As one would expect, a significantly higher number of farms belong to ethnic Latvians. The same is true with regard to agricultural associations and cooperatives. Cross-tabulating with the ethnic composition of the population at large, Juris Dreifelds found that the Latvians' share of private capital in industry was 30 percent and 48 percent in private commerce.[202] However, it appears that Dreifelds did not take into account such factors as the turnover quantities of the various enterprises or the total volume of the capital they represent. Therefore, one would probably be ill-advised to make any definite conclusions about the ethnic distribution of private capital in Latvia on the basis of his figures.

An important indicator of ethnic stratification in the economy and social life in any country is the differences in the levels of unemployment among the various ethnic groups. As is shown in Figure 4.19, the share of Latvians in the employed segment of the population is somewhat greater than average while their share among the unemployed is somewhat lower than the population at large. The figures for Russians and most other ethnic groups point in the opposite direction. In November 1996, 26 percent of the Russians in Latvia and 14 percent of the ethnic Latvians claimed that they had been unemployed at some time during the last half year while 53 percent of the Latvians and 45 percent of the Russians had never experienced unemployment. (33 percent of the Latvians and 29 percent of the Russian respondents were not in the labor force.[203]) Another survey, conducted in 1994 by the NORBALT

---

[201] Lieven 1993, 365.

[202] Ibid.

[203] Rose 1997a.

living conditions project, showed that Russians have a considerably higher probability of being unemployed than ethnic Latvians, all other background characteristics being equal. Within the Russian group, persons holding Latvian citizenship are better protected against unemployment than are non-citizens and citizens of other states.[204]

However, also these data ought to be treated with caution. Official Latvian unemployment statistics disregard several important factors. First and foremost they do not take into account the hidden unemployment, that is, the high number of cases when workers are sent on unpaid leave for an indefinite period of time, rather than being fired. Such bogus arrangements make it possible for the enterprises to avoid paying gratuity of discharge to laid-off workers. The workers, on their side, know that if they quit their job voluntarily, they will forfeit their right to this gratuity in perpetuity. Thus neither party is interested in a formal dismissal. The workers stay on without a job or a salary but are at the same time not considered unemployed.

While inattention to these dynamics tends to produce unrealistically low unemployment figures, other omissions have the opposite effect. Official statistics, inevitably, do not include employment in the "grey sector" (petty street peddling, shuttle trade, small-scale smuggling, and work "for cash" without a formal work contract—an arrangement which allows the worker to evade taxes and the employer to evade social security payments). It is widely believed that non-Latvians are more active in this "grey economy" than are the Latvians. If this really is the case, the real unemployment rates among the various ethnic groups are somewhat closer to their shares of the population at large than the official statistics would indicate.

Table 4.8 gives the responses we received in our survey regarding attitudes toward preferential employment policies. It comes as no surprise that more Latvians than non-Latvians want to give ethnic Latvians and citizens of Latvia preferred treatment on the labor market.

TABLE 4.8 Who Should Have Employment Priority in a Situation of Few Jobs?

	Ethnic Latvians	*Latvian citizens*	*Specialists*
Answers from Latvians	18.1	33.3	45.0
Answers from Russians	3.7	10.5	81.5
Other	3.2	17.8	74.9

---

[204] Aasland 1997, 113 and 115.

Differences of Perceptions

In the Communist period the Soviet Union was a single political unit
with one official ideology. This created the illusion that the country
and its inhabitants formed a uniform mass, having the same viewpoints
and opinions on all important issues. In reality, however, the various
ethnic groups living in Latvia had very different attitudes toward and
perceptions about the history and the legal status of the Latvian
republic.

Thus, the majority of the Russophones who arrived in Latvia after
the Second World War did not question the official version of the history of the Baltic states. (According to this version, what took place in
1940 was a socialist revolution; the USSR and the Soviet people played
a decisive role in the economic and social achievements of the Baltic
countries, etc.) In the opinion of Rasma Karklins, such perceptions pre-
disposed a certain segment of the Russophone population toward condescending and patronizing attitudes toward the Latvians.[205]

Among ethnic Latvians, on the other hand, an unofficial, oral version of the history of the country circulated alongside the official version and was passed on from generation to generation.[206] This version
remained unknown to the majority of the Russians right up to the introduction of glasnost.

Another important difference in the perceptions that predominate
among the major ethnic groups is the understanding of the Soviet nationality policy. To most Latvians, the Soviet regime had an unmistakable ethnic color: "Soviet" was identified with "Russian." One of the
main reasons for this was the language factor: The instruments of power
almost without exception used the Russian language. In addition, the
establishment of Soviet power in Latvia was on the popular level associated with the appearance in the country of scores of soldiers who
spoke Russian. Up to the very present, Latvians from very different
walks of life refer to the Soviet period as "krievu laiki" ("Russian
times").

The Latvians' perception of the Soviet power as an ethnically alien
rule led directly to their political rejection of this regime. It was therefore quite natural that the idea of restored statehood would enjoy great
popularity among the Latvians while most Russians never gave a
thought to it. The data reproduced in figure 4.20 show the dynamics

---

[205] Karklins 1986/1989, 52–53.
[206] On the role of oral history in Latvia, see Savdona 1994, 25–30.

FIGURE 4.20 Support for Latvia's Independence

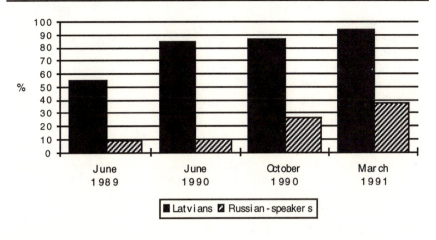

Source: Zepa 1992, 23.

FIGURE 4.21 Evaluation of the Threat of Extinction of the Latvian Nation

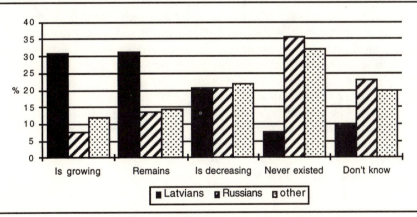

Source: Survey conducted by "Latvian Facts" in October 1995. See Chapter 6, appendix.

in the attitudes toward Latvian independence from the USSR, and the different trajectories of Russophone and Latvian opinions. Among the Russophones support for Latvian independence increased fourfold between 1989 and 1991, but still remained less than half of the Latvians' support.

Ethnic Latvians react very sensitively to any tendencies toward changes in the ethnodemographic situation in Latvia. They fear that if the Latvians should become a minority in the country, this would lead to radical changes in the ethnocultural environment, in the language situation, etc.[207] As late as 1996 more than 30 percent of the Latvians believed that the danger of the extinction of the Latvian ethnonation had still not passed away. Almost the same number of respondents believed that this danger in later years had become even more acute, while 35 percent of the non-Latvians at this time believed that no such danger existed (see Figure 4.21).

However, if in earlier years ethnicity seems to have been the most important factor determining people's attitudes toward basic values in Latvia, then in later years sociologists have detected ever more distinct differences of opinions along the age cohort divides which cut across ethnic divisions. The effect of this trend is most pronounced among the non-Latvian youth. As a result, the viewpoints of young Russophones and young Latvians are rapidly approaching each other.[208] In particular, the vast majority of the non-Latvian youth today regard Latvia as their motherland. Nevertheless, with regard to certain other issues such as citizenship, attitudes toward Russia, and the evaluation of some historical events, the viewpoints of Russians and Latvians are worlds apart. Thus, Russians and Latvians have basically the same perceptions about the general level of the threat against the security of the Latvian state, but disagree as to whence the threat is stemming. More than 40 percent of the citizens of Latvia believe that Russia is the greatest source of insecurity while only some 7 percent of the non-citizens believe so (Table 4.9).

---

[207] For an outline of these changes, see pp. 69–71 .

[208] In particular, this tendency has been registered by the leading Latvian sociologist Brigita Zepa, and discussed in the paper she presented at the conference "The process of the formation of political nations in the Baltic states," Riga, 17–18 October 1996. Comparative tendencies have been registered also in Estonian, cf. Axel Kirch's presentation at the same conference.

TABLE 4.9 Assessment of Main Threats to Peace and Security by Latvia's Residents

	Citizens	*Residents*
Neighboring countries (except Russia)	1.7	2.4
Russia	41.9	6.7
Ethnic minorities	5.4	1.4
Immigrants, refugees	14.0	5.3
Terrorism	54.4	47.5
Environmental pollution	57.5	55.2
Drugs, criminality	74.9	69.8
Losing national identity	26.1	15.8
Corruption	63.1	61.9

Source: Survey conducted by "Latvian Facts" in October 1995. See Chapter 6., appendix. The respondents were free to agree with more than one option on the list.

As the New Baltic Barometer III survey data reveals, Russians are much more pessimistic about the future prospect for Latvia's economy: only 33 percent believe that economic conditions will improve in five years, while 60 percent expect them to continue to be poor.[209] For ethnic Latvians, the corresponding figures are 43 percent on both counts. Also answers to the question "Are you the sort of person who works with others in the community to try to solve local problems" are revealing. Only 5 percent of Russians do this often, 22 percent sometimes, and 51 percent never. For ethnic Latvians, the figures were 8 percent, 31 percent, and 38 percent.[210]

Russophone Organizations

Traditionally, dominant tendencies within a group are analyzed through a description of the activities of political and social organizations created and run by the group members. For a number of reasons, however, this method may be applied to Latvia's Russian-speaking population only with some reservations. Most important is a very low level of social activity. According to the New Baltic Barometer III survey, only 2 percent of Russians claim to be members of any public or nonstate-sponsored organization[211] (for Latvians this figure is 9 percent[212]). Alienation from the state remains the dominant tendency

[209] Rose 1997a, 15.

[210] Ibid., 17.

[211] Ibid., 26.

[212] A prominent Latvian analyst Nils Muiznieks believes that to some extent this difference could be explained by the fact that the mass organizations with the largest member-

among the Russian-speaking population of Latvia. Passivity, insecurity, uncertainty about the future, lack of mobilization and fragmentation of the community are the most characteristic features.

There is no simple answer explaining why this is so. We will only
point to some possible causes: The Russophone community of Latvia
lacks strong social, political, and mental bonds which could have given
it a sense of common purpose and shared destiny. It has no authoritative, charismatic leaders. On the contrary, it is highly fragmented
and divided. The fast social changes going on around them, in which
the majority of the nontitulars have played a passive role only, have
left them bewildered and frustrated. Also, by the early 1990s the
"indigenization" of the Latvian political elite had already become an
accomplished fact and led to the marginalization of the Russians. Finally, one should not underestimate the strong desire of the vast majority of the non-Latvians to avoid open, interethnic confrontations. They
know only too well what kind of horrors violent ethnic conflicts have
led to in other parts of the former USSR. Generally, this trend has
much in common with the Soviet model of relations between an individual and a state: avoidance of any contact with the state whenever
possible.

During the perestroika period Russian intellectuals participated
actively in the new social and protopolitical movements. However,
while the social activity of Latvians was centered around the national
liberation movement, the activities of the Russians were more in line
with the mainstream democratization rallies in the rest of the then
Soviet Union.

In the late 1980s some ethnically based cultural organizations were
created within the Latvian Russophone community. The Baltic–Slavic
Society of Cultural Development and Cooperation (BSO), established
in July 1988, was the first association of its kind.[213] Initially, BSO included Russian, Ukrainian, and Belarusian sections, but at some point
the two latter sections were transformed into separate organizations.

The "International Front of Working People of the Latvian SSR," or
Interfront—established in late 1988, early 1989—was widely regarded
as "the Russian organization." Indeed, the overwhelming majority of
the Interfront supporters were Russian-speakers, and the organization

---

ships, the trade unions, comprise primarily teachers, doctors, and state servants, i.e. groups
in which ethnic Latvians prevail. Besides, a considerable part of Latvia's NGOs are 'restored organizations', that is, heirs to those that existed before 1940 (e.g. student corpora-
tions). Also these organizations are dominated by ethnic Latvians. Nevertheless, taking
even these factors into account, the differences in organizational activity among the various ethnic groups are striking.

[213] Chicherina 1989, 201; Kudriavtsev 1990, 9.

strongly opposed the drive toward independence and all attempts to strengthen the position of the Latvian language in society. At the same time, the Interfront leadership consistently avoided the use of "Russian" rhetorics, sticking instead to internationalist slogans in accordance with the general Communist program of the organization.[214]

In the early 1990s, a high level of politicization characterized all minority-run and particularly all Russian organizations in Latvia. Some of them overtly supported the Popular Front (e.g. LORK), while others leaned towards the Interfront. BSO officially kept neutral.

Restoration of Latvian independence and its official recognition by Russia and the international community significantly changed the situation for Russian organizations in Latvia. The Interfront was outlawed and ceased to exist. At the same time, the Resolution on citizenship adopted in October 1991, as well as some other steps of a nationalistic nature undertaken by Latvian authorities undermined the position of LORK and other Russophone organizations that had supported the Popular Front. Gradually, also LORK switched to a position of moderate opposition toward the government. In February 1996 several prominent LORK leaders, together with three Latvian writers, signed a letter to President Ulmanis strongly criticizing the Latvian minority policy.[215] However, LORK and its allies never moved close to Interfront positions, nor did they questioned the independence of Latvia.

The most ambitious attempt to create a broad Russian organization was undertaken in early 1991. A small group of activists designed an organization called The Russian Community of Latvia (ROL). The guiding principles of ROL were solidarity, justice, subsidiarity, and the need to help Russians adapt to conditions of market economy in a Latvian national state.[216] The initiators of ROL declared that they did not intend to challenge the political powers that be but rather wanted to cooperate with them.[217] They also stressed the necessity of creating a firm economic basis for the community. For a while, ROL indeed managed to bring together leaders from many other Russian organizations and to launch several enterprises under its auspices, even a Slavic Bank.

Before long, however, internal squabbles weakened the organization and eventually tore it apart. These conflicts lasted for several years.[218] ROL branches in some Latvian cities, *in casu* in Daugavpils, declared

---

[214] Kurakina and Tikhomirov 1991.

[215] *Diena,* 7 February 1996.

[216] Smekhov 1991, 8–9.

[217] *Baltiiskoe vremia,* 14 May 1991.

[218] *SM-segodnia,* 27 February 1996.

their independence from the Riga leadership.[219] The economic activities of ROL practically collapsed, and it gradually became only one among several competing Russian organizations emerging in 1991–1995.

Some new attempts to create unity among the Russian organizations continued to be made. In particular, in February 1995 the Latvian Association of Russian Societies was established,[220] somewhat later, the Center of Russian Culture in Latvia, and the Russian Cultural Autonomy Association. However, none of these organizations has ever acquired a real mass membership or can claim to represent the entire Russian population of Latvia.

In 1993 an attempt was made to create an Association of Russia's Citizens in Latvia. However, the Latvian Ministry of Justice refused official registration of this organization on the grounds that its activities were considered to be in breach of Latvian legislation.[221]

Several predominantly Russian organizations focus primarily on human rights issues. The Latvian Human Rights Committee, founded in 1990, is the leading NGO of this kind. The Committee deals with legal consultancy and litigation, prepares and disseminates declarations and appeals concerning human rights problems in Latvia (in particular, publishes monthly surveys of the human rights situation in Latvian Russian-language media), and organizing mass actions like pickets and meetings. In 1992–1994, the Committee concentrated on legal aid to persons who claimed that their rights had been violated in the process of registering the permanent residents of Latvia. With assistance from the Committee several thousand plaintiffs won law suits against the Department of Citizenship and Immigration. In January 1995, the Committee was admitted to The Federation Internationale des Ligues des Droits de l'Homme, F.I.D.H., and was later registered by the Latvian Ministry of Justice as a Latvian branch of this international organization.[222] Several leaders of the Committee are also active in the leftist Equal Rights movement, and the Committee is often blamed—not without reason—for mixing politics and human rights activities.

---

[219] *Dinaburg*, 6 October 1992.

[220] *Baltiiskaia gazeta*, 24 February 1995; *SM-segodnia*, 17 February 1995.

[221] *SM-segodnia*, 10 September 1993.

[222] *SM-segodnia*, 24 January 1995.

The Impact of the Russian Federation
on Latvian Nation-Building and Ethnic Integration

Russians in the Baltic states are often identified with Russia and even branded as "fifth columnists." Sociological surveys reveal that this point is ill-based. For most Russians Latvia and not Russia is their "home country." According to a British researcher there is not even a strong demand among them for closer ties with the Russian Federation.[223]

An important indicator of the feeling of belonging to Russia among Russophone communities in the Soviet successor states is the number of persons who have acquired Russian citizenship. Despite Russia's offer of citizenship to all citizens of the former USSR by registration, less than 9 percent of the Russian-speaking noncitizen population in Latvia have taken it, and many of those who have, did so on the eve of leaving for Russia. As pointed out on page 98, there is a striking difference in this respect between Latvia and Estonia. Apparently, the higher number of Russian citizens among the nontitular population in Estonia is connected with the compactness of the Russian communities in that country and their greater geographic separation from the Estonian communities. Most Russians in Estonia live in the capital and in the biggest cities of the Northeast. By contrast, the Russian population in Latvia is more evenly distributed throughout the urban areas (and, to a lesser extent, even in the countryside). Also, Russians with ancestral roots in the interwar state are much more numerous in Latvia than in Estonia. Thus, generally speaking, the Russian-speaking residents in Latvia are less Russia-oriented that are the Russophones in Estonia. Strong attachment to Russian language and culture does not necessarily imply a strong feeling of belonging to Russia as a state. Russia is definitely an important actor also in Latvian ethnopolitics, but an external one.

Relations between the nascent democratic state of Russia and the equally nascent independent states in the Baltics initially developed under the popular slogan of "For your freedom and ours." Boris Yeltsin's demonstrative visit to the Supreme Council of Latvia in August 1990[224] was a clear sign of support, and stood in sharp contrast to the negative attitude of the Gorbachev regime in Moscow. During this visit, Yeltsin spent many hours with the leaders of the Latvian Popular Front faction

---

[223] Rose 1997b, 42.

[224] *Baltiiskoe vremia*, 7 August 1990.

in the Latvian Supreme Council, and agreed to only one very brief meeting with representatives of the pro-Communist Equal Rights faction.[225]

In January 1991, Yeltsin came to Tallinn to sign treaties with Estonia and Latvia on mutual recognition of sovereignty. These treaties were immediately ratified by the Latvian and Estonian parliaments.[226] Many people in the Baltics believe that this move was crucial to stop the anticipated military invasion which had been prepared by the activities of Soviet OMON forces (special militia units) in Vilnius and Riga a couple of days earlier. Yeltsin also published an open letter to "The Peoples of the Baltics" expressing strong support for their independence struggle and also urging them to avoid interethnic confrontation.[227]

Russia was one of the very first states to recognize the independence of the Baltic countries after the abortive coup in August 1991,[228] thus leaving no choice for Gorbachev but to do the same, greatly alleviating the task of the Western democracies. The alliance between Russia and the Baltic states, however, was based on a temporary convergence of political goals rather than on a common ideology. In 1989–1991, the basic political conflict in the USSR ran between the regional elites (including the ethnic elites of the Soviet national republics) on the one hand, and the Soviet central authorities on the other. When the Soviet center collapsed, other interests and political alignments came to the fore.

After the 1993 parliamentary elections in Russia the two main opposition forces—the revived Communist Party and the various nationalist, "statist" alliances—became firmly established in the corridors of power. They actively used the topic of "the betrayal of compatriots abroad" as an effective political trump card against the Russian democratic leadership. Strict measures taken by Latvian authorities against the Russian-speakers in the field of citizenship and language policies, as well as persistent Latvian demands for the immediate withdrawal of former Soviet, now Russian, troops, also contributed much to the deterioration of Russian–Latvian relations. The main cause, however, was a crucial change in the strategic position of the Russian political elite: no longer in opposition to the Soviet Communist regime, it had become responsible for the development and the interests of the Russian state.

---

[225] *Edinstvo*, 20–26 August 1990.

[226] *LR AP Lemums* 1991. The text of the Latvian–Russian treaty was published in Russian in *Baltiiskoe vremia*, 17 January 1991.

[227] *Baltiiskoe vremia*, 21 January 1991.

[228] *Ukaz Prezidenta Rossiiskoi* 1991.

In the long run, the Moscow democrats could not afford to leave the subject of "Russia's interests" to the opposition alone. Official Russian rhetorics on Baltic issues became increasingly aggressive. In the fall of 1992 Russia prodded the UN into sending a fact-finding mission to Latvia and Estonia to investigate alleged large-scale violations of the human rights of the Russian-speakers. The mission made some critical remarks, but on the whole did not confirm Russia's allegations.[229] Russian authorities also began to link the problem of the status and rights of the local Russians to the issue of troops withdrawal. Foreign Minister Andrei Kozyrev accused Western states of ignoring serious human rights problems faced by Russian-speakers in Estonia and Latvia. Threats to the Russians, Kozyrev said, justified the continued presence of Russian troops. Kozyrev also maintained that the attitude of the West greatly helped Russian ultranationalists like Zhirinovskii to strengthen their positions.[230] In the upshot, an active intervention from the side of Western governments and intergovernmental organizations facilitated the signing of a treaty on troops withdrawal in April 1994.

The most characteristic feature of Russia's policies toward Latvia at this stage was a virtual consensus across the entire political spectrum on the necessity of strong-arm policies aimed at the protection of the compatriots in the Baltics.[231] However, the implementation of these policies remained rather weak and inconsistent.

President Yeltsin adopted several decrees related to the protection of Russians outside Russia.[232] The Russian Parliament also discussed several declarations and law projects on the Support of Compatriots, but did not adopt any of them.[233] Several organizations and institutions affiliated with the State Duma, the Russian Government, or the President's Administration were established to deal with the problem of the compatriots. However, the authority and financial resources of these institutions, as well as the degree of coordination between them, were insufficient for the task they were assigned.

More than once the possibility of economic sanctions against Latvia and Estonia was put on the Russian political agenda, but no such sanctions were ever implemented. Already in 1994 the Russian MFA had pointed out that sanctions would punish also those whom Russia

---

[229] Fall 1993.

[230] Quoted in *SM-segodnia*, 8 February 1994.

[231] See e.g. interview with one of the leaders of the Iabloko party, Viacheslav Igrunov, in *SM-segodnia*, 24 February 1995.

[232] In particular, *Ukaz Prezidenta Rossiiskoi* 1994.

[233] *Proekt Deklaratsii o podderzhke* 1994; *Proekt Zakona Rossiiskoi Federatsii* 1994. A new draft law was discussed by the State Duma in late 1997. *Proekt Federal'nogo Zakona* 1997.

wanted to defend.[234] In early 1997 the press service of President Yeltsin announced the adoption of a new concept of long-term policies toward the Baltic countries.[235] The main strategic goal of this concept was the elaboration of a constructive model for Baltic–Russian relations based on the promotion of regional economic integration and bilateral economic cooperation; the indivisibility of security; and respect for human rights and minority rights. For the first time since 1991, protection of the rights of compatriots in the Baltic states was officially mentioned only as a second priority goal, while the conclusion of "regional security guarantees" (to prevent the entry of the Baltic states into NATO) was singled out as the most urgent one.

Commentators in the liberal Russian press saw the adoption of this concept as a sign that "Russian-Baltic relations are no longer under the sway of political radicals." They also pointed to the clear commitment in the document not to use force or pressure in Russia's dealings with the Baltic states. At the same time, the commentators questioned the judiciousness of turning the problem of NATO expansion into the centerpiece of Russian–Baltic relations, and criticized the methods chosen for the protection of Russians in the Baltics as "hardly efficient."[236]

In any case, in 1996–1997 a new emphasis on business relations and attempts to exploit politically the neighboring states' strong economic dependence on Russia emerged as a clear trend in Russian policy toward the Baltics. Igor Iurgen, a member of the Russian governmental Council on Foreign and Defence Policies, maintained that Russian business must penetrate the Baltic markets as much as possible and create networks of joint ventures which may later provide an access to the markets of the European Union.[237] However, it is not clear to what extent the Russian political leadership may influence the investment strategies of Russian private business. The ongoing privatization in Russia will make its leverage in this respect ever-weaker. Russian businessmen who care about their profits will have dealings with Latvia in such areas as transit and banking regardless of what the Russian government thinks about Latvian policies toward local Russians. This point is often made semi-officially by Latvian politicians.

How have Russian policies toward the Baltics influenced Latvian nation-building? Three main aspects may be pointed out. First, Russia's actual policies, despite some noisy rhetorics to the contrary, have for the most part discouraged Baltic Russians from developing a

---

[234] *Izvestiia*, 10 March 1994.

[235] *Soobshchenie press-sluzhby* 1997.

[236] *Segodnia*, 14 February 1997; *Nezavisimaia gazeta*, 11 March 1997.

[237] *Biznes un Baltija*, 21 November 1997.

"pro-Russian" orientation. Few Russian organizations—be they cultural, political, or human-rights oriented—have ever received much practical assistance from Russia. Revealing is the fact that in the summer of 1997 the Russian ambassador to Latvia signed a letter appealing for donations for making the Palace of Peter the Great in Riga a Russian cultural center, rather than pledging Russian authorities to support this project financially, as had been hoped would be his course of action.[238]

Second, frequent (and often clumsy) official Russian statements lashing out against the policies of the Baltic states have intensified lingering fears among the Balts that Russia harbors everlasting imperial designs on their region. Such statements confirm their fears that Russia is a major and permanent threat to their independence. In this sense, Russia's policies have been a serious impediment in the development of an intercommunity dialogue in the Baltics, convincing Baltic leaders that the local Russophones are an inalienable part of the Russian nation and not a community worth discussing with separately. These perceptions have been actively exploited by Baltic radical–nationalist forces. In other words, Russian statements often give Baltic nationalists a good pretext for ignoring the demands of the local Russians.

Finally, while the active position of Russia at the international arena on the issue of minority rights in the Baltic states has rarely been endorsed by Western countries, it has nevertheless drawn their attention to the problems of Russians in the Baltics and induced them to urge the Baltic governments to soften their policies toward their Russian-speaking population. The role of Russia in this process, therefore, must be regarded as ambiguous.

Conclusions

The specific qualities of the ethnopolitical situation in Latvia since independence have been determined by a number of objective and subjective factors. In Latvia, the nationalist feelings which were widespread in practically all post-communist countries in Eastern Europe and the former Soviet Union were stimulated by the country's peculiar demographic make-up. Many Latvians feared that if the prevailing demographic trends continued the Latvian nation might arrive at a point where it would cease to exist. Therefore, the new legal structures were first and foremost geared toward a strengthening of the dominant positions of the ethnic Latvians in society.

---

[238] *SM-segodnia*, 30 June 1997.

At the same time, a constant pressure from European non- and inter-governmental organizations, combined with an almost total absence of Russophone political resistance, induced the Latvian leadership to adopt a somewhat more liberal attitude toward the nontitular groups than what they might otherwise have done.

In contrast to many other post-Soviet states, the politization of ethnicity in Latvia was largely channeled into the adoption of legal acts, not into pogroms or other kinds of violence. Formally, these acts were unrelated to the ethnic factor. Even so, the ethnic domination of the Latvians was secured through a consistent process of "state restoration." This approach gained legal and political support from the international community. A crucial point was the restrictive solution to the citizenship problem which secured the titular nation a firm control over the political institutions. This control, in turn, made it easy to put into effect the desired solutions also in other areas, such as language policy and educational policy.

By leading the nationalist sentiments into legal, and legalistic, channels, Latvia managed to avoid violent ethnic conflicts. In fact, hardly any serious deterioration of ethnic relations at the street level could be registered at all. A survey which was conducted by the Danish newspaper *Weekendavisen* in 1991–92 analyzed how the public hostility of the ethnic Latvians toward the Russophones was related to their personal lives and preferences. It turned out that the number of Latvians who would accept the Russians "as neighbors, but not as co-citizens" was three times as high as the number of those who reversed these preferences, that is, those who supported equal rights for all permanent residents but who on the personal level would prefer to have contact with members of the their ethnic group only.[239] In other words, the average Latvian would be three times as ethnocentric in the election booth as in his daily life. Interestingly, in the Lithuanian part of the same survey these correlations were reversed.

At the same time, the covert legitimation of ethnic dominance in Latvia—through citizenship, linguistic legislation, cadre policy, etc.—created long-term problems for the development of the political system into a universal, inclusive democracy. There were few incentives in this system to search for effective interethnic dialogue.

Among the Russian-speaking population of Latvia centrifugal tendencies—in Schermerhorn's typology—are not strong. Of the various options open to the Russian-speakers in Latvia emigration and return to Russia are among the least popular.[240] Several surveys indicate that

---

[239] Poulsen 1994, 25.
[240] See pp. 73-74.

large-scale emigration of Russian-speakers should not be expected. All in all, up to 10 percent of the non-citizens have chosen or will choose this option. The low number of persons who have acquired Russian citizenship, and the lack of consolidation around any "Russian party," also show the low popularity of this trend.

Instead, integration and accommodation are the most frequent choices of Latvia's Russian-speakers. Their centripetal tendencies do not, however, include a strong desire for full assimilation into an ethnocultural Latvian environment. Many Russophones choose what can be called " a Jewish model" of behavior: The current situation of Russians in Latvia has much in common with the traditional conditions under which Jews have been living in Europe (lack of political rights and land ownership rights, exclusion from state service, etc). The traditional "Jewish" response of industrious Russophone non-citizens is to engage in commerce, trade, and financial activities. The problems which they encounter they try to solve not by establishing effective social mechanisms but "by opening the purse." For example, rather than struggling for state-funded Russian-language education, children attend private schools or study abroad.

Another characteristic trend is the "European" orientation of a substantial part of the Russians in Latvia. In fact, Russian-speakers in both Latvia and Estonia are generally more in favor of joining the European Union than are ethnic Latvians and Estonians (66 percent vs. 52 percent in Latvia, and 78 percent vs. 59 percent in Estonia, in late 1996).[241] Many Russians seem to be more inclined toward an acceptance of liberal European values than are ethnic Latvians who are preoccupied with the problems of preserving their ethnic identity and are fearful of European "cultural intrusion." In pragmatic terms, also, a closer integration into Europe may increase the Russians' chances of competing with ethnic Latvians in Latvian society on an equal and equitable footing. Russian-speakers in Latvia who are oriented toward Europe may thus become a kind of social *avant garde* and play an important role in the process of integrating Latvia into Europe.

The "Jewish model" is compatible with the Latvian concept of nation-building as it implies that non-Latvians will not intervene into politics which basically will remain an arena for ethnic Latvians. Russophone businessmen will be concerned about political affairs only to the extent that politics affect their business. The "European model" runs contrary to "official" Latvian assumptions about Russian social behavior. This may perhaps explain why the European-oriented part of the Latvian political elite so far has failed to make use of this trend.

---

[241] Rose 1997a.

An external factor—the governmental relationship between Latvia and Russia—has to a significant degree influenced the ethnopolitical situation in Latvia. True, only a small part of the Russians in Latvia have taken Russian citizenship and the majority of them regard Latvia, not Russia as their fatherland. Still, the vicissitudes of Russian–Latvian relations, as well as the frequent changes in the political climate of Russia, have sharply influenced interethnic relations and political decisions in Latvia.

Under these conditions it comes as no great surprise that the political regime in Latvia has evolved in the direction of what an increasing number of researchers are calling "ethnic democracy," that is, a combination of certain general democratic principles with elements of ethnic favoritism. Graham Smith defines ethnic democracy as a combination of three elements: the core nation is institutionally pivotal beyond its numerical proportion within the national territory; individual civil rights are enjoyed universally; and certain collective rights are extended to ethnic minorities.[242]

A political regime based on the mechanisms of ethnic democracy may evolve further, into either "traditional," nonethnic democracy, or into ethnocratic structures and ever deeper ethnic segregation. Only time will show if any of these varieties will be realized in Latvia.

---

[242] Smith 1996, 200.

5

Political Integration in Kazakstan

Jørn Holm-Hansen

Civic vs. Ethnic Models of Integration

The successful integration of the citizens by means of political institutions is of primary importance for the legitimation of *civic* power in
newly established states. The civic model is based on active participation through political institutions. The *ethnic* model, on the other
hand, is based on the mere fact of belonging to some designated ethnic
group. Hence, in these models two very different modes of perceiving
man and his surroundings confront each other face on. Is a person's roots
an inseparable aspect of his political being, or can he liberate himself
sufficiently to operate in a public sphere in which ethnocultural
"neutrality" is an explicit objective?

States which base their legitimacy on ethnic ties are far less dependent upon political institutions for survival than states where civic
principles constitute the baseline. Titular citizens of ethnic states "hold
membership" automatically through their ethnic affiliation, whereas
citizens from nontitular groups more or less explicitly are "members" of
a second order. In some countries they are not even granted formal citizenship. Membership in ethnic states is accorded, or not accorded, by
birth. Through roots and heritage a person can belong passively and
collectively.

In contrast to this, the civic model presupposes active participation
by *individual people*. Inhabitants become members by virtue of their
participation. This model defines political institutions as important

FIGURE 5.1 Map of Ethnic Kazaks in Kazakstan

Map of ethnic Kazakhs in Kazakhstan

% = percentage of ethnic Kazakhs in the region (oblast')

(Based on figures from the Results of the all-Union census 1989 - *Itogi vsesoyuznoy perepisi naseleniya 1989 goda* - as presented in Gawecki, 1994)

□ Ust'-Kamenogorsk

□ East Kazakhstan 28,3 %

□ Taldy-Kurgan/Taldykorgan

□ City of Almaty 24,3 %
Almaty oblast' 45,5 %

□ Semipalatinsk /Semey 54,1 %

52,8 %

□ Petropavlovsk 19,1 %

□ North Kazakhstan

□ Kokchetav/Kokshetau 39,5 %

□ Pavlodar 29,9 %

□ Akmola 22,8 %

□ Arkalyk

□ Karaganda 19,2 %

□ Dzhezkazgan/Zhezkazgan 48,8 %

□ Dzhambul/Zhambyl 53,7 %

□ Shymkent 58,3 %

□ South Kazakhstan

□ Kostanay /Kustanay 17,9 %

□ Torgay 43,8 %

□ Kzyl-Orda 81,9 %

□ Aktiubinsk 58,3 %

□ Ural'sk

□ West Kazakhstan 57,4 %

□ Atyrau 81,3 %

□ Aktau

□ Mangyshlak/Mangystau 54,6 %

FIGURE 5.2 Administrative Map of Kazakstan

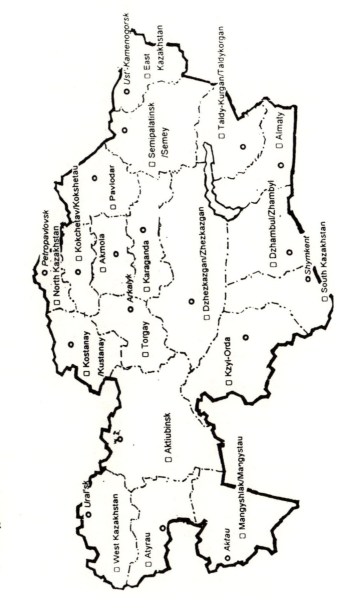

Administrative map of Kazakhstan

o = administrative centre of oblast'
☐ = oblast' (province)

instruments of integration. People participate through institutions. In order to attract people, political institutions have to be more than mere semblances. In other words, in the initial phase of a new state's history, as the basic elements of legitimization are being spelled out, the civic model is likely to require more in terms of democratic content than would the ethnic model.

This is an important reason why the civic model is weakly represented among the nation-building states of the former Soviet Union. Even in countries where there is a genuine will among power-holders to introduce democracy, the immediate applicability of the civic model is not evident. This is so because the civic model is based not only on the existence of democratic institutions, but first of all on long-term democratic *practices* and *habits*. The history of the twentieth century demonstrates that democracy can be turned off relatively easily, but it is much more difficult to turn it on. Making democracy work takes time.

By appealing to ethnicity, power-holders in new states have a ready-made and easy-to-understand framework on which to base legitimization. In Kazakstan, the only post-Soviet republic where no ethnic group had a majority at the outset of independence, it would be natural to have expected the nation-builders to emphasize civic aspects rather than focusing on ethnicity. Moreover, ethnicities are in flux in Kazakstan, not only among the multiethnic Russian-speaking population, but also among the titular Kazaks. The appropriation of "civic patriotism" rather than "ethnic nationalism" has not materialized in Kazakstan, however. As will be argued below, the situation is more one of *combining* and *balancing* these two models.

In this chapter I will start out by taking a close look at the doctrines and rhetorical maneuverings employed by the present Kazakstani authorities in an attempt to divine the most likely outcome, the political integration of all residents, or, alternatively, the political exclusion of segments of the population. Following this I will review the institutional reforms that have been implemented in Kazakstan. What happened during the process of creating new institutions and redefining the functions of the old ones? Did this result in a greater degree of social cohesion? Here both institutions and issues will be examined. The political institutions are classified into four groups, namely state institutions; advisory bodies; self-governmental and representative institutions; and nonstate organizations. I will further analyze the controversial issues of citizenship, language, and passport legislation.

Nation-building implies both the establishment of political institutions, which function adequately over the entire state territory, *and* the cultivation of a sense of community among the residents. In the present historic and demographic situation, the existence of a Kazakstani state is not self-evident. Kazakstani statehood is fragile; its borders are unfixed and the various segments of the population lack a common denominator that could set them off from the citizenries of other post-Soviet states. The common cultural denominator in Kazakstan, as elsewhere in the former Soviet Union, consists in a shared, post-Soviet, modern culture. There is, in addition, a common cross-ethnic frame of reference related to the fact that Kazakstanians live in the contemporary state of Kazakstan.[1]

Attempts at disrupting the common supraethnic, intra-CIS, everyday "street" culture, which is so strong in Kazakstan, would probably result in heated controversies. The attempts to "Kazakify" the image of Kazakstani state culture has already aroused protests not only from non-Kazaks, but from Kazaks as well. Ethnic nation-building is bound to be controversial in Kazakstan, whereas civic nation-building, on the other hand, is a very demanding task, as it is in all former Soviet republics, due to the systemic underdevelopment of everything civic under state socialism.

The Demographic Controversy

Throughout the twentieth century Kazakstan has been in a state of dramatic demographic flux. Agricultural reforms, Stalinism, war, work migration and post-Soviet nation-building are all factors that have had a deeper demographic impact on Kazakstan than on most other areas of the former Soviet Union. Therefore, and because the titular nation did not constitute a majority when Kazakstan was established as a state, demography forms an important part of the political consciousness both of leading nation-builders and their opponents. The Kazakstani debate on de-Sovietization and nation-building is to a large extent a debate over demographic issues.

The ongoing exodus of non-Kazaks—primarily Russians and ethnic Germans—combined with a higher birth-rate among Kazaks and an influx of "diaspora Kazaks"—has led to an increase in the Kazak proportion of the total population. Official sources, like the President's homepage on the Internet (1998), claim that the proportion of Kazaks already has increased to 50.6 percent.[2]

Passing the fifty-percent threshold is seen as an important psychological breakthrough by the supporters of Kazakstan as a nation-state

---

[1] 97 percent of the population of Kazakstan has lived in the republic for more than ten years, according to a survey carried out as part of this project.

[2] The website address is www.president.kz

for Kazaks (see below). This "magic" limit is treated as being analogous to the fifty-percent threshold in a plebiscite, where gaining a majority gives special rights. According to this way of thinking, 50.6 percent means that Kazakstan is not only quantitatively but also qualitatively more of a "Homeland of the Kazaks" than if a mere 49.9 percent of its population had been Kazaks.

Kazaks were among the ethnic groups that suffered most in demographic terms during the Soviet period. This holds true both regarding their relative proportion of the total population and in absolute figures. The first census to be carried out in the Russian Empire (1897) shows that in the territories now constituting Kazakstan, 82 percent of the population were Kazaks, or Kirgiz, as they were classified at the time. But as a result of labor surplus in the Russian countryside and the pre-Revolutionary Stolypin agricultural reforms, Russian settlers moved into the Steppes. In the years between 1896 and 1914, the Russian population increased by 214 percent resulting in a decrease in the Kazak proportion of the population to 70–75 percent. In the 1920s, 65 percent were Kazaks.

Collectivization policies affected the ethnic Kazak population severely, and the combined effects of persecution, famine, and emigration have been likened to genocide. Collectivization destroyed their traditional nomadic life based on livestock breeding. The cattle population was decimated by about 80 percent and 1.5 million Kazaks died from starvation and disease, or fled. Kazak households declined from 1,223,000 in 1929 to 565,000 in 1936.[3] At the same time Northern and Eastern Kazakstan were industrialized, almost exclusively by Russians. Figures presented by authors writing within the framework of ethnic nation-building, such as Makash Tatimov, claim that the total number of Kazaks decreased from 5.2 million in 1916 to 1.9 million in 1945.[4]

In the second half of the twentieth century, however, the Kazak share began to rise again despite waves of immigrating Russians. What was called The Virgin Lands Campaign started in 1954. Forty-one million ha traditional Kazak grazing land in Northern Kazakstan was converted into land for cereal crop cultivation. In addition, industrial enterprises were established in Kazakstan, most of them directly under the central government in Moscow. The military-industrial complex became a significant part of Kazakstani economic life. All this implied Russians moving in. However, the positive Russian immigration balance ended already in the 1960s.

---

[3] Olcott 1995, 184–5.
[4] Tatimov 1995.

In 1959 the Kazak percentage stood at 30, increasing slowly to 32.6 percent by 1970 and 36 percent by 1979. In 1989 it stood at 40 percent, 44.3 percent in 1994, and 46 percent in 1995.[5] The latter figures must be seen against a background of massive migratory movements. Since Kazakstan gained independence there has been a large net outflow of non-Kazak inhabitants. Emigration reached a peak in 1994 with a negative balance of 411,000. In 1996 this figure was reduced to 175,000. Altogether, in the period 1991–1996, net emigration reached 1.3 million.[6] Apart from the Kazaks all ethnic groups were reduced numerically.

For supporters of an ethnically based state the simple enumeration of Kazaks in Kazakhstan is not sufficient; ethnic brethren abroad also form an intrinsic part of the nation. This point of view is supported both by the Law on Independence and the Law on Citizenship which state that all Kazaks, wherever they happen to be, are automatically eligible to Kazakstani citizenship. A special program to boost Kazak immigration to the Motherland has been in operation since 1992.

According to official figures, in 1995 there was a total of 12 million Kazaks both in Kazakstan and throughout the world. Of these, 64.8 percent lived in Kazakstan, 20.6 percent in other countries of the Commonwealth of Independent States, and 14.6 percent elsewhere, i.e. China, Mongolia, Afghanistan, Iran and Turkey.[7] Diaspora Kazaks play a symbolic role in the official designation of Kazakstan as the "only Kazak state in the world." The first World Kurultay (World Assembly) of Kazaks from all over the globe was held in 1992. 154,941 ethnic Kazaks (35,300 families) immigrated to Kazakstan from abroad during the years 1991–1996. 85,000 came from CIS countries and the Baltic states; 62,000 from Mongolia; 4,600 came from Iran; 640 from China; and 418 from Afghanistan.[8]

Ethnic Kazak immigrants have come up against problems in adapting to the relatively modern life in their historical Motherland. Their poor knowledge of Russian makes it impossible for them to communicate properly in daily life at work, in shops and in the neighborhood.[9] This is particularly true of the Kazaks from Mongolia, who mostly come

---

[5] Smagulova 1996; *O demograficeskoi*1996, 42–45; Olcott 1995, 259.

[6] *CIS Migration Report* 1997, 56

[7] *Respublika Kazakhstan* 1996, 5.

[8] *CIS Migration Report* 1997, 61

[9] Mentioned by a spokesman of Kazak immigrants in the Kazak-language newspaper *Turkistan*, and quoted in *Kazakhstanskaia Pravda* 17 April 1996.

TABLE 5.1 Migration of Russians and Kazaks 1991–1996

		1991	*1992*	*1993*	*1994*	*1995*	*1996*
Emigrants	Total	255,000	369,000	333,000	480,639	309,632	229,412
	Russians		175,000	170,000	283,154	160,883	120,427
	Kazaks		13,400	12,400	14,491	10,883	9,543
Immigrants	Total	206,000	190,000	111,000	70,452	71,137	53,874
	Russians		69,300	46,600	31,220	34,415	24,043
	Kazaks		72,000	36,400	19,975	18,662	16,446

Source: Eschment 1998, 82.

from rural areas. A local official in charge of "internal policies," who held "Kazakification" to be a paramount goal, said that the influx of ethnic Kazaks from Mongolia to her municipality was of little help in this respect. The resettled diaspora Kazaks were "a relief only in quantitative, not in qualitative terms."[10] Quantitatively the resettled Kazaks contribute to the legitimization of an ethnically based nation-state. As a group, however, these newly arrived Kazaks have had to put up with aligning themselves with the rural poor Kazaks, socioeconomically the most marginalized stratum in the country, merely playing a symbolic role as carriers of pure national virtues. In this capacity they are useful for the rural newcomers to the cities in their intra-Kazak rivalry with the urban Kazaks.[11]

The dramatic demographic shift, however, has not been caused by diaspora Kazaks moving in, but by non-Kazaks moving out. Those leaving the country are mostly Russians and Germans. Since 1990 almost 65 percent of the ethnic Germans in Kazakstan have left, which means that only 370,000 Germans remain in the country.

Russians constituted the largest group of emigrants (58 percent); Germans 19 percent; and Kazaks only three percent in 1995. In 1996 the corresponding figures were 52.4, 25.7, and 4.1 percent.

In contrast, immigration figures show that (in 1994) 44.5 percent of immigrants to Kazakstan were Russian, 28.4 percent Kazak, and four percent German. (Table 5.1 shows the migratory flows over the last years.) Two years later the corresponding figures were 44.6, 30.5, and

---

[10] Holm-Hansen 1997, 81.

[11] Nurbulat Masanov claims that the intra-Kazak urban–rural cleavage is dominant in Kazakstani politics (Amrekulov and Masanov 1994; Masanov 1995 and 1996).

3.7. Immigration in most cases is *re*-immigration.[12] Some Russians come from other Central Asian republics.

In Kazakstan's inventory of ethnic groups one finds Chechens, Ingush, Germans, Meskhetian Turks, Koreans, and Poles. These are groups that were deported from their towns and villages in other parts of the Soviet Union during the Second World War because they were considered untrustworthy. Inspired by the German and Israeli examples of welcoming ethnic "conationals" back home, minority ethnopolitical leaders seek to obtain advantages from their historical homelands (see below). Among such favors is the opportunity to immigrate to the homeland. This is not feasible in most cases, but it helps to popularize the idea that everybody belongs to a historical homeland, thus weakening the foundation of an integrating, civic model of the state–nation relationship.

Why do people leave Kazakstan? The table above tells us that there is significant net emigration from Kazakstan, but we do not know whether this is due to post-Soviet Kazakstani strategies of nation-building that have been pursued. In fact, "Kazakification" of leading positions in the state administration started prior to Kazakstani statehood, already in the late 1970s under the rule of Dinmukhamed Kunaev. The proportion of Kazaks in leading positions under Kunaev superseded the proportion of Kazaks in the population as a whole. Kazaks also occupied leading positions in heavy industry, agriculture, and construction at that time. The Kazakstani division of the KGB was twice headed by a Kazak. "Kazakification," therefore, is more a continuous development than a sudden change following the collapse of the Soviet Union.

Net emigration from Kazakstan started in the sixties. The emigrants were primarily specialists, fleeing partly as a result of the relative economic backwardness in Kazakstan, partly because they were outcompeted by ethnic Kazaks who benefited from the combined effects of the educational boom and the "Kazakifaction" of higher cadres.[13] The dramatic *increase* in emigration came, however, with Kazakstani statehood.

Russian ethnopolitical leaders among the Cossacks and in Lad (see below) claim that Russians move out of Kazakstan because they face discrimination. Spokesmen of the present Kazakstani regime tend to maintain that people emigrate because of economic hardships that are part and parcel of a transition to a market economy.

---

[12] O *demograficheskoi* 1996, 57–59; CIS Migration Report 1997, 61; OMRI Daily Digest, 19 August 1996.

[13] Eschment 1998, 81.

A survey carried out in 1994 among people who had decided to emigrate from Kazakstan sought to determine the factors that would make the respondents change their mind and return. 48.6 percent said that they would stay if the economic situation improved; 44.8 percent would do the same if "convincing guarantees for the future of the children were given." 27.1 percent said that a halt to all ethnic discrimination would made them stay. 22.7 percent mentioned "double citizenship" and 17.7 percent "Russian as state language" on an equal footing as Kazak. Only 3.2 percent said they would emigrate anyway.[14]

This, and similar polls, suggest that reasons of economy rather than ethnicity lie behind people's decision to move. There is, however, good reason to see the two elements together. There is a widespread and overtly expressed feeling among nontitulars in Kazakstan that they are discriminated against. But it cannot be denied that, at the same time, people are experiencing an economy in crisis. When asked to pinpoint the main cause for leaving, economic insecurity dominates the responses, but if economy alone is the problem, it is difficult to explain why Russians incur the cost of moving just to migrate to another country in deep transitional crisis.

Returning to the question of whether present policies aim at the inclusion of inhabitants as citizens, or, alternatively, treat inhabitants according to ethnicity, it seems clear that the way in which demographic figures are presented in public reveals an underlying pattern of exclusion. High-ranking policy-makers, like senior expert of the Information and Analytical Center of the presidential apparatus, Makash Tatimov, call for measures which secure ethnic Kazak interests. Among such measures would be the development of a policy on migration that secures "the strategic goals and tasks to strengthen Kazakstan as a young and unitary state with a large territory." For Russians and other Europeans living in Northern and Eastern Kazakstan it is not difficult to interpret this statement as an invitation to leave. Tatimov even suggests that scientific prognoses, new legislation, and administrative decisions undergo a "demographic impact assessment."[15] Professor A.K. Kotov of the Institute of Law and State under the Academy of Science writes: "In order to protect the genetic fund of the Kazak nation processes of migration and re-emigration are regulated according to legal provisions by establishing quotas on entry to the country."[16] Professor Kotov maintains that such measures are taken in "all developed countries."

---

[14] Figures from *Karavan*, 21 January 1995, quoted in Eschment 1998, 88.
[15] Tatimov 1995.
[16] Baikhmanov et al. 1994, 73.

The whole debate on ethnicity and demography is based on figures which presuppose fixed ethnic identities. An analysis of the ethnic make-up of Kazakstan should not, however, be based exclusively on figures relating to official ethnic tags. Ethnicities indicated in official documents merely tell ethnic *origins* of an individual. In Kazakstan most non-Russian, non-Kazaks belong to the community of Russian speakers, and only on special occasions do they bring their original ethnicity to play.

Likewise, being a Kazak is not incompatible with belonging to the wide community of Russian-speakers. Most Kazaks move freely in and out of the various Kazak and Russian settings in daily life. A central unifying factor in Kazakstan is the Russian language. Almost everybody (86 percent of the total population, 75 percent of the Kazaks[17]), speaks, reads and writes Russian fluently, and inhabitants of the country's 83 cities and towns (56 percent of the total population are urban in this sense[18]) have also been sufficiently influenced by Soviet and post-Soviet experiences to find common cultural ground across original ethnic backgrounds.

Nation-Building: Political Rhetoric and Doctrines

All nation-builders have to answer two crucial questions: "Why are we a nation?" and "Why should there exist a state within these borders?"

In order to answer these two questions convincingly nation-builders in Kazakstan have a need for more elaborate explanations than nation-builders in, say, Latvia. Kazakstan gained its independence without much mental preparation among its inhabitants. Unlike Latvia, where the interwar experience of statehood played a significant role in boosting the drive for independence, perestroika activists in the Soviet Republic of Kazakstan never emphasized statehood. The power-holders in the new state—to a large extent the same people as those who governed in the Soviet Republic—therefore have had to compose an ex post facto justification for independence. This endeavor has proved a delicate task, and the doctrinal texts have been written in a conciliatory tone. This has been done partly in order not to undermine the authority of the political leaders, who have retained their positions from the

---

[17] See Arenov and Kalmykov 1995c.
[18] *O demograficheskoi* 1996, 47.

Soviet times, partly not to alienate the Slavic population, which would easily construe anti-Soviet propaganda as anti-Russian.[19]

In Kazakstan, nation-building doctrines are explicit. They are presented as authoritative documents written by the President after having been subject to some public debate and consultation in advance. President Nazarbaev has made several important speeches since 1991 in which he has outlined the fundamentals of the official version of Kazak national identity as well as of Kazakstani state identity. These speeches have been disseminated on a wide front by TV, radio, and most newspapers (usually in extenso).

President Nursultan Abishevich Nazarbaev is concerned about the lack of "societal consciousness" (*obshchestvennoe soznanie*). According to the President, the ideological debate "should create a basis for the formation of a societal consciousness, to replace the communist ideology that has broken down."[20]

Nation-builders have to explain a new political situation and structure by reference to concepts that can be understood and accepted by the population. However, official ideology is still established from the top down. It partakes therefore more of the nature of a prescriptive instruction on how to think about certain issues, than a crystallization of widespread beliefs or of an established consensus in the country. Statements from the political authorities may be divided into three groups: First, the rhetorical statements, which aim at the creation of a cultural community through emotional appeal. Second, doctrines which point out the limits of acceptable activities (e.g. nonseparatism, nonfederalism). Third, the officially acknowledged need of standardizing the historical past after the Soviet period, a Kazakstani "Vergangenheitsbewältigung" (coming to terms with the past).

The Main Documents. Five documents are of particular importance:
1. "Societal consolidation through ideas as a precondition for the progress of Kazakstan" (presidential speech in 1993);
2. "For peace and harmony in our common home" (presidential speech at the founding session of the Assembly of the peoples of Kazakstan, March 1995);
3. "Concept for the formation of a state identity in the Republic of Kazakstan";
4. "Concept for ethnocultural education in the republic of Kazakstan";

---

[19] Among Kazakstani Russians and Ukrainians 36 and 46 percent respectively consider the Soviet Union to be their Motherland. Thirteen percent of the Russians felt that Russia was their Motherland, according to the survey we carried out as part of this study.

[20] See *Sovety Kazakhstana*, 13 May 1993: "Nursultan Nazarbaev: "Nashi orientiry – konsolidatsiia, obshchestvennyi progress i sotsial'noe partnerstvo.' "

5. "Concept for the establishment of a historical consciousness in Kazakstan."[21]

The Main Models. Apparently, the official doctrines on state–ethnicity relationship are at cross-purposes. Officially Kazakstan is both a *multiethnic* state and a *nation-state* for the Kazaks. The ways in which these two main models are elaborated in official texts create openings for various interpretations. As for the multiethnic model, its architects have apparently had in mind two quite disparate models. First, multiethnicity is taken as supraethnicity. The inhabitants bound together in a republican spirit as "Kazakstanians," as citizens. Secondly, and somewhat out of alignment with the first model, multiethnicity portrays the inhabitants as "representatives of nationalities."

The authorities emphasize the various doctrines in different settings, seemingly in order to appease their listeners. This leads to a situation where no doctrines guide policy-making and implementation. Instead an official balancing act goes on between incompatible principles.

As for the institutional set-up of Kazakstan the doctrine-makers are less ambiguous. Kazakstan is a centralized (presidential) and unitary state (nonfederalism).

Model: Kazakstan as a Multiethnic State

Multiethnic (Civic) State. The "Concept for the creation of a state identity" recounts why all ethnic groups in Kazakstan are welcome to live there:

> Historically the state defended only the interests of the Kazaks as no other ethnic groups lived in the territory at that time. However, as time passed the Great Steppes began to receive representatives of other nations. In correspondence with this the functions and substance of the state changed. Remaining a national state the Republic of Kazakstan now expresses the interests of the whole population, irrespective of ethnic adherence. This new substance of the state is secured in our Constitution.[22]

It is possible to discern two different ways of defining "the people" within the official texts presenting the multiethnic model (the "Kazak Homeland" model will be treated separately). The one model of

---

[21] 1: Nazarbaev 1993; 2: Nazarbaev 1995; 3: *Kontseptsiia formirovaniia* 1996; 4: "Kontseptsiia etnokul'turnogo obrazovaniia" 1996; 5: "Kontseptsiia stanovleniia istoricheskogo soznaniia" 1995. [22] *Kontseptsia formirovaniia*, ibid., 26.

multiethnicity could be termed "integration," the other "multiple re-ethnification."

Integration. The integration model emphasizes the supraethnic *Kazakstani* character of the new state. This in contrast to the ethnona-tionalizing model, in which the state first of all is conceived of as *Kazak.* Kazakstan was noted for its integrating, supraethnic approach to nation-building during the first years of the new state. State symbols, like flags and the national anthem, were to form rallying points more than folklore and other potentially divisive phenomena.

A supraethnic—Kazakstani—loyalty to the state is one of the goals emphasized in the "Societal consolidation through ideas as a precondi-tion for the progress of Kazakstan" According to the President a Kazak-stani patriotism has to be encouraged: "Unfortunately the understanding that we are citizens of an independent, sovereign state of Kazakstan—and not the former USSR or CIS—is quite superficial."[23]

Attempts to balance the different principles of nation-building are evident in the "Concept for the creation of a state identity." After hav-ing explained why a nation-state for the Kazaks is necessary, the Con-cept presents a purely civic notion of the Kazakstani nation. The development of a state identity is described as the "establishment of a nation in the perspective of the state." The citizens in this state form one state irrespective of their ethnic background, and "belonging to it appears to them as the main identity marker."[24] If this is to be taken literally, it is a clear expression of an integrating approach that muf-fles the ethnic focus to the advantage of a civic approach.

In an article in the Almaty journal *Mysl'* the Kazakstani political scientist B. Abdygaliev presents a critique of this approach, which he calls the model of a "Kazakstani nation" (*natsiia*). The author claims that this model implicitly aims at making the inhabitants forget their ethnic origins, that ethnicity cease to be the platform from which group demands are made, in short, that ethnicity no longer form the basis of political mobilization.[25]

This, according to Abdygaliev, is a model of a "Kazakstani nation" that is technocratic and drawing too much on Western experiences. In his view the "polyethnic society" of Kazakstan consists of various eth-nicities with their own interests that should not be merged. The very concept of *natsiia* (as opposed to *narod* "the people/nation") is not only based on the anthropological (in the old meaning of the word) or ethnic origin of an individual, but also on sociocultural, historical and state

---

[23] Nazarbaev 1993, 25.
[24] Ibid., 26.
[25] Abdygaliev 1996b.

adherence—and is primarily a Western phenomenon. Kazakstan is not ready for this at the present stage, says Abdygaliev. Today, Kazakstan lives both in the modern world and in a world of preindustrial mentalities. To force the Western concept of "nation" onto the Kazakstani context would provoke nationalist reactions, he warns, preferring the model of a "nation (*narod*) of Kazakstan," a model that implies a re-ethnification of the population.

Re-Ethnification. Whereas in the integrative model unity and state identity are sought *above and beyond* ethnicities, the re-ethnification model seeks unity *through ethnicities* (in the plural). In this perspective individual people are "representatives of an ethnic group." This "collectivist" formulation is an inheritance from Soviet times, still frequently used.[26] In the Kazakstani context, "re-ethnification" takes place at the expense of the Russophone community.

At the founding congress of the Assembly of the Nationalities of Kazakstan in March 1995, Nazarbaev said that "we, in a way, more often talk about the relationship between the two nationalities, Russians and Kazaks. Why do we forget the interests of the other twenty percent of the Kazakstanians who have good reason to feel offended by this?"[27] The vast majority of this "twenty percent," however, are thoroughly Russified Poles, Germans, Ukrainians, and Koreans. They speak Russian, and Russian only.

Re-ethnification is also the objective stated in the "Conception for ethnocultural education in the republic of Kazakstan." The main aim of this conception is to strengthen "ethnic identification and state integration" at one and the same time. The school curricula will include courses in the history, culture, and beliefs of the ethnic groups of Kazakstan. Their heroes will be honored. The "Conception for ethnocultural education" states that the development of state identity takes longer time than the process of forming an ethnic identity. The successful rise of a state identity demands efforts from all ethnic groups in the state."

B. Abdygaliev[28] the political scientist who criticized the integrative model, provides a justification for re-ethnification, which he terms the model of "the people (*narod*) of Kazakstan." This model allows people both to be a "representative" of a defined ethnic group and an equal citizen of Kazakstan.

---

[26] The post-Soviet habit of defining individuals as "representatives" (*predstaviteli*) of their ethnic group may be interpreted as a manifestation of national romanticist ideas living on, treating nationality not as an "association of individuals, but rather as a collective appearance of an supra-individual substance" (Glotz 1990, 78).

[27] Nazarbaev 1995, 46.

[28] Abdygaliev 1996.

Model: Homeland of the Kazaks

In addition to defining Kazakstan as multiethnic, the doctrines state that the country is the homeland of the Kazaks. This latter model refers to the need to protect Kazak culture from the danger of extinction. The doctrinal "Concept for the formation of a state identity for the Republic of Kazakstan" states that

> Kazakstan is the ethnic center of the Kazaks. Nowhere else in the world do they possess a statehood that is concerned about the protection and development of the Kazaks as an ethnos of their culture, way of life, language, or traditions. It is first of all with regard to these qualities that Kazakstan should be defined as a nation-state.[29]

The document further states that

> the very logic of the development of the ethnos necessitates the rise of a state as the instrument for securing the material and spiritual conditions for the existence and development of a nation.[30]

The fact that the population of the state is multiethnic does not prevent the authors of the semiofficial booklet *The Establishment of the Sovereignty of Kazakstan* from referring to "the national nature of the state." This is even more significant since this "national nature" is not readily given as long as most ethnic Kazaks are thoroughly Russified, and this ethnic group still constitutes less than a majority. The authors, however, explicitly dispute the prediction of other scholars who foresee the development of "Kazakstanianness" (*kazakhstanskost'*) as a territorial principle.[31]

The question posed in *The Establishment of the Sovereignty of Kazakstan* is: Why is it that it is the Republic of Kazakstan, and not any other state, that has been established on this very territory? The short answer given is that it is the manifold historical factors that have led to the "ethnopolitogenesis" of the Kazak nation.[32] The very existence of the multiethnic state of Kazakstan relies on the existence of a Kazak nation:

> In legal terms, the territorial independence of present-day Kazakstan flows naturally from the ethnopolitical genesis of the Kazaks. This very nation,

---

[29] *Kontseptsiia formirovaniia* 1996, 26.

[30] Ibid.

[31] Baikhmanov, Vaisberg and Kotov 1994, 43–44.

[32] Ibid., 67.

which is legitimized by its historical destiny, constitutes, and will always constitute, the ethnopolitical basis for state independence of the republic of Kazakstan, and for this reason should be recognized as such by all Kazakstanians and by the world community without being suspected of nationalism. After all, what is a tree without roots, and what is the present without the past?[33]

Similar beliefs in the inevitability of ethnic nation-states lie behind the less doctrinal statements in the State Report on Demography, where the emigration of Russians and Germans from Kazakstan is presented as "a historically natural (*zakonomernyi*) process and normal reaction:" the emigrants choose a more prosperous Fatherland for themselves and their children to which they feel attached "ethnically and by tradition."[34]

Despite references to the natural character of an ethnic nation-state, Kazak nation-builders rarely claim that ethnic Kazaks have expressed a strong will to build "their own" state. However, on occasion they refer to the December events of 1986 as expressions of a popular longing for independence. In December 1986 there were riots in Almaty following the replacement of Communist Party first secretary Dinmukhamed Kunaev with an ethnic Russian from Russia, Gennadii Kolbin. The tenth anniversary of the events was soundly celebrated in 1996.

An official account of these riots was made by State Secretary (coordinator directly under the President) Abish Kekilbaev in an extensive article in *Kazakhstanskaia Pravda*.[35] Kekilbaev saw the December events as one of numerous acts of courage in the five thousand (!) years' longing for "the independent road to development upon which we have entered only now." In accordance with the official nation-building doctrine, Kekilbaev viewed the December events both as an expression of general, supraethnic wishes for a less authoritarian society, and also as an outburst of ethnic yearning for a nation-state. The state secretary emphasized the universal, cross-ethnic aspects of the protests (for more self-government at the republican level, less *diktat* from Moscow, "local cadres know better"). At the same time he also emphasized the boost in ethnic Kazak self-esteem, which followed the riots. The Kazaks found people to be proud of, namely the "heroes who, without weapons, stood up against the punitive machinery." At this moment, according to Kekilbaev, the Kazak nation collectively braved the propaganda apparatus and "conceived itself as a nation."

---

[33] Ibid., 72.

[34] *O demograficheskoi* 1996, 58.

[35] See *Kazakhstanskaia Pravda*, 12 November 1996, "Surovoe ispytanie nakanune peremen."

Land seems to be an important rhetorical marker, frequently mentioned by senator Zhabaikhan Mubarakovich Abdil'din, who led the preparatory work on the document "Formation of a state identity."[36]

First, Kazakstani statehood is justified as being the "native Kazak land" (*iskonnaia kazakhskaia zemlia*), as is stated in the 1995 Constitution. Kazakstan is the land where the forebears of the contemporary Kazaks lived: "From the fifteenth century this land served as the territory of an independent state, the Kazak khanate, the first state of Kazaks in history."[37]

Although Nazarbaev is usually reputed to adhere to civic principles in the construction of state institutions, some of his utterances belie this. In his keynote address to the first World Kurultay (Congress) of Kazaks he advocated a certain nationalization of state structures:

> first of all we aim at forming a strong presidential power in the republic. In this connection we emphasize the defense of national structures in the state construction in order to save them from being washed away (*razmyvanie*). Therefore, the interests of the titular population (*korennoe naselenie*) in certain cases have to be defined and considered separately.[38]

These views are repeated by Kazakstani specialists on constitutional law, who claim that Kazakstani state leaders and top-level officials must "know the needs of the population, and, above all, those of the titular nationality."[39]

State Borders

An important question for all nation-builders is why borders are where they are. The official Kazakstani nation-building doctrine accepts the borders drawn up by the Soviet authorities as inviolable. According to official parlance the national-state demarcation of 1924 resulted in "the unification of Kazak lands."[40] The following year, in 1925, the capital of the Kazak SSR was moved from Orenburg (now in Russia) to the deeply Central Asian town of Ak-Mechet (later renamed Kzyl-Orda). In 1929, the capital was moved once more, this time to Alma-Ata (now Almaty). Today, it is about to be moved to the predominantly Russian-European city of Astana (Akmola) in Northern

---

[36] Author's interview in Almaty, 25 September 1996.

[37] *Kontseptsiia formirovaniia*, 1996, 25—26.

[38] See *Kazakhstanskaia Pravda*, 2 October 1992, "Rech' Prezidenta N.A. Nazarbaeva na torzhestvennom zasedanii Vsemirnogo Kurultaia kazakhov."

[39] Baikhmanov, Vaisberg and Kotov 1994, 49.

[40] *Istoriia Kazakhstana* 1993, 300.

Kazakstan. These frequent transfers of the capital in and out of different "cultural zones" bear witness to the unsettled character of Kazakstan as an ethnopolitical unit.

The present borders of Kazakstan, which were established while Kazakstan was part of the Soviet Union, "corresponded fully with the historically formed settlement of the Kazak people. No changes of the borders are acceptable," according to the Concept.[41] This was also a theme in Soviet-style Kazak nation-building prior to independence. In a 1958 monograph the geographer S.Z. Zimanov claimed that the territorial extension of the Soviet Kazak Union Republic was coterminous with that of the Kazak population of the early 1800s.[42]

Continuity is an old theme in the doctrines of Nazarbaev. He has pointed out that contradictory opinions exist as to what the twentieth century has given the Kazak nation. Having ridiculed the Soviet propaganda of the seventies, he nevertheless goes on to say, "however, we cannot negate the history of the Kazaks from 1917 on." Rhetorically he asks whether one can deny

> the obvious fact that it was precisely in the first years of Soviet power that we got the chance to form a republic on our native territory, which during the preceding century was under threat of being divided up and parceled out among three regions? We were able to restore the integrity of the country, to officially define and consolidate its borders, and, in this way, to institute the legal basis for the establishment of our independent republic of today.[43]

The Kazakstani Nation-Building Model: Multiple Re-Ethnification

Nation-builders usually endeavor to establish national *unity*. In order to do so, they try to minimize the dividing factors in the population. In Ernest Renan's formulation

> The essence of a nation is that all the individuals have something in common and also that they have forgotten quite a lot of things.[44]

As we have seen from the above presentation of the various possible models for Kazakstani nation-building, its executors first of all *remind* the population of their original ethnic differences, and urge the citizens

---

[41] *Kontseptsiia formirovaniia* 1996, 25.

[42] As referred in Baikhmanov, Vaisberg and Kotov 1994, 68.

[43] See *Kazakhstanskaia Pravda*, 2 October 1992.

[44] Renan, 1882/1992, 42.

not to forget that they actually belong to several distinct ethnic groups. Without such reminders they might well have forgotten, since in their everyday life many non-Russian Kazakstani inhabitants—Kazaks and non-Kazaks alike—actually have forgotten their historical languages and are no longer familiar with ethno-folkloristic codes of conduct.

This policy of *multiple re-ethnification* does not seek to cleanse people of solely Kazak ethnicity. Rather, all ethnic groups, Poles, Koreans, and Germans, etc., are expected to find their "roots" irrespective of the time which has passed since their forefathers ceased to speak anything but Russian. In the rivalry between Kazak and Russophone cultures in Kazakstan universal re-ethnification must be regarded as an attack on the cross-ethnic Russophone identity.

In other words, the actually existing, cross-ethnic "everyday community" of Kazakstani inhabitants (who are Russian-speaking and have a post-Soviet frame of reference) is not allowed to develop as a basis for state loyalty. Instead, the state is defined and justified *through* the Kazaks. Kazakstan is the homeland of the Kazaks, and—according to the doctrine-makers—would not have been a state at all were it not for the existence of a Kazak nation. Individuals from a non-Kazak background are welcome to live in this state, the state demands loyalty from them and in return allows them to cultivate their "own" ethnic identities.

Seemingly, this is a liberal and inclusive model of nation-building since no one is forced to forsake his ethnicity. At the same time, the model can be perceived in an opposite manner, as an encouragement or prescription for *re-ethnification* of a population which is otherwise on the verge of being integrated by language, education, and common frames of references.

In official Kazakstani parlance, then, multiethnicity should not be understood as a model for ethnocultural integration. Multiethnicity should not be confused with "supraethnicity." A supraethnic model would have to be based on the premise that people are able and willing to downplay the significance of their original ethnicity and to develop a sense of common nationhood focused on the state as such. This would create a Kazakstani identity open to all citizens.

In Kazakstan, however, multiethnicity is officially understood as the ideal situation in which all Kazakstani citizens live by their original ethnicity. When this concept of multiethnicity is combined with the model of a Kazak homeland, ethnicity becomes highlighted in a way that may seem surprising for a country that often is portrayed as one in which state symbols form the main identity markers. In fact, it may seem that the leaders point to the "original" ethnicity of each individual in an endeavor to gain legitimacy. The Kazakstani power-holders deliberately miss the opportunity to create a common Kazakstani identity beyond configurations of ethnicities. The nation-building doctrines of Kazakstan envisage ethnic nation-building by a revival of not only one, but all the officially codified ethnic groups in Kazakstan.

Russophone Reactions
to the Nation-Building Models

Indifference or *resistance* to the new state is common among ethnic Russians, as well as among Russophones of other ethnic backgrounds. The Slavic Union Lad is the best organized of the Russian nationalist groups in Kazakstan, although it has difficulties in getting officially registered in some areas of the country. Lad is constantly under attack by the authorities for being disloyal. Lad defines itself as oppositional, and does not confine its activities to culture alone. Its leader Viktor P. Mikhailov does not believe in the Assembly of Kazakstan's Nationalities, which he finds "too close to the executive power."[45] Nonetheless the national administration of Lad has its headquarters in a government building together with the other national-cultural centers.

The main aim, according to the chairman of Lad, is that Russians in Kazakstan feel as in their Motherland (*Rodina*), the land where they were born. At the same time, Lad helps Russians wanting to emigrate to Russia, or to acquire Russian citizenship, with the practicalities involved. In this way Lad may be accused of making Kazakstan less Russian. On the other hand, if Russians in Kazakstan actually become citizens of the Russian Federation, it would strengthen the claim put forward by Lad that Kazakstan introduce the possibility of holding dual citizenship.

In interviews and conversations with people of North and East Kazakstan, it turned out that the words "us" and "our President" could just as easily mean the Russian Federation and Boris Yeltsin. This applied even to very young inhabitants of cities like Akmola and Ust-Kamenogorsk. A retired pilot and first secretary of the Communist Party in Semipalatinsk for thirteen years said, "Yes, I talk about Russia. I don't know anything about Kazakstan. There is no information about it."[46] This man, Nikolai Ulianov, was nonetheless still a "political person," one of the organizers of the "riot of the retired" in May 1996. The pensioners blocked the bridge over the river Irtysh

---

[45] Interview in Akmola 17 May 1996 with Viktor Petrovich Mikhailov.
[46] Interview in Semipalatinsk 22 September 1996 with Nikolai Matveevich Ulianov.

protesting pension arrears and lack of compensation for having lived next to the nuclear test site. The Slavic Union Lad was among ⸜the organizers.

Cossacks have featured in the forefront of anti-nation-building protests in Kazakstan. Originally Cossacks were soldiers of fortune and settlers who were assigned the task of defending the borderlands of the Russian Empire. Their descendants have organized all over the former Soviet Union, causing problems in places where they now find themselves *outside* Russia. The most famous of the Cossacks in Kazakstan is the former ataman (chieftain) of the Semirech'e Cossacks, Nikolai Gunkin. Gunkin does not accept that the Soviet Union has been dissolved, and portrays himself as a defender of the rights of ethnic Russians. In Kazakstan Cossack groups are allowed to register as "nonstate organizations" provided they do not suggest a split-up of Kazakstan.

In one of the most politically heated cities of Kazakstan, Ust-Kamenogorsk, various attitudes exist among Russian leaders who compete in trying to represent the non-Kazak majority population. Some of them sound extremist in their criticism, not shunning words like "apartheid," "genocide," and "traitors," but nevertheless take part in the official political institutions like, for instance, the regional *maslikhat* (council). This is the case for the rhetorically relatively extremist Nikolai Borisovich Ivanov, vice-chairman of the province council of Lad. Ivanov presents himself as a "gosudarstvennik" and "derzhavnik," meaning that he would like to see a strong, conservative Russian state as a superpower in the CIS territories. According to Ivanov the Kazakstani authorities aim at making non-Kazaks a "stateless, hired workforce as in Kuwait." The Russians working in the province administration "do not care about the Russians in the population. They take part in the ethnocratic game," according to Ivanov, who nonetheless represents Lad in the 39 member *maslikhat* of East Kazakstan.[47]

East Kazakstan province is represented in the lower chamber of Parliament—*Mazhilis*—by another member of Lad, Mikhail Nikolaevich Golovkov. He considers himself the "standard-bearer" of Russian-speakers in Kazakstan. He compares himself to the experimental Taganka Theater in Moscow during Soviet times, something the authorities put on show for the world to prove their tolerance.[48]

Interestingly, and seemingly paradoxically, Russian nationalist groups like Lad combine an implicit rejection of the new Kazakstani

---

[47] Interview 23 and 24 September 1996 in Ust-Kamenogorsk with N.B.Ivanov, one of eight representatives of the Slavic Bloc, which consists of Lad and two cultural-social organizations.

[48] Interview with Mikhail Nikolaevich Golovkov 25 September 1996 in Almaty.

statehood with active rallying against its policies. The more Lad contributes to mobilization against the regime, the more they redirect their co-Russians' attention from Moscow to Almaty. Over some years this may further the integration of Russians into Kazakstani statehood. They may remain oppositional, but they grow into aware citizens. The effect of this is to strengthen the civic model, which otherwise seems to have lost its explicit spokespersons in the Russophone community over the last few years.

Ethnicity and Legislation

The current Kazakstani Constitution (of 1995) is the second since independence. The first was adopted in 1993. The preamble of the 1995 Constitution treads a balance between the two models described above by defining the nation as "We, the people of Kazakstan, united by a common historical destiny, constituting statehood on the native Kazak land." This formulation is more inclusive than was the case in the 1993 Constitution, which additionally referred to Kazakstan as "the form of statehood of the Kazak nation."

The draft text for the first constitution was presented to the citizenry for consultation (*vsenarodnoe obsuzhdenie*) in the half-year from June to December 1992. Most controversial was the question of the official state language, even if questions pertaining to ownership rights, the role of the locally elected councils, and the Constitutional Court also constituted objects of debate. Concerned citizens pointed out that civil rights and human rights were not mentioned in the draft law.

Citizenship

Kazakstan applied the so-called "zero option" in awarding citizenship. All permanent residents at the time of Kazakstan's succession to independence became eligible for citizenship. In consistency with the unitary character of the Kazakstani state, which shall be achieved through nonfederalist means and through the rejection of all kinds of ethnoterritorial self-government, Kazakstani citizenship cannot be combined with citizenship of any other state. This was a provision in the 1993 Constitution which was retained in the present Constitution of 1995. Paragraph 10 states that citizenship of Kazakstan "is exclusive (*edinyi*)."

Diasporas and Dual Citizenship. Despite the "exclusive citizenship" laid down by the Constitution, the Law on Citizenship of 1991 allows ethnic Kazaks living abroad to gain Kazakstani citizenship without giving up their current citizenship.[49] Double citizenship is available to ethnic Kazaks only, not to other ethnic groups in Kazakstan. The official justification for this arrangement is that the Kazak nation deserves compensation for the tragedies inflicted upon it under Stalinism and World War II, which hit the Kazaks more severely than most other ethnic groups in the Soviet Union. However, also other ethnic groups— among them Germans, Chechens, Poles, and Koreans—were repressed, and moreover, unlike the Kazaks, they were repressed collectively on ethnic grounds. Today, these groups cannot hold dual citizenship in Kazakstan.

This issue of dual citizenship has aroused much debate and interlocks with the ethnicity complex. Predominantly Russian national organizations, like the Slavic Movement Lad demand that the right to dual citizenship must extend to all citizens. Such an arrangement would make daily life easier for local Russians who would like to operate as unconstrained as possible along the Russo–Kazakstani state border. Kazakstani nation-builders, for their part, fear the potentially separative effects of having large numbers of citizens with dual citizenship. The practical inconveniences resulting from the establishment of state borders crisscrossing the former Soviet Union, they insist, could be eased though increased integration of the CIS states.

To many Russians in Kazakstan dual citizenship would afford a sense of security: should the ethnopolitical situation in Kazakstan deteriorate they could move northwards into Russia. Dual citizenship would also formalize the bewilderment of many Russians: they live in a Russian "diaspora," but at the same time are full-fledged citizens of Kazakstan (see also Chapter 6 on Attitudinal and Linguistic Integration in Kazakstan). Russophone nationalist movements in Kazakstan such as the Slavic Movement Lad, have made dual citizenship one of their top priorities, and helping people acquire Russian citizenship one of their main social tasks.[50]

The official Kazakstani point of view is represented by the lawyer A.K. Kotov.[51] Kotov served as a member of the advisory commission to the President during the period of preparation of the draft

---

[49] Kolstoe 1995, 249–50.

[50] During a visit to the national headquarters of Lad in Akmola 17 May 1996, the author was told that Kazakstani authorities hindered the establishment of Russian consulates in several cities of the republic, among them, Ural'sk and Akmola. The scarcity of consulates raises the cost of acquiring a Russian citizenship in parts of the country. In Akmola the price would at that time have been 12–15 000 tengé (160–180 USD), but thanks to Lad, which collects and passes on applications to the embassy in Almaty, the price was limited upwards to only 2 000 tengé.

[51] Kotov 1995.

Constitution. Kotov presents a host of arguments against dual citizenship one of which is consideration of ethnic Russians in Kazakstan who chose Kazakstani citizenship from the beginning. Is it fair that they enjoy less access to Russia than fellow Russians with dual citizenship? Kotov also worries about hypothetical situations of dual citizens having to choose sides. What if a person is a citizen of two states, and these states become engaged in a conflict? Beneath this statement lies the fear that Russian irredentism may gain ground on both sides of the Russo-Kazakstani state border.

The conflict over dual citizenship brings the two main models of ethnicity–state relations to the fore. The provision that only diaspora Kazaks may obtain dual citizenship is a clear expression of the "Kazak Homeland" model. It presumes that ethnicity and territory go together in the case of Kazaks. In fact, most diaspora Kazaks may be said to be in a situation similar to the Germans, Poles, Turks, and others who were deported by Stalin: When they try to return "home" today, most of them move not to the area they actually came from, in Russia or another of the post-Soviet states, but to their ethnic homelands— Bundesrepublik Deutschland, Rzeczpospolita Polska, or Türkiye Cumhuryieti.

At the same time, the refusal to accede to the demands for dual citizenship from the ethnopolitical leaders of non-Kazaks may also be interpreted as an expression of the multiethnic, integrative state model. If the legitimacy of the new Kazakstani state is to be built on civic concepts, the citizens should be compelled to "stand with both legs planted" in the same state. Particularly in the Kazakstani situation, where a large number of the inhabitants perceive state borders as indistinct, permitting the holding of more than one citizenship might well be disintegrative. However, a strategy of legitimation based on citizenship instead of ethnicity would put the newly established semi-democracy of Kazakstan under strain since it would probably be successful only if the inhabitants feel that it is meaningful and important to be a citizen. Being a citizen becomes increasingly relevant the more democratic and depersonalized the state apparatus and the administrative procedures become. Therefore, in order to make Kazakstani *citizenship* the focal point of the citizens, rather than their *ethnicity* (which may induce a majority of them to look for their "original" citizenship abroad), the official policies of Kazakstan have to concentrate on giving citizenship a meaningful content.

State Language

As early as 22 October 1989 the Supreme Soviet of Kazakstan passed a Law on the Languages of the Kazak SSR. This was followed up by a governmental order of 1 July 1991 which declared that, as of 1995, the Kazak language should be considered and employed as the *formal language of the state*. From mid-1991, the number of schools at all levels providing education in Kazak grew sharply, and the use of Kazak in the administration accelerated. At the local and regional levels plans were made on how to carry through the transition to Kazak.

The policies of "Kazakifying" public life by means of a formal state language has been criticized from different perspectives. Proponents of "Kazakification" complain that Kazak is still a minority language, even among Kazaks in their daily life. Proponents of an ethnically neutral state protest that language policies are being used tacitly to oust non-Kazaks from their posts.

A survey of a representative group of Kazakstani citizens indicated that the Kazak language is more widespread now than previously.[52] However, the spread of Kazak has not been equal in all sectors of public life. Well over 50 percent of the respondents in 1996 were of the opinion that Kazak was proliferating in state bodies, education, and the mass media. Moreover, respondents indicated that the proliferation of Kazak in these sectors was greater in 1996 than in 1994. As reagrds the sectors of trade, service, public transport, science, and health care between 24 and 28 percent of the respondents had registered an increase in 1996, a lower proportion than in 1994. In other words, state administration and culture has witnessed a greater strengthening of the position of Kazak than has the manufacturing sector, where quotas and other forms of state regulation are more difficult to realize. These trends reveal a pattern of continuity between the present and the preindependence situation, when Kazakification was more successful in public administration and culture by a long chalk than in other sectors. Furthermore they highlight features of a kind similar to those in Latvia, where non-Latvians resort to commerce where they, "act like Jews" (see Chapter 4).

Language legislation has become one of the main arenas for ethnic policies and politics in Kazakstan. Both Constitutions (1993 and 1995) were passed only after long-drawn-out debates on the status of Russian and Kazak. Language has become a touchstone of the official willingness to integrate individuals from the nontitular population into the

---

[52] Arenov and Kalmykov 1997.

political and administrative structures of the country. In addition, the language question clearly also divides ethnic Kazaks along the urban/newly urbanized line (see below).

If the citizens are to be integrated through allegiance to state institutions, these institutions must have a high degree of ethnocultural "neutrality." It could be argued that the insistence on Kazak as *the* state language in central and local government institutions is incompatible with this kind of ethnocultural integration. Since Kazak is not the natural language of communication chosen by Kazakstani citizens (which will be shown later in this chapter) pushing Kazak through will have a disintegrating effect. In practical policy, however, the Kazakstani authorities have followed a middle course, assigning to Russian a status that formally is secondary, but nevertheless is an everyday language for "interethnic communication" to be "used on a par with Kazak in state and local bodies of self-government."[53]

The ambiguity of the official position, however, has provided for unclear practices, and grievances are frequent. People who are not sufficiently proficient in Kazak for professional purposes, complain that they are being marginalized; on occasion they are even being fired. Conversely, Kazak speakers lament that not enough is being done to implement the state policy of making Kazak the real state language, for instance by compiling an index of positions to be filled exclusively by individuals who master Kazak.

In official documents dealing with the language question, references are rarely made to "the Kazak language."[54] Instead, references are usually to "the state language" which, of course, is the same thing. This purely rhetorical move makes the requirement that civil servants master Kazak seem more reasonable. Who could object to state officials speaking the "state language"?

Official statements, furthermore, maintain that not only Kazak and Russian, but also the "original" languages of the smaller ethnic groups in the country must be cultivated and popularized. Creating multilingual individuals is one of the objectives listed in the "Conception of ethnocultural education in the republic of Kazakstan."[55]

The language debate must be understood in terms of the actual linguistic situation. Only a small part of the citizenry is able to use Kazak as a working language. Even among ethnic Kazaks operational knowledge of Kazak is far from universal. In a survey made in 1994 only 13 percent of the respondents said that they were able to "speak, read, and

---

[53] *Konstitutsiia* 1995, Article 7, 2.

[54] See: *Kazakhstanskaia Pravda*, 6 November 1996, "Kontseptsiia iazykovoi politiki Respubliki Kazakhstan."

[55] *Kontseptsiia etnokul'turnogo obrazovaniia* 1996.

write Kazak fluently." 71 percent of the ethnic Kazaks, however, said that they mastered the language to this degree; 51 percent of the ethnic Russians had no knowledge of Kazak at all, though a surprisingly high 25.5 percent said that they were able to understand spoken Kazak.[56]

According to polls carried out by the Parliamentary Center for Information and Analysis the state language has made progress as a working language in the "labor collectives" of the respondents, but is still not widely used.

Interestingly, the sense of discomfort caused by the language regulations in the state administration was less among ethnic Russians than among Kazaks. In one survey from 1994, 21 percent of the Kazaks said that the requirements of the Language Law had caused problems for them personally in their professional work. Only 17 percent of the Russians were of the same opinion despite the fact that only 2 percent of them have a command of Kazak.[57]

Two years later—in 1996 in a similar survey—these figures had changed. Of the Russians 9.9 percent confirmed that they had experienced problems in carrying out their professional duties by not knowing "the state language"; 14 percent of the Kazaks had had similar experiences. However, responding to a general question on discrimination 26.3 percent of the Russians said they were discriminated against because of their lack of knowledge of Kazak.[58]

In comparison one might note that a poor command of Russian also creates problems for Kazakstani citizens. 16.2 percent of Kazaks (and 5.3 percent of Russians) said that they had experienced problems due to

TABLE 5.2 Language of Executives in Kazakstani Work-Places (in percent)

Executives' work performed in ...	1994	1996
Kazak	5.9	12.3
Kazak and Russian	24.8	19.0
Russian	60.7	58.7

Source: Arenov and Kalmykov, 1997b.

---

[56] Arenov and Kalmykov 1995a.

[57] Arenov and Kalmykov 1995b. This survey was carried out in July 1994 among a representative group of 1169 Kazakstani inhabitants by the Center for Information and Analysis under the Supreme Soviet (now Parliament) of Kazakstan.

[58] See *Kazakhstanskaia Pravda* 29 November 1996, "Etnosotsial'nye otnosheniia cherez prizmu obshchestvennogo mneniia." Questions were posed to 1,761 respondents from seven "typical districts of Kazakstan."

TABLE 5.3 Percentage Claiming That They Have Experienced Problems in Carrying Out Their Profession Due to Lack of Knowledge in the "State Language"

	Ethnic Kazaks	Ethnic Russians
1994	21	17
1996	14	10

Sources: Arenov and Kalmykov, 1995a and 1995b, and *Kazakhstanskaia Pravda* 29 November 1996, "Etnosotsial'nye otnosheniia cherez prizmu obshchestvennogo mneniia."

poor knowledge of Russian. 16.1 percent of Kazaks and 4.6 percent of Russians had similar problems "occasionally."[59]

The debate over the language provisions in the Constitution has not only been one between spokespersons of non-Kazaks versus spokespersons of ethnic Kazaks. There was also a serious rift within the Kazak community itself. Urban dwellers of long standing stood against newcomers to the city. Most urban Kazaks have never learnt standardized Kazak as have those who have grown up in the provinces. Since independence the asset of a knowledge of Kazak has been used as a tool to get privileged positions, despite the provision in the final text of the Constitution that nobody shall be discriminated against on the basis of a lack of proficiency in Kazak (or Russian).

The requirement that they shall acquire a command of the state language is directed with greater intensity to all members of the titular nationality than to the nontitulars. Ethnic Kazaks are expected to be "national" and "genuine," and failure to live up to this standard may be more embarrassing than the strain from not belonging to the titular nation. In the spectrum of political parties the nonethnic approach is one of the main elements of *Novoe Pokolenie* (New Generation). *Novoe Pokolenie* has been called the movement of Russian-speaking Kazaks, frequently described as "Kazakstani Kazaks." One of the main slogans of this party is "We are all Kazakstanians." Co-chairman Kosykorpesh Esenberlin says that "They told us that we are *mankurty*, that we grew up on the street, that we have forgotten where our roots are."[60] As noted by one expert (in Russian: "referent") from the Northern Kazakstan oblast administration, those who are "marginal in relation

---

[59] Arenov and Kalmykov 1997b.

[60] See: *Karavan*, 17 February 1995, "Bez grafy 'natsional'nost'" and *Panorama*, 24 June 1995, "My prizyvaem narody Kazakhstana oshchutit' sebia edimym etnosom— kazakhstantsami."

to their traditional culture" are more able than others to adapt to modern civilization and foreign firms. This, on the other hand, has a reverse side: They lose contact with deeper values, becoming "economic animals" in a negative sense.[61] Conflicts internally among Kazaks over what it means "to be a Kazak" may well grow to become the main problem of nation-building. As illustrated in the table above, "Kazakification" strikes Kazaks more negatively than it does Russians in Kazakstan.

In this situation, the power-holders in the new state could have made Russian a state language as a codification of the actual situation. In that case, the almost universal knowledge of Russian in Kazakstan could serve as a unifying agent. On the other hand, the predominant position of Russian may also be seen as an aberration of the natural state of affairs in a nation-state. If that viewpoint is accepted, the authorities ought to pursue an anticipatory policy of assigning Kazak the highest status.

The debate over the language provisions was spurred not only by the rivalry over material benefits among different groups in the population. It had deep roots in two separate schools of thinking about man and ethnicity. The proponents of Kazak as the only state language considered the fact that large parts of the Kazak population no longer used their "mother tongue" to be an abnormality resulting from the brutality of an external system (the Soviet system, industrialization).

According to the "Kazak only" faction each nationality has its own language and ought to preserve it within its state borders. They see Kazakstan as the homeland of the Kazak nation. Therefore, efforts have to be made to "re-Kazakify" the ethnic Kazak part of the population. Awarding the Kazak tongue a constitutional status as state language, with or without the addition of Russian as a language of interethnic communication, is a basic step toward the reestablishment of "a just order." The *Kazak tili* movement clearly works within this frame of thought. *Kazak tili* means "Kazak language," and the members of the organization are first and foremost engaged in helping people learn Kazak and reviving Kazak traditions.[62]

Opponents to this "prescriptive" approach to the language issue proposed assigning Kazak and Russian equal status as state languages. Given the unequal starting points of the two languages, in practical

---

[61] Irgaliev 1995.

[62] Interviews carried out in Semipalatinsk 20 September 1996 with Mendigali Ospanov, vice-chairman of Kazak tili'in Semipalatinsk city, and 23 September 1996 in Ust-Kamenogorsk with Zhumabike Abilmazhinova, chairwoman of the provincial branch of Kazak tili and Toleukhan K. Kodabaev, chairman of the Council of Elders.

terms this would spell continued Russian dominance. Some participants in the debate believe that this is exactly what should be aimed at. Russian is without doubt *the* language of Kazakstan: everybody, with the exception of rural dwellers in the most remote districts of the country, make use of it freely without displeasure. Nurbulat Masanov, an ethnic Kazak, political scientist and "official" *enfant terrible*, says that if Kazakstan were to base itself on the part of the population which did not "bother to learn Russian" in the Soviet period the country would hardly ever be able to modernize. Masanov argues that the Kazak language is a phenomenon of the past. Kazakstan's communications with the outside world go through the Russian language, Masanov maintains. In his view the dominating cleavage in today's Kazakstan runs between urban Kazaks and Kazak newcomers to the cities who try to make rural roots a prerequisite for being a true Kazak fit for nation-building tasks.[63] Typical for spokespersons of this point of view, Masanov is a third generation intellectual—his grandfather was a student at the university of St. Petersburg. A Kazak-speaking Kazakstan, according to Masanov, will be isolated and inward-looking, provincialized and alienated from the achievements of world civilization.[64]

The *akim* (head of administration) in the town of Issyk, appointed in 1996, is an ethnic Pole. His name is Aleksandr Brichkovskii (Polish spelling: Brzyczkowski). Although a Pole, he commands the state language to the extent that he carries out some of his ceremonial tasks in Kazak. Brichkovskii says that "Knowing Kazak helps at work, especially when communicating with those who come from Mongolia and Karakalpakia."[65]

Language in Education

As an instrument for integrating inhabitants into the state as citizens nothing can compete with schools and higher learning institutions. Since Kazakstan has chosen to make Kazak the state language, the fate of that language in schools is of particular interest. As shown in Chapter 6 in this volume, Russian still dominates as the language of instruction. And, more surprisingly, the use of Kazak is not widening to any significant degree. Among respondents defining themselves as

---

[63] Amrelukov and Masanov 1994; Masanov 1995; Masanov 1996.

[64] Masanov 1995, 123.

[65] See the Kazak-language newspaper *Ana tili*, as quoted in *Karavan* 14 June 1996.

Kazaks, 57.7 percent had gone to Kazak-language schools; 66.4 percent of Kazak parents have their children study in Kazak. Only 3.2 percent of respondents defining themselves as Russian let their children study in Kazak, while 5.3 percent of "others" do the same. This means that Kazakstani parents either do not believe Kazak will be practiced as the state language, or they do not expect that their children will, or should, become involved in public affairs.

The number of Kazak parents choosing Kazak as the language of instruction for their children must be seen against the backdrop of the language they use at home. Surveys indicate that only one of four Kazak parents have their children speak only Kazak at home; at street level Kazak is even more marginalized. Kazak is a minority language among Kazak youth.

The Kazakstani press reports of a clear tendency for parents to withdraw their children from schools and kindergartens which switched from Russian to Kazak in 1991–92, i.e. from schools that use the "state language" as their language of instruction. Some of these schools have already gone back to using Russian as their preferred language, while others have simply been closed down. One reason for parents to withdraw their children from Kazak-language schools is that the general standard of these schools is considered to be far lower than their Russian-language counterparts. Among other things, it is reported that pupils do not learn proper Kazak in Kazak-language schools.[66]

The Department for Co-ordination of Language Policies under the Ministry of Education confirms the press reports about the closure of educational institutions using Kazak as the language of instruction. A basic flaw in the figures offered by the language policy department is the omission of any account on cut-downs on Russian-language alternatives. Economic recession and cuts in public spending have led to a general decline in Kazakstani education.

Kindergartens and preschools may serve as good indicators of the distribution and popularity of Kazak-language alternatives. The most recent trends can be seen by looking at the choices made for the very youngest groups. As showed in table 5.5, 436 Kazak-language preschool institutions were closed in 1996. This, however, was the result of a general reduction in funding for preschool institutions, a reduction that

---

[66] See for example *Kazakhstanskaia Pravda*, 31 May 1996, "Gosudarstvennyi iazyk: Tak kto zhe protiv?" and *Kazakhstanskaia Pravda*, 1 November 1996, "Edinyi moi iazyk..."

TABLE 5.4 Use of Language Among Kazak Children 1996 (in percent)

	Only Kazak	*Only Russian*	*Both*
At home	25.0	45.8	6.4
Among children of same age	15.2	52.0	8.1

Source: Arenov and Kalmykov, 1997a.

TABLE 5.5 Number of Teaching Institutions Using Kazak as Language of Instruction Closed in 1996

Preschool institutions	436
Primary schools	78
"Poorly developed schools"[a]	235
Boarding schools	15
Technical school	42

Source: Iazykovaia situatsiia, 1997.

[a] *Malokomplektnaia shkola,* i.e. schools, often located in the countryside, suffering from a lack of premises and teachers. Usually these schools work in two shifts.

TABLE 5.6 Primary Schools and Language of Instruction (1996–97)

Language	*Number of schools*
Russian	2,513
Kazak	3,382
Mixed	2,251
Uzbek	77
Uighur	15
Turkish	3
Tadzhik	2
German	2
Ukrainian	1
Total:	8,246

Source: Iazykovaia situatsiia, 1997.

also affected Russian-language kindergartens and preschools as well.[67] The total number of children losing their Kazak-language preschools amounted to 43,000. In northern and eastern Kazakstan very few Kazak children attend Kazak-language kindergartens and preschools. 2.5 percent of Kazak children in East Kazakstan oblast go to such educational institutions; 4 percent in Semipalatinsk.[68]

Despite cuts in 1997 a clear majority of primary schools in Kazakstan are Kazak-language schools. There is, however, reason to believe that these schools are small and mostly situated in the Kazak settlements, the *aul*. 906,500 pupils study in Russian-language schools. No figures are given for the other schools.

A great number of schools are mixed, which means that they offer training in various languages. In 301 mixed schools 14 languages other than Kazak and Russian are offered as the language of instruction. These schools clearly play a role in the strategies that I have termed "multiple re-ethnification." It is, however, worth noting that two years earlier, in 1995, there were 450 such schools. Lack of readers and other didactic material has led to closures, according to the Department, which adds that existing material is poorly adapted to Kazakstani conditions.[69]

Of particular interest are the technical and professional schools. Despite the fact that custom-made policies have been pursued since the sixties to counteract underrepresentation of ethnic Kazaks in technical professions, the Kazak language has never made any breakthrough in industry and technical sectors. As an illustration of this, only four percent of the books in the libraries of the technical universities are in Kazak, while the average for all universities and colleges is 20.3 percent.[70] About 25 percent of the Kazak students in the various technical and professional schools are taught in Kazak.

As late as the 1995–96 school year, 69 percent of the 260,000 university students of Kazakstan were studying in Russian, according to official statistics (see Table 5.7). 31 percent of the students chose to study their curriculum in Kazak despite the fact that 65 percent of them were classified as ethnic Kazaks. Only 25 percent of the students were ethnic

---

[67] See *Kazakhstanskaia Pravda*, 27 January 1996, "Khochu, chtoby novyi parlament nachal svoiu rabot zakona ob obrazovanii."

[68] *Iazykovaia situatsiia*, 1997, 14.

[69] *Ibid.*, 8.

[70] *Ibid.*, 15.

TABLE 5.7 Students at Institutions of Higher Learning in Kazakstan, 1995–96 School Year, by Language of Instruction

Oblast (County)	Absolute numbers	Studying in Russian	Studying in Kazak
Total	260,043	69.1	30.9
City of Almaty	80,785	63.8	36.2
Dzhambul/Zhambyl	13,177	65.2	34.8
East Kazakstan	11,617	87.8	12.2
Semipalatinsk/Semey	11,751	68.2	31.8
Pavlodar	7,318	80.6	19.4
Karaganda	30,566	81.9	18.1
Akmola (Tselinograd, Astana)	16,272	82.1	17.9
Kokchetav/Kokshetau	5,588	75.5	24.5
North Kazakstan	4,953	90.9	9.1
Taldykurgan/Taldykorgan	3,642	52.7	47.3
Kostanay/Kustanay	11,912	86.2	13.8
Dzhezkazgan/Zhezkazgan	4,806	56.8	43.2
Torgay	2,249	62.7	37.3
Kzyl-Orda	8,126	41.2	58.8
West Kazakstan (Ural'sk)	7,447	69.0	31.0
Aktiubinsk	8,755	64.7	35.3
Mangyshlak/Mangystau	3,270	81.1	18.9
Atyrau (Gur'ev)	7,759	58.7	41.3
South Kazakstan (Chimkent)	19,600	52.7	47.3

Source: Gosudarstvennyi komitet, 1996, 58–62.

TABLE 5.8 Students at Institutions of Higher Learning in Kazakstan, 1995–96 School Year, by Nationality

Nationality	Percentage of student body, 1995-96	Percentage of total population, 1 Jan. 1995
Kazaks	65.2	46.0
Russians	24.9	34.8
Germans	1.4	3.1
Ukrainians	2.3	4.9
Uzbeks	0.5	2.3
Tatars	1.3	1.9
Belarusians	0.4	1.0
Azeris	0.2	0.6
Others	3.8	5.4

Sources: O demograficheskoi 1996, 66; Gosudarstvennyi komitet, 1996, 58–62.

Russians (see Table 5.8).[71] In other words, the education boom among Kazak youth is not yet reflected in a corresponding position of Kazak as a university language.

Language in the 1993 Constitution. In the draft Constitution (Article 8) it is stated that

> In the Republic of Kazakstan Kazak is the state language. Russian is the language of interethnic (*mezhnatsional'nyi*) communication. The State guarantees the preservation of the sphere where Russian is used (*'sfera primeneniia'*) as the language of interethnic communication and will also ensure the free development of other national languages. It is forbidden to restrict the rights and freedoms of citizens on the grounds that they do not master the state language or the language of interethnic communication. (My translation)

As noted by the political scientist, Zh. Kh. Dzhunusova, this was a compromise formulation.[72] It was written into the draft text as a result of the discussions in the Supreme Soviet's eighth session while ten of its members voted against.

During the period of national consultation proponents of more controversial formulations suggested (a) that Kazak alone ought to be mentioned in the Constitution, and then as "State language," and (b), from the other side of the barricades, that both Kazak and Russian should be given status as state languages.

When the Supreme Soviet convened for its ninth session in December 1992 it was to discuss the draft Constitution. The Kazakstani president Nursultan A. Nazarbaev, in his capacity as chairman of the Constitutional Commission, presented the draft in the light of the public consultation. As described by Dzhunusova, practically all speakers touched upon the language provisions, which were the most controversial issue by far. Just as in the round of public consultations, the speakers of the Supreme Soviet were split into three groups: Kazak only; Kazak as state language with Russian as the interethnic mode of communication; and Kazak and Russian as state languages on an equal footing.[73]

In the upshot, at the next, or ninth, secession, a majority of the members of the Supreme Soviet voted in favor of the draft text quoted above, i.e. Kazak and Russian, but with different status. The ambiguity of this formulation meant that the language discussion has continued, and the exact meaning of the compromise had to be spelt out in a Law on Languages.

---

[71] *Gosudarstvennyi komitet* 1996, 58–62.

[72] Dzhunusova 1996, 121–122.

[73] Ibid., 123.

The Language Issue in the 1995 Constitution. Article 7 of the new Constitution states that "Kazak is the state language," and that "in state bodies and bodies of local-self-government Russian shall be used officially on a par with Kazak."[74] Even so, nobody is to suffer discrimination on the basis of insufficient skills in any of these languages. The article also states that the State shall endeavor to create the necessary preconditions for the study and development of the "languages of the people of Kazakstan."

The Language Law

A new law on the languages of Kazakstan was passed 11 July 1997. Its main aim is to improve implementation of the provisions in the Constitution, i.e. to reinforce Kazak as the state language. The law states that all citizens of Kazakstan are obliged to master Kazak, which it terms "the most important consolidating factor of the people of Kazakstan" (Art 1, § 4).

Throughout 1996 the draft language law was one of the most heated subjects of the political debate in Kazakstan, and much of the same disagreements were aired then as had emerged during the debate over the draft Constitutions.

In the 1989 language law the definition of Kazak as "state language" and Russian as "the language of interethnic communication" had been formulated together with an affirmation that "the functioning of Russian on an equal basis with the state language" would be secured by the Kazak SSR. This wording, as we have seen, later found its way into the 1993 Constitution. The law gave detailed regulations concerning how and where the state language was to be used.

One of the most controversial issues in the debate was the proposed "index of posts requiring a knowledge of the state language on the part of their incumbents." Such an index was about to be introduced in 1991, but the idea was watered down. One of the main proponents behind implementing such an index was Bakhytzhan Khasanov, director of the Center for the Strategy of Language Development and a sociolinguist. His center is subordinate to the Ministry of Science, and Khasanov took part in the working group that prepared the draft law on the languages of Kazakstan. He is a proponent of the view that there can be no Kazak nation without a Kazak language, and no Kazak language without a

---

[74] The wording in the Kazakstani Constitution is very similar to that of ethnically defined subjects of the federation in Russia, where the titular languages are "used on a par with Russian" in official settings. See: *Novoe Pokolenie*, no. 5, 1997, "Novyi zakon o iazykakh – trebovanie vremeni."

state in which it dominates. On the other hand, Khasanov adds that the Kazak language forms a classical example of a situation where the position of a language depends upon linguistic policies and nonlinguistic factors.[75]

Whereas much of the criticism of the present situation originates in allegations by state officials ousted for not mastering Kazak, Khasanov takes the opposite view. In his opinion the state administration is dominated by Russian-speakers, who pursue their own linguistic interests despite the fact that the Kazakstani state needs to protect itself by asserting Kazak as the state language.[76]

Khasanov has additionally claimed that the prestige of the Kazak tongue has suffered over the last few years and that its breadth of application is shrinking to the advantage of Russian. This is due to the fact that the implementation of the Constitutional provisions on the state language has been entrusted to "Russian-speaking officials."

Having achieved state sovereignty, Kazakstan has failed to achieve linguistic sovereignty, Khasanov asserts. Even in the absence of a language index it must be an absolute requirement that the *akims* at all levels master the Kazak language: "No akim can be out of contact with the Kazaks," he says. Also, all members of the Mazhilis need to know Kazak. Khasanov refers approvingly to the language indexes of the twenties and thirties, decades which, in most other respects, can hardly be said to have been beneficial to the Kazaks. The introduction of such an index would be followed up by a list of clearly defined language skills to be required of civil servants. Khasanov would like to see the skills to be attained before 2001 and 2006 for Kazaks and Russians, respectively.

The final law was passed 11 July 1997. It states in its Article 2 that it regulates not only language use in state affairs, but in the activities of nonstate organizations and local government, too. Language use in religious associations and in "interpersonal relations" is not subject to regulation. The state language is Kazak, in Article 5 termed "the most important factor through which to consolidate the people of Kazakstan." It is the duty of all citizens to master Kazak, but it makes no mention of any index of jobs requiring knowledge of Kazak. Article 6 is entitled "Usage of the Russian language" and states: "In governmental organizations and bodies of local self-government Russian shall be used officially on a par with Kazak." Non-state organizations are obliged to employ the state language, or, as stated in Article 8, "if necessary,

---

[75] See *Novoe Pokolenie*, no. 5, 1997, "Novyi zakon o iazykakh – trebovanie vremeni."

[76] See *Kazakhstanskaia Pravda*, 29 November 1996, "Priniatie zakona o iazykakh – mirovoi standart razvitiia iazykov."

other languages." The fact that nonstate organizations are subject to a slightly stricter regime as to language requirements than are state and local-self-government institutions, may evoke fears that the vagueness of the legislation could be used as a pretext for crack-downs on independent activities carried out by citizens who do not master Kazak. Similar suspicions are aroused by the wording in Article 18 that requires a minimum of 50 percent Kazak language in TV irrespective of the ownership of the channel. Cutbacks in Russian-language broadcasts in Kazakstan have already become a controversial issue in the country, arousing protests in wide circles of the population.

Passport Provisions (Indication of Ethnicity)

As part of the political mobilization of the citizens a campaign has been waged to encourage people to acquire new Kazakstani passports. Detailed descriptions have been given in the press about how to obtain the passport by applying to the local office of the Ministry of the Interior and bringing a photograph and the equivalent of 20 U.S. dollars in Kazakstani tengé.[77] In addition to spaces for first name, family name, patronymic, date of birth, and others there is an item for "ethnic origin," a homologue to the fifth line in Soviet passports tying people to often long-forgotten ethnic pasts. The article does not provide information about the optional indication of nationality, and reportedly such information is generally not given. Very few holders of Kazakstani passports leave the entry for "nationality" blank. The fact that ethnic classification is optional for the new passports is potentially to the advantage of a multiethnic, integration model, but not a significant one if ethnicity matters in everyday life.

Political Institutions and Integration

We have seen that Kazakstani nation-building balances between several doctrinal models. We have also seen that these models have coexisted in the official rhetoric and doctrines since 1991, and that citizenship and ethnicity alternate as a focus. In my opinion, the sum of this balancing act can be characterized as a drive for "multiple re-ethnification." At the same time, I suggest, all models presuppose the need to create loyalties to the state institutions.

---

[77] See *Iuridicheskaia gazeta* 22–29 April 1995, "Atribut gosudarstvennosti."

The important question then arises: are the political institutions of Kazakstan really integrative? This will be the main topic of this sub-chapter. The doctrines, the formal set-up, and the practices will be discussed. In other words, are the inhabitants of Kazakstan being molded into an everyday attachment/loyalty to the state through involvement in the political institutions? Or is the development of state institutions and the creation of a Kazak "state nation" intertwined to an extent that hampers the development of loyalty in non-Kazaks and "Russified" Kazaks?

In this chapter we will discuss whether civic and ethnic concepts compete also at the level of institution-building in the new Kazakstani state. In order to determine whether Kazakstan's political institutions are integrative or not it is necessary to perform an investigation on two different levels. First, we must ascertain whether the institutions are integrative in general. Are they merely fronts, or do they really function as *the* arena for political debate and policy-formulation? Second, if the political institutions really do function, are there open or hidden mechanisms that exclude parts of the citizenry from full participation?

Two important principles of Kazakstani nation-building determine the scope and directions of institution-building in the state. First of all, Kazakstan is a centralized state, the core of which is the vertical command line from the President down. "Governors" or *akims* at all levels of governance are accountable only to the President or to akims at a higher level. They are therefore in a position from which they with ease can outmaneuver autonomous local and regional self-governing bodies. Second, Kazakstan is a strictly unitary state; in stark contrast to the Russian Federation, no ethnically defined autonomous territories are allowed.[78]

The consequence of this is that the powerful political institutions are manned by people appointed directly or indirectly by the President. This significantly limits the chances of possible ethnopolitical groups or other counterelites to gain ground by utilizing the state apparatus and elected bodies. The absence of ethnically defined territories further reduces the opportunities of ethnopolitical leaders—and would-be leaders—to use ethnicity as a rhetorical tool.

In order to promote ethnic diversity the authorities encourage ethnic self-government through so-called national-cultural centers (see below). These centers may use the "Conception for ethnocultural education" as a platform for their work.

---

[78] The attempt to establish an autonomous German oblast in North Kazakstan in 1979 was curbed.

The activities of self-governing bodies nonetheless have to stick to strictly defined rules of conduct. There is no room for other cultural identities to function as organizational rallying points than the Soviet Union's ethnographic inventory of officially recognized ethnicities, that still are in use. It is not very probable that the institution of ethnocultural centers will be made use of by non-Russians who would like to develop, say, a Russophone identity.[79]

The President and His Vertical Line of Command

The presidential character of the Kazakstani political system has increased steadily since independence. In December 1991 the President was elected by a direct ballot, which marked the passage to a presidential system.[80] The Constitution of 1993 introduced the principle of the balance of powers, whereas the 1995 Constitution enhanced the powers of the President. Several decrees in late 1995 further strengthened the position of the President.

In the draft Constitution of 1993 it was suggested that only ethnic Kazaks may run for presidency. As Kazakstan was to become a nation-state for the Kazaks, the head of state ought to have an intimate understanding of their lives which only a co-national could possess. This argument, however, failed to sway the Parliament, and a compromise solution was found: the president must be able to speak perfect Kazak.[81]

Nation-building, also after state-centered Soviet socialism, implies the penetration of the state into all parts of the territory to exert power and pacify counterelites. The tough strategy for economic restructuring embarked upon by Kazakstan requires a state apparatus able to act in the face of popular resistance.

The argument is that reforms have to be carried out by leaders who are not accountable to the—allegedly only short-term—victims of such reforms. The akim of Semipalatinsk admitted that if the akim was to be elected, rather than appointed as is the case at present, "very few

---

[79] Scholars like Nurbulat Masanov argue in favor of maintaining the Russophone identity of large parts of the population (see Masanov 1995a and 1996a). Cultivating this identity along national-romanticist patterns, as they do in the national-cultural centers, would, however, seem paradoxical. [80] According to the secretary of the Senate Committee on Legislation and Legal Reform, Anatolii Kotov, this does not necessarily imply a rejection of parliamentarianism in Kazakstan. See *Kazakhstanskaia Pravda*, 27 August 1996, "Parlament nuzhen takoi, kakoi opredelila ego Konstitutsiia."

[81] Baikhmanov, Vaisberg and Kotov 1994, 49—50.

today would have voted for me. Indeed, there are very great costs resulting from the ongoing reforms."

His plea for unaccountability for heads of the regions and disavowal of representative bodies meddling in his work is underpinned by his conviction that "the laws of the market, just like the laws of mathematics, work in the same way everywhere."[82]

The Akim. The President exerts his influence through the vertical chain of executive command, the *ispol'nitel'naia vertikal'*, which is often simply referred to as "the presidential vertical" (*prezidentskaia vertikal'*). This command line is based on an akim (head of administration) for every level of governance, who is accountable only to the President and to akims on a higher tier. The akim heads the administration of the oblast or rayon. Rayon-level akims are appointed by the heads of the oblast administration. In this way a strong, vertical presidential power has been established, and the influence of the elected maslikhats—over the local administrations is very limited. "Multiethnicity requires a centralized state," according to Nikolai Ilich Akuev, an advisor to the President on institutional questions and member of the Constitutional Council.[83]

The akims control the only administrative apparatus at the regional level large enough to implement policies, the *akimat*. The maslikhat has no efficient apparatus of its own.

Debate on the Vertical Power Structure. The decisions to strengthen the vertical power structures to the detriment of the local councils were not passed without criticism. One example of this is an article by Grigorii Shparaga in the monthly sociopolitical journal *Mysl'*, published in Almaty. In this article Grigorii Shparaga criticizes the rapid growth throughout the nineties of the non-self-governmental administration (i.e. the akimat) in the country. According to him, vertical structures, like clans and (post-)Soviet industrial branches, can easily obtain control over this *ispolnitel'naia vertikal'*. And these groups—including "the bureaucratic-apparatchik nomenclatura"—are the real conservatives of Kazakstan, not the local councils, the author claims. The establishment of the new administration has "again" led to a flourishing of "protectionism, clan rule and corruption." Officials are accountable only to those on a higher level of the executive *vertikal'*, and for that reason oblivious to local problems, according to this political scientist.[84]

People in the executive *vertikal'* often refer to themselves as "the presidential team" (*prezidentskaia komanda*). The author of the *Mysl'*

---

[82] See *Kazakhstanskaia Pravda*, 18 May 1996, "Esli by dolzhnost' akima byla vybornoi, za menia by segodnia malo kto progolosoval."

[83] Author's interviews in Almaty 8 May and 27 September 1996.

[84] Shparaga 1994.

article warns that the strong position of local state—or rather, presidential—administration, somewhat paradoxically, may weaken the position of the president. As all heads of administrations are responsible solely to the President, all grievances of the local population may easily be taken all the way to the President who, in the last resort, is responsible for the entire vertical.[85] This situation is not very different from what the situation used to be under state socialism.

Is the Presidential Vertical Integrating? The dominance of the presidential vertical encourages the inhabitants to look to Almaty. Important matters are solved in the akimat. The ultimate decision-maker at a local level is the representative of the President, a man who can be replaced on short notice. Local power-holders or notabilities who fill up the maslikhat are of far lesser importance. This situation impedes the development of strong localism. Due to strong regional differences with respect to the ethnic composition of the population, tribal—*zhuz* in the vernacular—allegiances, and, not least, the generally high level of familiarity with the great Russian neighbor not only among Russians but also among Kazaks of the North and the East, nation-builders in Almaty are eager to restrain the development of localism and regionalism.

The Departments of Internal Policies. There is a special akimat department for internal policies *(otdel vnutrennoi politiki)* on both oblast and rayon levels. This department is responsible for issues related to the social sphere; institutions of culture; education; sport; health; NGOs; and nationalities.

The departments for internal policies play an important role in the regulation of matters relating to ethnicity because they deal with the national-cultural centers and oversee the establishment of special language classes in the schools to help national minorities maintain contact with their historical mother tongue. This department often carries out ethnicity-related surveys. "All our cases are dealt with by the department of internal policies," said the chairman of the national cultural center of the Uighurs in Almaty city.[86]

The tasks of the department are similar to those of the former ideology secretary, and in everyday parlance the department is sometimes termed "the ideology department." Grigorii Shparaga, a political scientist and former chairman of the Ust-Kamenogorsk Soviet of People's Deputies, asks whether a department for internal policies and social affairs is really needed. He maintains that this department is en-

---

[85] Dokuchaeva 1994a.
[86] Author's interview with Rakhimzhan Makhpirovich Kasymov, Almaty, 31 May 1996.

trusted with ideological security and censorship and that it "makes one think of ideological totalitarianism."[87]

Another view is presented by the head of the Department of Internal Policies in Akmola town:

> We suffer from an ideological vacuum. People need concrete concepts to live by. The Assembly of the Nationalities of Kazakstan has been established to develop such concepts, to achieve consolidation. I am glad I joined the Communist Party in the Soviet period. Through the Party I learnt implementation and personnel policy.[88]

The departments of internal policies help to establish links between the national-cultural centers and the processes of defining nation-building doctrines in Kazakstan (see below).

Ethnicity in the Oblast Administration. At the oblast level, as in other sectors of the state administration, allegations have been made that Kazaks are occupying ever more of the leading positions. This they do to an extent that far exceeds their relative ethnic strength in the population. In a path-breaking article published in December 1993 two Russophone journalists produced numerical details on what had been up to then almost a taboo subject: In Karaganda the ratio of Kazaks to non-Kazaks in the oblast top apparatus was six to two, in Pavlodar six to three, in the city of Almaty nine to two, etc.[89] Later, also Kazak social scientists have discussed the ethnic aspects of the "cadre policy" in even greater detail.

Tables 5.9 and 5.10 depict the situation in 1992 and 1993 respectively.[90] The figures clearly illustrate the predominant position of ethnic Kazaks in the regional administration. Perhaps most interesting is the significant overrepresentation of ethnic Kazaks in important industrial and political centers such as Almaty and the Northern and Eastern districts of the country.

---

[87] Shparaga 1994, 19.

[88] Author's interview with Ms Gulim Khamitovna Abdrakhmanova, Akmola, 16 May 1996.

[89] Giller and Shatskikh 1993. At the time, this article caused a sensation. Author's interview with Viktor Shatskikh, September 1996.

[90] The researchers of the Development Institute of Kazakhstan, who computed the figures in these tables, have operationalized "leaders of oblast administration" as: Heads of administration (*akims*); their deputies; chairmen of oblast soviets; leaders of the apparatuses, and secretaries of the oblast level committees of the Communist Party (for the 1993 figures this last category was omitted).

[91] Dzhunusova 1996, 79.

TABLE 5.9 Ethnic Composition of Leading Positions in Oblast Administrations in 1992 and 1993 in Relation to Ethnic Composition of Oblast Population: Percentage of Ethnic Kazaks

Oblast (County)	1992	1993	% of total population (1989)
Almaty/Alma Ata	60.0	77.8	45.5
City of Almaty	56.3	72.7	24.2
Dzhambul/Zhambyl	56.2	(-)	53.7
East Kazakstan	42.8	50.0	28.3
Semipalatinsk/Semey	50.0	45.5	54.1
Pavlodar	42.8	63.6	29.9
Karaganda	50.0	60.0	19.2
Akmola (Tselinograd, Astana)	50.0	50.0	22.8
Kokchetav/Kokshetau	28.5	44.4	39.5
North Kazakstan	28.6	40.0	19.1
Taldy-Kurgan /Taldykorgan	66.6	63.6	52.8
Kostanay/Kustanay	35.7	30.0	17.9
Dzhezkazgan/Zhezkazgan	60.0	(-)	48.8
Torgay	57.4	45.4	43.8
Kzyl-Orda	64.3	55.5	81.9
West Kazakstan (Ural'sk)	42.8	50.0	57.4
Aktiubinsk	50.0	70.0	58.3
Mangyshlak/Mangystau	56.3	50.0	54.6
Atyrau (Gur'ev)	54.5	70.0	81.3
South Kazakstan (Chimkent)	53.3	63.6	58.3

Sources: Galiev et al., 1994, 53–55 and the 1989 census as reproduced in Gawecki, 1994

TABLE 5.10 Ethnic Composition of Leading Positions in Oblast Administration in 1992 and 1993: Percentage of Slavs

Oblast (County)	1992	1993
Almaty/Alma Ata	35.7	22.2
City of Almaty	43.7	27.2
Dzhambul/Zhambyl	31.2	(-)
East Kazakstan	42.8	30.0
Semipalatinsk/Semey	43.8	54.5
Pavlodar	50.0	36.4
Karaganda	18.7	10.0
Akmola (Tselinograd, Astana)	28.6	40.0
Kokchetav/Kokshetau	35.7	33.3
North Kazakstan	73.3	40.0
Taldy-Kurgan/Taldykorgan	33.3	18.2
Kostanay/Kustanay	57.1	30.0
Dzhezkazgan/Zhezkazgan	26.6	(-)
Torgay	28.6	9.1
Kzyl-Orda	14.3	11.1
West Kazakstan (Ural'sk)	28.6	30.0
Aktiubinsk	43.2	10.0
Mangyshlak/Mangystau	25.0	20.0
Atyrau (Gur'ev)	27.2	10.0
South Kazakstan (Shymkent)	26.6	18.2

Source: Galiev et al., 1994, 53–55. (-) means no figures given

Representative Bodies

The Parliament. When Kazakstan gained independence, the very concept of a parliament was completely unknown as far as practical experience was concerned, as was the case in most other Soviet republics. To be sure, a Supreme Soviet of Kazakstan had functioned from 1938 to 1990, but its procedures can hardly be likened to those of a parliament. Throughout the period, it only passed 457 laws, all of them replicas of Union-level laws.[91]

Political life in Kazakstan since 1991 has resembled that of the Russian Federation in its tug-of-war between the presidential administration on the one hand and the representative bodies on the other. Parliament has been dissolved twice by the President after a conflict over competencies not very different from the one that ended in "Bloody October" in Moscow in 1993. The latest dissolution took place in March 1995 when the Supreme Soviet of Kazakstan was abolished.

The First Parliament (April 1990–December 1993). The parliament that served in the years immediately before and after the declaration of independence was elected after the Gorbachevian principles of glasnost had been introduced. Nevertheless, all oblast first secretaries of the CPSU managed to run unopposed and more than half of the newly elected deputies in the spring 1990 belonged to the nomenclatura.[92]

Even though it was elected relatively democratically, the new Supreme Soviet did not operate as a clearly defined counterweight to the President. Members of the presidential administration who had also been elected to the parliament, did not have to choose between the two branches of power but were allowed to serve in both capacities.

In a speech to the Supreme Soviet of Kazakstan in October 1993, President Nazarbaev announced the abolishment of the lowest-level elected bodies, the local soviets.[93] As he put it, "It is important that the representative and executive bodies merge into one single system of state executive power."[94] This subsequently led to the self-dissolution of the parliament as well.

By law the President was allocated all powers that hitherto had been in the hands of Parliament. In addition, an electoral code was passed that secured central control of the parties and candidates to run for a seat in the legislature. An electoral commission and the Ministry of Justice was to screen the candidates. This system, as well as the

---

[92] Ibid., 80.

[93] See *Izvestiia*, 14 October 1993, "Vsia vlast'– akimam!"

[94] See *Sovety Kazakhstana*, 14 October 1993, "Mezhnatsional'noe edinstvo i ekonomicheskii suverenitet – glavnaia i nadëzhnaia opora nashego prodvizheniia vperëd." See also Avtonomov 1995, 25.

general registration of movements and parties by the Ministry of Justice, has been judged as arbitrary, and favoring the old nomenclatura.[95]

The Second Parliament (April 1994–March 1995). The Parliament elected on 7 March 1994 was the first so-called professional Parliament in Kazakstan, which means that it was working on a permanent basis. A clear majority of its members came from posts in the state administration and in state-owned enterprises. Thirty-three members were actually heads of administration at district or local levels, which meant that they came from posts directly in the presidential line of command.[96]

Out of a total 176 members 42 were elected from the so-called "state list" (*gosspisok*) composed by the President. The President nominated a total of 70 candidates, which gave the voters some choice. The OSCE recommended that the state list be abolished, which it was not. The list was officially justified by the need to secure a fair representation of national minorities, women, and people from the sphere of culture.[97] 75 members were nominated by parties and independent groups, while 59 ran as independents. If no candidate achieves more than 50 percent of the votes cast in his constituency, a second round is held. In the second round only two candidates are permitted to run.

In accordance with electoral legislation passed by the preceding Parliament the number of constituencies was reduced to 135 from almost 300. Each constituency (*okrug*) was to elect one candidate. The presidential hand in the process was to be secured by an additional 42 MPs elected from a list consisting of 64 names nominated by the President. These candidates run on an oblast basis, three candidates per oblast, and two to be elected. The elections were held on 7 March 1994. The President's men won a majority of the seats. Only 23 members of the new Parliament were known to disagree with the main policies of the President.[98]

Despite the indisputable fact that the electoral laws and practices were shaped to produce a parliament close to the President, the Parliament was slow to enact the necessary changes to enable market reforms to take place, probably reflecting sentiments in their own electorates.

The second Parliament was dissolved officially by the Constitutional Court on the grounds that the Electoral Commission had adopted unconstitutional documents. Interestingly, some time before the

---

[95] Dixon 1996, 99.

[96] Dzhunusova 1996, 94.

[97] Dzhunusova 1996, 94; Dixon 1996.

[98] Dixon 1996, 99.

dissolution of the Parliament the President established an advisory body, the Assembly of the Nationalities of Kazakstan. Similar to the members of the first Parliament the second Parliament was also thoroughly coopted into the presidential branch of power and offered little resistance when the situation deteriorated. Only the political groups most aggressively opposed to the President protested.

The prevailing ethnopolitical tendencies cannot, of course, be determined on the basis of the ethnic composition of the Parliament alone. An ethnic Kazak does not necessarily have to be a Kazak nationalist. On various occasions, however, the second Parliament proved to have a penchant for Kazak nationalism. In December 1994 the President asked Parliament to carry out a preliminary vote on four issues to be changed in a new Constitution. What happened was that there was a majority both against two state languages and against changing the constitutional formulation in favor of Kazakstan being a state of "the self-determining Kazak nation."[99] In other words, Parliament turned down reforms that would have symbolized an "integrating state." Interestingly, even among the presidential nominees, a majority voted against the introduction of two state languages. Support for this proposition came first of all from the three northernmost oblasts, where 39 MPs were in favor and only 15 against. Of these 15 northerners, 13 were ethnic Kazaks.[100]

The Third Parliament. In August 1995, after the dissolution of the second Parliament, a referendum was held over a draft constitution. Not surprisingly, a majority endorsed the constitutional changes, among them the establishment of a two-chamber Parliament to replace the Supreme Soviet. Elections to a new Parliament were held in December 1995. This new Parliament consists of a Senate, and a lower chamber, the *Mazhilis*.

The new Parliament is to function within a strictly presidential system. At the inaugural meeting of the Parliament on 30 January 1995 President Nursultan Nazarbaev warned that he would not hesitate to dissolve it if it repeated the mistakes of the previous parliaments. The speaker of the *Mazhilis*, Marat Ospanov, later assured that it would follow "Asian traditions," i.e. not meddle in the wide-ranging affairs of the President.[101]

Nevertheless, the third Kazakstani Parliament has also been able to assert itself *vis-à-vis* the executive power branch. In clashes between the executive and representative branches of power, economic and

---

[99] Dzhunusova 1996, 107.

[100] Masanov 1995b, 27–28.

[101] See *OMRI Daily Digest*, 6 February 1996.

welfare issues have typically been in the forefront. In June 1996 a vote of confidence was taken in Parliament. Of the 106 members of the combined Senate and Mazhilis taking part, 76 voted for confidence.

The members to the upper chamber, the Senate, are elected indirectly in two-candidate constituencies, i.e. from each oblast; important cities having the status of "cities of republican significance"; and the capital.

The oblasts (counties) of Kazakstan are supposed to make use of the Senate to get their voices heard. The senators are elected by electors selected by the local *maslikhats*. As parties do not play a significant role in the maslikhats, the Senate also maintains a low party profile. Senators tend to be regional notabilities.[102]

In addition to the Senate's ordinary members seven senators are appointed by the President. It is commonly assumed that this is a provision that allows for the President to secure the representation of the smaller ethnic groups of Kazakstan.[103] Seven representatives of small ethnic groups in the Senate will compensate for the difficulties this category of candidates may meet in attracting a majority of the voters in the two-candidate constituencies for the Mazhilis.[104] On the other hand quota systems might make it even more difficult for non-Kazaks and non-Russians to run for an ordinary seat as quotas "teach" voters to look for ethnicity. On the other hand again, as noted in section above on nation-building: political rhetoric and doctrines, it seems that "multiethnic society" means a re-ethnified society.

I. Karsakov of the Almaty-based Development Institute of Kazakstan says that the need for a group of parliamentarians appointed by the President is caused by the fact that Kazakstan "is an interethnic (*mezh-natsional'nyi*), not a biethnic (*bi-natsional'nyi*) society."[105] However, the seven individuals actually picked by the President were not drawn from ethnic minorities. Four of them were Kazaks, two were Russians, and one was Ukrainian. Two of them were females, five were lawyers, four were directly employed in the presidential branch of power.[106]

The imbalanced relations of power between the executive and the representative powers, as envisaged in the Constitution, leads to a

---

[102] Mashanov 1995.

[103] Dzhunusova 1996, 179.

[104] Such problems exist, according to the chairman of the Turkish national-cultural center in Almaty. Because Turks are too dispersed throughout in the republic to have a chance of gaining a majority for their representative, the chairman considered it pointless to run for a seat in *Mazhilis* in the December 1995 elections. See Holm-Hansen 1997, 70.

[105] Karsakov 1995.

[106] See *Vesti Kazakhstana*, 25 January 1995, "Nursultan Nazarbaev naznachil senatorov."

certain brain drain away from the Parliament into the administration of the President. Well-known politicians may fear giving the impression that they are losers if they try to get into Parliament rather than into the presidential apparatus.

Several factors contribute to the lowered status of the Parliament. First of all, it simply has less power. Procedures have been introduced which authorize the President to dissolve Parliament. The members of the Parliament have no guarantees that they will be allowed to return to their ordinary jobs if they fail to be reelected. In 1995, though, thanks to a comprehensive rotation and reduction (20 percent) of the presidential and governmental administrations, many politicians and administrative officers who were left out in the cold with no portfolio ran for a seat in Parliament. According to M. Mashanov, of the Development Institute of Kazakstan, the intellectual capacities of the 1995 Parliament will prove to be inferior to those of the preceding Supreme Soviet.[107]

The Law on Elections of September 1995 was promulgated as a presidential decree. It included some important modifications: The number of members elected directly in one-man constituencies was halved. It now stands at 67. In the Supreme Soviet the figure was 135. This means that there are now more voters for each candidate (provided the turnout remains the same). This favors large parties, and—if people vote according to ethnicity—candidates from large ethnic groups.

The electoral campaign of November–December 1995 was carried out very discretely in comparison to the campaign that was being waged in Russia at the same time. During a stay in Almaty in the weeks prior to the elections I noted that most people appeared to be following the mass media coverage of the Russian campaign with a much keener interest than their "own" domestic electoral campaign. This seemed to be true irrespective of ethnic background and proximity to the power structures.

Among the candidates to the Mazhilis who had presented themselves as candidates by 5 November, 28 were Kazaks, 20 Russians, four Ukrainians, one German, one Korean, and one a Chechen. To the Senate there were 26 Kazaks, 14 Russians, and one Uighur by the same date.[108] After the first round, 32 of a total of 67 seats in the Mazhilis were filled (i.e. one of the candidates had attained more than half of the total votes cast in his constituency). Of these MPs 26 were Kazaks, four Russians, one was a Ukrainian, and one a Korean.

---

[107] Mashanov 1995.
[108] Ibid.

TABLE 5.11 The Ethnic Composition of the Kazakstani Parliaments (in percent)

Registered nationality	Parliament 1990–93	Parliament 1993–95	Parliament 1995–
Kazak	53	58	65
Russian	29	27	30
Ukrainian	7	6	3
Belarusian	1.5	-	-
German	4	2	1
Jewish	-	2	-
Others	5.5	5	2

Sources: Dzhunusova, 1996, 80 and 93; and information from the Giller Institute. Note on the 1995 Parliament: Figures apply for both Mazhilis (67 seats) and Senate (47 seats). There are only minor differences in the ethnic composition of the two chambers.

Interestingly, the candidates elected from North and East Kazakstan tended to be independent and "nonstate," i.e. neither holding positions in the "presidential vertical" nor running for presidential parties.

The figures in Table 5.11 must be read with caution. First of all one should bear in mind that the ethnic Kazaks are disproportionally present among the younger generations, not yet eligible to vote. This makes the overrepresentation of ethnic Kazaks in the legislature even more noteworthy. Second, one should be critical of the significance of ethnic labels. Ethnicity is a fleeting phenomenon in Kazakstan, even among Kazaks, and the fact that most members of Parliament are Kazaks does not necessarily imply that they are in favor of the "Kazakification" of the state. In many cases they may be basically Russophones with a poor knowledge of the "state language."

The President and the Parliament as Integrating Factors. As a parallel to the growth of the presidential powers in Kazakstan, the powers of the Parliament have shrunk. From the reinvention during the age of perestroika of the slogan "all power to the councils," the 1993 Constitution stated that the Parliament was "the only legislative and a high representative organ of the Republic of Kazakstan" (Article 62). The 1995 Constitution reduced the Parliament to "a high representative organ of the Republic, carrying out legislative functions." Now, not only the Parliament, but also the President and the government, can make laws.

Judging from statements by important politicians, Parliament is to constitute a smooth link in a streamlined system of power execution, dealing only in a technical sense with the processes of making laws. According to the chairman of the present Mazhilis, Marat Ospanov, the earlier parliaments have represented *the old* against *the new*, "the new" being the executive power. However, not even the introduction of presidentially appointed senators, or the fact that a great number of those elected belong to the presidential vertical, has made Parliament completely subservient to the executive power, and voices in Kazakstani newspapers often argue in favor of a more active Parliament.

Does the present Kazakstani Parliament bring about integration? In other words, is it conducive to a gradual shift of loyalties from substate, premodern, post-Soviet, or ethnic allegiances toward a state based on civic participation through the political institutions? On the one hand, the Parliament of Kazakstan is far more independent of, and self-assertive toward, the presidential administration than parliaments usually are in Central Asia. The Parliament has proved capable of raising important objections to the policies of the executive branch of power on crucial issues, like pensions and wages. It is noteworthy that the most heated issues in the controversies between the President/government and the Parliament are issues that are "non-ethnic" in the sense that they concern all citizens irrespective of ethnicity. This makes citizens of all ethnicities feel that they are together in the same boat. Focus on economic issues may help de-ethnify politics. On the other hand, also issues like state language and citizenship have caused a great deal of controversy. The conflict lines in these latter questions, however, basically run among various factions in the Parliament rather than between Parliament on the one hand and the President on the other.

The presidential office constitutes the main force among political institutions in official Kazakstani nation-building. As a unifying symbol, a protector of the minorities, and, at the same time, both a "true Kazak" *and* a Russified Kazak, Nursultan Nazarbaev so far has been able to fill this role. However, the underdevelopment of civic institutions and practices under state socialism cannot be healed by a well-functioning presidency alone. Far from it, what is needed are relevant institutions between the citizens and the head of state, among them a parliament. The present legislation of Kazakstan, forbidding parties promoting ethnic hatred and separatism, and with an electoral system that favors "catch-all" candidates, makes for an integrative parliament, equally important for all citizens irrespective of their ethnic background. In this perspective, the complaints from representatives of the presidential vertical that Parliament makes priorities which differ from those of the executive branch of power, may in effect prove to be complaints about integration.

The political element in nation-building consists in streamlining institutions and making them work with the same penetrative force in all geographic parts of the state. Such a consolidation of state presence

TABLE 5.12 Percentage Supporting President and Parliament

"Do you believe in...	Kazaks 1995	Kazaks 1996	Russians 1995	Russians 1996
strong presidential power?"	40.8	42.3	12.3	17.4
a parliamentary republic?"	4.0	5.1	4.4	3.4

Source: Ethnopoliticheskii monitoring, 1996, 12.

against localist and traditional elites could be a precondition for democratization and the participation of the citizens, but it could also imply a continuation of citizen weakness, and thereby hamper political integration.

If political integration is to take place through the institutions, a precondition is that these institutions are considered relevant. Do the inhabitants of Kazakstan actually find their political institutions relevant? In one survey the respondents were asked to say whether they had faith in the main political institutions of Kazakstan. Proponents of strengthening the Parliament received an unpleasant message from this survey.

These figures are noteworthy for two reasons. First, they show a dramatic difference between ethnic Kazaks and Kazakstani Russians as regards their faith in the presidency. The picture of "a good tsar" protecting his ethnic "nontitulars," is not sustained. Nurbulat Masanov, who presents these figures, is himself a highly profiled spokesman of the Kazaks who are opposed to Kazakification. Masanov interprets the figures as a reflection of strong paternalist tendencies among Kazaks. Second, the figures show a dramatically low support for "parliamentarism" both among Kazaks and Russians. Cross-ethnic integration through political institutions is not likely to take place as long as the figures remain as represented in these tables.

Table 5.12 reproduces questions about general faith in institutions. If one asks specifically about the capability of these institutions to promote the aim of interethnic stability, one gets somewhat different answers (Table 5.13). These figures are remarkably low, the importance of ethnic stability in the official rhetoric taken into consideration.

TABLE 5.13 Which Institution Guarantees Interethnic Stability? In percent

Institution	Kazaks 1995	Kazaks 1996	Russians 1995	Russians 1996
President	54.3	47.6	22.5	25.0
Government	22.4	19.9	17.3	14.7
Parliament	4.3	4.3	5.2	3.0

Source: Ethnopoliticheskii monitoring, 1996, 11.

Local and Regional Self-Government. In a nation-building context the establishment of local and regional self-government may work in two separate directions. On the one hand it may be conducive as it brings decisions closer to the population and thereby strengthens people's ties with the political institutions, thus relaxing premodern loyalties. On the other hand, local and regional self-government may be appropriated by premodern or modern elites using ethnicity or territoriality to seize power in a battle against centralized nation-building.

The caution with which the Kazakstani authorities have allowed the introduction of territorial institutions of self-government can be explained by a fear of letting territorially based counterelites utilize such institutions as platforms for their own advancement. The territorial self-government of Kazakstan has been designed to reinforce the unity of the state, which is one of the main elements in the country's nation-building doctrine. Substate units are not to be established on the basis of ethnicity. In Kazakstan, "ethnicity" and "territory" are to remain separate as sources of institution-building. This principle is based on the assumption that institutional arrangements may affect the development of mental patterns. Ethnoterritorial units would endanger the project of affirming Kazakstan as a state, as minorities are concentrated in the borderlands adjacent to their countries of origin, Russia and Uzbekistan. A similar situation of potential irredentism exists for the Turkic-speaking and Muslim Uighurs. They live predominantly in the oblast of Taldykorgan, bordering on the Chinese province of Xinjiang, named East Turkestan and Uighurstan among nationalists.

Regional differences manifest themselves not only through the ethnic composition, but also through the varying influence of the three Kazak "super-tribes"—or *zhuz*—in various regions of the country. Identities and loyalties among Kazaks follow zhuzto a large extent. References to zhuz as the independent variable in a wider sense— encompassing all kinds of lineage awareness—in Kazak decision-making has become commonplace. Some writers, like Nurbulat Masanov, explain the important events in recent Kazakstani history in the light of zhuz rivalries.[109]

Although Masanov and others may be accused of exaggerating the importance of lineage, the intra-Kazak zhuz cleavages remain a challenge to Kazakstani nation-builders because zhuz is closely connected to territory and culture. Each of the three zhuz inhabit a distinct

---

[109] Masanov 1996, 47–50. I am grateful to Shirin Akiner for advising against emphasizing the zhuz overmuch. Though by no means denying the importance of clans, she finds zhuz a far more complex and fluid concept than reflected in textbooks which draw upon early twentieth-century "revivalist" historians.

historical territory and are distinguished by particular cultural traits. The Great Southern and dominant zhuz is culturally closer to other Central Asian cultures. The cultures of the Middle and Little zhuz—whose territories are to the northeast and west of the country—are characterized by a close intertwining with Russian culture. Despite the fact that zhuz play an important role, the zhuz have not been institutionalized. It is entirely an informal and analytical concept and is at present not a basis of claims for self-government of any kind. As the zhuz are regionally based on the fringes of the large, "empty" Steppes, their significance would partly be manifested in regional contention.

Some regions have significantly better access to material assets such as industries and raw materials, and local elites make use of them in much the same way as in the Russian Federation. The rayon-level units are too small to be able to develop into strong anti-centralist platforms. The oblast, on the other hand, may have the strength to do so.

The History of Territorial Self-government. Kazakstan has retained the three levels of substate administration which existed in Soviet times, as the table 5.14 depicts.

As early as the summer of 1991 a conflict broke out between the presidential authority and the elected authorities at the local—rayon—level.[110] The present maslikhats of Kazakstan were elected on 7 March 1994. According to the Constitution of 1995 the maslikhats (local, elected councils) are to constitute a local counterbalance to state power as represented by the akim and his apparatus, the akimat. In interviews with people working within the maslikhat, this elected council is often described as a "counterweight" (*protivoves*). At the same time they criticize central authorities for not allowing stronger local self-government. Spokespersons of stronger local and regional

TABLE 5.14 Type and Number of Administrative Units (1996)

Administrative unit	Number of units
Oblast: County	19
Rayon: Municipality	220
Aul, selo: Villages	Several thousands

---

[110] Dzhunusova 1996, 143–146.

self-government are able to voice their opinions despite the semi-authoritarian character of Kazakstan. Direct comparisons with the Russian federation are made:

> At times political brawls in Russian guberniia (regional) legislatures are shown on the TV, whereas our oblast maslikhat is unusually silent.[111]

The provisions for local self-government given in the 1995 Constitution confirm the separation of the local maslikhats from the local executive bodies.[112] This creates a situation of weak links between the self-government authorities and the local executive bodies. As a result the activities of the maslikhat are basically restricted to monitoring the activities of the local administration, and the head of this administration remains in the line of command of the President.

The maslikhat meetings are chaired by a secretary elected at each session for that specific term alone. The tasks of the secretary are purely technical; he is therefore in no position to offset the akim in any sense. The system of rotating the holder of the position of chairman further weakens the position of self-government in a country where the combination of personality and position often has proved to be far more important than the position itself.

The members of the maslikhats are elected in one-man constituencies. Interviews with maslikhat officials indicate that it is very seldom that more than one candidate runs in each constituency. Very often the candidates are picked by the akim among his most entrusted men heading enterprises, institutes, and schools. Candidates rarely run as party alternatives, and even if they do, their party affiliation is never indicated on the ballot.

Table 5.15, based on information submitted in the respective regions, gives an impression of the relative strength of the maslikhats (elected) as compared to the akimats (executive, central state representative):

TABLE 5.15 The Relative Size of Maslikhat and Akimat in Three Localities

Town	Members of the maslikhat	Employees in the maslikhat	Employees in the akimat
Kaskelen	36	6	250
Shymkent	47	7	73
Akmola	26	7	100

Source: Holm-Hansen 1997, 55.

---

[111] See *Kazakhstanskaia Pravda*, 15 June 1996, "Maslikhat ne stremitsia rulit'."

[112] *Konstitutsiia Respubliki Kazakhstan* 1995, Part VIII.

As for the administrative level above the rayon, the Soviet structure of districts—the oblasts—has been retained. Only minor changes have been made. In August 1990 the internal boundaries of Kazakstan were redrawn increasing the number of oblasts to 20 as against 18 previously. The new additions were designated Mangystau and Torgay, which are Kazak names. Land was taken from two Russian-named oblasts (in Kasak: oblys), Gur'ev and Tselinograd (later renamed Atyrau and Akmola, respectively). The number of oblasts where ethnic Kazaks were dominant was increased by two. Kazaks comprise a majority in Mangystau and are the largest single group in Torgay.[113]

In April 1997, Torgay oblast was split into two parts. One joined with Akmola/Astana, the new capital, the other with Kostanay. As a part of the same presidential decree Taldykorgan oblast was incorporated into Almaty oblast. As pointed out above, Taldykorgan has a significant Uighur population and borders the Xinjiang Autonomous Uighur Province of China.[114]

Since independence, a large number of Kazakstani cities, streets, etc. have been given new names.[115] In the majority of the cases a Kazak toponym was substituted for a Russian-sounding name, and the changes have therefore been interpreted as attempts to deprive certain places of their Russian identity. One of the officials involved in the renaming of place-names—officially designated the "toponymic policies"—claims that the names given by the forefathers should be respected. Russian transcriptions and loan translations of Kazak toponyms should therefore be replaced by Kazak versions as close as possible to the original ones.[116] The policy of naming places in post-Soviet Kazakstan has first of all affected the oblasts inhabited predominantly by ethnic Russians. Ural'sk oblast—which derived its name from its geographical location in the Urals, became "Western Kazakstan." Tselinograd—named after the Virgin Lands campaign of the fifties—got back its old name of Akmola, or Aqmola in the official Kazak transcription to Latin characters. In this spelling "k" has become "q." That the name of the country itself is written "Kazakstan" and not "Qazaqstan," forms an exception to the rule.

The Debate on Territorial Self-Government. The strict vertical line of command is frequently debated by scholars writing in Kazakstani newspapers and journals. Professor of philosophy, Alban Balgimbaev,

---

[113] Mangystau and Gur'ev had been split up earlier, in the 1970s, and been rejoined during the short reign of Gennadii Kolbin. See Olcott 1995, 258, The reasons behind these frequent reshufflings seem to have been initially economic but increasingly ethnopolitical.

[114] See RFE/RL Newsline, 24 April 1997, "Major overhaul of Kazak civil service."

[115] See, e.g., *Kazakhstanskaia Pravda*, 17 September 1992; *Sovety Kazakhstana*, 14 May 1993.

[116] Abdrakhmanov 1997.

writes that this line of command is useful for central and regional levels, but that local akims should be independent from akims higher in the hierarchy. Instead, they ought to be subordinated to the local councils. Professor Balgimbaev calls for a more distinct drawing of the lines between executive and representative power in order to let "civil society" and the political system coexist "to the benefit of the political ideal."[117]

Vladimir Gaaga, head of the organizational department of the Kokshetau oblast maslikhat, asserts that people were better off when "the local soviets had their own executive bodies. Then there was a direct link between making decisions and their implementation." His description of the present situation is that "We are called not to rule, but to transmit the mood of the population to the executive power."[118]

One viewpoint often represented in the Kazakstani debate—well-known in contemporary West European debates on similar issues—portrays the provinces as the motors of development. In a newspaper article the leader of the apparatus of the akim of South Kazakstan oblast, Nurdaulet Sarsenov, argues in favor of taking into account the specificities of each region. He argues in favor of decentralization of economic decision-making: "Decentralization of economic administration assumes that each region lives within the limits of its budgetary revenues."[119]

This article was followed up by another where the author warns against allowing the akim and the akimat to take the lead in development questions. Kazakstan does not need miniature replica of the presidential vertikal', he says. He distinguishes between the methods of achieving common state goals (strictly bureaucratic) and regional goals (more flexible). Seemingly inspired by contemporary Western models, the author suggests that coordinating committees should be set up in which representatives from the central authorities and the state sector, the local authorities, local industry and business, and local inhabitants could meet to coordinate local development projects.[120]

Territorial self-government in Kazakstan does not seem to form a platform for ethnopolitics. A vocal self-government lobby is clearly visible, but the concerns of its spokespersons are decentralization and increased power to the elected bodies. Ethnopolitical goals are not mentioned. As in the case of Parliament, however, the central authorities

---

[117] See *Kazakhstanskaia Pravda*, 13 June 1996, "Politicheskaia sistema: Ideal i real'nost'."

[118] See *Kazakhstanskaia Pravda*, 15 June 1996, "Maslikhat ne stremitsia rulit'."

[119] See *Kazakhstanskaia Pravda*, 27 June 1996, "Na smenu zhestkoi tsentralizatsii idet initsiativa regionov."

[120] See *Kazakhstanaia Pravda*, 20 August 1996, "Na smenu zhestkoi tsentralizatsii idet ...zhestkaia tsentralizatsiia?"

around the President do not seem willing to take the risk of channeling state loyalty from the citizens to institutions of territorial self-government. They evidently fear that local elites, out of the reach of the presidential line of command, might be too zealous in their application of this loyalty.

Consultative Bodies:
Assembly of the Nationalities of Kazakstan

On 1 March 1995 the President issued a decree calling for the establishment of a new consultative body, the Assembly of Peoples of Kazakstan. Its objectives were to promote the revival of the various ethnic groups living in Kazakstan and to ensure that the interests of these groups are taken into consideration when laws were drawn up. When parliament was dissolved in March 1995 the President was accused of planning a dictatorship with a loyal Assembly of Peoples to serve as a fake parliament. And in fact, at its first meeting on 24 March 1995, the Assembly of Peoples suggested a referendum on the prolongation of the term of office of the president until the year 2000. Such a referendum was indeed held late in April and the proposal received overwhelming support.

Today, the Assembly of Peoples may be perceived as a parallel—and partly rival—*advisory* structure to the weak representative bodies, the Parliament and the maslikhats. The members of the Small Assembly of Peoples at the district level and the Assembly of the Nationalities at the national level are selected from among the leaders of the various national-cultural centers. They are nominated by the centers, but confirmed by the akim and the President. These assemblies are to serve as "advisory-consultative" bodies for the President and the akims, as the President himself notes: "In the most difficult times the Assembly has served as an body of genuine, popular representation."[121] The President is here referring to the period in 1995 when he had dissolved the Parliament. But apart from being alternative institutions of—indirectly elected—popular representation, the main task of the assemblies is to foster "Harmony and Unity."

Not surprisingly, the Assemblies have been involved in the processes of formulating a state ideology. Interestingly, Nazarbaev chose a highly charged event for the Assembly's first activity. The Assembly was to participate in the memorial day celebrations of the historical pact entered into by the three zhuz leaders Tole bi, Kazybek bi, and

---

[121] Nazarbaev 1996, 173.

Aytek bi that was to take place in the town of Ordabasy in the oblast of South Kazakstan. Ordabasy had been chosen for this event because, in this place 200 years ago, representatives of the three Kazak zhuz gathered under the leadership of the great *batyrs* (Kazak: heroic warriors) in order to unite in the struggle against the invasion of the Dzhungan khanate. "This fusion of forces gave the nation the strength to win," Nazarbaev asserted.[122] By such actions Nazarbaev "builds the nation" in two senses, both by speaking to the nationalities of Kazakstan, and by expressing clear statements in favor of unity across the intra-Kazak zhuz branches.

The Assembly has played a prominent role in several national celebrations. Not all celebrations are of equal interest to all Kazakstani citizens, and by filtering them through the Assembly the authorities dampen the impression that they are totally organized from above, while enhancing the impression that they concern more people than the ethnic segment directly related to the commemoration. One example is the anniversary of 1,100 years of the Slavonic literary language. Formally a result of a suggestion by the Archbishop of Almaty and Semipalatinsk this event was celebrated with the patronage of the Assembly of Peoples. Likewise the 150th anniversary of the birth of Abai, the "father of Kazak literary language" and hero of Middle zhuz Kazaks especially, was celebrated under the aegis of the national-cultural centers.

Each oblast, city/town, and rayon administration is obliged to work out systems for effective contact with the national-cultural centers of the various ethnic groups in order to satisfy the national demands in their region, the President said in his ideological speech in 1993. Such contacts are now assured by the oblast-level Small Assemblies of the Nationalities which work in close contact with a department established under the oblast akim to deal with these questions.

The members of the Small Assemblies of Nationalities are chosen on the recommendation of the national-cultural centers and other nongovernmental organizations. These assemblies exist at oblast level and formally serve as advisory bodies for the akim.

The President often plays the role of "protector" of the ethnic groups in Kazakstan, i.e. the smaller ones. At the founding meeting of the Assembly of Peoples in March 1995 the President emphasized the role of the non-Kazak, non-Russian parts of the population, which, according to the President, amount to 20 percent of the population. In order to reach this figure he was obliged to include Belarusians and Ukrainians

---

[122] See *Sovety Kazakhstana*, 13 May 1993: "Nursultan Nazarbaev: 'Nashi orientiry— konsolidatsiia, obshchestvennyi progress i sotsial'noe partnerstvo.'"

as non-Russians, which is a dubious maneuver in the Kazakstani setting. In addition, he also had to disregard the fact that most diaspora nationalities have been thoroughly Russified. Germans, Poles, and Koreans have to attend language courses to be able to speak their mother tongue.

Some nationalities have specific problems originating in the recent past. Individuals belonging to nationalities that had been accused of collective treason during the last World War and deported to Kazakstan, such as Poles, Kurds, Germans, Meskhetian Turks, Chechens, and others, are eligible for state-funded compensation. The national-cultural centers may be important helpers in the rewriting of history and the rehabilitation of people from these nationalities.

The central administration of the Assembly of Peoples has seven employees and forms a part of the presidential apparatus. The deputy head of the secretariat of the Assembly of Peoples, Oleg Dymov, an ethnic Bulgarian, has termed the system "an institution of diplomacy of the peoples enabling the nationalities to regulate conflicts themselves."[123] Traditionally hostile ethnic groups are represented by people who have to work on the same floor in the same building, relating to the same institutions within the public administration, following the same rules. The system of ethnic self-government, however, will probably have little influence on any conflicts arising between the two large ethnic groups in the country, Russians and Kazaks. This conundrum is an aspect of the larger conflict between the well-established Russian and post-Soviet culture on the one hand and the burgeoning Kazak state-bearing culture on the other. For the prevention of other possible conflicts, however, it may be an effective tool. In Central Asia, outbursts of ethnic violence have so far almost invariably involved people from smaller, Asian nationalities, like the Meskhetian Turks, not the larger nontitular groups. The prevalence of small nationalities in the Kazakstani system of ethnocultural self-government induces ethno-leaders of these nationalities to act through the institutions.

Very often, ethnocultural leaders have problems attracting their potential flocks. Among the material instruments making the Assembly of Peoples interesting to parts of the population, is the system of university entry quotas for students registered as belonging to "smaller nationalities," (officially termed "representatives of national minorities").[124]

---

[123] Author's interview in Almaty 27 September 1996 with Oleg Grigorevich Dymov, deputy head of the executive secretariat of the Assembly of Peoples of Kazakstan.
[124] Author's interview with Dymov.

Ten percent of all student places at the universities are reserved for this category of students. In the 1995–96 school year—the first year of the quota system—a total of 2,682 students were accepted on the basis of quota distributions. All would-be students, regardless of ethnic background, compete for the remaining 90 percent of the places. This means that all institutions of higher learning have to reserve ten percent of their places for minorities. Apparently, this has not been very popular among faculty heads. An indication of this is that in order to force all universities, regardless of institutional links, to apply the quota system in its second year, a special "law of governmental rank" was passed.[125]

The members of the admission committees administering the quota system are not professionals from the universities, but leaders of the national-cultural centers. This is quite significant as it gives these officially sanctioned ethnocultural leaders real power. It helps them create the ethnocultural communities they can hardly be said to have had hitherto. Individuals registered as belonging to the smaller nationalities in Kazakstan usually do not identify very strongly with their ethnic affiliation, but rather see themselves as members of the greater Russophone community. Under the quota system young people may begin to feel more attached to their official ethnicity since it is thanks to it that their entry to university may be secured.

Non-State Organizations

A host of civic organizations has been set up in Kazakstan since the late eighties. They are officially registered in accordance with specific laws for NGOs (*obshchestvennye organizatsii*), trade unions, and religious organizations. All civic organizations operating at a national level in Kazakstan have to be centrally registered with the Ministry of Justice. Organizations with a regional scope of activities are registered at the regional level. About 600 organizations (trade unions, and organizations for veterans, women, youth, etc.) are registered at the national level, whereas 3,000 organizations are registered at the regional level.[126]

---

[125] See *Kazakstanskaia Pravda*, 18 May 1996 "V vuz—s 'blagosloveniia' Assamblei Narodov Kazakhstana."

[126] Author's interview with Ms Mugul'sum Mukhametkazievna Amirova 20 November 1995. Ms Amirova is the head of the department dealing with NGOs in the Ministry of Justice.

Political Parties

The relative freedom for parties to organize and voice their criticism in Kazakstan may serve an integrative purpose. Even if parties are small and insignificant they may have symbolic value by indicating that everybody is part of the state. If the state allows relatively radical criticism, then there is reason to feel at home.[127]

However, when it comes to direct policy-making, nongovernmental, or nonstate, organizations do not play any significant role in Kazakstan. Political parties do not mobilize large followings. The only exception to this is the Communist Party of Kazakstan, which has a genuine mass basis, and claims to have 45,000 members. In 1995, 22.7 percent of CPK members were ethnic Kazaks, while more than 50 percent were Russians.[128] Today, the chairman of the party, himself an ethnic Kazak, claims the party is equally strong among Russians and Kazaks. However, under no circumstances is he in favor of diluting or eradicating ethnic identities: "National feelings come from the blood. They are congenital," he said.[129] The Communist Party is strongly in favor of strengthening the representative branch of power.

The most influential party, however, is not CPK but the Party of National Unity of Kazakstan (*Partiia Narodnogo Edinstva Kazakhstana* or PNEK). In 1995, 43.2 percent of its members were Kazaks.[130] This party is genuinely a "nomenclatura" creation, boasting the great administrative capabilities of its candidates. PNEK is pro-government and pro-President, and offers an additional coordinating network for central power-holders. It is a party for policy output, not voter input. Its main goals are stability, interethnic harmony, democracy, and a social market economy. "At the present, we are oriented toward all social strata, but after the success of economic reforms, we will become a party of the middle classes," the vice-chair of the party claims.[131]

The Party National Congress of Kazakstan (*Partiia Narodnyi Kongress Kazakhstana* or PNKK) is an heir to a genuinely nonstate

---

[127] The human rights activist and social democrat Evgenii Zhovtis is pessimistic with regard to the future of parties and NGOs in Kazakstan after the revision of the laws pertaining to social organisations in 1996. The new laws, he maintains, are old-fashioned, leaving merely decorative tasks to parties and groups. Author's interview in Almaty, 18 September 1996.

[128] Babakumarov, Buluktaev and Kusherbaev 1995, 59.

[129] Author's interview in Almaty, 19 September 1996 with Serikbolsyn Abdil'gaevich Abdil'din.

[130] Babakumarov, Buluktaev and Kusherbaev 1995, 59.

[131] Author's interview in Almaty, 21 November 1995 with Sergei A. Diachenko.

organization of the late 1980s, the Nevada-Semipalatinsk movement. This movement campaigned against nuclear tests in both the U.S. and in Kazakstan, and is widely accredited for the closure of the test site in Semipalatinsk. The PNKK was heavily dependent upon the figure of Olzhas Suleimenov, a popular poet, who was appointed ambassador to Rome. This was a shrewd move of the President by which he weakened one of the main oppositional groups. PNEK, like the Socialists, started out as one of his main supporters.[132]

At the outset, the Socialist Party was the presidential party *par excellence*. A legal heir to the Communist Party, it tried to find a place for itself in the new state structures, but soon lost its close contacts with the President. The Socialist Party has developed into one of the oppositional forces, focusing on economic and social policies.

Azamat (which is Kazak for "Citizen"), is a kind of Popular Front, rallying nonradical but outspoken critics of the presidential policies. The respected sinologist and son of a popular national author, Murat Auezov, is one of the three chairmen of Azamat. Auezov is considered the main personality of this front whose membership is slight. His cochairman, Petr Svoik, is also vice-chairman of the Socialist Party and perhaps the most profiled non-Kazak politician in the country. Azamat is a loose alliance of various groups and movements, such the Independent Trade Unions, and might, in the event of a change of guards in the President's office, form an alternative power elite.

Kazak nationalist parties and groups, like Zheltoqsan, Azat, and Alash, were very active in the first years after independence, but have later become almost invisible. Azat has not issued any regular publications since 1993. The main objective of these groups has been Kazakification of the state, mixed with suspicion of foreign investments. Some groups, like Alash, are strongly in favor of pan-Turkic unity. Alash has stated that it aims at the creation of an Islamic pan-Turkic state from Vladivostok to Istanbul. It is in favor of sending Russians "back" to Russia. The group has taken its name from Alash, the legendary forefather of the Kazaks and father of three sons named Alchin (Small Horde), Aktol (Middle Horde) and Usun (Great Horde).

The function of the Kazak nationalist groups has changed since the late eighties and early nineties. As spokespersons of the "Kazak cause," they started out as defenders of a minority in the Soviet Union,

---

[132] Suleimenov got into trouble with the Soviet authorities in 1975 after having written *Az i ia* (which in medieval Russian can be read either as *Alpha and Omega* and *I and me*. At the same time it sounds like *Asia* in modern Russian). In this work he tried to demonstrate the common roots of Kazak and Turkish cultures. In 1989 he was a co-founder of the Nevada-Semipalatinsk movement. One of Suleimenov's catch phrases is "You don't light the torch of freedom in a powder keg."

but suddenly found themselves as defenders of a dominant ethnic group in the middle of a nation-building process. Moreover, they now have to play the role of defending the "winning cause" without being let into the circles of power. The Kazak nationalists live at the political fringes of nation-building Kazakstan.

Some Kazakstani critics of nation-building policies in Kazakstan explain the apparent decline of the Kazak nationalist groups by their very success. Their goal of the Kazakification of the state has been achieved, according to a semi-dissident political scientist from Semipalatinsk.[133] Today, the Kazak nationalist groups focus on social degradation resulting from the economic reform policies of the present authorities. "Our relations to the nomenclatura are tense, due to the fact that people are hungry," says one of the founders of Zheltoqsan, now an ideologist in Azat. In the autumn of 1996 Azat held talks with other opposition groups, such as Azamat and the Communists, in order to find a common ground for mobilizing on the basis of social grievances in the population.[134] One year later news agencies reported that an odd group of organizations had gathered to discuss the establishment of an opposition front. The Kazak nationalist party Azat stood shoulder by shoulder with Russian nationalist Lad. Azamat, the Communist Party and the Socialist Party also took part. Apparently nonethnic concerns were in the forefront.

At the other end of the spectrum, in terms of both economic and ethnic policies, but still within the Kazak community, one finds the *Novoe Pokolenie* (New Generation). Novoe Pokolenie has been labeled the movement of Russian-speaking Kazaks. The business-like character of the movement is evident.[135] Its founding declaration of February 1995 was signed by representatives of the largest companies of Kazakstan, such as Alemsistem, Butia, Astana-Holding and others.[136] The combination of business success and rejection of ethnification is not particular for Kazakstan, and parties and groups of this kind are found also in other former Soviet republics. However, the Russification of the indigenous elite was deeper in Kazakstan than in most other Soviet republics, and the social basis for Novoe Pokolenie is therefore potentially strong.

Political parties in Kazakstan are working under difficult conditions, due to both unsettled rules for their activities and to low levels of citizen participation. Since independence most of the relatively

---

[133] Author's interview in Semipalatinsk 21 September 1996 with Leonid Anatol'evich Syromiatnikov.

[134] Author's interview in Almaty 19 September 1996 with Khasen Kozhakhmetov.

[135] See *Karavan*, 17 February 1995, "Bez grafy 'natsional'nost'."

[136] Dzhunusova 1996, 161.

influential parties have turned their back on the President. This holds
true for such different groups as the Socialist Party, PNKK, and the
Kazak nationalist groups.

Trade Unions

A major issue in Kazakstani politics is social security. Wage and
pension arrears are no less widespread in Kazakstan than in the other
parts of the post-Soviet realm. Strikes and protests are frequent. In
mid-October 1996 a Day of Poverty was arranged all over Kazakstan to
protest the drastic decline in real income suffered by large groups of the
population. The President made a speech on 5 November in which he
criticized the trade unions and nonstate organizations for not behaving
responsibly in a difficult phase of Kazakstan's history.

Since the mid-nineties open political unrest in Kazakstan has been
centered around economic and social policies. Demonstrations, strikes,
and road blockades are frequent. The largest demonstration in
Kazakstan since independence was held on 30 May 1997. Several
thousand demonstrators protested wage arrears and price hikes for
heat, electricity, water and rent. The radical character of the
demonstrations was underscored by slogans calling for the resignation of
the Parliament and the President. Nazarbaev was called a false leader
of the Kazak nation.[137]

Trade unions are at variance with the government over the unemployment figures, which are at an unruffling four percent according to
official statistics. The Federation of Trade Unions holds the unemployment rate to be around 25–28 percent.[138]

Independent trade unions formed a part of the early de-Sovietizing
institutions in Kazakstan. The Kazakstan Independent Trade Union
Center and *Birlesu* were founded on November 1–2 1989 as a
"sociopolitical organization" uniting enterprise and cooperative managers, private farmers, and workers. After the unsuccessful *coup d'état*
in Moscow in August 1991 *Birlesu* joined with several independent trade
unions forming a new association called *Proftsentr*. The leader of *Birlesu*, Leonid Solomin, was elected chairman of this new organization.

The combination of business and labor in one organization, called the
Independent Trade Union to distinguish it from the old trade unions, is a
commonplace in the former state-socialist world, reflecting the special
situation of having to build market mechanisms and private enterprises

---

[137] See *RFE/RL Newsline*, 30 May 1997.
[138] *RFE/RL Newsline*, 26 January 1998.

and to defend worker interests. At the same time it continues the practice of the old state-controlled unions in which both managerial staff and ordinary workers had to be members.

The strike in the mines of Kentau in the province of Southern Kazakstan in the summer of 1992 is an example of how the national question and the labor question converge. Here, a strike committee was formed by independent trade unionists. A Kazak, A. Kozakhmetov, and a Russian, Gennadii Nikitin, were elected co-chairs of the committee. At the suggestion of Nikitin, Kozakhmetov was elected first co-chair, as Nikitin believed this post should be held by an ethnic Kazak. This was done to please Kazak tili which not only cultivates and promotes the Kazak language, but also monitors vacant leading positions and makes loud protests if they are not filled by ethnic Kazaks. Reportedly, the sentiment among the workers on strike were clearly non-nationalist: "We all work together and have common interests. I like my Russian co-worker more than a Kazak from the plant administration," one Kazak worker said.[139]

National-Cultural Centers

Ethnopolitical leaders in Kazakstan have no legal means permitting them to exploit territory as a rhetorical platform for their activities. Ethnicity is strictly separated from territorial units in Kazakstan due to the principle of the unity of the state. Instead, a system of nonterritorial, ethnocultural self-government has been established under the auspices of the President.

The basic units in the system of ethnocultural self-government are the national-cultural centers that legally are nongovernmental organizations, independent of the state. The centers have exclusively cultural, not political, tasks, and are not assigned any formal authority in their respective ethnic communities. Not surprisingly, representatives of the national-cultural centers offer diverging answers as to the nationality policies of the present Kazakstani leadership.[140]

Unlike territorial self-government the system of ethnonational self-government is the apple of the eye of the President and plays a significant role in his plans for regulating ethnicity. In his May 1993 speech Nazarbaev said that the role of the national-cultural centers should be

[139] See *Central Asia Monitor*, No. 5 1992, "Strikes in Kazakstan: An Advisor's Account." This article is a personal report from the US AFL-CIO representative Ludmila Alexeeva.

[140] Based on author's interviews in November 1995 and May/June 1996 with representatives for national-cultural centers of the local Poles, Meskhetian Turks, Chechens, Russians (Lad), Armenians, and Uighurs.

to achieve interethnic harmony. Therefore, the centers of the ethnic groups will be supported by the state. In Nazarbaev's words these centers

> constitute the heart of the preservation of national self-consciousness, or-
> ganizational mechanisms for support and development of national tradi-
> tions, cultures, and the original spirituality of the nations and national
> groups. These national-cultural centers have to take the initiative in achiev-
> ing harmony between people not only of different nationalities, but also of
> different religious confessions.[141]

National-cultural centers have been operating since 1991, officially registered with the Ministry of Justice since 1992. They have to undergo a thorough procedure before being allowed to register.[142] Most registrations pass without any problems as long as the centers stick to some basic rules. These rules are: nonseparatism, nonracism, and nonhatred. To "clean up the system" it was decided in December 1995 that registration of all national-cultural centers had to be made anew.

The national-cultural centers work in close contact with the administration of the oblast akim. In the apparatus of the akim there is a dedicated department dealing with the local Small Assembly of Peoples. The Department for Internal Policies deals with the national-cultural centers. Both departments are part of the presidential vertikal', which underscores the strong ties between the centers and the President.

All ethnic groups of Kazakstan enjoy the same right to establish national-cultural centers, but have very different degrees of access to external resources. Germans, Koreans, Poles, Jews, and Turks have good ties with the foreign service's cultural departments and the ministries of education of their respective "homelands."

Chechens, Tatars, and Uighurs may have a "homeland," but not one which can act as a protector or patron. Chechen and Uighur groups do not easily fit into the systems of ethnocultural self-government as they often adopt positions that are contrary to those of Kazakstan's main neighbors. This is the case in the Chechen-Moscow conflict and the problems in the Chinese province of Xinjiang. Ethnocultural leaders of all these nationalities, however, stress the importance of their "homeland" abroad, ranging from Germany to "East Turkestan" (the Xinjiang province of China).

---

[141] See *Sovety Kazakhstana*, 13 May 1993: "Nursultan Nazarbaev: 'Nashi orientiry— kon-solidatsiia, obshchestvennyi progress i sotsial'noe partnerstvo."

[142] Author's interview with Ms Mugul'sum Mukhametkazieva Amirova, head of the department in charge of registration of NGOs at the Ministry of Justice, 20 November 1995 in Almaty.

It is noteworthy that most leaders of national-cultural centers pay homage to the main elements in Nazarbaev's rhetoric in interviews, etc., most often, though, by referring to the arch-Soviet concept of *druzhba narodov* —the friendship of the peoples. There are also remnants of the Soviet times in the way leaders of the centers perceive themselves. The leader of the Almaty city Uighur center told me that the centers do a lot of work for the state without remuneration. He particularly mentioned their activities in the area of education and their "work with people, and the efforts we make in explaining the policies of the government. Earlier, party functionaries received wages to do this. We do not get anything."[143]

National-Cultural Centers: Instruments for Multiple Re-Ethnification

The system of national-cultural centers and assemblies of the nationalities is one of the specificities of the Kazakstani set-up of political institutions. The centers function along the semidemocratic lines that characterize Kazakstan. They are not entirely nonstate and self-governmental, neither are they a part of the state apparatus. They are not professional advisory or consultative bodies. Nevertheless, they are useful tools in the communication between the authorities and the population. For issues pertaining to ethnicity (language, festivals, compensation for oppressed people, etc.) the centers' task is to represent the people in accordance with ethnic criteria, and bring their wishes to the President through the assemblies. At the same time, the authorities make use of the centers in their efforts to implement the doctrine of multi-ethnicity through multiple re-ethnification. This system is dependent upon willing ethnopolitical elites. If these elites were to start to demand a territory of their own, as they became wont to during Soviet times, they may opt for federalization or secession. In that case, the Kazakstani system of ethnocultural self-government would fall apart.

The national-cultural centers are useful in helping the authorities to achieve some of their main objectives. First, the centers help the authorities in *coopting* would-be leaders. Ethnopolitical counterelites often describe the state in which they live as oppressive and the nationalizing processes as alienating "their ethnic group." Their claims may be more or less accurate, but minority leaders may feel dependent upon such an image to gain support among their potential followers. The

---

[143] Interview with Rakhimzhan Makhpirovich Kazimov, Almaty, 31 May 1996.

streamlined system of ethnic representation in Kazakstan is well suited to prevent processes of this kind, at least among ethnic leaders of small nationalities. The project of asserting the Kazak character of the Kazakstani state is concomitant with the revival and promotion of small-nation ethnicity also for other nationalities.

The system of ethnocultural self-government offers numerous positions for local, regional, and national elites, which try to position themselves as spokesmen of their respective ethnic group. So far, the system seems to have been able to absorb this category of leaders. In Kazakstan there is a widespread belief—which is quite well-founded—that problems are first of all solved in direct conversations with the President or his representatives. In interviews with leaders of national-cultural centers it was often mentioned that the present system gives them opportunities to speak directly with the President, or, more often, his representatives. For a potential political leader it is therefore very important to be able to portray himself as one who has access to the President or at least to his vertical power line. This is exactly what the assemblies offer as they are *pri Prezidente* ("under the President").

The political capital earned from contacts with the presidential apparatus is complete with direct economic remuneration. This applies in particular to the leaders of so-called diaspora nationalities. There are direct material benefits to be gained from being in contact with the "Motherland," be it Korea, Germany, Israel, Turkey, or Poland. One example of this is the hand the ethnocultural leaders have in the game of whom to send for representation or education in the "homeland." This is the kind of power people in post-Soviet societies know how to relate to. For the Kazakstani authorities the goodwill won in Germany, Korea, Turkey, and Poland each time a local folklore group performs is of great importance.

Second, *re-ethnification* is among the main objectives of the nationality policies pursued by the present regime. In Kazakstan, ethnic representation is confined to the national-cultural centers, which seek to revive and underscore the meaning of the "original" ethnic adherence of each citizen. National-cultural centers contribute to the popularization of the idea that ethnicity is, or rather should be, fixed once and for all.

The names of the local national-cultural centers clearly reflect how their founders think. German centers are usually called "Wiedergeburt." The Union of Polish centers is named "Wiez" (the Link) and the Turkish Union is simply called "Türkiye." When asked about their main tasks the leaders of the centers mention "language training," and "the revival and cultivation of national traditions." This conforms with the Concept on Language Policies, which assigns the "language-building" of the smaller tongues to the national-cultural centers in cooperation with ethnic homelands.[144]

If successful, the activities of the national-cultural centers will "roll back" the influence of Russian culture. The Russophone community of Kazakstan will be split up. The effect of the work of the national-cultural centers is not only that they separate ethnic issues from political and territorial claims. They also contribute to the revival of dormant or by-passed ethnic sentiments.

This strategy, however, is risky. First of all because it may trigger counteractions. Second, because it means destroying the adhesive that already binds Kazakstani citizens together. This adhesive consists of the Russian language which everyone is able to use, and in a common post-Soviet framework of references connected with the experiences of living in Kazakstan right now. This cultural common denominator for people from all ethnic groups could have formed the basis for a Kazakstani identity.

Conclusions

Some states are deprived of the possibility of covering only one, or basically one, nationality. Kazakstan is one of them, simply because no ethnic group has a substantial majority. Therefore, Kazakstan often has been presented as a new state dependent on its ability to develop supraethnic loyalties. And, indeed, in the period immediately following independence, the state symbols were focused upon as common rallying points for inhabitants of all ethnic backgrounds.

The picture of a state forced by circumstances to reject the ethnic model of nation-building, was established. However, beneath the civic rhetoric, many observers were able to detect practices of quite another kind. Domestic critics have accused the state apparatus of undertaking a zealous Kazakification, even to the extent of making Kazakstan an ethnocracy.[145]

My analysis of the disputes over some selected political issues (citizenship, state language), of the development of core political institutions (executive, representative, advisory, and nonstate) as well as of official doctrinal statements, lead to the conclusion that Kazakstani nation-builders are attempting to achieve several incompatible goals at the same time. They are trying simultaneously to ethnify the state

---

[144] See *Kazakhstanskaia Pravda*, 6 November 1996, "Kontseptsiia iazykovoi politiki Respubliki Kazakhstan."

[145] Amrelukov and Masanov 1994, 108–9; Masanov 1995, 121–24.

and to integrate the population on a supraethnic basis. Furthermore, they implement policies which presuppose clear ethnic identities in the population, whereas such clarity is far from evident in all cases.

Basically, Kazakstan is resolved to be a unitary state in which all kinds of internal ethnoterritorial units are anathema. The new and rebuilt state institutions are all included in, or in practice subordinated to, a strictly vertical command line headed by the President. The set-up of Kazakstan's political institutions is designed for policy output rather than for citizen input. However, contrary to most other Central Asian republics, there are institutions of territorial self-government that are able to assert themselves, at least verbally, when confronted with the "vertical line of command" of the President. Also, while weak, the Parliament is not totally bridled by the presidential apparatus. There are political parties, nonstate organizations, and trade unions in Kazakstan which in practice define their own goals and carry out activities that would have been unthinkable in, say, Uzbekistan.

To some extent, Kazakstan's political system is open for participation from others than those belonging to the vertical power structures of the President. Therefore there are tendencies, although weak, of inhabitants approaching the political institutions actively as citizens. This approach competes with the passive ethnic approach, where individuals relate to the state through their ethnicities, as passive, "inborn" members of the community. The decisive channel of influence nevertheless remains the presidential vertical. This fact eases the nation-building penetration of institutions into all nooks and crannies of the new state. The result is that the development of strong localist political platforms is restrained.

The explicit principle of nonethnicity which is applied to the core political institutions is not matched by a similar clarity as to the definition of the "people" of Kazakstan. Officially, Kazakstan is portrayed as a nation-state for Kazaks *and* as a multinational community at the same time.

The multinational model has two disparate meanings. One of them in a purely civic way states that the citizens form one state irrespective of their ethnic background, and "the belonging to it appears for them as the main identity marker," as stated in one doctrinal document.[146] This integrative definition of multiethnicity is confronted by a multiple re-ethnification definition, in which all residents are perceived as representatives of their "original" ethnic group. I will argue that this definition hardly matches the actual situation of Kazakstan, where large parts of the population have complex ethnic identities, and very few

---

[146] *Kontseptsiia formirovaniia* 1996, 26.

practice a "purist" approach to these issues in their daily lives. Nevertheless, rigid, fixed ethnicities and ethnically defined nation-states are portrayed as "logical" and "natural" by the Kazakstani nation-builders.

In one of the doctrinal documents it is explicitly stated that "the strategy of ethnocultural education is geared toward the achievement of two mutually linked goals: ethnic identification and state integration."[147] Calls made by central state nation-builders for a diversification of the population through an all-out re-ethnification may seem surprising. The aim of nation-building is, one would suppose, to create, not to scale down, common identities.

The apparent discrepancy stemming from the strong insistence on nonethnicity in state institutions combined with an equally strong insistence that "original" ethnicities matter, is partly solved by the establishment of ethnocultural advisory bodies to the President. *National-cultural centers* for the various ethnic groups represented in Kazakstan have been set up as nonstate organizations to preserve, promote, and develop national languages and traditions. At regional and national levels, these centers form advisory *Assemblies of the Nationalities*. These bodies are working directly with the regional akims and the President, and represent an alternative to the popularly elected channels of influence (local and regional maslikhats and the parliament). Even if the smaller nationalities are the focus of most of the rhetorics connected with these ethnocultural activities, also Kazak and Russian groups take part.

The seemingly weak and insignificant national-cultural centers may play an important role in preventing an ethnification of politics in Kazakstan. So far, the issues in Kazakstan which have brought the political temperature to boiling point (strikes, road blockades, demonstrations) have primarily been related to cross-ethnic economic and social problems. Equally open to all ethnic groups the national-cultural centers have first of all activated would-be ethnocultural leaders of the smaller ethnic groups.

In Kazakstan, the smaller ethnic groups potentially play a strategic role. In Central Asia ethnic violence has mostly involved people of smaller ethnicities. Through the set-up of national-cultural centers and Assemblies of Nationalities ethnocultural leaders have a framework for ethnopolitical diplomacy and reconciliation.

However, as my treatise shows, the purpose of the national-cultural centers is to strengthen ethnic identities and they may thereby also prepare the ground for ethnic conflicts. Being ethnic pays, not only for

---

[147] *Kontseptsiia etnokul'turnogo* 1996.

the center leaders themselves, but also for the average youngster, as a special quota system helps people from the smaller ethnic groups into the universities. The ethnocultural leaders have a say about whom to admit to the universities under these quotas, which make up ten percent of the total number of students at a given faculty. The function as middleman between Kazakstan and economically important states, like Germany or Korea, played by the leaders of the ethnocultural centers, confers great honor. The role as advisors to the President and his representatives further enhances the significance of the ethnoleaders.

Furthermore, the national-cultural centers operate with an explicit goal of ethnocultural revival. If the smaller ethnic groups of Kazakstan ever get reanimated, it would be tantamount to 20 percent of the Kazakstani population breaking away from the Russophone community. From an ethnically defined nation-building perspective this would be a gain as the relative strength of the ethnically revived Kazaks would increase.

My conclusion is that the Kazakstani system of ethnocultural self-government may look like overcoming ethnicity, but in practice it is creating and recreating ethnic boundaries between people.

Kazakstan follows the tracks of ethnically focused nation-building despite the fact that no ethnic group constitutes a majority of the population. The Kazakstani combination is one of *multiple re-ethnification*. Not only the titular nationality, but all nationalities, are to be revived. The application of a civic model, with its emphasis on political institutions and the contents of citizenship, would have been a striking novelty in the post-Soviet area.

6

Attitudinal and Linguistic Integration in Kazakstan and Latvia

Irina Malkova, Pål Kolstø, and Hans Olav Melberg

Superordinate / Subordinate Relationships

As discussed in Chapter 3 we understand by ethnic integration societal and political processes facilitating greater voluntary participation of ethnic minorities in society at large. The subordinate groups must themselves be interested such participation and the superordinate (dominant) group must accept it. A high degree of integration is achieved when the resultant vector of both groups is "centripetal" in Schermerhorn's sense of the word.

Integration is multidimensional, involving both cultural and structural (organizational and political) aspects. Below, we will examine the attitudinal preconditions for social integration in Latvia and Kazakstan, by identifying some trends in the attitudes and perceptions of both the titular nationality and the nontitulars in these two countries. This we do on the basis of large-scale surveys conducted in both countries.[1] Some of the questions in our questionnaires touched upon structural incorporation in Schermerhorn's sense, others upon cultural trends.

---

[1] For a methodological description of these surveys, see the appendix to this chapter.

TABLE 6.1 Time of Residence (proportion of total in percent) [2]

Time of residence	Latvia	Kazakstan
less than 3 years	1.8	1.6
from 4 to 10 years	3.0	1.3
more than 10 years, but not whole life	20.7	18.9
since birth	74.3	77.9
D/K	0.3	0.3
A/F	1,563	1,000

Demographic Stability

As pointed out in Chapter 5, several official Kazakstani and Latvian documents distinguish between the indigenous population on the one hand (the Kazaks / the Latvians) and the nontitular population on the other. The latter half is often referred to as "the immigrant population." We wanted to find out to what degree this dichotomy corresponds with the actual demographic make-up of the countries, and asked how long the respondents had been living in their present country of residence (Table 6.1).

The distribution of responses in both countries is remarkably similar. It appears that fresh immigration to Kazakstan and Latvia has practically stopped. The vast majority of permanent residents are born and raised in the country in which they are now living.[3]

A Nation of Minorities?

As a first inroad into the relationship between superordinates/subordinates in Latvian and Kazakstani society we tried to identify the minority groups in each society. We first addressed the question "from within," asking the respondents if they consider themselves to be a member of a minority, then "from without," asking whom they regard as belonging to the minorities.

To the question "Do you consider that you belong to an ethnic minority?" we received the following replies (Table 6.2).

---

[2] In the following, the response categories "don't know" and "no answer" will be abbreviated as "D/K" and "N/A." The entry "A/F" in the last row of the column will give the absolute figures from which the percentages have been calculated.

[3] The indigenization of the nontitular nationality in Kazakstan and Latvian may increase further in the future as a result of outmigration: Those who arrived last are often also most prone to leave first. As a result, the percentages of nontitulars with deep historical roots in the country increase among those who stay behind (Kolstø 1996b).

TABLE 6.2 Do You Consider That You Belong to an Ethnic Minority?

	Latvia	*Kazakstan*
yes	31.1	13.8
no	55.3	71.4
D/K	13.6	14.6
A/F	1,563	1,000

TABLE 6.3 Do You Consider That You Belong to an Ethnic Minority in Kazakstan?—Ethnic Breakdown[a]

	Kaz	*Rus*	*Ukr*	*Germ*	*Kor*	*Tatar*	*Uigh*	*Cauc*	*Euro*
yes	3.7	9.3	22.9	56.1	73.3	15.6	56.3	61.5	45.2
no	85.6	75.3	52.1	31.7	20.0	59.4	31.3	23.1	35.5
D/K	10.7	15.4	25.0	12.2	6.7	25.0	12.5	15.4	19.4
A/F	376	408	48	41	15	32	16	13	31

[a] Kaz = Kazaks, Rus = Russians, Ukr = Ukrainians, Ger = Germans, Kor = Koreans, Uigh = Uighurs, Cauc = Caucasians, Euro = Europeans.

TABLE 6.4 Do You Consider That You Belong to an Ethnic Minority?—Ethnic Breakdown. Latvia[a]

	Lat	*Rus*	*Ukr*	*Bel*	*Poles*	*Lith*	*Jews*
yes	18.1	36.6	67.3	70.6	77.3	57.1	82.4
no	70.0	44.7	23.0	14.7	20.5	35.7	11.8
D/K	11.9	18.7	9.6	14.7	2.3	7.1	5.9
A/F	858	486	52	68	44	14	17

[a] Lat = Latvians, Bel = Belarusians, Lith = Lithuanians.

In Kazakstan, more than half of the nontitulars rejected this category for themselves. In Latvia, a significantly larger percentage of the population regards themselves as members of an ethnic minority group. These aggregate figures, of course, obscure significant differences among the various ethnic groups in each country (Table 6.3 and 6.4).

The concept of a minority is, as a matter of course, linked to numbers: small groups are more likely to regard themselves (and be regarded) as minorities than are large groups. However, the distribution of minorities in society cannot be established by arithmetics alone, it is also very much a matter of perceptions.

In Soviet ideology it was repeated time and again that all citizens of the Soviet Union had equal rights and obligations irrespective of nationality. Officially, every Soviet citizen could settle down wherever he liked and make a living for him or herself in every corner of the country without suffering discrimination, and this notion was firmly engrained in most people's mind. Against this backdrop, the very idea of "national minorities" had negative connotations. To be listed among the minorities to many people implied that he or she was not a full-fledged member of society.

The highest numbers of those who regard themselves as minorities in both countries are found in nontitular groups without historical roots in the area. Germans, Koreans, and Caucasians were deported to Kazakstan before or during World War II and were denied basic civil rights. While the collective charges against them were repealed under Khrushchev, an echo of the discrimination they underwent lingers on, both in their own self-understanding and in the popular consciousness. In Latvia, Jews more than any other group regard themselves as a minority, but this self-perception is common also among the smaller Slavic groups—Ukrainians, Belarusians, and Poles (from 67 to 77 percent).

In both countries, small national groups with historical roots in the area were less inclined to regard themselves as a "minority": Lithuanians in Latvia, and most Muslim nontitulars in Kazakstan, such as Tatars and Uzbeks. These groups often live in compact settlements in areas where their forbears have been living for ages.

Quite remarkable are the differences in the responses of the Slavs in the two countries. The number of Russians and Ukrainians who regard themselves as members of a minority group is three to four times higher in Latvia than in Kazakstan. This cannot be explained by differences in group size since the Russians in Latvia make up almost the same proportion of the total population in this country as do the Russians in Kazakstan, approximately 31 percent in Latvia and 34 percent in Kazakstan. For the Ukrainians the figures are 3 percent and 5 percent, respectively.

In Kazakstan, as many as three-quarters of the Russians and more than half of the Ukrainians insisted that they did not belong to a minority culture.[4] In itself, this does not necessarily indicate a high degree of integration into society. On the contrary, acceptance of a minority status may be a step in a process of transferring the focus of identity from the USSR to the new nationalizing state, that is, from a centrifugal to a centripetal orientation. If this is the case, it would probably be correct to say that in this respect the Russians in Latvia have more centripetal orientations than their coethnics in Kazakstan.

However, the different perceptions of the Russophones in Latvia and Kazakstan may perhaps also reveal different semantic connotations of the word "minority." In Kazakstan, the answers may be more influenced by the negative Soviet attitude toward the concept of "minorities," while the Latvian residents probably have been more exposed to Western ideas about "minority status" and "minority rights." For instance,

---

[4] The self-perception as "non-minority" among Ukrainians in Kazakstan is probably often a reflection of their membership in the larger Russophone community rather than of their Ukrainianness.

the official title of the OSCE representative Max van der Stoel, who in Latvia is widely seen as a staunch champion of the interests of the non-titular population, is "High Commissioner of National Minorities."

One would perhaps not expect any member of the titular nationality in either country to ascribe a minority status to themselves. However, 3.7 percent of the ethnic Kazaks put themselves in this category while another 10 percent of the Kazaks found it hard to answer this question. Probably this reflects attitudes among Kazaks living in compactly European cities in the north with a Russophone culture. No less than 18 percent of the Latvians in our survey considered themselves as members of a minority group and another 12 percent found it difficult to answer. One of reasons behind the marked differences between the Latvians on the one hand and Kazaks on the other, may be the fact that our Latvian pollster asked "Do you consider that you belong to an ethnic minority?" without indicating any country of reference, while in the other survey Kazakstan was spelled out as the country of reference.

Who, then, do belong to the minorities, in the perception of the Kazakstani and Latvian populations? As one can see from the tables below, the viewpoints differ:

TABLE 6.5 Who Are Considered to Belong to a Minority Group?

Response	*Latvia*	*Kazakstan*
1. All, except the Latvians (/Kazaks)	31.9	12.3
2. All, except the Latvians (/Kazaks) and the Russians	38.1	32.3
3. There are no national minorities in Latvia (/Kazakstan)	4.8	29.6
Another answer	0.6	1.3
D/K	24.6	24.5
A/F	1563	1000

TABLE 6.6 Who Are Considered to Belong to a Minority Group?—Ethnic Breakdown. Kazakstan

	Kaz	*Rus*	*Ukr*	*Ger*	*Kor*	*Tatar*	*Uigh*	*Cauc*	*Euro*
1.	15.9	15.3	21.2	20.0	-	16.7	30.0	12.5	25.0
2.	42.5	43.8	39.4	60.0	83.3	16.7	20.0	75.0	15.0
3.	40.9	39.3	39.4	10.0	16.7	66.7	40.0	12.5	55.0
A/F	376	408	48	41	15	32	16	13	31

TABLE 6.7 Who Are Considered to Belong to a Minority Group?—Ethnic Breakdown. Latvia

	Lat	*Rus*	*Ukr*	*Bel*	*Poles*	*Lith*	*Jews*
1.	41.2	45.4	40.0	54.5	42.1	18.2	23.5
2.	54.3	45,6	50.0	43.6	47.4	81.8	70.6
3.	4.3	9.0	10,0	1.8	10.5	-	5.9
A/F	604	377	50	55	38	11	17

No more than 15.9 percent of the ethnic Kazaks reserved the category of "non-minority" for themselves only. 42.5 percent in this group believed that they shared this status with the Russians, while all other groups should be regarded as minorities. An approximately equal number of Kazak respondents did not think that any ethnic group should be categorized as "minority."

Interestingly, the distribution of Russian answers in Kazakstan to this question was almost identical with the Kazak distribution: 15.3 percent for "all except the Kazaks," 43 percent for "all except Kazaks and Russians," and 39 percent for "no minorities." These data indicate that attempts made by certain Kazak intellectuals to elevate the Kazaks to a status of "a state-bearing nation" has not been met by a positive response among the population at large, not even among ethnic Kazaks. Representatives of the formerly repressed nationalities tend to regard both the Kazaks and the Russians as a combined, oppressive majority. Among the rest of the population the "Soviet" attitude remains strong: "We have no ethnic minorities."

In Latvia, the picture is different. Here, the tendency to regard the titular nation as the only nonminority group is twice as strong as in Kazakstan. This tendency is somewhat more pronounced among the Latvians themselves, but the differences among the various ethnic groups to these questions are not glaring. Thus, the congruence of perceptions among the various population groups seems to be equally strong in both countries, with the vector pointing somewhat more in the direction of clear-cut distinction between superordinate titulars and subordinate nontitulars in Latvia.

Social Stratification

Recent sociological and statistical studies have shown that members of the titular nationality tend to take over an increasing number of prestigious jobs in official administration and state enterprises in most newly independent countries.[5] We tried to see if we could find any traces of ethnic stratification in the labor market reflected in our survey, but no clear and unequivocal tendencies were to be found.

We asked the respondents which qualities they believed are most essential in order to succeed in society today. We gave the following categories to choose from: 1. religious faith, 2. personal qualities, 3. nationality, 4. education, 5. gender, 6. profession, 7. property and income.

---

[5] Kaiser 1995.

TABLE 6.8 Qualities Believed to be Essential to Succeed in Kazakstan

	Important	rather important	not very important	not imp. at all	D/K	coeff.[a]
property and income	57.9	23.0	7.0	7.3	4.8	1.62
education	55.3	25.3	7.8	9.1	2.5	1.70
individual qualities	45.2	30.6	12.9	5.4	5.9	1.77
profession	47.0	26.5	11.7	10.8	4.0	1.86
religious faith	21.6	18.7	24.9	27.1	7.7	2.62
ethnicity	13.3	16.2	26.1	39.5	4.9	2.97
gender	7.7	10.8	25.1	50.3	6.1	3.26

[a] This coefficient is arrived at by multiplying the number of respondents who have chosen a particular gradation by the weight number of this alternative. The figures for the various alternatives are then added up and divided by the total number of respondents in the said group. A low coefficient indicates strong agreement with the statement. Complete agreement among all members of the group gives the coefficient 1, and complete disagreement gives the coefficient 4. For more on the use of coefficients, see the appendix.

TABLE 6.9 Qualities Believed to be Essential to Succeed in Latvia

	Important	rather important	not very important	not imp. at all	D/K	coeff.
property and income	34.9	44.3	13.5	4.4	2.8	1.82
education	40.4	42.8	11.7	2.8	2.3	1.72
individual qualities	35.3	46.1	12.8	3.3	2.6	1.79
profession	36.9	43.9	13.5	3.3	2.4	1.78
religious faith	5.8	19.5	43.8	26.6	4.2	2.83
ethnicity	17.5	37.5	27.8	13.4	3.8	2.30
gender	7.5	23.9	36.8	28.2	3.6	2.79

The respondents could indicate four degrees of importance: 1. "Important," 2. "rather important," 3. "not very important," and 4. "not important at all."

Our respondents in both countries clearly distinguished between two main categories of qualities: four important ones and three unimportant. Ethnicity was regarded as a not particularly important quality to succeed in society, while most people saw wealth as an important prerequisite for success (table 6.8 and 6.9).

Logically then, the majority of our respondents ought to see no connection or only a weak link between ethnicity and economic success in their country. Indeed, when we proceeded to ask, "in your opinion, in which ethnic group do we find richest people in Kazakstan/Latvia?" roughly half of the respondents ticked off for "independent of nationality." Others, however, were prepared to single out certain nationalities as more wealthy than others.

Here we hit upon a striking difference between Kazakstan and Latvia. While 28.6 percent of the respondents in Kazakstan though the Kazaks were the wealthiest, only 5.5 percent in Latvia believed that the titular nationality also was the most wealthy group (Table 6.10).

Broken down by ethnic groups the following pattern emerged (Table 6.11 and 6.12): The Russian were clearly convinced that the Kazaks were better off than themselves (41.6 percent against 27.9 percent). At the same time, they were also slightly more inclined than the Kazaks to believe that opulence may be found also among Russians (11.2 percent as against 9.3 percent). The Jews were singled out as wealthy by many Koreans, but by few Russians or other Europeans.

In Latvia, a rather different picture emerged. In this country, the *Russians*, and not the titular nationality, were singled out as the group in which one most likely would find the greatest number of rich people. While this perception could be found also among the Russians themselves, it was particularly pronounced among the ethnic Latvians. The Latvians tended to regard their own group as economically underprivileged. While 3.8 percent expected to find most rich people among their own group, almost four times as many, or 13.8 percent, expected to find them among the Russians.

In both Latvia and Kazakstan the answers we received may reveal either actual differences in the distribution of wealth in society or perceived differences produced by ethnic stereotypes or other circumstances. For instance, affluent Kazaks often have very visible positions in society as local community leaders and high profile businessmen. Rich people from other groups may often lead more secluded lives. When we asked our Kazakstani respondents to state their own income, we found very little difference between the Kazaks and the Russians: a monthly income of 2,434 tenge among the Kazaks and 2,381 tenge among the Russians (the national average was somewhat lower: 2315 tenge).

Generally speaking, the problem of income estimation is one of the hardest in sociological science, and it is particularly tricky in post-Soviet societies. In very many cases the sums listed do not represent the entire family income, but only the salaried wages. Already under communism profits on the side were frowned upon and, indeed, were usually illegal under the existing laws. Today, extra earnings are often hidden for another reason: tax evasion. For these and other reasons we are unable to determine whether the stereotype ideas correspond to the actual distribution of wealth in society among ethnic groups or not. But as regards the attitudinal preconditions for ethnic integration, the perceptions themselves are what count.

TABLE 6.10 In Which Ethnic Group Do We Find Richest People?

	Kazakstan	Latvia
Latvians	-	5.5
Kazaks	28.6	-
Russians	8.1	11.3
Jews	7.1	4.9
other nationalities	6.2	2.3
foreigners	4.7	6.5
independent of nationality	40.1	49.7
difficult to answer	5.2	19.8

TABLE 6.11 In Which Ethnic Group Do We Find Richest People?—Ethnic Breakdown. Kazakstan[a]

	Kaz	Rus	Ukr	Germ	Kor	Tatar	Uigh	Cauc	Euro
Kazaks	27.9	41.6	31.3	39.0	26.7	21.9	50.0	23.1	32.3
Russians	9.3	11.2	4.2	9.8	6.7	12.5	-	-	9.7
Jews	11.7	5.4	8.3	9.8	26.7	6.3	6.3	7.7	3.2
Others	6.1	8.3	6.3	12.2	6.7	-	12.5	7.7	9.7
Foreigners	8.5	3.7	6.3	2.4	13.3	6.3	-	7.7	-
Independent	46.5	48.4	50.0	46.3	40.0	59.4	25.0	53.8	51.6
D/K	7.4	4.2	6.3	4.9	6.7	9.4	12.5	-	12.9
A/F	376	409	48	41	15	32	16	13	31

[a] Note: The figures do not add up to 100 since the respondents were allowed to indicate more than one ethnic group. See the appendix for more information on this.

TABLE 6.12 In which ethnic group do we find richest people?—Ethnic Breakdown. Latvia

	Lat	Rus	Lith	Ukr	Bel	Pol	Jew	Other
Latvians	3.8	7.7	8.7	6.3	6.7	4.9	14.3	6.3
Russians	13.8	9.8	0.0	6.3	4.4	9.8	0.0	6.3
Jews	3.6	6.7	0.0	6.3	11.1	7.3	0.0	0.0
Other	2.4	1.7	0.0	0.0	0.0	7.3	0.0	12.5
Foreigners	4.9	6.4	17.4	18.8	11.1	14.6	7.1	0.0
Independent	50.7	50.2	39.1	43.8	40.0	41.5	57.1	62.5
D/K	20.7	17.5	34.8	18.8	26.7	14.6	21.4	12.5
A/F	550	297	23	16	43	41	14	16

Political Identities and Allegiances

Patriotism

In order to identify centrifugal and centripetal attitudes on the axis of political identification we asked: "Are you proud of being a Latviets/Kazakstanian?" "Kazakstanian" (*Kazakstanets*) is a relatively recent neologism, comparable to *rossianin* in the Russian Federation. The Russian word *Latviets* belongs to the same semantic category, implying "a Latvian national" in the political/civic, not the ethnic sense. An affirmative answer to our question would therefore imply a high degree of "patriotism" rather than ethnonationalism.[6]

In theory, all ethnic groups in Kazakstan should be able to subscribe to "Kazakstanianness" in equal measure, and as we have seen, it is an important goal of Nazarbaev-style nation-building to make them do so. The figures given below indicate that his endeavors are met with mixed results.

FIGURE 6.1 Are You Proud of Being a Latviets/Kazakstanian?

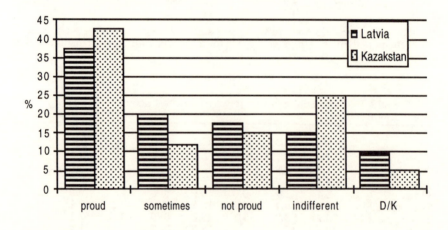

---

[6] In Latvian there is no equivalent to *"Latviets"* as a noun, although there is an adjective, *Latvijas*, corresponding to the Russian *"latviiskii."* From this word we constructed the word group *"Latvijas iedzivotajs"* ("inhabitant of Latvia").

TABLE 6.13 Are You Proud of Being a Kazakstanian?—Ethnic Breakdown

	Kaz	*Rus*	*Ukr*	*Germ*	*Kor*	*Tatar*	*Uigh*	*Cauc*	*Euro*
yes	69.9	25.4	25.0	19.5	26.7	46.9	37.5	38.5	19.4
sometimes	10.6	11.0	25.0	14.6	20.0	-	6.3	7.7	16.1
no	4.8	25.9	16.7	14.6	6.7	6.3	18.8	7.7	19.4
indifferent	11.7	31.5	27.1	41.5	40.0	43.8	18.8	38.5	35.5
D/K	2.9	6.1	6.3	9.8	6.7	3.1	18.8	7.7	9.7
A/F	376	409	48	41	15	32	16	13	31

TABLE 6.14 Are You Proud of Being a Latviets/Latvijas Iedzivotajs?

	Lat	*Rus*	*Lith*	*Ukr*	*Bel*	*Pol*	*Jew*	*Other*
yes	55.1	17.2	21.7	12.5	4.4	12.2	14.3	18.8
sometimes	19.3	21.9	17.4	18.8	26.7	14.6	0.0	31.3
no	11.8	22.2	17.4	37.5	31.1	34.1	50.0	12.5
indifferent	7.5	24.2	43.5	18.8	24.4	19.5	14.3	18.8
D/K	6.4	14.5	0.0	12.5	13.3	19.5	21.4	18.8
A/F	550	297	23	16	43	41	14	16

Only slightly more than half of the total sample in each country experienced "pride" in their country constantly or sometimes, while approximately 40 percent were either not proud or indifferent.

No doubt, the high degree of alienation indicated by these figures to a large degree reflects the countries' dire economic position which affects the well-being of the great majority of their residents. In addition, negative attitudes among the Russophones may express discomfort caused by real or perceived Kazakification/Latvification of society. For whatever reasons, it is clear that the nontitular ethnic groups are considerably less proud of their country than are the titular groups.

In Kazakstan, three attitudinal categories emerged. First, 80 percent of the Kazaks were proud of being "Kazakstanians"; Second, between 60 and 80 percent of the non-Russophone minorities (Uighurs and Uzbeks) were "proud of being a Kazakstanian," while less than 50 percent the Russophones responded positively.

Again, we believe, the operational value of the Russophone category has been confirmed. To be sure, on this issue we found clear variations also *within* the Russophone group: the Russians score as low as 36.4 percent while the Ukrainians, which in many other aspects of our survey follow the Russians like a shadow, mustered a far greater share of proud Kazakstanians: 50 percent. In contrast, the Germans had an even less developed sense of being "Kazakstanian" than the Russians.

Also in Latvia civic patriotism was clearly more developed among the titular nationality than among other ethnic groups. Apparently the

Soviet notion that the eponymous ethnic group somehow were the "proprietors" of Soviet republics still lingers on. It should be a cause for concern among Latvian nation-builders that as little as 5–22 percent of the non-Latvians associate their country of residence with feelings of pride. The highest score was found among ethnic Lithuanians, a Baltic people culturally and linguistically related to the Latvians, while the lowest we found among the Belarusians. This latter figure is probably related to the fact that the number of immigrants is particularly high among the Belarusians: Only 31 percent were born in Latvia, as against 49 percent among the Russians.

Motherland

However, people may be strongly attached to their country even if they do not feel proud of it. As the British saying goes: "Right or wrong, my country." You may even *love* a country you don't see any reason to be proud of, much as you may love your delinquent brother or a pitiable drunkard of a father. When we asked "which country do you regard as your motherland?," we received answers which sometimes differed significantly from the previous ones (Table 6.15).

In Kazakstan, slightly more than half of the respondents regarded Kazakstan as their motherland. This result can of course be regarded as either "a half full" or "a half empty" glass of water. Nevertheless, we assume, it must be discouraging news to today's Kazakstani nation-builders. They can take some solace from the fact that another 10 percent in our survey ticked off for "the Kazak SSR" as the country with which they identified. This choice may be regarded as a hybrid between a Kazakstani and a Soviet identity. We surmise that some people who identify territorially with Kazakstan, but not politically with the present regime, have preferred this option. In addition, 26 percent of our respondents retained a strong identification with the Soviet state.

Support for the option "Russia, my motherland" was weak, less than 7 percent. This surely must be good news for Kazakstani nation-builders and will assuage fears of impending irredentism. Even in East Kazakstan, an oblast widely believed to be a hotbed of Russian irredentism, only 5.3 percent of the respondents claimed that they regard Russia as their motherland. This, in fact, was lower than the national average.

TABLE 6.15 Which Country Do You Regard as Your Homeland?

	Latvia	*Kazakstan*
Kazakstan	-	51.9
Latvia	65.8	-
USSR	8.0	26.1
Latvian SSR	12.4	-
Kazak SSR	8.0	10.3
Russia	4.7	6.8
Another country	3.9	2.9
I have no motherland	3.6	1.4
D/K	1.6	0.6

TABLE 6.16 Country Identification—Ethnic breakdown. Kazakstan

	Kaz	*Rus*	*Ukr*	*Germ*	*Kor*	*Tatar*	*Uigh*	*Cauc*	*Euro*
Kazakstan	73.1	39.9	27.7	46.3	33.3	53.1	56.3	15.4	32.3
USSR	13.3	35.7	45.8	29.3	40.0	9.4	18.8	38.5	32.3
Kaz SSR	12.2	9.5	6.3	9.8	-	21.9	-	15.4	6.5
Russia	1.1	13.0	6.3	4.9	13.3	3.1	-	-	9.7
Other	0.3	0.2	12.5	7.3	-	6.3	25.0	7.7	16.1
None	-	1.5	-	2.4	13.3	3.1	-	23.1	-
D/K	-	0.2	2.1	-	-	3.1	-	-	3.2
A/F	376	409	48	41	15	32	16	13	31

TABLE 6.17 Country identification—Ethnic Breakdown. Latvia

	Lat	*Rus*	*Lith*	*Ukr*	*Bel*	*Pol*	*Jew*	*Other*
Latvia	88.7	41.1	47.8	12.5	37.8	34.1	28.6	12.5
USSR	0.5	17.8	0.0	18.8	17.8	17.1	42.9	0.0
LSSR	7.1	21.5	13.0	6.3	11.1	17.1	0.0	31.3
Russia	0.2	11.4	0.0	6.3	2.2	0.0	0.0	12.5
Other	1.1	1.0	30.4	50.0	17.8	17.1	21.4	31.3
None	0.4	2.4	4.3	0.0	6.7	4.9	0.0	6.3
D/K	2.0	4.7	4.3	6.3	6.7	9.8	7.1	6.3
A/F	550	297	23	16	43	41	14	16

It is hardly surprising that the vast majority of the ethnic Kazaks identify with Kazakstan, either in its contemporary or in its Soviet incarnation. (It is perhaps more puzzling that as many as 15 percent do not.) Among the Russians, almost equal numbers ticked off for "Kazakstan" and "USSR," while another 9.5 percent went for the in-between category of "the Kazak SSR."

Ukrainians and most other Russophones in Kazakstan have retained a stronger Soviet identity than have the Russians. Somewhat surprisingly, not a single Korean regarded Korea as his or her mother-land.[7] By contrast, 7.3 percent of the Germans and 25 percent of the Uighurs have "another" homeland, presumably Germany and Xinjiang. The Tatars are strongly attached to Kazakstan in territorial and po-litical terms: 75 percent identified with either "Kazakstan" or "the Kazak SSR." This was far more than in any other nontitular group.

Even fewer persons in Latvia than in Kazakstan identified with Russia as their homeland, and even more importantly, Soviet nostalgia seemed to be far less widespread. A good 78 percent of the respondents ticked off for either Latvia or the Latvian SSR. This seems to be a solid basis to build a civic Latvian nation-state upon.

To be sure, there are differences among the various ethnic groups re-garding country identification in Lativa as well. The tendency to iden-tify with "Latvia" was twice as strong among the ethnic Latvians than among non-Latvians. Among the nontitular groups, the Russians stood out as most attached to Latvia/Latvian SSR as their homeland (62 percent compared to 49 percent Belarusians, 28 percent Jews, and only 19 percent Ukrainians!). This probably reflects the greater rootedness of the Russians. As the Russians are much more numerous than all other nontitular groups combined, also this seems to be good news for Latvian nation-builders.

Cultural Identities and Forecasts

Linguistic Forecasts

Will Latvian and Kazakstani societies in the future be dominated by one or two linguistic cultures? If the answer is "one," which one will it be? If it turns out to be the state language, this will be an indication of successful nation-building based on strong elements of the titular cul-ture. On the other hand, if it is Russian, this will indicate that the Russophones may have been integrated into the nationalizing state though still retaining a large measure of their own culture.

We asked: "How important do you think it will be to master Kazak/Latvian and Russian in your oblast ten years from now?" The respondents were given a choice between five possible answers: 1. very important; 2. important; 3. not so important; 4. not important at all; 5. difficult to answer. We elicited the reactions illustrated in Figure 6.2.

---

[7] 13 percent regarded Russia as their homeland. This may reflect on the fact that they were deported to Kazakstan from the far eastern territory of the RSFSR.

FIGURE 6.2 How Important Do You Think It Will Be to Master Kazak and Russian in Your Oblast Ten Years From Now? (All Respondents)

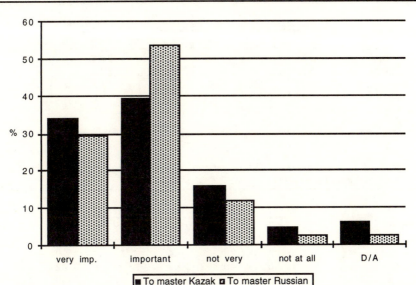

As we can see, most people believe that a good command of both languages will remain rather important. If we combine the categories "very important" and "important," a mastery of Russian rather than Kazak is singled out by more respondents as an essential skill also in the future (83 percent as against 73 percent).

Broken down by ethnic group, we get the results in Table 6.18. The two dominant nationalities, the Kazaks and the Russians, as it were, "exchanged compliments": 67.3 percent Kazaks expected Russian to remain important as a means of communication in the oblast in which they are living. Almost the same number of Russians expected that knowledge of Kazak will remain or become important. However, as seen from the opposite angle, this also means that almost 25 percent of the Kazaks believed that in ten years' time a good command of Russian will become dispensable while almost 30 percent of the Russians continue to think that they will be able to do without a good knowledge of Kazak also in the years to come.

In the residual group of "others," in which presumably few people have a vested interest in the development of any of these language over the other, there is a clear preference for Russian: 83 percent vs. 64 percent. If we dare regard the "others" as impartial umpires, Russian will

TABLE 6.18 How Important Do You Think It Will Be To Master Kazak and Russian in Your Oblast Ten Years From Now?—Ethnic Breakdown

	Kazaks		Russians		Other	
	Kazak	Russian	Kazak	Russian	Kazak	Russian
very imp.	57.7	15.7	17.6	40.6	24.4	31.9
important	31.1	51.6	46.2	51.6	39.9	51.2
not very imp.	6.9	20.7	23.0	5.1	17.8	9.4
not at all imp.	0.5	3.7	6.8	1.2	8.0	2.8
D/K	3.7	1.5	6.4	1.5	9.9	4.7
A/F	376		409		213	

Table 6.19 How Important Will Command of the Kazak Language be in Your Oblast Ten Years From Now?

	Very	Imp.	Not very	Not at all	D/K	A/F
Almaty	28.3	42.5	15.0	4.7	9.4	127
Kzyl-Orda	77.3	17.3	1.3	-	4.0	75
Zhambyl	60.7	29.3	6.4	0.7	2.9	140
Karaganda	22.6	48.1	13.2	1.9	14.2	106
East Kazakstan	11.5	34.5	38.1	8.0	8.0	113
Semipalatinsk	34.4	58.1	5.4	1.1	1.1	93
Akmola (Astana)	26.2	40.8	21.5	7.7	3.8	130
North Kazakstan	12.7	30.4	26.6	21.5	8.9	79
Atyrau	60.0	34.0	2.0	2.0	2.0	50
West Kazakstan	19.5	56.1	20.7	-	3.7	82

Table 6.20 How Important Will Command of the Russian Language be in Your Oblast Ten Years From Now?

	Very	Imp.	Not very	Not at all	D/K	A/F
Almaty	37.8	46.5	8.7	2.4	4.7	127
Kzyl-Orda	6.7	46.7	30.7	9.3	6.7	75
Zhambyl	15.7	49.3	25.7	5.0	4.3	140
Karaganda	21.7	72.6	4.7	-	0.9	106
East Kazakstan	45.1	44.2	10.6	-	-	113
Semipalatinsk	20.4	68.8	7.5	1.1	2.2	93
Akmola (Astana)	48.5	47.7	0.8	0.8	2.3	130
North Kazakstan	34.2	57.0	5.1	3.8	-	79
Atyrau	16.0	58.0	22.0	4.0	-	50
West Kazakstan	30.5	56.1	11.0	1.2	1.2	82

stand the ground, and for all practical purposes remain the "language of interethnic communication" in most parts of Kazakstan.[8]

As regards people's expectations of the future, variations among age groups are highly relevant. Young people will inevitably be more able to make an impression on the future society than will the older generations who are gradually leaving the social scene. We therefore made breakdowns also by age groups but did not find any significant trends and will therefore not burden readers with a detailed presentation of the results.

Broken down by oblast, the expectations regarding the future of the Russian and Kazak languages in Kazakstan clearly reflected the demographic distribution of the population (Table 6.19 and 6.20). The compactly Kazak oblast of Kzyl-Orda confidently expected Kazak to become important or very important, while almost 40 percent believed that they will be able to do without Russian ten years from now. By contrast, large groups in the compactly Russophone oblasts in East Kazakstan and Northern Kazakstan believed that command of the state language will not be important by the year 2006 (46 percent and 48 percent, respectively). At the same time, the 10 percent in Eastern Kazakstan and 9 percent in Northern Kazakstan who expected Russian to become more or less redundant are higher figures than we found in some other oblasts: Karaganda, 4.7 percent; Semipalatinsk, 8.6 percent; and Akmola—the future capital—only 1.6 percent! In this latter oblast more than 96 percent expected Russian to remain an important language in the future.

In Latvia, our survey revealed a completely different picture. The determination of the Latvian authorities to force the non-Latvian population to learn Latvian has been high and seems to be yielding results. Also in the communist period the language of the titular group was clearly more prestigious in Latvia than was the language of the titular group in Kazakstan. From this better starting point Latvian is today establishing itself as the dominant medium of communication in independent Latvia.

The combined support in Latvia for the two options "very important" and "important" to master Russian is only half of what it was in Kazakstan (49 percent as against 85 percent). The predictions regarding the future of the Russian language did not vary as much by region as we had expected: The strongest support we found in Latgale (54 percent) and the lowest in Zemgale, but even here it amounted to a substantial 40 percent.

---

[8] Kolstø and Malkova 1997.

FIGURE 6.3 How Important Do You Think It Will Be to Master Latvian and Russian in Your Oblast Ten Years From Now?

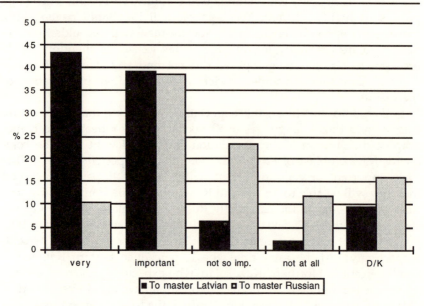

The faith in the future of Latvian as a vital language of Latvia is widespread. While we did find some geographical nuances this conclusion is basically true even for the most Russophone region, Latgale (73 percent support). In Vidzeme, less than one percent thought that they would be able to get along without a command of Latvian in ten years time.

The ethnic breakdown revealed that both among the Russians and among other non-Latvian ethnic groups more people believed in the future importance of Latvian than in the future importance of Russian. Among the Russians, the difference was 12 percentage points (73 percent as against 61 percent), among other nontitular groups, slightly lower (68 percent as against 59 percent).

Generally speaking, more people in Latvia than in Kazakstan were hesitant and found it difficult to pick one of the options in our questionnaire. Uncertainty regarding the future of Russian was widespread in Latvia (15.8 percent) while only 2.5 percent of the respondents in Kazakstan were unable to express an opinion on this issue. We do not

TABLE 6.21 How Important Do You Think It Will Be To Master Latvian in Your Region in Ten Years?

	Very	*Imp.*	*Not very*	*Not at all*	*D/K*	*A/F*
Riga	41.9	37.7	8.4	2.4	9.6	332
Kurzeme	33.8	42.4	6.5	3.6	13.7	139
Zemgale	43.8	40.3	4.9	1.4	9.7	144
Vidzeme	62.6	33.5	0.0	0.9	3.1	225
Latgale	25.6	47.5	10.6	2.5	13.8	160

TABLE 6.22 How Important Do You Think It Will Be To Master Russian in Your Region in Ten Years?

	Very	*Imp.*	*Not very*	*Not at all*	*D/K*	*A/F*
Riga	12.7	40.9	23.6	11.8	10.9	330
Kurzeme	10.1	38.1	18.7	7.2	25.9	139
Zemgale	9.7	31.3	23.6	11.1	24.3	144
Vidzeme	10.6	33.9	23.8	17.2	14.5	225
Latgale	6.3	47.5	25.0	10.0	11.3	160

TABLE 6.23 How Important Do You Think It Will Be To Master Latvian And Russian In Your Region In Ten Years?—Ethnic Breakdown

	Latvians		*Russians*		*Other Groups*	
	Latvian	*Russian*	*Latvian*	*Russian*	*Latvian*	*Russian*
Very	55.3	5.6	30.3	19.3	24.8	10.5
Important	35.6	33.6	43.1	42.0	45.3	47.4
Not so Imp.	2.7	27.3	10.4	17.6	10.5	21.5
Not at all	1.1	18.0	3.0	5.1	4.3	4.8
D/K	5.3	15.5	13.1	15.9	14.7	16.2
A/F	550		297		153	

have any good explanation for this apart from the conjecture that the "Russian" issue may be more politically sensitive in Latvia than in Kazakstan.

To conclude: the linguistic forecasts of the populations in Latvia and Kazakstan are clearly different. In Latvia, a clear majority in all groups and all regions expect the state language to gain in public importance at the expense of Russian. Also in Kazakstan a majority of the respondents gave the thumbs-up for Kazakstan, but certainly not to the detriment of Russian. On the contrary, *more* people expected Russian to remain an important medium of communication. If our respondents are correct in their gut feeling Kazakstan will *not* become linguistically Kazakified, Kazakstan will remain a bilingual country, with Russian as the most important medium of communication in all spheres of life. The only exceptions to this will be in remote villages and, perhaps, in official correspondence. In Latvia, on the other hand, the language of the titular group will become firmly established as the dominant medium of interethnic communication.

Linguistic Preferences in Schools

Do the residents of Latvia and Kazakstan in their private lives act upon the linguistic forecasts they made to our pollsters? In order to find the answer to that question we tried to detect the current trends in school choices. The respondents were asked about the language of instruction in the school they had attended in their youth as well as the language of instruction in the school to which they were sending their children. In combination, these two questions were intended to bring out the dynamics of language change in the educational system. Of course, many respondents did not have children of school age. Most young people but also some others fell into this category. This meant that the samples we were working with in response to the second question were considerably smaller than in respect to the first question.

As table 6.24 shows, no drastic changes have taken place in the school system in Kazakstan. The percentage receiving education in Kazak has increased by 3.5 percentage points in the course of one generation. Education in minority languages has been more than halved while the vast majority of the Kazakstani youth still receive their education in Russian.

There may be a number of different reasons why so many parents have chosen the same language of instruction for their offspring as they received themselves. In many places the school choice may be severely limited. If no new schools are opened in the neighborhood offering education in a new language, the children may have to be bussed long distances if they insist on a particular kind of instruction.

Kazakstani school authorities no doubt would like to see as many children as possible switching to Kazak-language instruction, but there is little evidence of a forceful school policy in Kazakstan. Also, as pointed out by Jørn Holm-Hansen above,[9] Kazak language schools are reputed to be of poor quality in terms of staff, student body, facilities, textbooks, and results.[10] This seems to be a major reason why so few pupils are tempted to enroll in them, even while such enrollment would presumably increase considerably their command of the state language.

---

[9] Page 184 above.
[10] Dave 1996.

Table 6.24 Parents' vs. Children's Language of Instruction in School. Kazakstan

In what language...	did you study in school?	are your children studying?
Russian	74.0	72.7
Kazak	22.0	25.5
Another	4.0	1.8
A/F	992	643

TABLE 6.25 Language of instruction in school, parent generation—Ethnic breakdown. Kazakstan

	Kaz	Rus	Ukr	Germ	Kor	Tatar	Uigh	Cauc	Euro
Russ.	42.5	99.0	91.7	92.7	100	87.5	68.8	84.6	74.2
Kaz.	57.7	0.7	-	4.9	-	3.1	-	-	-
Other	0.5	1.5	12.5	4.9	-	9.4	31.3	15.4	25.8
A/F	376	408	48	41	15	32	16	13	31

TABLE 6.26 Parents vs. Children's Language of Instruction in School—Ethnic breakdown. Kazakstan

In what language ...	did you study in school?			are your children studying?[a]		
	Kazaks	Russians	Other	Kazaks	Russians	Other
Russian	42.5	99.0	83.1	40.1	98.2	89.3
Kazak	57.7	0.7	2.8	66.4	3.2	5.3
Other	0.5	1.5	15.5	0.9	0.7	6.1
A/F	369	408	213	232	280	131

[a] The percentages add up to more than 100 percent because the respondents were allowed to indicate more than one category if they had children at different schools.

The breakdown by ethnic group shows that the vast majority of the non-Muslim, non-Turkic population received their education in the Russian language. The same is true of the Tatars and Caucasians. The largest—but not overwhelmingly large—part of the Kazaks were educated in their mother tongue. Among all other groups the numbers who have attended Kazak-language schools are very small.

Two-thirds of the Uzbeks have received a national language education. This is the highest percentage after the Russians, surpassing even the Kazaks. However, many of the minor ethnic groups in our sample, including the Uzbeks, are so small that there can be no question of representativity. In the following, therefore, we will reduce our categories to three: Kazaks, Russians and "others."

The share of Russians studying in Kazak today is more than four times as high as in the parent generation but is still only minute (up from 0.7 percent to 3.2 percent.). Among the "others," a doubling has occurred, from 2.8 percent to 5.3 percent. As for the Kazaks, an increase of nine percentage points can be registered, from 57.7 percent to 66.4 percent.

Will these tendencies last? As David Laitin has pointed out, it depends on the expectations of the Kazakstani population. They will only switch to Kazak-language schools if they believe that a good command of the state language will increase their career chances. This, in turn, hinges on the credibility of the linguistic Kazakification campaign. If and only if the shift in the direction of Kazak-language instruction reaches a critical point, will it become imperative for the others to follow suit. A stampede or, in Laitin's terminology, a "cascade," will set in. People therefore watch each other to see how many are making the move. To be the first one to switch to the new state language makes no sense if few others come after; on the other hand, it can be detrimental to the career to be last in line.

Based on a thoughtful analysis Laitin reached the conclusion that in Kazakstan no cascade will occur. His research indicated that too many ethnic Kazaks disregard the calls for Kazakification in their private lives. Even those who publicly clamor for Kazakification, surreptitiously undermine its credibility by their own school choices. Most Kazaks believe that ideally all parents (or at least all Kazaks) ought to send their children to Kazak schools, but as long as the quality of the Russian schools remains superior they remain unwilling to sacrifice the future of their children on the nationalist altar.[11]

---

[11] Laitin 1998, 133–139.

As for Latvia, David Laitin predicted rather different outcomes. In this country, he concluded, a mass movement in the direction of integration and assimilation of the Russians was highly probable. On a number of indexes the Russophones in Latvia were more open to the goals of the titulars than their coethnics in the other three countries included in his comparative research, Estonia, Ukraine and Kazakstan. For instance, half of all Russians in Latvia answered affirmatively when asked whether Latvian should be the sole state language. This was far more than in any of the other three countries.[12] The social constraints in this country for linguistic accommodation were very small. "Russians in Latvia do not scorn fellow Russians who are seen to be speaking Latvian as much as Russians in [Estonia and Kazakstan]." Also, ethnic Latvians do not scorn non-Latvians for their attempts to speak their language as much as titulars in the other three republics.[13]

Our findings seem to confirm Laitin's conclusions. Already in the parent generation Latvian was the most common language of instruction in Latvia, slightly more popular than Russian. Among the generation attending schools in Latvia today, the gap between these two language as a means of instruction is rapidly widening.

While more than 40 percent of the ethnic Kazaks stated that they had received a Russian-language education, less than 15 percent of the ethnic Latvians did. We realize that under the new political realities some Latvians may have been ashamed to acknowledge that they had attended a Russian school and have taken recourse to a lie here. However, if that should be the case this in itself would be additional

TABLE 6.27 Parents vs. Children's Language of Instruction in School. Latvia

In what language ...	*did you study in school?*	*are your children studying?*
Russian	47.0	40.6
Latvian	49.6	57.1
Other	3.3	2.3

TABLE 6.28 Parent vs. Children's Language of Instruction in School—Ethnic Breakdown. Latvia

In what language ...	*did you study in school?*			*are your children studyng?*		
	Latvians	*Russians*	*Other*	*Latvians*	*Russians*	*Other*
Russian	14.0	96.6	67.7	8.7	81.2	70.0
Latvian	84.4	2.7	15.7	89.9	18.3	21.8
Other	1.6	0.7	16.3	1.4	0.5	8.2

---

[12] Ibid, 205.

[13] Ibid, 256.

evidence supporting our conclusion that Latvian is rapidly gaining and Russian losing in prestige in Latvian society today. Few if any Kazaks would feel a similar shame.

The share of Russians attending Latvian language schools has increased almost sevenfold in one generation, up from 2.7 percent to 18.3 percent.[14] The momentum of this trend is so strong that Laitin's cascade metaphor seems justified. However, more than 8 percent of the ethnic Latvians still prefer Russian schools.[15]

This breakdown also reveals that education in minority language has been dramatically reduced in Latvia (as in Kazakstan). While Russian is still the most popular language among the "other" group, it has not gained from the tendency of the smaller groups to abandon education in their minority languages. On balance, all minority pupils who have changed to another language of education than their parents have chosen a Latvian school.

Cultural Self-Identifications

The language question is of course intimately related to questions of cultural self-identification. For years, an active cultural exchange among the peoples of the Soviet Union on the basis of Russian culture created a symbiosis generally referred to as "Soviet culture." Among some groups the common Soviet element in this composite culture was stronger, among others, the local or national element dominated. Also today a large part of the population continue to regard themselves as bearers of a "Soviet" culture. In our Kazakstani survey, in fact, this was the most common identity we registered. The respondents were given the following alternatives: 1. "I consider myself a representative of Kazak culture"; 2. "I consider myself a representative of Russian culture"; 3. "I consider myself a representative of Soviet culture"; 4. "I consider myself a representative of European culture"; 5. "I consider myself a representative of Asian culture." They could be in complete or partial agreement (1 and 2), or partial or complete disagreement (3 and 4) with these assertions.

An identification with Soviet culture does not necessarily imply a political content such as attachment to Communist ideology or to the Soviet political system. While this may indeed be case for some respondents, for others it may first and foremost signal an identification with Soviet multiculturalism, with the Soviet variety of the melting

---

[14] Of these, 60 percent live in Riga.

[15] Of these, more than 40 percent live in Latgale.

TABLE 6.29 Cultural Self-Identification. Kazakstan

	fully agree	agree somewhat	disagree somewhat	fully disagree	D/K	coeff.
Soviet culture	38.9	24.6	6.9	21.5	8.1	2.12
Russian culture	28.8	26.4	10.3	26.0	8.5	2.37
Kazak culture	32.0	12.4	10.6	34.8	10.2	2.54
Asian culture	12.2	13.8	9.8	45.1	19.1	3.09
European culture	5.7	11.0	15.8	51.5	16.0	3.35

TABLE 6.30 Coefficients of Cultural Self-Identification—Ethnic, Educational and Geographic breakdown. Kazakstan

Ethnic group	Kaz	Rus	Soviet	Europe	Asian
Kazaks	1.3	3.2	2.6	3.5	2.4
Russians	3.5	1.6	1.7	3.3	3.7
Ukrainians	3.0	1.8	3.8	3.1	3.5
Germans	3.3	2.1	1.8	2.6	3.8
Koreans	3.1	2.3	1.6	3.3	2.1
Tatars	2.8	3.0	2.4	3.7	2.9
Uighurs	3.2	3.7	3.7	3.5	1.9
Uzbeks	2.3	2.8	2.3	3.5	1.7
Caucasians	3.5	2.8	2.7	3.7	2.9
other Europeans	3.5	2.4	2.1	2.9	3.5
other Asians	2.6	3.3	2.8	3.8	1.0
Education					
incomplete medium	2.8	2.3	2.0	3.7	3.4
medium	2.5	2.5	2.1	3.3	3.1
medium specialized	2.5	2.3	2.3	3.4	3.1
incomplete higher	2.5	2.4	2.5	3.2	3.0
higher education	2.4	2.3	1.9	3.1	2.8
Location					
capital	3.1	2.2	1.7	3.3	3.1
oblast center	2.6	2.1	2.0	3.4	3.2
other city	3.0	2.0	1.8	3.3	3.4
industrial town	2.6	2.5	2.2	3.3	3.1
village	2.2	2.7	2.4	3.3	2.8

pot. To the children in many ethnically mixed families—in which the great grandparents may represent 3–4, even up to 8 different ethnic groups—the ethnic identity written into their Soviet passports must seem grotesquely inadequate. The category of "Soviet culture" may be the residual choice they arrive at having rejected all the others we suggested to them.

Next to Soviet culture, the most popular identification is with "Russian culture," followed by "Kazak culture." The more generalized identity choices of "European" and "Asian" cultures did not strike a chord in very many hearts in Kazakstan.

Of course, these identity choices are heavily influenced by the respondents' ethnic self-identification.

It comes as no surprise that the vast majority of the ethnic Kazaks identify with Kazak culture. Of the nontitulars, however, only the Uzbeks tend to identify somewhat with this culture. Among all other groups dissociation with Kazak culture is very pronounced: among Russians, "other Europeans," and Caucasians, as high as 3.5. It is also evident from our survey that identification with this culture is much more marked in the countryside, the less dynamic segments of society, than in the more pulsating towns and cities. The endeavors of some Kazak academicians to make Kazak culture "the integrating principle of the entire polyethnic population of Kazakstan,"[16] will be an uphill endeavor, to put it mildly.

All nationalities except Uighurs and Ukrainians identify to some degree with Soviet culture. The strongest scores on this point we found among Koreans, Russians, and Germans. The degree of identification with the sunken Soviet Atlantis grows with the level of education, up to a certain point: among persons with a completed higher education it drops again sharply. At the same time, the capital is clearly more Sovietized than the countryside. Of all groups, only the Germans show some attachment to European culture, while the Russians with a coefficient of 3.3 are far removed from it.

The cultural hierarchy which we found in Latvia differed significantly from the one we found in Kazakstan. If Soviet culture was the *most* popular identification in Kazakstan it was least popular in Latvia. Identification with Latvian took an undisputed first place but, of course, primarily among the ethnic Latvians (See Table 6.32).

---

[16] See above, p. 166–169.

TABLE 6.31 Latvia. Do You Consider Yourself as a Representative of ...?

	yes	partly	no	D/K	coeff.
Soviet culture	5.2	18.2	55.3	21.2	2.72
Russian culture	15.2	18.6	51.0	14.8	2.66
Latvian culture	47.3	22.1	20.5	10.0	1.85
European culture	7.5	23.5	39.4	29.6	2.24

Table 6.32 Cultural Self-Identification—Ethnic, Educational and Geographic breakdown. Latvia

Ethnic group	Latvian	Russian	Soviet	Europe
Latvians	1.2	3.1	2.8	1.9
Russians	2.7	1.8	2.6	2.6
Ukrainians	2.5	2.3	2.7	2.8
Belarusians	3.0	2.4	2.6	2.9
Poles	2.5	3.5	3.3	3.0
Lithuanians	2.1	3.3	3.0	2.6
Jews	3.1	3.2	3.3	3.2
Education				
incomplete medium	2.0	2.6	2.7	2.3
medium	1.9	2.7	2.8	2.3
medium specialized	1.9	2.6	2.6	2.1
incomplete higher	1.6	2.8	2.7	2.0
higher education	1.8	2.7	2.8	2.2
Location				
capital	2.2	2.5	2.8	2.5
oblast center	1.8	2.7	2.7	2.3
other city	1.7	2.5	2.7	2.2
village	1.5	2.9	2.7	1.9

The identification with the "titular culture" was slightly stronger among ethnic Latvians in Latvian than among ethnic Kazaks in Kazakstan (coeff. 1.2 vs. coeff. 1.3), but identification with Russian culture among ethnic Russians was somewhat *weaker* in Latvia than in Kazakstan (coeff. 1.8, as against coeff. 1.6) While Russians in Kazakstan overwhelmingly rejected Kazak culture as their focus of identity (coeff. 3.5) the responses of their ethnic brethren in Latvia revealed a more or less neutral attitude towards a Latvian identification (coeff. 2.7). Russians in Latvia also identified much more strongly with Europe than did Russians in Kazakstan. Among Ukrainians and Poles in Latvia, identification with Latvian cultural was stronger than among the Russians (but weaker among the Belarusians and the Jews). On balance, these results show stronger centripetal tendencies among the Russophone population of Latvia than among the Russophones of Kazakstan.

The Future of the Kazak and Latvian Nations

As pointed out above (p. 188–189), parts of the Kazak intelligentsia today assert that the limited role of the state language in Kazakstani society may lead to the disappearance of the Kazak nation as the bearer of this language. In our survey we tried to gauge how much support this notion enjoys. We asked, "The view has sometimes been expressed that the extinction of the Kazak nation is possible. Do you think that the possibility of the extinction of the Kazak nation exists?" We got the answers reported in table 6.33.

As one can see, this idea did not have many adherents. Half of those who expressed an opinion categorically disagreed, while one-third were more inclined to disagree than to agree. Less than 10 percent of the answers expressed agreement.

In the southern oblasts, where the concentrations of ethnic Kazaks are highest, this idea found least support. The assertion was met with more sympathy in the northern oblasts of Semipalatinsk, Atyrau, and Akmola, but also here the support was far from overwhelming. Until 1990, Semipalatinsk was the site of the main nuclear testing ground in the Soviet Union which was closed down only after prolonged pressure from various grass-roots movements and scathing criticism in the media. The highly charged nuclear issue has obviously sensitized the

TABLE 6.33 Do you think that the possibility of the extinction of the Kazak nation exists?

Answer	Percentage
agree completely	2.4
agree somewhat	5.6
difficult to say	12.0
disagree somewhat	26.4
disagree completely	46.9
difficult to answer	6.7

TABLE 6.34 Do You Think That The Possibility of The Extinction of The Kazak Nation Exists?—Ethnic Breakdown

	Kazaks	Russians	Others
agree completely	2.2	2.1	4.1
agree somewhat	8.9	4.5	3.6
difficult to say	8.7	15.6	15.3
disagree somewhat	25.1	31.6	28.1
disagree completely	55.0	46.2	49.0
A/F	358	377	196

TABLE 6.35 Do You Think That the Possibility of the Extinction of the Latvian Nation Exists?—Ethnic Breakdown

	Latvians	Russians	Others
yes, and the risk is growing	30.9	7.6	1.9
yes, there is some risk, but it is not growing	31.2	13.2	14.2
there was a risk but now it is decreasing	20.7	20.8	21.9
there has been no risk	7.5	35.6	32.0
difficult to answer	9.7	22.8	20.1

population in Semipalatinsk to the issue of survival. Their reactions to our question probably reflect their fear of genetic deformations and other diseases inflicted by nuclear exposure rather than linguistic and ethnic concerns.

At the same time, Semipalatinsk, as well as Atyrau—another northern oblast which in the survey expressed worry about the future of the Kazak nation—have high percentages of ethnic Kazaks, 51 percent, and 67 percent, respectively. Indeed, as regards variations among the ethnic groups, we found the highest number of alarmists among the Kazaks themselves.

However, somewhat surprisingly, the Kazaks also registered the highest number of optimists. This seeming paradox can be explained by the fact that comparatively fewer Kazaks than non-Kazaks found it difficult to answer this question. Apparently, the topic has been discussed more among Kazaks, and they have to a larger degree made up their mind on the issue.

In Latvia, the polling institute we engaged formulated the questions regarding the future of the Latvian nation slightly differently from the questions used in Kazakstan. They chose to focus on growing/decreasing risks, and the Latvian and Kazakstani figures are therefore not readily comparable. With this caveat we present the Latvian findings in Table 6.35.

In spite of the fact that Latvian language and Latvian culture seem much better entrenched in Latvian society than Kazak language and traditional culture in Kazakstan, anxiety about the future of the titular nation is clearly more widespread in Latvia than in Kazakstan. The fear, however, is primarily held by ethnic Latvians, and is far less among other groups. More than 60 percent of the Latvians believed in the possibility of the extinction of the Latvian nation, half of these even thought that the risk was growing. Thus, there seems to be a certain popular support for the ethnocentric nation-building policies pursued by the Latvian authorities.

The Future of Russian Culture
in Kazakstan and Latvia

Our question about the future of the Russian culture was addressed in a somewhat different key. The future of the Russian nation as such, of course, depends only to a very limited degree on developments in Kazakstan and Latvia, and so we asked "What will happen to the future of the culture of the Russians in Kazakstan/Latvia?" We got the following answers:

TABLE 6.36 What Will Happen to the Culture of the Russians in Kazakstan in the Future?

	Latvia	Kaz
1. It will remain as it is today	48.8	40.8
2. It will fall under the influence of Kazak culture	-	17.0
2. It will fall under the influence of Latvian culture	25.1	-
3. It will form a separate branch of Russian culture	2.8	16.6
4. It will fall under the influence of West European culture	10.5	3.5
5. It will be Americanized	5.6	2.5
no answer		19.6

A majority of those who expressed an opinion on this question in both countries thought that Russian culture will remain more or less as it is today. Among those who expected a change, only a small minority in Kazakstan foresaw a development in the direction of West European or American cultures while this was regarded as a much more likely scenario in Latvia. Roughly a fifth in Kazakstan and a fourth in Latvia supported the prognosis that it will fall under the influence of the culture of the titular nationality.[17]

How, then, was the distribution of answers among the various ethnic groups? In calculating the percentages in the table presented below, we have disregarded the N/A ("no answer") group. We arrived at the following score:

TABLE 6.37 What Will Happen To The Future of the Culture of The Russians in Kazakstan?—Ethnic Breakdown. Kazakstan

	Kaz	Rus	Ukr	Germ	Kor	Tatar	Uigh	Cauc	Euro
1.	62.6	41.1	35.9	46.7	50.0	70.4	33.3	57.1	40.9
2.	13.9	27.1	28.2	26.7	8.3	14.8	33.3	14.3	27.3
3.	17.7	24.4	28.2	16.7	33.3	11.1	22.2	-	13.6
4.	3.5	3.6	5.1	6.7	8.3	3.7	11.1	14.3	9.1
5.	2.3	3.9	2.6	3.3	-	-	-	14.3	9.1

[17] The alternatives we offered to the respondents in this case were not always mutually exclusive. Very possibly, many people may think that Russian culture is somewhat different from—but nevertheless a branch of—mainstream Russian culture, due to a certain influence from the titular culture. If they thought that this kind of influence has been strong for a long time already, they might have wished to indicate alternatives 1, 2 and 3 at the same time. Since under the rules of the game they could only indicate one alternative, we registered support for the alternatives which the respondents felt gave the most adequate description of the future situation.

TABLE 6.38 What Will Happen To The Future of the Culture of The Russians in Latvia?—Ethnic breakdown

	Lat	Rus	Ukr	Bel	Pole	Lith
1. It will remain as it is today	51.7	47.5	32.7	55.9	29.5	35.7
2. It will fall under the influence of Latvian culture	27.4	21.2	21.2	20.6	36.4	35.7
3. It will come under the influence of the culture of Russia	2.9	2.1	-	7.4	2.3	7.1
4. It will fall under the influence of West European culture	9.3	10.9	25.0	8.8	15.9	-
5. It will be Americanized	6.2	4.3	9.6	1.5	9.1	14.3

The expectation that the culture of the Russians in Kazakstan will not undergo significant alterations found most support among the Kazaks and other Asian nationalities. The Russians themselves, as well as heavily Russified groups such as Ukrainians and Germans, were far less likely to take a static view of Kazakstani Russian culture. More than a quarter of the respondents in these three categories believed that Russian culture will fall under the influence of Kazak culture.

While Russians in Kazakstan are not obliged to view the predicted Kazakification of their own culture as a cause for worry or regret, we nevertheless think that very many of them do so. We find support for this in their responses to questions regarding political attitudes referred to above.

On this question the Latvian responses differed little from the ones we elicited in Kazakstan. Also in this country roughly three-quarters of the titular group believed that the local Russian culture would remain basically unchanged. Two-thirds of the Russians themselves thought so, too. Not unnaturally, more respondents in Latvia, a European country, expected the local Russian culture to become Westernized.

Asking next "Do Russians in Kazakstan/Latvia differ from Russians in Russia?" we received a remarkably wide variety of answers (Figure 6.4). It is perhaps not surprising that almost 23 percent in Kazakstan and nearly 18 percent in Latvia found it difficult to answer this question since very many of the respondents have probably never been to Russia and thus lack the wherewithal to make a comparison. Among those who did express an opinion as many as 61 percent in Kazakstan and 86 percent in Latvia believed that the local Russians indeed behave and

FIGURE 6.4 Do Russians in [Your Country] Differ From Russians in Russia?

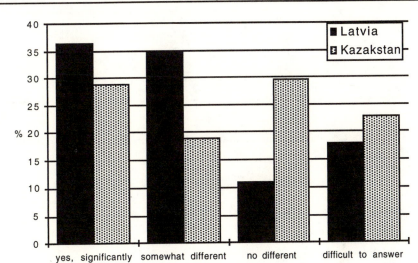

bear themselves differently to the core group in Russia, either significantly or somewhat. In particular, the Latvian figures here are remarkably high. Let us look at how these answers were distributed among the ethnic groups in each country (Table 6.39 and 6.41).

There is a remarkable congruity between Kazak heterostereotypes (Kazak perceptions of local Russians) and the autostereotypes of the local Russians: just under 50 percent in both groups (48.9 percent and 48.3 percent) believed that Russians in Kazakstan are different from Russians in the Russian Federation, either somewhat or significantly. Thus, in a sense, we can say that there is greater agreement *between* Kazaks and Russians on this issue than *within* each of these groups since both nationalities are divided almost evenly into two halves.

With the exception of the Tatars and the Uzbeks, between a fourth to a third of the respondents in all groups think that Kazakstani Russians differ from their ethnic brethren in Russia. Also, with the same two exceptions, half of the respondents either saw no significant differences or found it difficult to answer.

As the breakdown by oblasts we present below shows, the replies varied with the size of the local Russian group as well as with distance from Russia. The respondents in Kzyl-Orda—the demographically least Russianized oblast in our sample—saw the greatest distinctiveness of Kazakstani Russian culture (66.7 percent) (Table 6.40).

TABLE 6.39 Do Russians in Kazakstan differ from Russians in Russia?—Ethnic Breakdown

	Kaz	Rus	Ukr	Germ	Kor	Tatar	Uigh	Cauc	Euro
significantly	31.6	27.9	22.9	29.3	33.3	9.4	37.5	30.8	32.3
somewhat	17.3	21.3	29.2	19.5	6.7	6.3	6.3	7.7	25.8
no different	26.9	33.0	25.0	19.5	20.0	59.4	18.8	23.1	25.8
D/K	24.2	17.8	22.9	31.7	40.0	25.0	37.5	38.5	16.1
A/F	376	409	48	41	15	32	16	13	31

TABLE 6.40 Do Russians in Kazakstan differ from Russians in Russia?— Breakdown by oblast

	significant	somewhat	no diff.	D/K	A/F
Almaty	42.5	19.7	16.5	21.3	127
Kzyl-Orda	66.7	10.7	8.0	14.7	75
Zhambyl	31.4	20.0	25.7	22.9	140
Karaganda	13.2	18.9	37.7	30.2	106
East Kazakstan	30.1	18.6	30.1	21.2	113
Semipalatinsk	19.4	14.0	33.3	33.3	93
Akmola	22.3	23.8	32.3	21.5	130
North Kazakstan	12.7	16.5	45.6	25.3	79
Atyrau	36.0	26.0	36.0	2.0	50
West Kazakstan	18.3	18.3	37.8	25.6	82

TABLE 6.41 Do Russians in Latvia Differ From Russians in Russia?—Ethnic Breakdown

	Lat	Rus	Lith	Ukr	Bel	Pol	Jew	Other
significantly	35.2	41.6	34.8	25.0	24.4	31.7	28.6	37.5
somewhat	34.8	35.1	30.4	50.0	37.8	19.5	50.0	43.8
no	8.7	11.1	4.3	25.0	22.2	19.5	21.4	12.5
D/K	21.3	12.2	30.4	0.0	15.6	29.3	0.0	6.3
A/F	549	296	23	16	45	41	14	16

TABLE 6.42 Do Russians in Latvia differ from Russians in Russia?—Breakdown by region

	significant	somewhat	no	D/K	A/F
Riga	34.7	41.1	10.0	14.2	331
Kurzeme	36.0	30.2	12.2	21.6	139
Zemgale	33.3	35.4	11.1	20.1	144
Vidzeme	48.0	26.9	4.8	20.3	227
Latgale	25.2	37.1	20.1	17.6	159

The population in the three oblasts with the heaviest concentrations of Russophones—Karaganda, East Kazakstan and North Kazakstan—were far less inclined to see important cultural differences among Kazakstani Russians and "Russia–Russians." These are the regions which are located closest to Russia and in which the economic, cultural, and person-to-person links with Russia are most developed. At the same time, as we have seen, the population in East Kazakstan and North Kazakstan (together with the population in Akmola, another northern oblast), were least inclined to believe that Russian culture will remain constant in the future.

In Latvia, the perception that the local Russians are significantly different from Russia–Russians was most widespread among the Russians themselves (41.6 percent, more than 5 percentage points above the evaluation of the ethnic Latvians). This differed from Kazakstan where this view had stronger support among the titular nation than among the Russians. It is somewhat more surprising that this attitude was less common in Latgale, a region with many old Russian settlements, than in Riga where a much larger percentage of the Russians are recent immigrants (Table 6.42).

Moving from generalities to specifics, what exactly do the perceived peculiarities of the local Russian culture consist in? In order to achieve operationable lists of putative qualities to analyze we had to present the respondents with ready-made alternatives rather than give them a chance to formulate their own descriptions. We realize that in this way we may in some sense have preempted the issue, and important qualities may perhaps have eluded us. However, we do not think that this is necessarily the case. The list of qualities to choose from was compiled on the basis of numerous conversations with Russophones and others in various post-Soviet states over the last years.[18] Even so, we warn against overinterpretation of our findings. We suggested a large number of possible responses:

1. more active and industrious
2. more cultured and better educated
3. more internationalist
4. more hard-working and diligent
5. less given to drinking
6. more individualistic
7. less drawn into conflicts
8. more open and gregarious
9. more hospitable

---

[18] For a more detailed discussion of this see Kolstø 1996b.

10. more tolerant toward the views and opinions of others
11. less attached to national traditions and customs

Almost all of these qualities have a normative tint, but the value put on them may vary somewhat from society to society: in most cases agreement must be regarded as more complimentary of the local Russians than disagreement. There are, however, some moot points.

First, while in many Western societies individualism (quality 6) is regarded as a virtue, in Soviet ideology it was frowned upon. Our local team in Kazakstan believed that this would be regarded as a negative description in their country while our Latvian collaborators thought that in Latvian society it would be regarded as neutral, depending upon the situation. Second, the term "internationalism" (quality 3) is closely associated with Soviet ideology, and is likely to be regarded as invidious in Latvia, a relic of the discarded Soviet past, but is still used by Russian activists in Kazakstan as a positive self-identification.[19] Third, "attachment to traditions" (quality 11) is perhaps more likely to be highly valued in traditional societies than in modern or modernizing societies. However, even in modern societies this may be regarded as a rare but valuable quality. In fact both our Latvian and Kazakstani team believed that it would be seen as definitely positive in their society.

The respondents could choose from four levels of agreement: 1. agree completely; 2. more or less agree; 3. more or less disagree; 4. disagree completely. Below, the rows have been rearranged in a such a way that the alternative for which the highest agreement coefficient was registered is ranked first, followed by the others in descending order.

TABLE 6.43 Perceived Peculiarities of Russian Culture. Kazakstan

	fully agree	agree somewhat	disagree somewhat	fully disagree	D/K	coeff.
more internationalist	47.2	26.8	11.3	5.9	8.8	1.74
more hospitable	42.6	30.0	10.3	6.9	10.3	1.80
more open and gregarious	41.7	32.7	12.4	6.5	6.7	1.83
more hard-working, diligent	42.1	28.5	13.8	6.9	8.6	1.84
more tolerant	34.8	31.7	13.0	6.5	14.0	1.90
less drawn into conflicts	30.4	32.9	17.6	7.8	11.3	2.03
more active and industrious	34.2	26.2	22.0	9.2	8.4	2.07
less given to drinking	36.3	21.4	17.6	13.0	11.7	2.09
more cultured and educated	34.0	26.8	19.9	10.7	8.6	2.09
less attached to traditions	26.8	27.5	21.2	10.5	14.0	2.18
more individualistic	14.5	21.6	27.9	14.9	21.2	2.55

---

[19] See, e.g., the article "We are internationalists," *Iuzhnyi Kazakhstan* 10 November 1992.

TABLE 6.44 Perceived Peculiarities of Russian Culture in Kazakstan. Kazak and Russian Ranking Lists

Kazaks	coeff.	Russians	coeff.
more internationalist	1.8	more internationalist	1.7
more hardworking, diligent	1.8	more hospitable	1.7
more open and gregarious	1.9	more tolerant	1.7
more active and industrious	2.0	more hardworking, diligent	1.8
more cultured and educated	2.0	more open and gregarious	1.8
less drawn into conflicts	2.0	less drawn into conflicts	2.1
more hospitable	2.0	less given to drinking	2.1
more tolerant	2.0	less attached to traditions	2.1
less given to drinking	2.2	more active and industrious	2.2
less attached to traditions	2.2	more cultured and educated	2.2
more individualistic	2.4	more individualistic	2.6

TABLE 6.45 Perceived Peculiarities of Russian Culture. Latvia

	fully agree	agree	disagree somewhat	fully disagree	D/K	coeff.
more active and industrious	18.9	29.6	12.3	6.9	32.3	2.11
more hard-working, diligent	17.5	26.9	15.9	12.8	26.9	2.33
more open and gregarious	15.4	31.1	16.1	12.6	24.8	2.34
more cultured and educated	17.0	30.2	16.5	15.2	21.1	2.38
more internationalist	13.8	25.8	17.0	11.6	31.8	2.39
more hospitable	14.5	27.2	18.4	12.7	27.2	2.40
more tolerant	12.6	29.5	13.8	13.9	30.1	2.41
less attached to traditions	15.9	27.2	20.3	15.2	21.4	2.44
less drawn into conflicts	11.4	24.8	18.4	18.1	27.3	2.59
more individualistic	7.2	20.3	20.0	12.3	40.2	2.63
less given to drinking	7.6	15.6	20.6	25.0	31.2	2.92

TABLE 6.46 Perceived Peculiarities of Russian Culture in Latvia. Latvian and Russian Ranking lists

Latvians	coeff.	Russians	coeff.
more active and industrious	2.07	more tolerant	1.87
more internationalist	2.32	more hard-working, diligent	1.96
more open and gregarious	2.39	more cultured and educated	1.96
less attached to traditions	2.43	more active and industrious	2.12
more hard-working, diligent	2.58	less drawn into conflicts	2.12
more hospitable	2.63	more hospitable	2.14
more individualistic	2.64	more open and gregarious	2.25
more cultured and educated	2.69	less attached to traditions	2.37
more tolerant	2.84	more internationalist	2.39
less drawn into conflicts	2.91	more individualistic	2.61
less given to drinking	3.06	less given to drinking	2.65

As can be seen, the prevalent opinion in Kazakstan is that local Russians are a qualitatively better lot than Russians in Russia. Taken together, the respondents were inclined to agree with the positive value assessments they were offered. Only on one quality was the assessment clearly different from the others: individualism.

These two lists are more remarkable for their similarities than for their differences. Importantly, both groups put internationalism on top and individualism at the very bottom. On only two qualities—hospitality and tolerance—was the difference in the respective scores more than 0.2 points. On both of these the Russians were more inclined to give themselves a good testimonial than were the Kazaks. On the other hand, the Kazaks more than the Russians themselves tended to see the Russians in Kazakstan as industrious and cultured compared to Russia–Russians. We may perhaps permit ourselves to view the Kazak answers as evidence of positive attitudes toward Russians among the titular nationality in Kazakstan: "our" Russians are better than other Russians.

The Latvian ranking order differed from the one we found in Kazakstan. First, even though respondents in Latvia, as we have seen, are more inclined to see the local Russians as somehow different from Russia–Russians in general (more than 71.3 percent as against 47.7 percent in Kazakstan) they were less inclined to agree with the particular character traits we gave them to choose from. This might indicate that we were less successful in identifying the peculiar traits of Latvian Russians than of Kazakstani Russians (or perhaps, more correctly, in identifying the most common stereotypes of Latvian Russians than of Kazakstani Russians). Even so, with a 2.5 score as the break-off point between "agreement" and "disagreement," a majority of the respondents also in Latvia expressed more agreement than disagreement on 8 out of 11 qualities.

On the Latvian list, internationalism had receded to fifth place, while individualism also in this country was regarded as a not very typical character trait of the local Russians. The two most popular identifications were with high activity and hard work. These character traits, as pointed out in Chapter 2 (page 40), are widely regarded as typical of "the Baltic way of life" and an echo of "the Protestant work ethic."

However, while we found a remarkable concurrence of views in Kazakstan with regard to the assessment of the local Russians, the Russian character profiles composed by the various ethnic groups in *Latvia* differed from each other in significant ways.

It appears that Russians in Latvia were inclined to hold relatively self-congratulatory opinions of themselves while ethnic Latvians took a much dimmer view of their Russian neighbors. Only on four points—activity, openness, internationalism, and weak attachment to traditions—did the ethnic Latvians tend to agree with our suggestions. Of these, the latter two qualities should probably be regarded as negative assessments—or ambiguous at best.

Latvians were less willing to give the local Russians credit for higher diligence, hospitality, or individualism compared to Russians in Russia. They definitely did not think that "their" Russians were more cultured, tolerant, and sober or less conflictual than other Russians. On these quality traits, they gave the Russians as low score as 2.69 to 3.06, a real slap in the face. Only on the issue of drinking habits did the Russians themselves tend to agree with these negative assessments. As regards culture, tolerance, and ability to avoid conflict they gave themselves 0.7 to 1.0 higher scores than did the Latvians! This contrasts sharply with the situation in Kazakstan. On no quality assessment in Kazakstan was there greater disagreement than 0.3 points between the Russians on the one hand, and the titular nation on the other.

The lack of congruence between Russian autostereotypes and Latvian heterostereotypes of Russians in Latvia is so marked that it may allow for relatively robust conclusions. The Russians seem to be saying: "We are clearly different from our ethnic brethren in Russia, and the reason for this is that we are more like you Latvians." This may be interpreted as a centripetal message. However, the Russians in Latvia are met with a rather terse retort from the ethnic Latvians: "Certainly you are different from Russians in Russia, but not in the ways you think. And don't think that we necessarily hold you in higher esteem for that reason."

Ways and Means to
Foster Ethnic Integration

We suggested to our respondents a string of possible means and ways to promote ethnic integration. The titulars and the nontitulars are entering the interethnic arena from opposite sides, as it were, and it did not make sense to suggest the same kinds of solutions to all of them. Instead, we offered one package of remedies to the Kazaks and the Latvians, on the one hand, and another to the nontitulars in both countries, on the other.

TABLE 6.47 Kazak Perceptions of How to Best Promote Interethnic Consolidation

	1	2	3	4	D/K	coeff
Help the non-Kazaks learn Kazak	74.9	16.1	3.4	0.8	4.8	1.27
Get rid of national prejudices	43.1	36.5	6.9	4.5	9.0	1.70
Support non-Kazak cultural societies	29.6	37.6	12.4	8.5	11.9	2.00
Study the costumes of other peoples	29.4	32.5	14.0	11.9	12.2	2.10
Enhance the opportunities to use Russian language	26.5	35.2	18.8	11.4	8.2	2.16

TABLE 6.48 Latvian Perceptions of How to Best Promote Interethnic Consolidation

	agree strongly	agree somewhat	disagree somewhat	disagree strongly	D/K	coeff.
Increase the influence of Latvian culture on the non-Latvians	52.2	29.6	4.9	2.4	10.8	1.36
Get rid of ethnic prejudices built up over the last fifty years	40.9	30.9	7.9	4.9	15.4	1.46
Help non-Latvians learn Latvian	61.8	21.4	6.2	7.2	3.4	1.52
Support non-Latvian cultural societies	25.3	35.1	13.9	12.6	13.2	1.88
Promote the political activity of the national minorities	18.6	23.2	23.9	17.7	16.6	2.08
Enhance the opportunities to use Russian language	5.9	7.6	21.6	57.5	7.5	3.16

The Kazaks were asked to evaluate the following suggestions:

1. Help them learn Kazak
2. Increase the opportunities to use Russian language
3. Get rid of ethnic prejudices
4. Support non-Kazak cultural societies
5. Study the customs of other peoples

As the table shows, the vast majority of the Kazaks singled out "help them learn Kazak" as their preferred panacea to interethnic problems in Kazakstan. This is perhaps somewhat surprising since the enthusiasm for learning Kazak is less than overwhelming among the ethnic Kazaks themselves. As we have seen, as many as 40 percent of the Kazaks in our sample have children who study in Russian schools. At the same time, promotion of "the state language" is an essential aspect of official Kazakstani nation-building policy, at least on the face of it. We therefore assume that the high score on the need to teach Kazak to the nontitulars may have been boosted by "the Political Correctness factor."

The Kazaks agreed that they ought to contribute to the elimination of ethnic prejudices and in general were not opposed to any of the other proposals we suggested either. However, also on these points considerations of "political correctness" may have influenced their answers. They may also have observed that the survey was being organized by a Russophone polling institute affiliated with the largest opposition paper in the country. Taking these circumstances into account, we may perhaps be justified in seeing Kazak support for the three last proposals on our list as less than enthusiastic.

Among ethnic Latvians the two most popular solutions by far were to help the nontitulars learn Latvian and to increase the influence of Latvian culture. The Latvians adamantly rejected the idea of enhancing opportunities to use the Russian language. The coefficient of 3.16 agreement with this suggestion stood in sharp contrast to coefficient of 2.16 among the Kazaks! If these answers convey real attitudes—and not only what the respondents thought the pollster wanted to hear—while the Kazaks are willing to see their country remain bilingual and bicultural, the Latvians are not. These figures indicate a groundswell of popular support for the "one-community concept" of the Latvian nation-builders. Also the somewhat lukewarm support for the suggestion that the national minorities should become more politically active, corroborated this conclusion.

A parallel bundle of questions were presented to the nontitular groups in our sample. We asked if they believed that they could contribute to the improvement of interethnic relations by:

1. Learning Kazak/Latvian
2. Sending their children to Kazak-/Latvian-language schools
3. Take part in the activities of minority cultural organizations
4. Strive for genuine equality in all spheres of life
5. Study Kazak/Latvian traditions
6. Get rid of national prejudices

As usual, the respondents were offered a four-graded scale of agreement possibilities (Table 6.49 to 6.52).

The non-Kazaks believed that the most important thing they could do to improve the interethnic climate, would be to strive for genuine equality. Implicitly, they expressed the view that today the equality among the ethnic groups of Kazakstan leaves something to be desired. Like the Kazaks' preference for teaching the Russians better Kazak this choice must probably be regarded as more provocative than accommodating.

At the same time, our nontitular respondents in Kazakstan were rather indifferent to the work of the various national cultural centers; neither did they oppose them, nor did they support them. They were generally inclined to agree that they ought to learn the Kazak language and Kazak traditions but they were ill-disposed toward the suggestion that they ought to send their children to Kazak schools. They remain strongly committed to the Russian language as their first language, and will only agree to study Kazak as a second language in Russian schools, as they do today. Their willingness to gain a reasonably good command of the state language may in some cases be less than sincere.

As the following breakdown shows, the fiercest opposition to a Kazak-language upbringing stemmed not from the Russians, but from some smaller groups: Uighurs, Germans, and Koreans. However, the Russians, Ukrainians, and Caucasians were trailing not far behind.

On the issue of struggle for genuine equality, the Europeans were clearly more unyielding than the Asians (1.3–1.4 as against 1.6–1.7). On this question, the Caucasians joined the Europeans. Our suggestion that national prejudices may be a problem produced a strikingly similar alignment: the Asians were clearly more skeptical about this suggestion than were the Europeans. On the other hand, the Asians were much more ready to start studying Kazak, perhaps because they already have some skills in this language. These clear patterns we see as yet another confirmation of our thesis that there exists a separate subgroup of "Russophones" within the body of nontitulars in Kazakstani society.

Among the various types of settlements, the inhabitants of the capital city and Almaty oblast were least interested in joining national cultural organizations. This is remarkable, since these organizations, most of which have few local branches, usually are clustered in the capital. Thus, a greater accessibility of such organizations does not seem to increase their popularity; rather the opposite is true. This observation makes us doubt somewhat the sincerity of the determination to work for full equal rights which so many respondents avowed. While the vast majority of the nontitulars were willing to strive for greater equality in the abstract, they recoiled from entering the available arenas where this struggle can be waged in practice.

TABLE 6.49 Nontitulars' Perceptions on How to Contribute to the Improvement of Interethnic Relations in Kazakstan

	1	2	3	4	D/K	coeff
Strive for genuine equality	58.8	30.3	2.2	1.4	7.2	1.42
Get rid of national prejudices	51.9	26.3	3.0	3.4	15.4	1.50
Learn Kazak	25.8	41.5	14.4	9.9	6.3	2.09
Study Kazak traditions	20.4	49.2	15.2	6.6	8.7	2.09
Take part in the activities of minority cultural organizations	13.1	32.4	17.6	15.9	21.0	2.46
Sending their children to Kazak-language schools	5.1	19.4	26.3	39.3	9.9	3.11

TABLE 6.50 Nontitulars' Perceptions on How to Contribute to the Improvement of Interethnic Relations —Ethnic breakdown. Kazakstan. Coefficients

Ethnic group	Learn Kazak	Attend Kazak schools	Participate in cultural societies	Strive for equality	Study Kazak traditions	Get rid of prejudices
Russians	2.1	3.1	2.5	1.4	2.1	1.5
Ukrainians	2.2	3.1	2.4	1.4	2.0	1.5
Germans	2.4	3.4	2.1	1.4	2.1	1.5
Koreans	2.0	3.2	2.6	1.6	2.3	1.8
Tatars	1.7	2.9	2.2	1.4	2.2	1.6
Uighurs	2.5	3.5	2.2	1.7	2.2	1.2
Uzbeks	1.3	1.9	2.7	1.7	1.4	2.8
Caucasians	1.9	3.1	2.2	1.4	1.9	1.3
Other Europeans	1.9	3.0	2.3	1.3	2.2	1.3
Other Asians	1.4	2.6	2.3	1.7	2.1	2.2
Education						
Incomplete medium	2.0	3.0	2.4	1.4	2.1	1.5
medium	2.1	3.1	2.5	1.4	2.1	1.5
vocational	2.0	3.1	2.4	1.4	2.1	1.5
incomplete higher	2.1	3.3	2.7	1.4	2.1	1.4
higher education	2.2	3.2	2.4	1.4	2.1	1.6
Location						
capital	1.9	3.4	3.0	1.7	2.4	1.4
oblast centers	2.2	3.1	2.3	1.4	2.2	1.3
other cities	2.2	3.1	2.5	1.4	2.0	1.6
industrial towns	2.0	3.0	2.6	1.2	1.9	1.4
countryside	2.0	3.1	2.4	1.5	2.0	1.7

TABLE 6.51 Nontitulars' Perceptions on How to Contribute to Ethnic Integration in Latvia

	Agree strongly	Agree somewhat	Disagree somewhat	Disagree strongly	D/K	Coeff
Learn the Latvian language	70.8	24.0	1.4	1.3	2.6	1.28
Non-Latvians must strive for political equality with the indigenous population	53.2	28.4	7.5	3.8	6.8	1.48
Non-Latvians must participate actively in the cultural organizations of the minorities	41.4	39.9	7.5	3.4	7.8	1.57
Non-Latvians must send their children to Latvian-language schools/kinder-gartens in order to facilitate their integration into Latvian society	45.1	30.4	15.0	4.7	4.8	1.70
Non-Latvians must accept Latvian traditions and other cultural values	31.9	33.9	17.3	7.0	9.9	1.80

TABLE 6.52 Non-Titulars' Perceptions on How to Contribute to the Improvement of Interethnic Relations—Ethnic Breakdown. Latvia

Ethnicity	Learn Latvian	Attend Latvian schools	Participate in cultural societies	Strive for political equality	Accept Latvian traditions
Russians	1.26	1.74	1.54	1.45	1.78
Ukrainians	1.33	1.73	1.81	1.40	1.77
Belarusians	1.35	1.68	1.65	1.75	1.83
Lithuanians	1.07	0.99	1.50	1.36	1.14
Poles	1.27	1.52	1.50	1.64	1.93
Jews	1.47	1.88	2.00	1.35	2.65
Other	1.33	1.37	1.37	1.50	1.50
Education					
Incomplete medium	1.29	1.73	1.73	1.78	1.93
medium	1.28	1.78	1.55	1.48	1.80
vocational	1.29	1.58	1.64	1.39	1.70
incomplete higher	1.42	1.97	1.58	1.84	2.03
higher education	1.29	1.79	1.61	1.58	1.94
Location					
capital	1.41	1.86	1.65	1.51	1.83
oblast centers	1.22	1.63	1.47	1.47	1.91
other cities	1.12	1.58	1.61	1.35	1.48
countryside	1.17	1.47	1.52	1.54	1.70

Due to circumstances over which we did not have complete control, the list of questions presented to our respondents in Latvia were sometimes slightly different from those that were included in the Kazakstani questionnaire. The discrepancies, however, are not dramatic, and we are able to draw some rather startling comparative conclusions, in particular with regard to linguistic integration.

In Kazakstan, as we have seen, there was strong disagreement between the Kazaks and the Russians regarding the utility of the titular language as an instrument of integration: 76 percent of the Kazaks strongly agreed that the best way to promote interethnic consolidation was to help the nontitulars learn Kazak; 26 percent of the Russians were of the same opinion. In Latvia, on the other hand, 71 percent of the nontitulars believed that they ought to learn the state language while only 3 percent disagreed.

Equally interesting from a conflict perspective are the differences of opinion on whether increased nontitular political representation will help integrate the nontitulars. More than 40 percent of the ethnic Latvians disagreed that "Promotion of the political activity of the national minorities" was a good way of advancing integration. By contrast, more than 80 percent of the nontitulars in Latvia thought that striving for political equality was a good way of improving interethnic relations. Clearly, efforts of the nontitulars to be integrated into the Latvian political nation are met with a large measure of skepticism from the titular ethnic group.

The Russophones were quite willing to send their children to Latvian schools: the coefficients were around 1.7 for all major Slavic groups. This is more clear evidence of strong centripetal tendencies among the Russophones in Latvia.

Conclusions

The information revealed by our surveys can by organized under four headings. First, the extent of the current cultural and linguistic divisions. Second, the degree to which the subordinate groups want to be integrated. Third, whether the superordinate group accepts the integration of the subordinates. Fourth, the respondents' expectations of future developments.

On the first issue, the surveys indicated that we were dealing with two divided societies. For instance, on the question of cultural self-identification the Russophones and the titular nationalities clearly considered themselves to belong to different groups, but the perceived cultural distance was far more pronounced in Kazakstan than in Latvia.

In Kazakstan, the coefficient for identification with Kazak culture among the Russians was as high as 3.5, indicating strong disagreement with the statement that they were representatives of the titular nationality's culture. This may be unsurprising but the result is still valuable in the sense that it transforms what may have been prejudices into well-grounded beliefs. In Latvia, by contrast, the coefficient of the Russians was considerably lower: 2.7. Among some of the other nontitular groups the coefficient was even lower. This finding was less obvious, and indicates that, as seen from the perspective of the Russophones, Latvia is only a moderately divided society.

The responses we got from the ethnic Latvians, however, indicated that they tend to disagree with this view. They regard the local Russians as rather different from themselves and also tend to guard their status as "state-bearing nation" much more jealously than do the Kazaks. Twice as many ethnic Latvians than ethnic Kazaks regarded themselves as the sole nonminority group in their respective eponymous state. The Russians in Latvia were clearly prepared to defer to the Latvians on this issue. Even more Russians than Latvians accepted that Latvians are the only nonminority group in Latvia. Thus, in the perception of all major groups in Latvia there seems to be a clearer ranking of superordinates/subordinates than in Kazakstan.

Our surveys also revealed that although the nontitulars are culturally distinct from the titular group, most of them did not identify strongly with their putative ethnic homeland. For instance, in both countries only a minority of the local Russians—11 percent and 13 percent—ticked off for "Russia" as their motherland, while more than 40 percent considered Latvia/Kazakstan to be their homeland. This low degree of attachment to their ethnic homeland among the largest nontitular group must be good news for nation-builders who are concerned about Russian irredentism. At the same time, it also indicated that the potential for large-scale, culturally motivated emigration of the nontitulars is limited.

In Kazakstan, a sizable group among the Russophones—in the range of one-third—still cling to the defunct Soviet state as the country they identify with. In Latvia, support for the Soviet option in all nontitular groups was less than 20 percent.[20] If we regard identification with Latvia, respectively Kazakstan, as centripetal, and identification with "Russia" or "another country" as "centrifugal," then identification with the Soviet Union may be seen as undecided or transient. With this classification the political orientation of the majority of the nontitulars in

---

[20] The only exception was the Jews. This group, however, counted only 14 individuals; the finding, therefore, can not be regarded as very reliable.

Latvia is centripetal. In Kazakstan, on the other hand, the issue is as yet undecided, and may to a large degree be influenced by the actual nation-building policies as well as by the economic performance of the Kazakstani state.

In sum, the situation can be described as one with two quite distinct cultural groups who both claim the right to live in the country. These claims need not be irreconcilable, but they suggest that a precondition for peace is a willingness to adjust—that the titulars must accept the nontitulars as members of society, and the nontitulars must want to be members of this society. What did the survey tell us about this?

Questions which discussed what should be done to promote interethnic consolidation often revealed strong disagreements. In Kazakstan, most disagreements concerned issues of *linguistic* integration while in Latvia there were primarily strong disagreements with regard to *political* integration. In both countries, the titular ethnic group very much wanted the nontitulars to learn the state language. In Latvia, the Russophones expressed a high degree of readiness for this, while in Kazakstan they did not. In Latvia, however, the Russians also wanted to get a chance to participate more actively in Latvian political life, but were rebuffed in this by the ethnic Latvians.

The upshot of all this seems to be that while all groups may want closer integration, they differ greatly on exactly what it is that promotes integration. Thus, even if the superordinate group accepts integration and the subordinate groups want to be integrated, there is still scope for conflict since they disagree on how integration is best promoted. The importance of this conflict, however, depends on the fourth issue—expectations of the future.

In our surveys, the Russophones largely disagreed with the statement that one good way of promoting integration would be to send their children to Latvian/Kazakstani schools. However, if they expect the importance of the Latvian/Kazak language to grow in the future (as revealed in our surveys), they may nevertheless send their children to Latvian/Kazak schools. Hence, disagreement on the means to foster integration need not indicate that people's actual behavior will lead to further separation. In fact, we think that one of the most significant findings from our surveys was that there had been a sevenfold increase in the percentage of Russians attending Latvian schools (and a fourfold increase in Russians attending Kazak schools but from a much lower base). One plausible explanation of the difference between Latvia and Kazakstan, is that the Russians in Latvia to a greater extent than the Russians in Kazakstan expect the native language to become more important. This illustrates the importance of expectations for integration.

Social integration involves several actors: titulars and nontitular groups. Integration, furthermore, has several dimensions—political, cultural and linguistic. Strong centripetal tendencies in the political dimension do not necessarily go hand in hand with equally strong tendencies in the cultural dimension.

With regard to most questions in our Latvian survey we found a strong willingness among the Russophone respondents to integrate in Latvian society on the conditions set by the Latvian authorities but not an equally strong willingness of the ethnic Latvians to welcome them into the Latvian fold on these terms. However, this Latvian unwillingness is not so great that it should be labeled "forced segregation." The social scene in Latvia seems to vacillate between positions "A" and "C" in Schermerhorn's typology (see Figure 3.1, p. 53).

In Kazakstan, on the other hand, there seems to be a somewhat greater willingness among the titular group to accept the Russians and to want them to integrate into Kazakstani society. In many respects the Kazaks themselves also partake more in Russian culture than do the ethnic Latvians. However, in general the cultural cleavages between the two major groups in Kazakstan are nevertheless so deep that under no circumstances is an amalgamation of them into one culture an option. What remains is structural incorporation. On this issue, the willingness of the ethnic Russians to integrate is ambiguous. On the one hand, they do not seriously challenge the political superiority of the Kazaks, on the other, they have not wholeheartedly transferred their political allegiance to this state. The social scene in Kazakstan seems to vacillate between positions "B" and "C" in Schermerhorn's typology.

Methodological Appendix

There are at least two main questions one should ask before interpreting statistical evidence. First, is the sample representative of the larger population? Second, do the statistical procedures produce misleading differences? The first point can be examined by looking at the distribution of respondents according to gender, age, ethnicity, geographic location and educational level. The second requires us to mention some of the statistical difficulties we encountered.

The Surveys

Kazakstan. The survey in Kazakhstan was organized by the Giller institute in Almaty (507–511,11 Chaikovsky Street) among 1,000 respondents in Kazakstan between May and October 1996. This institute is run by the *Karavan* complex which also publishes the largest Russophone opposition paper in Kazakstan, *Karavan*. Interviews were conducted on 53 different locations in 10 oblasts. These oblasts were chosen from all parts of the country: the south (Kzyl-Orda and Zhambyl), the north (Akmola [Astana] and North Kazakstan), the northeast (Semipalatinsk and East Kazakstan), the northwest (Atyrau and West Kazakstan), the center (Karaganda), and the capital city with surroundings (Almaty). In each oblast residents of both the oblast center and other cities, of industrial towns, and of the countryside were included in the survey. In order to ensure maximum representativity the person in each household whose birthday was closest to the date when the visit of the pollster took place, was interviewed. Only persons older than 18 years of age were included. Questionnaires were produced

TABLE 6.53 Distribution of respondents by oblasts. Kazakstan

Oblast	percent
Almaty	12.7
Kzyl-Orda	7.5
Zhambyl	14.0
Karaganda	10.6
East Kazakstan	11.3
Semipalatinsk	9.3
Akmola	13.0
North Kazakstan	7.9
Atyrau	5.0
West Kazakstan	8.2
No answer	5.0
Total	*100*

TABLE 6.54 Distribution of Respondents by Educational Levels. Kazakstan

level	percent
incomplete medium	13.7
medium	30.0
medium specialized	31.6
incomplete higher	4.7
higher education	19.7
difficult to answer	0.3
total	100

TABLE 6.55 Distribution of Respondents by Age. Kazakstan

age	percent
under 20	3.8
20–29	20.1
30–39	24.2
40–49	21.1
50–59	12.8
60–69	10.5
older than 69	7.4
no answer	0.1

in two versions, one in Russian and one in Kazak. The interview was conducted in the language the respondent was most comfortable with.

In general, the sample gives a reasonably accurate cross section of the inhabitants of the republic of Kazakstan. There is a slight overrepresentation of persons with higher levels of education, which is not unusual in contemporary Kazakstani surveys. One of the reasons for this is a certain discrepancy between official educational statistics on the one hand and the actual number of graduates on the other. An increasing number of students have studied at private institutions of learning which not always are officially licensed. Even so, they regard themselves as belonging in the category of persons with higher education. In addition, it is more common that persons with low levels of education refuse to be interviewed.

As regards the distribution of age groups, there is a slight underrepresentation of the younger cohorts. One of the reasons for this is the higher mobility of the youth which makes them less accessible for interviews. Many youngsters travel from the villages to the cities where they live semilegally, or they travel abroad as *Gastarbeiters* for shorter or longer periods of time.

The ethnic composition of the sample is shown in Table 6.56.

TABLE 6.56 The Ethnic Composition of the Kazakstani Sample

Nationality	percent
Kazaks	37.6
Russians	40.9
Ukrainians	4.8
Germans	4.1
Koreans	1.5
Tatars	3.2
Uighurs	1.6
Uzbeks	0.8
Caucasian nationalities	1.3
other European nationalities	3.1
other Asian nationalities	0.9
No answer	0.2

The ethnic distribution in the sample we regard as accurate. The percentage of Kazaks is lower than in the official statistics, but one must bear in mind that these statistics include all age-groups, also children under 18 years of age. Since the birth rates of the Kazaks are higher than among the other ethnic groups in the country they are overrepresented in the lowest cohorts which were not covered by our survey. Thus, the number of Russians in our survey is three percentage points above the number of Kazaks. This we regard as perfectly normal.

Latvia. The Latvian data have been compiled from two separate surveys. The first was conducted by the company Latvian Facts in October 1995. A representative sample comprising 1,563 respondents was selected in accordance with the social, demographic, and territorial structure of the population of Latvia. Formalized interviews were conducted in the capital, in Latvia's major cities, in small towns, and in the countryside. The questionnaire was printed in two versions, Latvian and Russian. Computer input and data processing made use of SPSS for Windows software.

The second Latvian survey was conducted by the Laboratory of Sociological Research at the Daugavpils Pedagogical University (Parades street 1, 227, Daugavpils LV–5400 Latvia) in September 1997. This survey covered the questions dealing with language in education, perceptions of the future importance of the languages, the new rich, homeland perceptions, civic pride and the perceived differences between Russians in Latvia and Russians in Russia.[21]

The survey covered 1,000 respondents in all five administrative regions of Latvia—Riga, Kurzeme, Zemgale, Vidzeme, and Latgale. The respondents were picked through a five-stage selection process:

---

[21] The findings on these questions are reproduced in tables 6.10, 6.12, 6.14, 6.15, 6.17, 6.21, 6.22, 6.23, 6.27, 6.28, 6.29, 6.43, 6.44, 6.48, and 6.50.

1. the number of persons to be interviewed in each region. Rather than polling an equal number of respondents from each region, the number of interviews in each region corresponds to its share of the total population of Latvia: Riga: 332, Kurzeme 139, Zemgale 144, Vidzeme 227, and Latgale 160.
2. The area was chosen by lottery.
3. The municipality within each area was chosen by lottery.
4. The household was chosen by lottery, the procedure depending upon the type of settlement.
5. Within each household the person whose birthday was closest to the date when the visit of the pollster took place, was interviewed. Only persons older than 18 years of age were included.

Questionnaires were produced in two versions, one in Russian and one in Latvian. The interview was conducted in the language with which the respondent was most comfortable.

As expected the deviations from the national ethnic composition of the population are greatest in the smaller groups. By and large, we believe the cross section in the sample is very accurate.

In the last Soviet census from 1989, the male population comprised 46.5 percent of the total Latvian population. In working age and above, however, the male population was significantly smaller: 44 percent. Since 1989 the relative share of the adult male population has decreased further, due to the shorter life expectancy of men, the withdrawal of the Russian army, and short-term emigration in search of work.

TABLE 6.57 The Ethnic Composition of the Samples (Latvia)

	population[a]	1995 survey	1997 survey
Latvians	55.1	54.9	55.0
Russians	32.6	31.1	29.7
Lithuanians	1.3	0.9	2.3
Ukrainians	2.9	3.3	1.6
Belarusians	4.0	4.4	4.3
Polish	2.2	2.8	4.1
Other	1.9	2.6	3.0

[a] *Source: Latvija. Parskats par tautas attistibu. Riga 1996, 16.*

TABLE 6.58 Samples by Educational Levels. Latvia

Education	Official data[a]	1995 survey	1997 survey
higher education	13.6	18.2	11.1
incomplete higher	-	7.2	6.5
medium and specialized medium	53.7	54.2	56.2
incomplete medium and below	32.7	20.3	25.1
difficult to say/no answer	-	0.3	1.1

[a] *Source: Statistical bulletin. Labour force in Latvia*, Riga 1996, 27.

TABLE 6.59 Age Distribution. Latvia

Age	1989 Census	1995 survey	1997 survey
18-29 years -	27.6	24.1	26.0
30-59 years -	50.3	57.7	50.0
60 years and older	22.1	18.2	24.0

Our polling institute had aimed for a 42:58 ratio of males to females in the sample for the 1997 survey. In the final result, the ratio was 41:59 in the 1997 survey and 49:51 in the survey from 1995.

In the surveys the distribution of the respondents according to levels of education was as presented in Table 6.58.

The respondents covered by the survey were all 18 years or older, and the distribution among the age groups were therefore inevitably slightly different.

In sum, statistically speaking it seems that our surveys were reasonably representative of the population at large.

Statistical Problems

We encountered certain statistical problems which the reader should be aware of, for the most part caused by somewhat insufficient coordination between the three surveys. For instance, on the question of self-identification the Kazaks could choose between four alternatives (ranging from complete agreement to complete disagreement), while the Latvian polling institute used only three options (agree, partly, disagree). If we had calculated the coefficients in the usual fashion, they would not be comparable. The first would have a maximum value of 4; the second of 3—and we could not say that a coefficient of 2.7 in the second survey indicated more disagreement than, say, 3.1 in the first survey. To make the coefficients comparable, we made the theoretical range equal by assigning the value 1 to "agree," 2.5 to "partly" and 4 to "disagree." The controversial point, of course, is whether this weighting is correct. Assuming that "partly" is equally far from "disagree somewhat" and "agree somewhat," we thought the weighting was justified. There is, however, scope for disagreement.

More generally, the use of coefficients eliminates some types of information. For instance, a coefficient of 2.5 in the mentioned example of cultural identification could either represent a population in which most people partly agreed to the statement, or in which there were an equal number of people who strongly disagreed and agreed. If this were the case, the same coefficient would clearly require different interpretations. While this might be a problem for the smaller groups, we did not find it to be a large problem for comparison across major groups. Empirically speaking, after examining the details behind the coefficients we compared, we did not find that the problem above was a serious one.

A more important problem, however, is that comparison of coefficients can be misleading when there are significant differences in the number of people who did not answer the question. For instance, a coefficient of 2.7 for one group and 2.9 for another, does not necessarily imply that more people in the second group disagree with the statement, since the first group may have a large "don't know" percentage which pulls the coefficient down. This problem also explains the 0.99 value in table 6.52, and it implies that one should always consider the size of the "don't know" alternative before drawing conclusions based on coefficients. One could, of course, try to solve this problem by calculating the coefficients based on the percentages after eliminating the "don't know" answers. On the other hand, a large "don't know" category might be seen as an important piece of information which should be allowed to pull the coefficient down.

A final problem which should be mentioned, was that the Kazakstani respondents were allowed to choose more than one alternative to the question, "In which ethnic group do we find most rich people?," while the Latvians were only allowed to indicate one group. About 15 percent of the respondents in Kazakstan chose to mark more than one ethnic group. This means that the sum adds to more than 100, and, accordingly, one should not infer that if 60 percent think the Russians were the most wealthy people the same people necessarily believe that the Kazaks were less wealthy. Remembering this, the data are perfectly interpretable on their own as indicators of attitudes in each country, but they are not fully comparable.

7

Comparisons and Conclusions

Pål Kolstø

Cultural diversity, Stability, and Democracy

Stated in the broadest possible terms, the interrelationships between the three variables mentioned in the subheading above have made up the subject matter of this book. These interrelationships have provoked heated arguments among academics as well as among practitioners. Human rights experts maintain that the right to a cultural identity is an unalienable democratic right. Hence, in a genuine democracy, there will always be at least a potential for cultural diversity. In the wake of the collapse of Communism in Eastern Europe such viewpoints were brought to the surface in the ensuing debate. For instance, the Copenhagen meeting of the Conference on the Human Dimension of the CSCE in 1990 stated that persons belonging to national minorities have the right to freely express, preserve, and develop their ethnic, cultural, linguistic, or religious identity and to maintain and develop their culture in all its aspects. The meeting further affirmed that "respect for the rights of persons belonging to national minorities [...] is an essential factor for peace, justice, stability and democracy in the participating states."[1] Thus, not only democracy but also social stability, it was claimed, flows from good minority regimes. This view was based on the premise that inequitable relations between cultural groups can become a smoldering source of resentment and anger which will not die out until all groups in society get their due share of goods and influence. In this

---

[1] *Copenhagen Meeting* 1990, 40.

statement, then, all three elements of our triad are combined in a positive and vital interlinkage with each other.

Others have had their doubts as to the inevitability of these linkages, and even of the possibility to combine them all at the same time. Some have argued that cultural diversity may go together with only one of the other two elements of the triad, not with both at the same time. Political stability is attainable also in plural societies, it is said, but you may have to jettison democracy in order to achieve it. If you can not have it both ways, the argument goes, political stability and the avoidance of civil war must be preferable to political pluralism and democracy. A societal system which is quintessentially democratic but unsustainable is of little lasting value to its members. If cultural diversity enhances democracy but contributes to the breakdown of states, democracy may be bought at a too high price. This is a favorite argument of political leaders in many illiberal states, also in the former Soviet Union, but it is entertained by political scientists as well.

In a study of pluralism in Africa dating from 1969 Leo Kuper argued in general terms that cultural diversity and democracy are an impossible combination. With reference to G.M. Smith he distinguished between two types of mechanisms by which groups may be held together within the same society: integration and regulation by domination.

> Integration rests on common values and common motivation at the individual level and on the functional relations of common institutions at the societal level. It presupposes cultural homogeneity. [...] Cultural diversity or pluralism automatically imposes the strictest necessity for domination by one of the cultural sections. It excludes the possibility of consensus, or of institutional integration, or of structural balance between the different sections, and necessitates nondemocratic regulation of group relationships.[2]

It is likely that few researchers will subscribe to such bombastic determinism today, but many will lean toward similar positions.[3] The American expert on democracy, Robert A. Dahl, for one, has remarked that democracy is "significantly less frequent in countries with marked subcultural pluralism."[4] One might perhaps argue that even if this was true in the past, the movement toward greater liberalism and tolerance in the modern world has widened the scope for a combination of

---

[2] Kuper 1969, 14.

[3] For an overview of some of these positions, see Lijphart 1971, and Drobizheva et al. 1996, 22-39.

[4] Dahl 1989, 254ff. Dahl uses the term "polyarchy" rather than "democracy." In his vocabulary, however, this is not something different from democracy but represents his attempt to give democracy a precise and operationable content.

democracy and cultural pluralism. In the postindustrial "permissive society," one might think that state authorities would be less concerned about the cultural life of the citizens than they used to be. However, it is worth noting that one of the most influential theoreticians of nationalism in the last decades, Ernest Gellner, saw historical development as moving in the opposite direction. He pointed out that cultural diversity had worked well in the past, in traditional societies, and indeed had sometimes been invented where it was previously lacking. However, in Gellner's view such diversity had ceased to be an option under the conditions of modern nationalism and nation-building.

> The establishment of pervasive high cultures (standarized, literacy- and education-based systems of communication), a process rapidly gathering pace throughout the world, has made it seem, to anyone too deeply immersed in our contemporary assumptions, that nationality may be definable in terms of shared culture. Nowadays people can live only in units defined by a shared culture, and internally mobile and fluid. Genuine cultural pluralism ceases to be viable under current conditions.[5]

Classical nation-building theory pointed out that those European states which historically were pioneers in the development of democratic institutions, also pursued a consistent and conscious policy of cultural homogenization of their populations. To be sure, the early nation-building theoreticians were primarily preoccupied with political institutions, participation, etc., and less with cultural issues. However, Charles Tilly, for instance, explicitly remarked that, in his view, increased homogeneity followed almost without exception as an important result of nation-building.

> Almost all European governments eventually took steps which homogenized their populations: the adoption of state religions, expulsion of minorities like the Moors and the Jews, institution of a national language, eventually the organization of mass public instruction. The tolerance of the states of South-eastern Europe for linguistic, cultural, and religious diversity stood in sharp contrast to the intolerance of their North-western brethren, and surely stood in the way of effective state-making. The failure to homogenize increased the likelihood that a state existing at a given point in time would fragment into its cultural subdivisions at some time in the future.[6]

In this perspective, cultural homogenization is not only a concomitant *effect* of nation-building, but also a precondition for the survival of the nation-state.

---

[5] Gellner 1983/1990, 54–55.

[6] Tilly 1975, 43–44.

Thus, some Western researchers have tended to take the cultural pluralism in the societies they study for granted and have discussed the viability of democracy under such plural conditions. Others have focused on changes in the cultural landscape in the direction of greater homogeneity and have seen them as steps in the direction of stable democracies. Both of these research traditions were implicitly premised on the assumption that cultural pluralism, democracy, and stability in the long run would prove to be an impossible combination.

Consociationalism

This premise was forcefully challenged by the theory of consociationalism which sprang up in the 1960s and 1970s. This theory may be regarded as a massive attempt to refute what we could call "the Kuper thesis." In his ground-breaking works, *The Politics of Accommodation* and *Democracy in Plural Societies*, Arend Lijphart studied precisely states that are both democratic *and* marked by clear cultural divisions. The four states he concentrated on were The Netherlands, Belgium, Switzerland, and Austria. These states have traditionally had strong, distinct subcultures organized along ideological and religious lines, such as Catholicism and socialism. In one state, Austria, social peace broke down in the interwar period, resulting in a bloody civil war. After World War II, the Austrian community leaders agreed upon a number of mutual concessions in order to avoid such disasters occurring in the future. Although the other three states had not experienced similar traumas, the elites also in these countries opted for a number of self-imposed constraints which restricted the workings of democracy as this political model was understood in the classical, liberal sense. Lijphart divided the various devices of accommodation that were introduced into four categories: mutual veto; grand coalitions; an electoral system of proportional representation—with or without a quota system for distribution of high offices in the state; and finally a high degree of autonomy for each cultural segment. Such autonomy could take the form either of territorial government or institutions which confer some self-government on the segments.[7]

In a consociated state, in Lijphart's interpretation, cultural diversity is neither an impediment to the development of democracy nor an extraneous or irrelevant factor. On the contrary, it is in a sense the very stuff from which this variety of democracy is made. Culture is the structuring element of society. At the same time, the state as such is not

---

[7] Lijphart 1977, 21–44.

associated with any of its constituent cultural groups. On the contrary, it is elevated above all ethnic divisions.

Lijphart identified several conditions under which consociated democracy would be most likely to develop. The cultural segments in society should preferably be clearly delineated and identifiable. While the segments ought to be separated from each other on the ground, their respective elites, nevertheless, ought to be intimately integrated and to cooperate closely at the top. In the opposite case, Lijphart believed, the segmental elites would have little leeway to pursue accommodation. Whenever there are several competing elites within each segment, those elites that are willing to cooperate with their counterparts in the other cultural segments will be liable to outflanking from rival, less accommodating groups.

In addition, Lijphart identified a number of objective conditions conducive to the development of consociated democracy which did not depend upon the attitudes or actions of the elites. Among these *size* was important: consociationalism will enjoy the most favorable conditions in countries which are not very large but also not too small. In addition, the number of cultural divisions in society plays an important role, the optimal number being three or four. Two is a very unfortunate number, Lijphart believed. "In a society with two segments of approximately equal size, the leaders of both may hope to win a majority and to achieve their aims by domination instead of cooperation."[8]

Consociationalism is a "model" in two different meanings of the word. On the one hand, it is a theoretical model distilled from a large empirical material, designed to give a better understanding of the workings of democracy in certain types of societies. On the other hand, it is also offered by its proponents as a normative model to be emulated by the leaders of other states in the world with marked cultural cleavages that want to promote the development of stable democracy in their country. Lijphart himself discussed at length the potential of consociationalism in Third-World countries, and later authors have done so with respect to the Soviet Union[9] and to Soviet successor states. However, those researchers who have assessed its potential in Latvia and Kazakstan, have uniformly rejected it as inapplicable.[10] While some preconditions in these countries may be regarded as conducive to consociationalism, other circumstances seem to militate against this model. And, most importantly, the political will of the ruling elites seems to be lacking.

---

[8] Lijphart 1977, 55.

[9] Kommisrud 1996, 268ff.

[10] Aasland 1994, 260–1; Laitin 1998, 351–363.

As we have argued above, the cultural pillars in Kazakstan are clearly distinct from each other. On this account, a cultural autonomy scheme would clearly be feasible. Since each of the two major cultural groups dominate in their own halves of the country, autonomy could also theoretically take the shape of territorial federalism.

However, the factor of *size* is clearly a drawback. The huge republic of Kazakstan is vastly different from the small European states which Lijphart analyzed. The bipolarity of the cultural structure is even more deleterious. Central Kazakstani authorities clearly fear that a federalization of the state into two constituent parts, or, indeed, any measure of autonomy granted to the north, may prove to be a stepping stone in the direction of secession. And as Holm-Hansen has demonstrated in Chapter 5, Kazakstan is today run as a strongly centralized state.

Furthermore, the cultural pillars of Kazakstani society are not headed by homogeneous elites. In fact, it seems to have been an important objective of Kazakstani nationality policy to nip in the bud the emergence of *any* strong elites among the nontitulars. All cultural-cum-political organizations that might aspire to a leadership role in the Russophone community—such as Birlesu and Lad—have been thoroughly and successfully harassed into marginality. Some Russophones have been drawn into the state apparatus but not in a capacity as community leaders. Non-Kazaks (as well as most Kazaks) in Nazarbaev's entourage do not represent any constituencies at all, but merely themselves, the apparatus, and their possible professional qualifications.

One could perhaps argue that the official status accorded to the Russian language in the 1995 Kazakstani constitution goes some way toward a recognition of a two-community state. This, however, would be a misinterpretation of Kazakstani cultural politics. The concessions made to the Russian language are first and foremost a recognition of the fact that this is the preferred medium of communication of practically *all* cultural segments in Kazakstani society, including the Kazak political elites.

At a CSCE conference in Almaty in February 1996 devoted to "questions of interethnic harmonization in NIS countries. The Kazakstani case," spokespersons of some Kazakstani national cultural centers suggested that concrete steps ought to be taken to redress the underrepresentation of ethnic minorities in the *Mazhilis*. Had this appeal been heeded it might have represented a small step toward the introduction of consociationalism in Kazakstan. However, first deputy prime minister Nagashbai Shaikenov, one of the most influential thinkers in the Kazakstani government, retorted that "if we make an attempt to fill up the Parliament on the basis of proportional ethnic representation, then we would have to do the same with regard to [other] social groups as well."[11] Without discussing the validity of Shaikenov's argument we may observe that it is based on an implicit rejection of consociationalism as a conflict-reducing mechanism in plural societies.

In Latvia, the size of the country is far more propitious for consociational arrangements than in Kazakstan. The geographical and also the cultural separation of the two segments, on the other hand, is far less marked. The crosscutting cleavages between the groups are stronger. These circumstances are less conducive to consociational arrangements.

Certain policy measures undertaken by Latvian authorities could be seen as an instinctive recognition of the merits of consociational democracy. For instance, the reluctance of Latvian authorities to mix Latvian and non-Latvian pupils in the same schools will have the effect of isolating the main cultural segments in society from each other and may strengthen their distinctiveness. Such arrangements will perpetuate and reinforce the plural structure of Latvian society. The same is true with regard to the retention of an ascriptive nationality entry in Latvian passports. Also, if the Latvian law on cultural autonomy had been filled with real content this might have been a step to promote the autonomization of the cultural segments.

However, Latvia no more than Kazakstan may be regarded as a country moving in the direction of consociationalism or even semiconsociationalism. The crucial factor of *power-sharing* and *mutual accommodation* is conspicuously lacking also in this country. Rather than being a neutral zone of cooperation between the various cultural groups, the Latvian state is clearly identified with and set to serve first and foremost the interests of one cultural segment, the titular nation. The Latvian Law on Cultural Autonomy seems to be based on a clear compensatory idea: cultural autonomy is granted to the ethnic minorities as a kind of compensation for the absence of political power-sharing.

As Antane and Tsilevich have shown, the concept of a "two-community state" has been broached in the Latvian nation-building debate. If implemented, this concept might have led to a consociational structuring of Latvian politics. However, the "two-community state" is anathema to ethnically Latvian politicians of all shades. As David Laitin dryly remarks: "consociation was ruled out because the titulars, by moving first and decisively, successfully negated that opportunity."[12]

So far, it seems, consociationalism has worked well only in those cases where the cleavages in society have been of an ideological or

---

[11] As quoted in *Panorama*, 1 March 1996.
[12] Laitin 1998, 355.

confessional nature, the so-called "spiritual families" of small European nations. This model has not to the same degree been able to regulate *ethnic* conflicts, at least not in the long run. In fact, when ethnolinguistic divisions came to the fore in one of the pioneer countries of consociationalism, Belgium, the time-tested consociational measures of conflict reduction were largely ineffective.[13]

The fact that consociational arrangements and low levels of communal violence are sometimes found in the same country, does not necessarily mean that the latter is caused by the former. The path of causation may also be going in the opposite direction: the relatively high degree of moderation and fluidity that characterize the cleavages in small European countries is what has made consociationalism work there in the first place.[14]

Finally, some critics of consociationalism have maintained that this model may perhaps not be as democratic as it appears. First, it makes politics the exclusive domain of the elites while the political involvement of the common members of society is actively discouraged.[15] What is more, a political system which channels political power through the existing cultural segments of society will tend to reify these segments. New cultural groups which were not in existence when the system was created will be left out in the cold. In addition, individuals who do not belong to any segment at all, or are born into one of them but do not want to express their interests through them, will be deprived of a political voice.[16] These objections are quite relevant in Latvia and (perhaps even more so) in Kazakstan, where loyalties and cultural identities are very much in flux.

The debate for and against consociationalism will no doubt continue. The model is not a spent force. However, it is clearly more applicable to some kinds of conflicts than to others. As we have seen, Lijphart himself counted bipolar societies among those not readily amenable to consociational solutions.

Stability Through Domination

Control and Hegemony

An alternative means to achieve stability in plural societies has been discussed by Ian Lustick. He points out that, empirically, most

---

[13] Barry 1975, 502–04; Hooghe 1993, 64–65.

[14] Horowitz 1985, 572.

[15] See, e.g., Lustick 1979, 334.

[16] Brass 1991, 339–342, as summarized by Drobizheva et al. 1996, 29–31.

societies in the world which are characterized by deep vertical cleavages have achieved political stability without having recourse to consociationalist methods. In these states, stability will almost invariably be accounted for by the effective exertion of superior power of one group over the other(s). The common denominator in the political system of all these societies Lustick calls "control." Like Lijphart, Lustick presents his empirical generalization not only as a theoretical but also as a normative model. He claims that "in some deeply divided societies, the effective subordination of a segment or segments by a superordinate segment may be preferable to the chaos and disorder that might accompany the failure of Consociationalism."[17]

Lustick's category of control is very wide. As I understand it, it is basically synonymous with Schermerhorn's category of domination and I will make no distinction between the two terms. Lustick points to the relationship of Jews and Arabs in Israel; Tutsi and Huti in Burundi; Russians vs. the non-Russians in the Soviet Union; and blacks and whites in South Africa as typical control systems. Thus, he includes into his category also apartheid and other ethnocratic regimes.

Most of the countries on Lustick's list have two dominant ethnic cultures,[18] but the numerical relationship between them is unbalanced: One of the groups is demographically dominant. These cases, therefore, are not readily comparable to the situation in Latvia and Kazakstan. This does not mean, however, that the bipolar cultural makeup of "our" two countries is unique. As pointed out in Chapter 1, we may find countries also on other latitudes which are not only marked by clear cultural divisions, but where the major cultural segments are two in number and of roughly the same size. Three such countries—Guyana, Malaysia, and Fiji – have been analyzed by R.S. Milne in a comparative study of 1981. In this study he found certain regularities in the political structures which are very similar to what we have found in Latvia and Kazakstan. These observations corroborate our assumption that—besides other factors such as geography, economy, and the idiosyncrasies of the political elites—cultural bipolarity is an important factor behind the dynamics of nation-building processes in Latvia and Kazakstan.

The political systems of Guyana, Fiji and (after 1971) Malaysia,[19] cannot be characterized as consociationalism and neither are they

---

[17] Lustick 1979, 336. While this may be true, the chaos and disorder that might accompany the failure of control models, as exemplified by the horrors of genocide in Rwanda in 1994, may be no less catastrophic than a failure of consociationalism.

[18] In the case of the non-Russians in the Soviet Union, this was a residual category and not a coherent group.

[19] The political system which existed in Malaysia before 1969 has indeed been characterized as "a reasonably successful consociational democracy in the Third World." See Lijphart 1977, 150. In 1969 serious ethnic riots costing hundreds of lives led to the introduction of a

based on the stark oppression of one group over another. Regular elections to national and local assemblies are held on the basis of universal suffrage and multiparty voting. R.S. Milne defined them as systems of "hegemony." Since cases of stark oppression are excluded from this definition, "hegemony" is a considerably narrower category than Lustick's "control."

The common feature among the three cases in Milne's study, as he saw it, is that one ethnic group has managed to dominate political life and the state apparatus (but not necessarily other social spheres such as the economy). The measures employed to ensure hegemony were sometimes formal—such as constitutional and other legal provisions, explicit ethnic quotas, etc.—and sometimes informal and implicit, such as ethnic screening of job applications. In the latter case, the ethnic character of the state is not officially acknowledged, but nonetheless plain for all to see.

Hegemonic relations in Latvia and Kazakstan, as we have seen, follow the typical pattern of Soviet successor states: the titular nation dominates over nontitular groups. Above, I have interpreted this constellation as basically a legacy of Soviet nationality policy. In the USSR it was implicitly understood that the Union republics in some sense "belonged" to the titular nations, perhaps as a compensation for their relatively smaller career possibilities at the all-Union level.[20] However, in all three countries studied by Milne the indigenous or "oldest" population group is in control too. This is true both in those cases where the ruling group has a slight numerical edge over the other group and also when they represent a slight demographic minority. The group which may pose as "the sons of the soil" regards itself as "the rightful successor to the colonial power" (which in all cases was Britain).

Even more importantly, this claim to hegemony has tacitly, albeit grudgingly, been accepted by the nonindigenous communities. This recognition has made them "adopt, or acquiesce in, arrangements which limited participation but also limited the possibility of violence."[21] The most tenuous claim to seniority by residence duration is presented by the Africans in Guyana. The fact that this country has experienced more frequently recurring ethnic bloodshed than the two others is,

---

twenty-month period of emergency rule and constitutional amendments which severely restricted the political opportunities of the minorities. The post-1969 Malaysian system has moreover been characterized by reference to consociationalism. Diane Mauzy calls it "coercive consociationalism in an authoritarian state" (Mauzy 1993/1995, 113). This, however, is clearly to stretch the concept of consociationalism very far.

[20] Laitin 1991.

[21] Milne 1981, 10.

perhaps, not fortuitous. Since both major groups in Guyana are made up of immigrants, although with different arrival times, the latest arrivals, the Indians, have not as readily been prepared to defer to the rule of the Africans.

Milne maintained that any political balance which is attained in bipolar states without hegemony is temporary and precarious. It will be a prelude to a fierce, potentially violent, competition *for* hegemony and adds to the power of the extremists in both groups. An hegemonic regime, on the other hand, will be likely to provide more lasting stability. By imposing limitations on the political activities of the other cultural segment a moderately authoritarian and moderately nationalizing government will reduce the appeal of the nationalist radicals among its own ranks. This may prevent a rigid polarization of politics along ethnic lines. In a free-for-all competition, on the other hand, extremists on both sides will be able to feed on each other, and outbid the more moderate leaders of both communities.

Up to a point, Milne's analysis seems to fit well the situation in Latvia and Kazakstan. In both of these countries the radical nationalist parties on both sides of the cultural divide have been kept under control. Kazak groups such as Zheltoqsan, Alash, and Azat have been marginalized to the point of virtual extinction. By comparison, the success of the Fatherland and Freedom Party and the LNNK in Latvia has been significantly greater. These nationalist parties have been included in ruling coalitions and in 1997 the Fatherland and Freedom Party even got the prime minister post. Following Milne, we may see this as a consequence of the larger element of pluralism and competition in Latvian politics compared to the situation in Kazakstan. In bipolar societies, democratization of politics may easily lead to ethnification of politics. At the same time, however, their cooption into positions of power sometimes seems to have had a moderating effect on the Latvian nationalist radicals.

In Guyana, African control has been indirect and informal, while in Malaysia, the privileges of the titular group have been spelled out much more explicitly. On this score, Latvia conforms to the Malaysian situation,[22] while Kazakstani politics in many respects resembles more closely the situation in Guyana. Malaysian authorities have made no bones about the ethnic character of their state. An important part of the ethnic power of the Malays has been their ability to formulate rules of the game which favor themselves. All state symbols derive from Malayan culture, and after a transitional period when both Malay and English were official languages, this status was accorded to Malay

---

[22] See also Barrington 1995.

only. There has been some clamor among Chinese interest groups for the establishment of Chinese as a second state language, but to no avail.[23]

Since the 1950s, official Malaysian ideology has explicitly distinguished between the *bumiputra*—meaning indigenous—population, and the rest. State authorities are expected to promote *bumiputra* interests above the interests of other groups. The *bumiputra* category includes not only ethnic Malays but also some small, nonimmigrant, autochthonous minorities, particularly on Borneo, which, taken together, made up roughly 9 percent of the total population when the system was introduced.

As we have seen, the Latvian state has singled out among the nontitulars the autochthonous Livian group for special protection. While this decision has a superficial resemblance to the *bumiputra* policy the motivation behind it cannot be the same. The Malaysian nontitular groups, which are included in the *bumiputra*, raised the share of the indigenous population from 47 to 56 percent. Thus, the important 50-percent threshold which the Malays were unable to surpass alone at the time when the system was introduced, was surmounted.[24] The Livs, however, number less than two hundred individuals, and the special concern for the survival of this near-extinct group does not in any way raise the combined numerical strength of the "sons of the soil" category. Rather, it may probably be interpreted as an almost costless way of improving the minority rights record of the Latvian state.

In official rhetoric, the ruling African elite in Guyana is less explicit about ethnicity than are the Malays. In fact, the regime presents itself in ideological, not ethnic terms, as socialist, not African. Also, certain initiatives have been launched by Guyana state authorities to establish a supraethnic national ideology, embracing all cultural groups. These initiatives bring to mind Nazarbaev's official propagation of a supraethnic, all-Kazakstani state. However, just as Kazaks overwhelmingly dominate in the Kazakstani state apparatus, practically all leaders of the Guyana ruling party, as well as the bulk of the bureaucrats in the state administration, happen to be Africans.

In both Guyana and Kazakstan the apparatchiks know how to make use of their power. The following outburst from a despairing Indian in Guyana might sound strangely familiar to many Russians in Kazakstan:

> We know what is happening. It is oppression by administration. [...] The democratic safeguards are there on paper; but the oppressor can get round them. He can always use the administration. An application is delayed, even

---

[23] Milne 1981, 57.

[24] The *bumiputra* share of the population is on the rise and was approaching 60 percent by the mid-1990s.

for years; a file is lost; an employee is dismissed; a teacher is transferred to a distant spot. On the surface, all purely administrative decisions. But everyone knows the intention is to silence the protesters. And to warn the others.[25]

The explicit arrangements which are designed to secure ethnic Malays control of the Malaysian state are justified, *inter alia*, by their lower standard of living, as compared to the Chinese. In this way, lack of economic power is compensated for, as it were, by political power. In addition, specific programs have been elaborated to increase the relative wealth of the *bumiputra*. A stated goal of the New Economic Policy, which was introduced in 1970, was to raise the ownership share of bumiputra in business from 4 to 30 percent by 1990.

Again, the economic motivation behind the Malaysian ethnic policy has its parallels in Latvia. A large number of Latvian laws restrict the economic opportunities of non-citizens, albeit often in ineffective ways.[26] The economic inequalities prevailing between the Latvians and the Russians are difficult to quantify, but they are certainly not as glaring as the corresponding disproportionalities in Malaysia. Nevertheless, our survey discovered that there is a widespread *feeling* among ethnic Latvians that the Russians are eating soup from the same bowl with a bigger spoon. In our survey almost 14 percent of the ethnic Latvians thought that most of the new rich in Latvia can be found among the Russians, while less than 4 percent thought that the moneybags hailed from among their own ranks. A group of Latvian researchers assert that, according to the prevalent view, "the majority of the *nouveaux riches* are Russians."[27] I surmise that these perceptions contribute to a kind of compensation syndrome in Latvia similar to the one which is very strongly felt in Malaysia.

In Kazakstan, on the other hand, our survey revealed no such compensation syndrome among the ethnic Kazaks, and notions of exploitation are also absent from the ethnic debate. As our survey showed, among the respondents in Kazakstan who believed that wealth and ethnicity are related, three out of four, even among ethnic Kazaks, believed that most rich people were to be found in the Kazak group. At the same time, very many, also of the Russians, would claim that Kazak peasants on dissolved state farms are more indigent than any other group.[28]

---

[25] Milne 1981, 123.

[26] Opalski, Tsilevich, and Dutkiewicz 1994.

[27] Mezs et al. 1994, 21. This very vague statement is taken from an article which otherwise abounds in exact factual information.

[28] Author's interviews in Almaty, Semipalatinsk and Ust-Kamenogorsk, September 1996.

By comparing Latvia with Malaysia and Guyana with Kazakstan I do not want to imply that behind-the-scenes manipulations are absent in the Latvian variety of hegemonic control or that Kazakstani authorities do not make certain explicit references to the Kazaks as an indigenous group with special rights. In fact, as we have seen, sometimes they do just that. I only want to identify some similarities and regularities and point out the fact that some of these patterns cut across the post-British/post-Soviet dichotomy.

Both the Latvians and the Kazaks have achieved a monopolization of the political power which far surpasses the degree of ethnic hegemony found by Milne in the countries he studied. In Fiji, Malaysia, and Guyana also the nondominant ethnic groups were important players in the political game. Sometimes they were able to muster strong, moderate parties which entered into cooperation, even coalitions, with moderate parties representing the dominant group. In such coalitions, the party of the nondominant group was the junior partner and accepted certain policy decisions which clearly favored the other group. Their reward was that they were able to keep a hand on the steering wheel and had a voice where decisions were being made. At other times, some members of the non-dominant ethnic group were included into the leadership of the ruling party.

However, since R. Milne wrote his comparative study in 1981 both Malaysia and Fiji have taken long strides in the direction of stronger political hegemony of the titular group. Since the early 1980s and the accession of Dr. Mahathir Mohamad as prime minister, the Malaysian state has clearly become more repressive. "Accommodation has been marginalised, and ethnic relations have deteriorated."[29] Even so, there have been no serious ethnic clashes. In Fiji military coup-makers in 1987 oversaw the promulgation of a new constitution which assigned disproportionately higher representation to ethnic Fijians over other groups. "Further, in all major areas such as taxation, civil service appointments, recognition of religion, Fijians were accorded preferential treatment."[30] Moreover, in this country these opportunities were brought about without bloodshed.

These later developments in Malaysia and Fiji have reinforced the similarities between the political systems found in Latvia and Kazakstan, on the one hand, and in the bipolar former British colonies on the other perhaps even more than they were before. In post-Communist Latvia and Kazakstan, no political parties representing the Russophone communities, neither moderate nor extremist, have been able to

---

[29] Mauzy 1993/1995, 113.
[30] Premdas 1993/1995, 251.

play important roles. Nor have Russophones been included into governments or ruling parties in a capacity as community leaders. In Kazakstan, all ethnic representation is channeled through the nonpolitical, nonindependent national-cultural centers.

In Latvia, the most important reason behind this situation is clearly the fact that the majority of the nontitular population has been deprived of political rights. This has resulted in what Vello Pettai has called "stability through disenfranchisement."[31] This solution to the bipolarity challenge is unique among the states in our material. Only in one of the countries studied by Milne, Malaysia, has citizenship been an issue at all. In this country, however, the citizenship debate ended with granting citizenship rights to the vast majority of the Chinese and other immigrant groups within a short period of time.

No strong Russophone parties have emerged in Kazakstan either despite the fact that all Russians in this country are eligible for automatic citizenship. And, as we have seen, also among those Russophones in Latvia who have been granted citizenship rights there has been scant political mobilization. Internal factors within the Russophone community, such as intracommunal squabble, a dearth of leaders, etc., probably provide some explanation for this situation in both countries. In addition, the policies of the nationalizing regimes are important. In Kazakstan, Russophone parties and social organizations are allowed to register and operate legally, but the role of political parties in general are severely circumscribed. Candidates for local or national elections are not allowed to indicate their party affiliation on the ballot. In this situation, most do not bother to join a party at all. Also in Latvia, the authorities are generally reluctant to recognize Russophone organizations, let alone cooperate with them. Still, the general climate for political activity in this country must be regarded as far better than in Kazakstan.

Ethnic Democracy

As pointed out above, the democratic qualities of consociationalism have been questioned. There is even more reason to ask whether political systems based on *hegemony* may be regarded as democratic. Even so, some authors claim to have identified a combination of domination and democracy which they have labeled "ethnic democracy." This term was first coined to describe the political system of Israel and, in particular, the relationship between the Jewish majority and the Arab

---

[31] Pettai 1997.

minority in that state. Sammy Smooha believes that the Israeli case demonstrates the viability of ethnic democracy as "a distinct type of plural society. In such states the dominance of a certain ethnic group is institutionalized along with democratic procedures."[32] Ethnic democracy is a system of domination by an ethnic elite rather than by the entire superordinate group. The elite pursues its own narrow goals as well as the goals of the larger ethnic community as they define them, and tend to see these goals as coinciding.

All state symbols in Israel are drawn from Jewish history and Jewish traditions. The Arab minority enjoy full political rights, but there has never been an Arab cabinet minister or even a director-general of a government office. Unlike the Orthodox Jews, which constitute another distinct cultural segment of Israeli society, the Arabs have never been invited to join a coalition government.

In a comparative study of conflict regulation Sammy Smooha and Theodor Hanf suggest that ethnic democracy may serve not only as a descriptive but also a normative model, "a viable option for non-democratic, deeply divided societies." They acknowledge, however, that compared with other varieties of democracy, such as liberalism and consociationalism, ethnic democracy must be regarded as "least democratic." Smooha and Hanf also believe that ethnic democracy will not be applicable to all kinds of societies. They expect that a successful ethnic democracy arrangement is most likely to emerge when the dominant group has certain specific characteristics: it is strongly influenced by integral, exclusive nationalism; it has sufficient control of the state to curb the resistance of the minority, and it constitutes a clear-cut demographic majority.[33]

Thus, we see that the fathers of both consociationalism and the ethnic democracy model are disinclined to include bipolar states with two groups of approximately equal numerical strength among the states to which their model can be successfully applied. Apparently, they find the communal tensions in such states too intractable to be solved by the remedies they can offer. These hapless social creatures are thrown, as it were, like hot potatoes between the theoreticians: Smooha and Hanf claim that even if the ethnic democracy model will not work in bipolar states, *consociationalism* may. Among the fundamental conditions for a stable consociational democracy they identify—in spite of Lijphart's explicit words to the contrary—a "lack of a clear-cut majority (the existence of *two* or more ethnic groups *more or less equal in size*)."[34]

---

[32] Smooha 1990, 410.

[33] Smooha and Hanf 1992, 45.

[34] Ibid. Emphasis added.

Nevertheless, a leading expert on Latvian ethnic politics, Graham Smith, concludes that the model of "ethnic democracy" fits the Latvian political landscape better than any rival model.[35] In this evaluation he finds support in Richard Mole, Aadne Aasland, and Anton Steen,[36] and, as we have seen, in the contribution of Antane and Tsilevich to this volume.[37]

Formally, the restrictions on citizenship rights in Latvia are based on historical and legal reasons only. However, the ethnic motivation behind them is transparent. If anyone ever had any doubts about this, they were dispelled in March 1995 when amendments to the citizenship law granted ethnic Latvians the right to be naturalized without fulfilling the requirements demanded of other groups.

In addition, all aspects of symbolic nation-building in Latvia are based on the culture, history, and traditions of ethnic Latvians. A telling example of this is the preamble to the 1992 Latvian language law. The special status accorded to the Latvian language, and the detailed sanctions meted out to violators of the provisions contained in this law, are justified with the following words: "Latvia is the only ethnic territory [sic] in the world which is inhabited by the Latvian nation. One of the prerequisites for the existence of the Latvian nation and for the preservation of its culture is the Latvian language."[38] This piece of legislation is clearly based on an ethnic understanding of the nation-state. In the eyes of the Latvian legislature, the state is not an arbiter among the country's different linguistic groups but the defender of the interests of one of them. Latvia seems to fit well Smooha's criterion of a country with a strong strand of integral nationalism in the political elite.

In their contribution to this volume Antane and Tsilevich point out that over the last years the Latvian debate on ethnopolitics has been influenced to some degree by Western political ideas. If the idea of "the Latvian nation" during perestroika and in the first period afterwards was understood exclusively in ethnic and ethnocratic terms, then in later years the civic variety of this concept has been gaining some ground. Even so, the Latvian language still does not have a special term for a "Latvian national" in the civic sense comparable to the neologism *rossianin* which enriched the Russian political vocabulary during perestroika. While a Russian citizen in Latvia may call himself a *latviets* when he speaks Russian, when he speaks Latvian he must use a combi-

---

[35] Smith, 1996.

[36] Smith et al. 1994, Aasland 1994, 260; Steen 1997, 359–60.

[37] See also Kolstø and Tsilevich 1997.

[38] Guboglo 1994, II, 36.

nation of at least two words to explain that he is in fact a Latvian national.

On the practical, political level, the involvement of international organizations has left a distinct imprint on the formulation of Latvian ethnic politics. Due to strong objections from the Council of Europe and the OSCE High Commissioner for National Minorities Max van der Stoel, some of the most questionable aspects of the Latvian citizenship law, from the European point of view, were weeded out in 1994, in particular, the ethnically determined quota system. In 1996, van der Stoel stepped up the pressure further, asking the Latvian authorities to consider the abolishment of the "window" system as well and to make nationality entry into Latvian passports voluntary.[39]

While Latvia does not always heed the advice and recommendations of the representatives of the international community, the very fact that pan-European institutions are present in Latvia, monitoring the human rights development, seems to have a moderating effect on ethnic politics in this country. Since Latvia is aspiring for membership in several Western organizations such as the EU and NATO, the need to have a well-polished minority record—real or apparent—plays a more important role in Latvian politics than it does in Kazakstani politics. As regards Kazakstan, the international community seems to have been relatively less concerned with the development of democracy and relatively more concerned with the need to preserve political stability. There have been fewer warnings against discriminatory policies and no strong protests against the development of an authoritarian regime in this country.

Can the "ethnic democracy" model be extended to the political system of Kazakstan? To be sure, Kazakstan has granted the resident Russophone population citizenship rights on far more generous terms than has Latvia. Also, the Kazakstani constitution proclaims the entire package of political and civil rights and freedoms to all of its citizens in often more sweeping ways than Latvia does. Arguably, there is less systemic political marginalization of the nontitulars in Kazakstan than in Latvia. However, the problem with Kazakstan, as Jørn Holm-Hansen points out, is more a question of whether the Kazakstani political system may be described as democratic at all in any meaningful sense. Are popularly elected organs such as the parliament and the *maslikhats* the real loci of Kazakstani politics? While not

---

[39] van der Stoel 1996a and 1996b.

dismissing them as mere caricatures or facades, we will nevertheless maintain that the political power and decision-making processes in Kazakstan run very much outside of these institutions.

Traditional paternalistic patterns of authority, embodied in the zhuz structures and in the presidential apparatus, are still very important. From the former, the non-Kazaks are excluded as a matter of course; from the latter, they may be, and are indeed to some degree included. The cases where nontitulars are drawn into top positions in the Kazakstani state, however, smack of tokenism. This has created a situation in which, in the opinion of Bhavna Dave, few Russians want jobs in the state structure. "Isolated Russians in an all-Kazak apparatus are regarded as an anomaly, and often face in-group ridicule for allegedly 'going native'."[40]

The ethnic hoof of symbolic nation-building in Kazakstan may be somewhat more hidden than in Latvia, but is nevertheless not difficult to detect. The massive redesignating of Russian toponyms into Kazak names, even in compactly Slavic-dominated areas, is one clear indication. The central features of the Kazakstani coat-of-arms are the winged horse of Kazak myth and the smoke-wheel of the nomadic yurt, symbols with which European residents of Kazakstan hardly feel any strong emotional attachment.[41] At the same time, the proponents of integral nationalism have been sidelined more effectively in Kazakstan than in Latvia. The leaders of the Kazakstani state should more appropriately be called "pragmatic nationalists."

Stability Through De-Bipolarization

The above analysis of ethnic stability through the hegemony of one group is based on the implicit premise that the societal bipolarity is a given. This, of course, is not necessarily the case. The cultural identities of the citizens may change and the numerical ratios among the groups may be upset. Such processes may unfold by their own dynamics and/or be actively promoted by the powers that be.

In a bipolar situation strategies for stability through hegemony may be regarded as short-term policies, with *de-bipolarization* as a long-term objective. In both Latvia and Kazakstan, as we have seen, the state authorities have designed elaborate programs to alter the cultural distribution of the population away from the volatile bipolar situation. Below, we will single out for closer scrutiny some actual and

---

[40] Dave 1996a, 60.
[41] Akiner 1995, 61.

potential means and ways which may lead to this goal in these countries.

Integration

Integration, as we have used this term in this book, may be either cultural or structural. One way to soften the bipolarity of a society is to reduce the salience of cultural differences in the population. If these differences are completely eradicated the bipolarity will be eliminated and a homogeneous society will arise.

In both Latvia and Kazakstan we have identified groups which may be regarded as bicultural by dint of their bilingualism, upbringing in ethnically mixed families, or otherwise. In Kazakstan, many such people occupy important positions in the state apparatus and in the more dynamic spheres of the Kazakstani economy, such as the burgeoning private business sector. These groups, one would assume, could take a lead in a cultural integration drive. Indeed, as we have seen, a group of Russian-speaking Kazak businessmen calling themselves "The New Generation" have been exhorting the peoples of Kazakstan to develop an identity as "a single ethnos"—"Kazakstanians." In order to facilitate this identity shift this group wants to eliminate the nationality entry in the passports; introduce Russian as a second official language; and delete all passages in the constitution and other legal documents which make special reference to the ethnic Kazaks.[42] If this appeal had been heeded by the authorities, a major step would have been taken in the direction of deliberate cultural homogenization of the population (although, of course, this nation-building policy would not necessarily achieve its goal).

The New Generation created an uproar. The businessmen were denounced as *mankurty*, sons of the asphalt (rather than of the soil), who had lost their roots and identity. Undeterred, they turned their loose network into an organized movement, which, however, can hardly be characterized as a smash hit. Thoroughgoing assimilation—either through mutual acculturation or through the immersion of the nontitulars into the titular culture—is resisted by most representatives of the minorities as well as by the titular group. This is the case also in Latvia. In this country, even the expressly "internationalist" Equal Rights movement is vehemently opposed to all and any government policies that may be construed as assimilatory.

---

[42] Azimov 1995.

A less radical way to achieve integration in a bipolar society would be to invite the nontitulars into common political and social structures without asking them to forgo their cultural identity. Seemingly, a signal in that direction was given when new passports were issued in Kazakstan in 1996–97. In these documents the entry of ethnic classification is officially optional.[43] This might perhaps be interpreted as a conscious step to de-emphasize ethnicity as a social category. However, it seems that the citizens are usually not informed about their right not to register their nationality, and the overwhelming majority of the population still fill out this entry.[44] Also, Russian names may easily be distinguished from typically Kazak names, and will be increasingly so as ever more Kazaks drop the Russian-inspired "ev" or "ov" suffix from their surname.

In both Latvia and Kazakstan integration is touted by the authorities as a priority goal. In contrast to "assimilation" "integration" enjoys the support also of most of the minorities. However, this convergence of goals may be more apparent than real. As pointed out above, "integration" may mean very different things to different people, and no consensus has been formed in either country as to what this term shall imply. In an August 1995 article a Kazakstani professor hailed integration as the optimal solution to the ethnic problems of Kazakstan, infinitely superior to "assimilation." Integration, however, will be a protracted process, she believed, fraught with conflicting tendencies. The end result would—hopefully—be the formation of "a Kazakstani nation." In her view, this nation would be held together not only by common statehood and citizenship, but also by shared cultural bonds. While all ethnic groups in Kazakstan would retain their separate identities, they would nevertheless learn from and adopt to each other. In a process of mutual acculturation they would develop "a distinctive mentality as Kazakstanians."[45]

The major obstacle on the road toward this radiant future lies in the resistance of a large part of the Russian population of Kazakstan, this researcher believed. These people do not understand that, after independence, the two major groups, the Kazaks and the Russians, are going through significant changes of status. From being in a subordinate position the Kazak ethnos has been transformed into a titular nation. The Kazak ethnos has rectified the historical injustice done to them and restored their ancient right to their historical homeland, to their soil, language, mores, and traditions. "From being a 'junior brother,' the

---

[43] *Kazakhstanskaia pravda* 4 April 1996, 6.

[44] I am grateful to Shirin Akiner for providing me with this piece of information.

[45] Baitenova 1995a.

Kazaks have been turned into the leading ethnos, the indigenous nation." As a concomitant effect of the elevation of the Kazaks the Russians have been reduced "from a status as the senior brother to becoming
an ordinary ethnos, or even better: they are acquiring the status of an
ethnic group."[46]

It is difficult to see how this version of integration can gain wide
support among the nontitular population in Kazakstan, and indeed, if
such a total status reversal as is described here is a necessary element of
integration. A Western expert on ethnic relations in Kazakstan concludes that "it is doubtful that the nationalizing government genuinely
desires full integration of the Russian-speaking population into the
Kazakstani state, let alone its assimilation."[47]

As for Latvia, the restrictive laws and other official regulations are
ostensibly directed not against any particular ethnic group but against
the non-citizens. At the same time, the non-citizen population is made
up massively of nontitulars. The British researcher Neil Melvin draws
a conclusion regarding integration politics in Latvia which is very similar to the one Dave draws for Kazakstan: "There can be no doubt that
the laws adopted in Estonia and Latvia were intended to prevent the
majority of the settler community from integrating into the newly independent societies."[48]

However, even when political authorities make no efforts to promote
social integration, or even try to retard it, integration may take place as
a spontaneous, unguided social process. In a recent comparative study of
Latvia, Estonia, Ukraine, and Kazakstan, the American political scientist David Laitin found significant differences in the readiness of the
Russophone population in each country to adapt to the nationalizing
agendas of the ruling titular groups. In Kazakstan, he found very little
willingness among the nontitulars to learn the local language and to
adapt to Kazak culture. Only 23.2 percent of the Russians in this country
thought that all permanent residents ought to have facility in the titular language—as against 70.7 percent in Latvia. On the basis of these
findings, Laitin concluded that in Kazakstan a homogeneous national
culture based on the titular language was out of the question.[49]

Our own surveys corroborate this view. Almost two-thirds of the
Russophone respondents in Kazakstan believed that the Kazak language will be an important medium of communication in their oblast of
residence ten years from now. However, very few Russians in our sample

---

[46] Ibid., 28.
[47] Dave 1996a, 62.
[48] Melvin 1998, 43.
[49] Laitin 1998, 155–157.

were taking any practical steps to prepare themselves for a Kazakified future: only 3.2 percent were sending their children to schools with instruction in the Kazak language. The main reason for this, obviously, was that a solid majority in all groups in our survey—Europeans as well as Kazaks—believed that *Russian* will remain an even *more* important language in Kazakstan in the foreseeable future.

In Latvia, these perceptions were markedly different. In this country there was a strong expectation in all regions and among all ethnic groups and age groups that Latvian will be a far more important language than Russian ten years from now. And importantly, the non-Latvians also act upon this assumption. An increasing number among them are sending their children to schools with Latvian as the language of instruction. While less than 3 percent of the Russian parents had graduated from Latvian schools themselves, more than 18 percent now had children in Latvian schools.

With regard to political orientations among the non-titular groups in the two countries, the differences were less sharp than with regard to cultural orientations, but even on this score the Russians in Latvia revealed somewhat stronger centripetal tendencies. More than 60 percent of the Russians in Latvia regarded Latvia (or the LatSSR) as their motherland, while slightly less than 50 percent of their compatriots in Kazakstan did so.

As pointed out above, since the adoption of the Latvian citizenship law in 1994 the speed of naturalization has been very slow. The reasons for this are as yet not very clear, and must be studied further before any definite conclusions can be drawn.[50] Some observers see it as evidence of weak centripetal orientations among the Russophone population. My own hunch, however, is that in very many cases the reluctance to submit an application for citizenship is a reaction against a state which began its existence by defining them out of the political body of which they had regarded themselves as legitimate members, and quite a few had even supported its independence in the March 1991 referendum.[51] If this interpretation is correct what we are witnessing seems to be a case in which initially centripetal political orientations among (some members of) the subordinate group have been redirected outwards under the

---

[50] In August 1997 a working group was established in Latvia to study the problems of the naturalization process. This group includes representatives of the National Human Rights Office, the State Language Teaching Program, the Citizenship and Immigration Board, the President of Latvia's Minority Consultative Council as well as several nongovernmental organizations. The project is funded by, among others, the Soros Foundation–Latvia and the UND.

[51] Kolstoe 1995, 118–19.

influence of negative attitudes among the politically dominant elites in the superordinate group.

We also found evidence of dismissive attitudes among the ethnic Latvians toward the centripetal orientations of the Russophones in Latvia in our survey. Members of the titular nationality in Latvia took a decidedly less positive view of their Russophone neighbors than did the titular ethnic group in Kazakstan. The strong reluctance to let the Russophones into Latvian schools is further evidence of the same. While Latvian authorities are strongly opposed to a two-community state, some of its policies as well as the attitudes of the ethnic Latvians impede the transition to a one-community state.

Even so, the *cultural* orientations among the Russophone in Latvia remain basically centripetal. In sum, there seem to be stronger tendencies toward integration among the nontitulars in Latvia than in Kazakstan. The willingness to integrate among the Russophones in Kazakstan is almost exclusively political and structural and certainly not linguistic.

Multiple Re-Ethnification

Rather than *de-emphasizing* ethnicity as a means to move away from the cultural bipolarity of society, state authorities in Latvia and (particularly) Kazakstan have opted for what amounts to the diametrically *opposite* course. They are trying to resuscitate half-forgotten ethnic identities and trigger ethnic revivals among both the titulars and the nontitulars. This is what Holm-Hansen in his contribution to this volume has dubbed "multiple re-ethnification."

As pointed out in Chapter 2, the Soviet ethnic taxonomy continues to exert considerable influence on the nation-building debate in most, if not all, of the successor states. When defined in these categories, the titular groups in the former Soviet republics are by definition composed of only one "nationality" each while the Russophone community everywhere is a multiheaded entity. Therefore, a re-ethnification strategy will have the double effect of consolidating the Kazak/Latvian group and splitting up the nontitulars. Should the official nationality gain in paramountcy as identity marker among the Russophones, this cultural community would disintegrate into its constituent parts. The appropriate metaphor for the ethnic patterns in Latvia and Kazakstan would then no longer be two equal neighbors eyeing each other across a cultural fence, but one strong, self-assured giant in each country surrounded by a large number of dwarfs.

The Latvian decision to retain and reinforce the mandatory ethnic categorization of the population in official documents clearly falls into this pattern. In this country, the nationality of the permanent residents—citizens and non-citizens alike—is decided by their parental extraction only, not by their self-perception. This system locks the population into rigid ethnic compartments.

For a while, nontitulars in Latvia were also encouraged to send their children to minority schools. A Latvian nationality expert claims that "the ethnic school system in Latvia is rapidly expanding."[52] However, Antane and Tsilevich found little evidence of this: less than one percent of the Latvian population is today attending minority schools.

The ethnic minorities in Latvia have established around twenty cultural centers. In September 1996 they arranged a cultural festival of minority cultures called *Latvijas Vainags* ("Garland of Latvia") which has been seen as proof of the "rebirth" of the ethnic minorities.[53] However, the attitude of Latvian authorities toward these centers has been rather lukewarm. The financial support offered by the state is minimal, and the Latvian expert on minorities quoted above claims that such support would violate the principle of cultural autonomy and represent an unwarranted interference into the affairs of the minorities.[54]

In several cases ethnic groups in Latvia which have organized around cultural societies have began to express quite critical attitudes toward state policies in the fields of citizenship, language policy, etc. (This has been the case, for instance, with the Ukrainian societies). Thus, a re-ethnification policy may strengthen the political opposition among the nontitulars, and the state authorities seem have concluded that it is better to keep them poorly organized. In any case, the response on the part of the minorities themselves has also been weak.

It seems that the initiatives in the drive for a re-ethnification of the nontitular, non-Russian Latvian population has been taken over by individual groups of enthusiasts. Among them we find the Multicultural center in Daugavpils which cooperates with Secondary School No. 3 in Kraslava. In this experimental school, the pupils are urged to refind, or simply find, their "roots" in their respective ethnic cultures. At the same time, they are encouraged to develop an identity as Latvians in the civic sense and also to learn about and respect the cultures of the other ethnic groups studying at the same school.[55]

---

[52] Vebers 1997, 148.

[53] Ibid.

[54] Ibid., 160.

[55] Fleishman 1995.

However, the drive for multiculturalism seems to be an uphill struggle. The Latvian sociologist Elmars Vebers sees the Daugavpils experiment in multiculturalism as an attempt to establish an alternative to the national state and, for that reason, as unacceptable.[56] What is more, many minority members in Latgale seem to be skeptical about multiculturalism. They believe that it would be better for them to send their children to a Latvian language school: this choice, they surmise, will enhance the career chances of the offspring later in life.[57]

In Kazakstan, it seems, the policy of re-ethnification is pursued more determinedly. Nazarbaev hails the ideal of "polyculturalism" as a progressive factor in the development of Kazakstani society.[58] In the state museum in Almaty the cultures of all major ethnic groups in Kazakstan are extolled in separate expositions. Kazak integration experts suggest that there ought to be published multiethnic encyclopedias, cooking books, literary anthologies, studies of ethnic folk crafts, and so on.[59] The Kazakstani leaders clearly prefer the trichotomic model of "Kazaks–Russians–Others" to the dichotomic model of "Kazaks vs. Russophones."

Jørn Holm-Hansen interprets, with good reason, the Kazakstani program of multiple re-ethnification as, in effect, a strategy of divide and rule. The Ukrainians, Poles, Germans, Belarusians, and members of other smaller Russophone groups are invited to turn to the ethnic roots of their forbears in order be weaned away from the embrace of the Russians. The special affirmative action programs for the recruitment of minority students into institutions of higher learning include all nontitular nationalities—with the exception of the Russians.

In the regional buildings of the Assembly of the Nationalities of Kazakstan various ethnic group have their own offices, and sometimes teaching facilities as well, for the resurrection of their forgotten languages. In some cases, the main reason why minority members visit the national cultural centers seem to be a desire to migrate to a more prosperous putative homeland. Migration plans are clearly part of the reason for the ethnic revival among Germans, Jews, and even Poles, not only in Kazakhstan but, as Tsilevich and Antane point out, also in Latvia. By leaving, these people do not contribute to a greater cultural

---

[56] Vebers 1997, 162.

[57] The author's impression after a visit to Daugavpils and Kraslava in May 1995.

[58] Nazarbaev 1994, 19.

[59] Baitenova 1995a. See also Absattarov, R. 1995.

heterogeneity in their former homeland, but rather to an increased ethnic homogeneity in the Russophone group.

In Semipalatinsk the door to the office of "The Slavic Lad Movement" in the building of the Assembly of the Nationalities of Kazakstan, was locked when we visited it in September 1996. Instead, we found the local Lad activists, who promote a common Russophone identity, in their homes: they lack the means to man their office and do not feel welcome in the Assembly building either. In the largest office, at the top of the stairs, the representative of the *akim* holds court, keeping a close eye on the activities of his underlings.

Apparently, the policy of re-ethnification in Kazakstan has met with a measure of success. When a leader of the Slavic Lad movement in April 1995 appealed to the voters not to endorse the prolongation of Nazarbaev's term in office beyond the five year period he was elected for, some Belarusian, Ukrainian, and Polish spokesmen criticized Lad for this stance. A Kazak researcher saw this as evidence of these nations' greater loyalty. Not the Russophones, but the *Russians* alone were the main opponents of the Kazaks, she believed. Such analyses drive wedges into the Russophone group, splitting it into smaller, politically less powerful and more manageable components.[60]

However, other elements of the policies pursued by the authorities in Latvia and Kazakstan may be counterproductive to the re-ethnification campaigns. In both countries, nation-building is heavily charged with the ethnic culture of the titular group. The Latvians, respectively the Kazaks, are groomed as "the state-forming people." In Malaysia, R.S. Milne observed that a similar policy of ethnic nation-building reinforced and even created new ties among the nontitular population. The Malays have so defined their own ethnic group, and the privileges belonging to it, that immigrant groups are motivated to regard themselves as constituting a single category—non-Malays.[61] There is much evidence that the same dynamics are at work in Latvia and Kazakstan. Thus, different aspects of the nation-building policies in these countries seem to be working at cross-purposes, (deliberately) weakening Russophone solidarity and (inadvertently) strengthening it at the same time.

---

[60] Baitenova 1995a.

[61] Milne 1981, 7 and 132–33. Donald Horowitz has pointed out that not only the nontitulars, but also the titular nation in Malaysia is an amalgam of several historically distinct subgroups. These groups tended to speak separate languages, to be endogamous and often mutually hostile and violent. The arrival of the Chinese in the nineteenth century changed this. By the end of World War II a strong, coherent Malay identity had, for most purposes, superseded these lesser loyalties. Horowitz 1975, 127–132.

Demographic Changes

If the demographic structure is altered a bipolar society may reach a higher degree of cultural homogeneity without having recourse to either integration or re-ethnification. To be sure, neither Latvia nor Kazakstan has embarked upon a policy of large-scale expulsions. However, a deliberate, ethnically motivated migration policy has led to a distinct rise in the titular nation's share of the total population in both countries. The Latvian borders are for all practical purposes sealed for immigrants from the former Soviet Union. At the same time, the return of ethnic Latvians to their historic homeland and the return of the Russians to *their* putative homeland is actively encouraged.

In the Soviet period there was always a high degree of population exchange among the republics.[62] Today, too, people continue to leave Latvia for various reasons, in search of a better job, to marry, etc. In addition, a number of nontitulars now leave because of their sense of discomfort in a state which is now seen as "belonging to the Latvians." Thus, increasing emigration without any immigration of nontitulars combined with a positive migration balance for the ethnic Latvians is slowly but surely shifting the titular/nontitular ratio further away from the bipolar situation.

However, as Antane and Tsilevich demonstrate, the outmigration of nontitulars from Latvia peaked in 1992 and has been steadily and rapidly decreasing since that year. While there are some differences in the natural growth rates among the various ethnic groups in this country, these demographic variations are so small that they will not contribute to any perceptible population shifts in the foreseeable future. The potential for further homogenization of Latvian society through demographic change seems, therefore, very limited.

The Kazakstani migration law of 1992 contained explicit preferential treatment of Kazaks. This provision has since been scrapped, but the migratory flows of the various ethnic group nevertheless continue to go in opposite directions. In 1996 the Kazaks were the only ethnic group with a positive migration balance. The outmigration of Russophones in that year was more than 180,000, compared with less than 10,000 in the Kazak group.[63]

If the differences in natural growth between the titular and nontitular population in Latvia are negligible, in Kazakstan, they are significant. If the Kazaks also in the future continue to raise far larger

---

[62] Lewis et al. 1976.
[63] *CIS Migration report* 1997, 58.

families than the Russophones the growth of the Kazak nationality will rapidly outpace the growth of the non-Kazak groups, even without an ethnically slanted migration pattern.

Ian Bremmer and Cory Welt have remarked that "[i]f Nazarbaev believed that the Russians would comprise up to 40 per cent of Kazak-stan's population indefinitely, it is conceivable that he would seek some kind of power-sharing arrangement with them."[64] Indeed, the expected demographic shifts in the country are an important disincentive for accommodation and "consociationalism" in the Kazak leadership. This may perhaps not come through very clearly in Nazarbaev's own speeches, but permeates the writings of his advisors nevertheless.

Demography is one of the favorite themes in the Kazak nationality debate. According to official sources, the share of the Kazak group increased from 39.7 percent in 1989, to 44.3 percent in 1994 and 46 percent by 1 January 1995.[65] A Kazak demographic dominance is predicted to be in place in the course of the first decade of the next century.

In the Kazakstani debate these figures and extrapolations are used to drive home two points. First, this development will break the resistance of Russophone activists against the Kazakification of the state. Second, it allegedly also justifies the present overrepresentation of Kazaks in the state apparatus and in elected offices. A group of researchers from the semi-official Institute for the Development of Kazakstan has claimed that

> while the major ethnic groups have different degrees of representation in the examined structures, the differences are not so large to give cause for concern. The dynamics of ethnic representation, in our view, go in the same direction as the ethno-demographic development in the country.[66]

One might expect the growth of "nationality power" (to use Rasma Karklins' expression),[67] to follow demographic tendencies with a time-lag of one generation. After all, not infants but adults fill public offices. However, as we have shown, the political influence of the ethnic Kazaks in contemporary Kazakstan is clearly *running ahead* of their demographic weight.

With a terminology reminiscent of Oswald Spengler's culturology M. Tatimov, a senior member of the presidential analytical center in Kazakstan, has divided the nations of the world into "young" and "old" by the criterion of their demographic development. A nation is

---

[64] Bremmer and Welt 1996, 196.

[65] *O demograficheskoi* 1996, 66.

[66] Galiev et al. 1994, 43.

[67] Karklins 1986/1989, 77–100.

"old" if the older age cohorts dominate over the age groups of children and youngsters. In Tatimov's typology the Russians, the Balts, and the Ukrainians are old nations.

Whenever two "old" nations dominate on the same territory, they will tend to engage in a kind of "psychological cold war" for control, Tatimov maintains. Kazakstan, however, is in a much more favorable situation since one of the two competing nations in the country, the Kazaks, is young. The Kazaks, therefore, will win out without engaging the Russians in direct confrontation, just by biding their time. The ethnic battle, as it were, will be fought in the bed chamber, where the Kazaks inevitably will be victorious.

However, the Kazakstani state authorities ought not to sit back smugly awaiting this happy outcome. Instead, they should actively strengthen the natural trends by "an effective demographic policy, supporting and promoting the full manifestation of the historically objective tendencies in the development of our population." In addition, the state should pursue a migration policy geared toward the strategic aim of "consolidating the Republic of Kazakstan as a young, unitary state."[68]

What the Future Holds:
A Few Glimpses into the Crystal Ball

The dominant mood among Kazak nationality experts seems to be triumphalism. Kazak intellectuals tend to rest assured that in the present ethnic rivalry the Kazak side will win out without taking recourse to any extreme measures. The decisive factor of *time* is on their side. The sanguine views of the Kazak researchers go against the grain of most Western analysts who, in later years, have been predicting growing interethnic and intraethnic violence in Kazakstan.[69] In fact, the tranquil scenario of the Kazak expertise may easily be turned on its head. In 1993 a Cossack deputy to the Kazakstani Supreme Soviet saw the equal strength of the two main cultural groups in Kazakstan as one of the basic preconditions explaining the virtual absence of ethnically motivated bloodshed in the country. Since neither group could hope to prevail over the other, both were inclined to compromise and accommodate.[70]

---

[68] Tatimov 1995.

[69] Bremmer and Welt 1995; Bremmer and Welt 1996; Kaiser and Chinn 1995.

[70] Viktor Vodolazov in *Rossiiskaia gazeta*, 20 February 1993.

If the Russophones are feeling that they are gradually losing (demographic and political) strength *vis-à-vis* the titular nation, they may conceptualize the situation as a closing window of opportunity. They will have to act before it is too late. They must make a last-ditch defense before they have become so numerically and politically weakened that they are no longer able to stem the ongoing tide of Kazakification. However, when we visited Almaty, Semipalatinsk, and Ust-Kamenogorsk in September 1996, we saw few signs of Russian or Russophone mobilization. Whether this shows that "the window of opportunity" has already closed or we were witnessing the proverbial lull before the storm, we cannot tell.

Russophone spokespersons in Kazakstan maintain that a massive outmigration will have detrimental consequences and effect all ethnic groups alike. The deputy director of the Kazakstani state committee on nationality policies, Natalia Loginova, herself an ethnic Russian, has warned that "if the emigration turns into a panic, it will simply be a catastrophe for Kazakstan."[71] It will drain the country of valuable human and intellectual resources which are needed in the economic development. A massive exodus of nontitulars will lead to deteriorating living standards among those who remain behind, indeed, these effects are already being felt, she claims.

If the economy continues to contract, this may easily lead to social unrest. Many local observers in Kazakstan whom we spoke to see hunger riots as a more likely scenario than interethnic confrontations. In order to forestall such dire consequences the Kazakstani leadership may try to undertake measures to halt the Russian emigration and even to lure back those who have left. Certain such steps have already been taken by the leadership in the neighboring state of Kyrgyzstan, with partial success.

Many observers we have spoken to in Kazakstan also predict that a mass departure of Russians may lead to intensified intra-ethnic rivalries among various segments within the Kazak group. When there is no longer any need to keep a common front against the Russophones the zhuz divisions as well as urban–rural Kazak antagonism may spring out into full blossom. Thus, many Russophones insist that their presence in society has a stabilizing effect on intra-ethnic relations within the dominant Kazak group.[72] Should the dominant Kazak community fall apart into various interest groups and cultural segments a whole new political game will open up which we cannot pursue here.

---

[71] Loginova 1995, 41.
[72] Conversations in Almaty and Semipalatinsk, September 1996.

However, the prognoses for rapid changes in the ethnodemographic makeup of Kazakstan may be exaggerated. In the late 1990s there are certain signs of decreasing population growth among the ethnic Kazaks, primarily for two reasons. Urban Kazaks have a family structure more similar to the Russians, and as ever-more Kazaks move to the towns and the cities, they tend to have fewer children. But also in the Kazak *auls* the population growth seems to be abating, as least temporarily, as a result of falling standards of living and health. Rural mortality, including infant mortality, it is being claimed in Almaty, is on the rise.

At the same time, the outmigration of Russophones from Kazakstan peaked in 1994, two years later than in Latvia. Most of those Russophones in Kazakstan who wanted—and were able—to leave seem to have done so already. While Kazakstan had a negative migration balance of 411,000 in 1994, the deficit had dropped to 238,000 individuals in 1995 and to 175,000 in 1996.[73] In combination, the newest trends in population growth among titular and nontitular groups in Kazakstan seem to indicate that the Kazakstani authorities probably cannot rely on demographic change as a decisive means to eliminate the ipolar structure of society in the foreseeable future.

Another important factor influencing ethnic stability is economy. Few people will deny that the Kazakstani economy in the 1990s is in dire straits. A contracting economy, leaving smaller pieces of the cake to everyone, may easily lead to increased social tension. At the same time, semi-official Kazakstani sources insist that "the fall in living standards, and the stratification into rich and poor have affected all national groups in equal measure. Therefore, no one has any reason to bear a grudge against the other groups."[74]

However, there is no reason to believe that the economic development will affect all *individuals* in the same way. While most Kazaks have become poorer, a few have grown richer. The post-Communist economy in Kazakstan—while not exactly a capitalist market economy—has contributed to the creation of new cleavages within the titular nation, between the destitute and the well-off, which may lead to new fragmentations within the titular group.

In Latvia, integration into the Western, capitalist economy is proceeding much faster than in Kazakstan. Primarily for that reason, new socio-economic stratifications seem to be crystallizing more rapidly. Even if it proves true, as many Latvians insist, that Russophones are in control of important sectors of the Latvian economy today, there is every reason to believe that an increasing number of ethnic Latvians

---

[73] *CIS Migration Report* 1997, 56.
[74] Arenov 1996.

will join the ranks of the more prosperous business community. The ethnopolitical effects of this development are difficult to predict. On the one hand, it may lead to increased interethnic competition and hostility on the economic arena. On the other hand, Russian and Latvian businessmen may conclude that they have common interests against other groups in society, such as workers and the state bureaucracy. This may contribute to a restructuring of the Latvian political landscape away from ethnic issues into a more "Western-style" axis of economic liberals vs. adherents of state intervention in the economy.

The Latvians are more consolidated as an ethnic group than are the Kazaks and it is not likely that cultural or regional divisions among them will become an important political factor in the future. Also in this country the relative numerical strength of the titular nation is likely to grow but the demographic shifts will be slow. It will probably take several generations before Latvian nationalists will reach their longed-for goal of a 75–25 percent Latvian ethnic dominance, if that day ever dawns at all.

The Latvian citizenship law provides for the gradual inclusion of the nontitulars into the body politic on certain conditions, most importantly, that they learn the Latvian language. If this process should gain speed the majority of the Russophones will achieve citizenship some time in the future. In theory at least, an ethnic redistribution of the citizenry may lead to a situation in which the mechanisms of ethnic democracy will no longer work. Anton Steen expects that "in the future, when more Russians are given citizenship and the right to vote in elections, more interethnic tensions will probably develop."[75] So far, however, the speed of the naturalization process has been exceedingly slow. If it does not accelerate this scenario may be overtaken by other events.

Another scenario envisages Russian mobilization outside of the political system, in streets riots, civil disobedience, etc. However, this is not likely to happen in Latvia. Resentment and anger do not necessarily lead to collective action in any form.[76] The prevalent mood in Latvia today that "politics is the domain of the ethnic Latvians" will probably linger on for a long time. Even as the non-Latvians are granted political rights, they will not necessarily use them to the same extent as the ethnic Latvians, as the situation in the late 1980s and early 1990s showed. The vast majority of the Russophones seem resigned to the fact that politics is off limits to them and they will not make any attempt to challenge the Latvians in that arena.

---

[75] Steen 1997, 358.

[76] Smith and Wilson 1997.

Also, two aspects of Latvian society are likely to serve as important safety vaults against ethnically motivated unrest. The political and cultural marginalization of the nontitulars in Latvia has not to the same extent led to their social or economic marginalization. While the Russophones may have poor chances of improving their status as a group, they may invest their time and energy in the promotion of their private careers. Even if the Latvians have monopolized the arenas of politics and state bureaucracy, there are other ladders available for ambitious and mobile nontitulars. To some extent, these ladders serve as social lightning rods, channeling the energy of the nontitulars away from collective action towards a striving for individual betterment.

Finally, while the non-citizens in Latvia are deprived of basic *political* rights, their nonpolitical, individual human rights are generally respected. Latvia may perhaps not qualify yet for the designation *Rechtstaat* in the full sense of the word, but it is certainly not a lawless society either. Latvian laws, while far from flawless, are not empty declarations, but increasingly provide the groundwork for societal interaction. These conditions a majority of the Russophones seem prepared to put up with, although, some of them at least, with clenched teeth.

Summing Up

The historical record shows that an ethnic structure of society of the kind that Donald Horowitz has called "centrally focused systems"— with two distinct, major cultural groups of roughly equal size—does not necessarily, probably not even normally, lead to a fierce struggle for control of the state. There are several reasons for this and some regularities may be pointed out. Obviously, even if two groups are of equal size numerically they may be very unequal in other respects, for instance with regard to access to resources, inner cohesion, social structure and the will to rule. Even in a bipolar situation Schermerhorn's dictum often seems to be true: "the probability is overwhelming that when two groups with different cultural histories establish contacts that are regular rather than occasional or intermittent, one of the two groups will typically assume dominance over the other."[77] The group which achieves superior status in bipolar situations often seems to be the one which is able to pose as "the sons of the soil." In the former Soviet Union this tendency is reinforced by the Soviet manner of regulating ethnic

---

[77] Schermerhorn 1970, 68. See p. 52.

FIGURE 7.1 Congruent and Incongruent Orientations Toward Centripetal and Centrifugal Trends of Subordinates as Viewed by Themselves and Superordinates

Tending towards integration

	A	B
Superordinates	Cp	Cf
Subordinates	Cp	Cf
	Assimilation Incorporation	Cultural pluralism Autonomy

Tending towards conflict

	C	D
Superordinates	Cf	Cp
Subordinates	Cp	Cf
	Forced segregation with resistance	Forced assimilation with resistance

Cp = centripetal trends, Cf= centrifugal trends

relations—the formalized ethnic ascription system and the ethnically defined federation.

Once the elites of the titular ethnic group are entrenched in positions of political power they have the opportunity to formulate the rules of the game to suit themselves and their own ethnic group. In both Latvia and Kazakstan the Russophones today seem to lack both the will, the opportunities, and the resources to eject them from these positions. The titular elites are therefore free to pursue their nationalizing policies as deeply and as fast as they seem fit, provided that they are not restrained by other factors such as economic considerations or the involvement of the international community or of Russia.

Even as the balance between the two major cultural-linguistic groups shifts somewhat from the 50–50 mark, Latvia and Kazakstan will remain basically bicultural in the foreseeable future. In Latvia, the Russians seem prepared for a high degree of acculturation, but their centripetal orientations are frustrated by the attitudes of the superordinate group. In Kazakstan, the Russians do not intend to jump over the cultural divide even if the attitudes they are met with among the members of the titular nation in this country are more sympathetic than are being faced by their coethnics in Latvia. Controversy, however, may arise over the political integration which they are being denied. While neither of our two cases fit neatly into any of the four boxes in Schermerhorns's typology, we may locate their approximate positions somewhere between A and C for Latvia and B and C for Kazakstan.

Horowitz points out that policy-makers may want to reshape the ethnopolitical structure in their respective countries away from the instability of a centrally focused system toward a system resembling those of India and Tanzania. In his book he discusses several such devices: accommodation (federalism, cultural autonomy, consociationalism), partition, and preferential treatment of one group over the other(s).[78] Among these, preferential treatment is clearly the favored device among state leaders in both Latvia and Kazakstan. In addition we have in our study identified strategies for de-bipolarization as an important element of the nationalizing policies in the two countries. One possible way to shift the ethnosocial structure of society away from the bipolar situation is ethnic integration. Integration, however, is not among the preferred options of the nationalizing leaderships in either Latvia or Kazakstan. Instead, the state authorities in these two countries bank on other means to achieve de-bipolarization such as strategies for ethnodemographic shifts. In Kazakstan, a determined policy for the re-ethnification of the population is also a conspicuous and noteworthy element in this strategy.

---

[78] Horowitz 1985, 41 and 563–680.

Bibliography

General Literature

Aasland, Aadne 1996. "Russians outside Russia. The New Russian Diaspora," in Graham Smith (ed.), *The Nationalities question in the post-Soviet States*. London: Longman, 477–498.

Acton, John Emerich Edward Dahlberg 1862/1967. *Essays in the Liberal Interpretation of History*. Chicago: University of Chicago Press.

Anderson, Barbara A. and Brian D. Silver 1983. "Estimating Russification of Ethnic Identity Among Non-Russians in the USSR," *Demography*, 20, 4 (November), 461–89.

Anderson, Benedict 1983/1994. *Imagined Communities*. London: Verso.

Arutiunian, Iu.V. (ed.) 1992. *Russkie. Etnosotsiologicheskie ocherki*. Moscow: Nauka.

Barry, Brian 1975. "Review article: Political Accommodation and Consociational Democracy," *British Journal of Political Science*, 5, 4, 477–505.

Barth, Fredrik (ed.) 1969. *Ethnic Groups and Boundaries*. London: Allen & Unwin.

Bendix, Reinhard 1977. *Nation-building and Citizenship*. Berkeley: University of California Press.

Berger, Peter L. and Thomas Luckmann 1966/1976. *The Social Construction of Reality*. Harmondsworth: Penguin books.

Birch, Anthony H. 1989. *Nationalism and National Integration*. London: Unwin Hyman.

Brass, Paul 1991. *Ethnicity and Nationalism, Theory and comparison*. New Delhi: Sage.

Brubaker, Rogers. 1993. "Political dimensions of migration from and among Soviet successor states," in Myron Weiner (ed.), *International migration and security*. Boulder CO: Westview, 39–64.

Brubaker, Rogers 1996a. "Nationalizing states in the old 'New' Europe – and the new," *Ethnic and Racial Studies*, 19, 2 (April), 411–437.

Brubaker, Rogers 1996b. *Nationalism Reframed. Nationhood and the national question in the New Europe*. Cambridge: Cambridge University Press.

Carrère d'Encausse, Hélène 1979. *Decline of an Empire. The Soviet Socialist Republics in Revolt*. New York: Newsweek.

Carrère d'Encausse, Hélène 1992. *The Great Challenge. Nationalities and the Bolshevik State, 1917–1930*. London: Holmes and Meier.

CIS Migration Report (1996) 1997. Geneva: IOM International Organization for Migration.

Connor, Walker 1994. *Ethnonationalism. The Quest for Understanding*. Princeton: Princeton University Press.

Copenhagen meeting 1990. *The Document of the Copenhagen Meeting of the Conference of the Human Rights Dimension of the CSCE*. Copenhagen.

Dahl, Robert A. 1989. *Democracy and its Critics*. New Haven: Yale University press.

"Data on Ethnic Intermarriages," 1990. *Journal of Soviet Nationalities*, 1 (Summer) 160–174.

"Declaration of compatriots rights. 2nd world congress of Russian communities" 1994. *Survey of Baltic and post-Soviet politics*. Sakala centre, Tallinn, (February), 18–22.

Deutsch, Karl 1963. "Nation-building and national development: Some issues for political research," in Karl Deutsch and William J. Foltz (eds.), *Nationbuilding*. New York: Atherton, 1–16.

Drobizheva, L.M, A.R. Aklaev, V.V. Koroteeva and G.U. Soldatova 1996. *Demokratizatsiia i obrazy natsionalizma v Rossiiskoi Federatsii 90-x godov*. Moscow: Mysl'.

Folz, William 1974. "Ethnicity, Status, and Conflict," in Wendell Bell and Walter E. Freeman (eds.), *Ethnicity and Nation-building. Comparative, International and Historical perspectives*. Beverly Hills: Sage, 103–16.

Friedrich, Carl J. 1963. "Nation-building?," in Karl Deutsch and William Foltz (eds.), *Nation-building*. New York: Atherton, 27–32.

Gasprinskii, Ismail bey (Gaspirali) 1993. *Rossiia i Vostok*. Kazan: Tatarskoe knizhnoe izdatel'stvo.

Gellner, Ernest 1983/1990. *Nations and Nationalism*. Oxford: Blackwells.

Gladney, Dru C. 1996. "Relational alterity: Constructing Dungan (Hui), Uygur, and Kazakh identities across China, Central Asia, and Turkey," *History and Anthropology*, 9, 4, 445–477.

Gleason, Gregory 1990. *Federalism and Nationalism. The Struggle for Republican Rights in the USSR*. Boulder CO: Westview.

Glotz, Peter 1990. *Der Irrweg des Nationalstaats: europäische Reden an ein deutsches Publikum*. Stuttgart: Deutsche Verlags-Anstalt.

Hallik, Klara 1994. "On the international context of the interethnic relations in Estonia," paper presented at the conference "Democracy and Ethnopolitics," Riga March 9–11, 1994.

Hodnett, Grey 1979. *Leadership in the Soviet National Republics*. Oakville: Mosaic Press.

Hooghe, Liesbet 1993. "Belgium: From Regionalism to Federalism," in John Coakley (ed.), *The Territorial Management of Ethnic Conflict*. London: Frank Cass.

Horowitz, Donald L. 1975. "Ethnic identity," in Nathan Glazer and Daniel P. Moynihan (eds.), *Ethnicity. Theory and Experience*. Cambridge MA: Harvard University Press, 111–140.

Horowitz, Donald L. 1985. *Ethnic Groups in Conflict*. Berkeley: University of California Press.

Kaiser, Robert J. 1994a. *The Geography of Nationalism in Russia and the USSR*. Princeton: Princeton University Press.

Kaiser, Robert J. 1994b. "Ethnic Demography and Interstate Relations in Central Asia," in Roman Szporluk, (ed.), *National Identity and Ethnicity in Russia and the New States of Eurasia*. Armonk: Sharpe, 230–65.

Kaiser, Robert J. 1995. "Nationalizing the Work Force: Ethnic Restratification in the Newly Independent States," *Post-Soviet Geography*, 36, 2, 87–111.

Kappeler, Andreas 1992/1993. *Russland als Vielvölkerreich*. Munich: C.H.Beck.

Karklins, Rasma 1986/1989. *Ethnic Relations in the USSR. The Perspective From Below*. Boston: Unwin Hyman.

Katz, Zev, Rosemarie Rogers and Frederic Harned (eds.) 1975. *Handbook of Major Soviet Nationalities*. New York: Free Press.

Kohn, Hans 1946. *The Idea of Nationalism*. New York: Macmillan.

Kolstø, Pål, 1993a. "The New Russian Diaspora. Russians Outside Russia. Minority Protection in the Soviet Successor States," *Journal of Peace Research*, 30, 2, 197–217.

Kolstø, Pål, 1993b. "National Minorities in the Non-Russian Soviet Successor States of the Former Soviet Union," *RAND report DRU–565–FF*, November.

Kolstoe, Paul (Kolstø, Pål) 1995. *Russians in the Former Soviet Republics*. London/Bloomington: C.Hurst/Indiana University Press,.

Kolstø, Pål, 1996a. "Nation-building in the Former USSR," *Journal of Democracy*, 7, 1, 118–132.

Kolstø, Pål, 1996b. "The new Russian diaspora – an identity of its own? Possible identity trajectories for Russians in the former Soviet republics," *Ethnic and Racial Studies*, 9, 3, 609–639.

Komarova, O.D. 1980. "Ethnically mixed marriages in the Soviet Union," *GeoJournal Supplementary Issue*, 1, 31–34.

Kommisrud, Arne 1996. *Stat, nasjon, imperium. Habsburgmonarkiet, Tsar-Russland og Sovjetunionen*. Oslo: Spartacus.

Kozlov, V.I. 1982. *Natsional'nosti SSSR, Etnodemograficheskii obzor*. Moscow: Finansy i statistika.

Kuper, Leo, 1969. "Plural Societies: Perspectives and Problems," in Leo Kuper and M.G. Smith (eds.), *Pluralism in Africa*. Berkeley: University of California press, 8–25.

Laitin, David D. 1991. "The National Uprisings in the Soviet Union," *World Politics*, 44, 1, 139–77.

Laitin, David D. 1995. "Identity in formation: the Russian-speaking nationality in the post-Soviet diaspora," *Archives européenes de sociologie*, 36, 2, 281–316.

Laitin, David D. 1996a. "Language and Nationalism in the Post-Soviet Republics," *Post-Soviet Affairs*, 12, 1 (January–March), 4–24.

Laitin, David D. 1996b. "National Revival and Competitive Assimilation in Estonia," *Post-Soviet Affairs*, 12, 1 (January–March), 25–39.

Laitin, David D. 1998. *Identity in formation. The Russian-speaking populations in the Near Abroad*. Ithaca: Cornell University press.

Lewis, Robert A, Richard H. Rowland and Ralph Clem 1976. *Nationality and Population Change in Russia and the USSR*. New York: Praeger.

Liebich, André 1995. "Nations, states, minorities: why is Eastern Europe different?," *Dissent*, (Summer) 313–17.

Lijphart, Arend 1971. "Cultural Diversity and Theories of Political Integration," *Canadian Journal of Political Science*, 4, 1, 1–14.

Lijphart, Arend 1977. *Democracy in Plural Societies*. New Haven: Yale University Press.

Lustick, Ian 1979. "Stability in deeply divided societies: Consociationalism vs. control," *World Politics*, 31, 3, 325–344.

Mauzy, Diane 1993/1995. "Malaysia: Malay political hegemony and 'coercive consociationalism'," in John McGarry and Brendan O'Leary (eds.), *The politics of ethnic conflict regulation*. London: Routledge, 106–127.

Melvin, Neil 1995. *Russians Beyond Russia. The politics of National Identity*. London: Royal Institute of International Affairs.

Melvin, Neil 1998. "The Russians: Diaspora and the End of Empire", in Charles King and Neil J. Melvin (eds.), *Nations abroad. Diaspora politics and International Relations in the Former Soviet Union*. Boulder, CO: Westview press, 27–57

Mill, John Stuart 1861/1946. *On Liberty and Considerations on Representative Government*. Oxford: Basil Blackwell.

Milne, R.S. 1981. *Politics in Ethnically Bipolar States*. Vancouver: University of British Columbia Press.

Motyl, Alexander J. 1993. *Dilemmas of Independence. Ukraine After Totalitarianism*. New York: Council on Foreign Relations Press.

Nahaylo, Bohdan and Victor Swoboda 1990. *Soviet Disunion. A History of the Nationalities Problem in the USSR*. London: Hamish Hamilton.

Naselenie SSSR 1988, statisticheskii ezhegodnik 1989. Moscow: Finansy i statistika.

Natsional'nyi sostav naseleniia SSSR 1991. Moscow: Finansy i statistika.

Neumann, Iver B. 1993. "Russia as Central Europe's Constituting Other," *East European Politics and Societies*, 7, 2 (Spring) 349–370.

"Osnovnye napravleniia gosudarstvennoi politiki Rossiiskoi Federatsii v otnoshenii sootechestvennikov, prozhivaiushchikh za rubezhom," Postanovlenie Pravitel'stva Rossiiskoi Federatsii 31 August 1994, no. 1064, reprinted in *Russkoe slovo* (Chisinau), 24–30 October 1994.

Pavlovich, Matthews 1980. "Ethnic Impact of Russian Dispersion in and Beyond the RSFSR," in Edward Allworth (ed.), *Ethnic Russia in the USSR. The Dilemma of Dominance*. New York: Pergamon, 294–305.

Pearson, Raymond 1983. *National minorities in Eastern Europe*. London: Macmillan.

Pipes. Richard 1974/1979. *Russia under the old Regime*. Harmondsworth: Penguin.

Pipes, Richard 1975. "Reflections on the Nationality Problems in the Soviet Union," in Nathan Glazer and Daniel P. Moynihan (eds.), *Ethnicity. Theory and Experience*. Cambridge MA: Harvard University Press, 453–65.

Premdas, Ralph R. 1993/1995. "Balance and ethnic conflict in Fiji," in John McGarry and Brendan O'Leary (eds.), *The politics of ethnic conflict regulation*. London: Routledge, 251–274.

Proekt Deklaratsii o podderzhke Rossiiskoi Federatsiei rossiiskoi diaspory o pokrovitel'stve rossiiskim sootechestvennikam 1994 (unpublished draft).

Proekt Federal'nogo Zakona O gosudarstvennoi politike v otnoshenii sootechestvennikov v gosudarstvakh-uchastnikakh Sodruzhestva Nezavisimykh Gosudarstv, Latviiskoi Respublike, Litovskoi Respublike, Estonskoi Respublike i drugikh gosudarstvakh 1997. 19 March (unpublished draft).

Proekt Zakona Rossiiskoi Federatsii o sodeistvii rossiiskim sootechestvennikam za rubezhem 1995. (unpublished draft).

Rabushka, Alvin and Kenneth A. Shepsle 1972. *Politics in Plural Societies. A Theory of Democratic Instability*. Columbus: Bell and Howell.

Renan, Ernest 1882/1992. *Qu'est-ce qu'une nation? et autres essais politiques*. Paris: Presses Pocket.

Rokkan, Stein 1975. "Dimensions of State Formation and Nation-building: A Possible Paradigm for Research on Variations within Europe," in Charles Tilly (ed.), *The formation of national states in Western Europe*. Princeton: Princeton University Press, 562–599.

Schermerhorn, R.A. 1970. *Comparative ethnic relations: A framework for theory and research*. New York: Random House.

Shanin, Theodor 1985/1986. *Russia as a "developing society."* London: Macmillan.

Shibutani, Tamotsu and Kian M. Kwan 1965. *Ethnic Stratification. A Comparative Approach*. New York: Macmillan.

Silver, Brian D. 1978. "Ethnic intermarriage and ethnic consciousness among Soviet nationalities," *Soviet Studies*, 30, 1 (January), 107–16.

Simon, Gerhard 1986/1991. *Nationalism and Policy Toward the Nationalities in the Soviet Union*. Boulder: Westview.

Sisk, Timothy D. 1996/1997. *Power Sharing and International Mediation in Ethnic Conflicts*. Washington DC: United States Institute of Peace.

Slezkine, Yuri 1994. "The USSR as a Communal Apartment, or How a Socialist State Promoted Ethnic Particularism," *Slavic Review*, 53, 2, 414–452.

Smith, Anthony D. 1986. *The Ethnic Origins of Nations*. Oxford: Blackwell.

Smith, Anthony D. 1991. *National Identity*. Harmondsworth: Penguin.

Smith, Anthony D. 1992. "Introduction: Ethnicity and Nationalism" in Anthony D. Smith (ed.), *Ethnicity and Nationalism*. Leiden: E.J.Brill, 1–4.

Smith, Graham (ed.) 1990/1992. *The Nationalities Question in the Soviet Union*. London: Longman.

Smith, Graham and Andrew Wilson 1997. "Rethinking Russia's Post-Soviet Diaspora: The Potential for Political Mobilisation in Eastern Ukraine and Northeast Estonia," *Europe-Asia Studies*, 49, 5, 845–64.

Smooha, Sammy 1990. "Minority status in an ethnic democracy: The status of the Arab minority in Israel," *Ethnic and Racial studies*, 13, 3, (July), 389–413.

Smooha, Sammy and Theodor Hanf 1992. "The Diverse Modes of Conflict-Regulation in Deeply Divided Societies" in Anthony D. Smith 1992 (ed.), *Ethnicity and Nationalism*. Leiden: E.J.Brill, 26–47.

Snyder, Jack 1993. "Nationalism and the Crisis of the Post-Soviet State," *Survival*, 35, 1, 5–26.

"Soobshchenie press-sluzhby Prezidenta Rossiiskoi Federatsii" 1997. 11 February.

Stalin, I.V. 1946. "Marksizm i natsional'nyi vopros" in I.V. Stalin, *Sochineniia*, vol. 2, Moscow: OGIZ, 290–367.

Strayer, Joseph R. 1963. "The Historical Experience of Nation-building in Europe, in Karl Deutsch and William J. Foltz (eds.), *Nation-building*. New York: Atherton, 17–26.

Sugar, Peter F. 1969/1994. "External and Domestic Roots of Eastern European Nationalism," in Peter F. Sugar and Ivo Lederer (eds.), *Nationalism in Eastern Europe*. Seattle: University of Washington Press, 3–54.

Suny, Ronald Grigor 1993. *The revenge of the past. Nationalism, Revolution, and the collapse of the Soviet Union*. Stanford CA: Stanford University Press.

Susokolov, A.A 1992. "Natsional'no-smeshannye braki sredi russkogo naseleniia v raznykh regionakh strany," in Iu. V. Arutiunian (ed.), *Russkie. Etnosotsiologicheskie ocherki*. Moscow: Nauka, 191–222.

Szporluk, Roman (ed.) 1994. *National Identity and Ethnicity in Russia and the New States of Eurasia*. Armonk: Sharpe.

Tilly, Charles 1975. "Reflections on the History of European State-making," in Charles Tilly (ed.), *The formation of national states in Western Europe*. Princeton: Princeton University Press, 3–83.

Tishkov, Valery 1997. *Ethnicity, nationalism and conflict in and after the Soviet Union. The Mind Aflame*. London: Sage.

Titma, Mikk and Nancy B. Tuma 1992. *Migration in the Former Soviet Union*. Cologne: Berichte des Bundesinstituts für ostwissenschaftliche und internationale Studien no. 22–1992.

Ukaz Prezidenta Rossiiskoi Federatsii "Ob osnovnyh napravleniiakh gosudarstvennoi politiki Rossiiskoi Federatsii v otnoshenii sootechestvennikov, prozhivaiushchikh za rubezhem" 1994. No 1681, 11 August.

Vasil'eva, Ol'ga 1991. "Novaia natsiia? Russkie v SSSR kak natsional'noe men'shinstvo," *XX vek i mir,* 7 (July), 15–19.

Zaslavsky, Victor 1982/1994. *The Neo-Stalinist State.* New York: Sharpe.

Zaslavsky, Victor 1992. "Nationalism and Democratic Transition in Postcommunist Societies," *Dædalus,* 121, 2, 97–121.

Zaslavsky, Victor and Yuri Luryi 1979. "The Passport System in the USSR and Changes in Soviet Society," *Soviet Union/Union Sovietique,* 6, part 2, 137–53.

Østerud, Øyvind 1978. *Utviklingsteori og historisk endring.* Oslo: Gyldendal.

Literature on Latvia

Aasland, Aadne 1994. "Russians in Latvia. Ethnic Identity and Ethnopolitical Change." University of Glasgow: Institute of Russian and East European Studies. Ph.D.-dissertation.

Aasland, Aadne (ed.) 1996. *Latvia: The Impact of the Transformation.* The NORBALT Living Conditions Project. Oslo: Fafo Report 188.

Aasland, Aadne 1997. "Ethnic groups and Living Conditions: A Study of Unemployment in the Baltic Countries," in Aadne Aasland, Knud Knudsen, Dagmar Kutsar and Ilze Trapenciere (eds.), *The Baltic Countries Revisited: Living Conditions and Comparative Challenges.* Oslo: Fafo (Fafo Report no. 230), 105–119.

Abyzov, Iurii 1992 "Ostzeiskii kompleks rossianina – i sovremennost'," *Diena* (Riga), 11 April; *ibid,* 16 April; Subbotnii den', 25 April, p. 13; ibid. 30 April, p. 13.

Antane, Aina 1991. "Some Aspects of Cultural Autonomy of Minorities in Latvia 1920–1934 and Today." paper presented at the symposium "National Identity in the Baltic States and Croatia/Slovenia," Oslo, 5–6 September 1991.

Apine, Ilga 1994. "Osobennosti etnicheskikh konfliktov v Latvii," in V.Tishkov (ed.), *Etnichnost' i vlast' v polietnichnikh gosudarstvakh.* Moscow: Nauka, 257–274.

Baltic Media Book 1996. Riga: Baltic Media Facts Ltd.

Baltiiskaia Assambleia Tallinn 13–14 maia 1989. 1989. Tallinn: Valgus.

Barrington, Lowell 1995. "Citizenships and the 'Nation-builder's Dilemma:' Ethnicity, Nation-building, and State-building in Newly Independent States." Paper prepared for the annual meeting of the American Political Science Association, August 31 – September 3, 1995, Chicago.

Birckenbach, Hanne-Margret 1997. *Preventive Diplomacy through Fact-finding. How international organisations review the conflict over citizenship in Estonia and Latvia.* Hamburg: Lit Verlag.

Bojars, Juris 1992. "The Citizenship and Human Rights Regulation in the Republic of Latvia." *The Finnish Yearbook of International Law,* 3, 331–352.

Brubaker, Rogers 1992. "Citizenship Struggles in Soviet Successor States." *International Migration Review,* 26, 2, 269–91.

Bungs, Dzintra 1994. "Local Elections in Latvia: The Opposition Wins," *RFE/RL Research Report,* 3, 28 (15 July), 1–5.

Ceturta tautas skaitisana Latvija 1935.g. 1936–1939. Riga.

Chicherina N.G. 1990. *Grazhdanskie dvizheniia v Latvii 1989.* Moscow: Center of Studies of Inter-Ethnic Relations.

Citizenship and Language Legislation in the Newly Independent States of Europe. Seminar held in Copenhagen January 9–10, 1993. Copenhagen: The Danish Center for Human Rights and The Danish Helsinki Committee.

"Comments on the Draft citizenship law of the Republic of Latvia. Strasbourg, 24 January 1994," *SM-Segodnia* 24–26 February 1994.

Constitutional law "Cilveka un pilsona tiesibas un pienakumi" 1995. Adopted 10.12.1991, in *Latvijas Republikas Pamatlikumi.* Riga: Kamene, 18–24.

Council of the Baltic See States 1996. Commissioner of the CSCE on Democratic Institutions and Human Rights, including the Rights of Persons belonging to Minorities. Annual Report. Presented at the V Ministerial Session, Kalmar, 2–3 July.

Darbaspeks Latvija/Labour Force in Latvia 1996. Riga: Statistikas biletens.

Dreifelds, Juris 1984. "Demographic Trends in Latvia," *Nationalities Papers,* 12, 1, 40–84.

Dreifelds, Juris 1996. *Latvia in Transition.* Cambridge: Cambridge University Press.

Druviete, Ina (ed.) 1995. *The Language Situation in Latvia. Sociolinguistic Survey.* Part 1. Riga: Latvian Academy of Science.

Druviete, Ina (ed.) 1996. *The Language Situation in Latvia and Lithuania.* London: Macmillan.

Eide, Asbjørn 1992. *Human Rights Aspects of the Citizenship Issues in Estonia and Latvia.* European Bank for Reconstruction and Development, London. Reprinted in Hanne-Margret Birckenbach 1997. *Preventive Diplomacy through Fact-finding. How international organisations review the conflict over citizenship in Estonia and Latvia.* Hamburg: Lit Verlag, 96–116.

"Estonia Today" 1996. Information Division of the Press and Information Department, Ministry of Foreign Affairs, WWW http://www.vm.ee, 21 February.

Etnosituacija Latvija (fakti un komentari) / The ethnic situation in Latvia (facts and commentary). 1992. Riga: Ethnic Studies Center.

Fall, Ibrahima 1993. *Summary of the Report on a Fact-Finding Mission to Latvia (November 1992).* Reprinted in Hanne-Margret Birckenbach 1997. *Preventive Diplomacy through Fact-finding. How international organisations review the conflict over citizenship in Estonia and Latvia.* Hamburg: Lit Verlag, 117–138.

Fehervary, Andrash 1993. "Citizenship, Statelessness and Human Rights: Recent Developments in the Baltic states," *International Journal of Refugee Law,* 5, 3, 392–423.

Fleishman, Arkadii 1995. "Multikulturalizm, nash prioritet," *Kultura un vards,* January 1995.

Goeckel, Robert F. 1995. "The Baltic Churches and the Democratization Process," in Michael Bourdeaux (ed.), *The Politics of Religion in Russia and the New States of Eurasia.* Armonk: Sharpe, 202–25.

"Grozijumi Nolikuma par valsts valodas lietusanu nosaukumos un lietosanu informacija, 25.07. 1995"; *Saeima un Ministru Kabineta,* 16 August 1995.

Guboglo, M.N. 1994. *Perelomnye gody. Tom 2. Iazykovaia reforma – 1989. Dokumenty i materialy.* Moscow: Tsimo.

Iedzivotaju migracijas procesi Latvija 1995.gada. 1996. Analitiskie materiali. Pielikums Latvijas statistikas ikmenesa biletenam No.2.

Iedzivotaju starpvalstu migracija 1992. un 1993. gada menesos. 1993. Latvijas vestnesis, 22 September.

Izglitibas iestades Latvija 1995/1996. macibu gada sakuma. 1996. Riga: Statistiskais biletens.

Kamenska, Angelita 1994. *Valsts valoda Latvija*. Riga: Latvijas cilvektiesibu un etnisko studiju centrs.
Kamenska, Angelita 1995. *The State Language in Latvia: Achievements, problems and prospects*. Riga: Latvian Center for Human Rights and Ethnic Studies.
Karklins, Rasma 1987. "The Analysis of National Cadre Politics," *Journal of Baltic Studies*, 18, 2, 167–175.
Karklins, Rasma 1994. *Ethnopolitics and Transition to Democracy*. Washington: The Woodrow Wilson Center Press.
Kolstø, Pål and Boris Tsilevich 1997. "Patterns of nation-building and political integration in a bifurcated postcommunist state: Ethnic aspects of parliamentary elections in Latvia," *East European Politics and Societies*. 11, 2, 366–91.
Krickus, Richard J. 1993. "Latvia's 'Russian Question'," *RFE/RL Research Report*, 2, 18 (30 April), 29–34.
Kudriavtsev, Il'ia 1990. *Spravochnik politicheskikh i obshchestvennykh organizatsii Latvii s kommentariami*. Moscow: Moscow Public Bureau of Information Exchange.
Kurakina, T. and Tikhomirov, V. 1991. *Pochemu pogib Interfront?* Riga: Latvian Association of Russia's Rebirth.
Kuzmitskaite, Loreta 1992. "Ob aktual'nosti issledovaniia etnicheskikh stereotipov," *LZA vestis*, 10, 9–10.
Lange, Falk 1994. "The Baltic States and the SCSE," *Journal of Baltic Studies*, 25, 3, 233–248.
Latvia. Human Development Report 1995. Riga: UNDP.
Latvia. Human Development Report 1996. Riga: UNDP.
Latviesu nacijas izredzes 1991. 1990.g. 28. septembra konference, Riga: Zinatne.
Latviia – ch'ia ona rodina? 1994. Konspektivnyi otchet o konferentsii, sostoiavsheisia 29 aprelia – 1 maia 1994 goda v Institute Gete v Rige. Riga: Vaga.
Latvija citu valstu saime: Kulturali-saimniecisks apskats 1939. Riga.
Latvija skaitlos/Latvia in figures 1996. Riga: Latvijas Republikas Valsts statistikas komiteja.
Latvijas demografijas gada gramata 1995. Riga: Latvijas Republikas valsts statistikas komiteja.
Latvijas demografijas gada gramata – Demographic Yearbook of Latvia 1996. Riga: Latvijas Republikas Valsts Statistikas komiteja.
Latvijas PSR Tautu foruma materiali 1988.g. 11–12.decembris. 1989. Riga: Liesma.
Latvijas Republikas Augstaka Padome 1991. Riga: LR AP kanceleja.
Latvijas Republikas Izglitibas likums 1991. *Diena* (supplement), 26 July.
Latvijas Republikas Pamatlikumi 1995. Riga: Kamene.
Latvijas Republikas pasvaldibu velesanas 1994.g. 29.maija. 1994. Oficials izdevums. Velesanu rezultati. Riga: Centrala velesanu komisija.
Latvijas Republikas 5.Saeimas velesanas 1993. Oficials izdevums. Riga: LR Centrala velesanu komisija.
Latvijas Republikas 6.Saeimas velesanas 1995. Par kandidatu sarakstiem un deputatu kandidatiem nodoto balsu skaits. Riga: LR Centrala velesanu komisija.
Latvijas Republikas 6.Saeimas velesanas 1996. Oficials izdevums. Riga: LR Centrala velesanu komisija.
Latvijas statistiska gada gramata 1920 1921. Riga.
Latvijas statistikas ikmenesa biletens/Monthly Bulletin of Latvian Statistics 1996.
Latvijas vestures apcerejumi (no 1940.g. lidz musdienam) 1990. Riga: Zvaigzne.
Levits, Egils 1987. "National Elites and Their Political Function within the Soviet System: The Latvian Elite," *Journal of Baltic Studies*, 18, 2, 176–190.

Lieven, Anatole 1993. *The Baltic Revolution, Estonia, Latvia, Lithuania and the Path to Independence.* New Haven: Yale University Press.

Likums par Latvijas izglitibas iestadem. Latvijas Tautas Padome, 8. decembri 1919.g.

Likums par Latvijas nacionalo un etnisko grupu brivu attistibu un tiesibam uz kulturas autonomiju 1995. Adopted 19 March1991. Latvijas Republikas Pamatikumi. Riga: Kamene.

Likums par mazakuma tautibu skolu iekartu Latvija. Latvijas Tautas Padome, 8.decembri 1919.g.

LR AP Lemums Par liguma ìPar Latvijas Republikas un Krievijas Padomju Federativas Socialistiskas Republikas starpvalstu attiecibu pamatiem ratificesanu 1991, 14 January.

LR Ministru kabineta noteikumi Nr.271 "Kartiba, kada privatajam izglitibas iestadem tiek pieshkirts valsts finansejums," 1996. 23 July.

Malek, Martin 1994. "Sprachenpolitik im Baltikum," *Osteuropa*, 44, 10, 926–37.

Mezgailis, Bruno 1985. *Padomju Latvijas demografija: struktura, procesi, problemas.* Riga: Zinatne.

Mezgailis, Bruno and I. Katkovska 1992. *Latvija dzivojoso etnosu demografiskais raksturojums.* Riga: Valsts statistikas komiteja.

Mezgailis, Bruno and Peteris Zvidrins 1973. *Padomju Latvijas iedzivotaji.* Riga: Zinatne.

Mezs, Ilmars 1994. *Latviesi Latvija. Etnodemografiskais apskats.* Riga: Zinatne.

Mezs, Ilmars 1995. *Parmainas Latvijas iedzivotaju etniskaja sastava 20.gadsimta.* Riga: LZA Vestis, 5–6, l.

Mezs, Ilmars 1997. *Data from the State Archive of the Republic of Latvia.*

Mezs, Ilmars, Edmunds Bunkse and Kaspars Rasa 1994. "The Ethno-Demographic Status of the Baltic States," *GeoJournal*, 33, 1, 9–25.

Meyer, Jan De and Christos Rozakis 1992. "Human Rights in the Republic of Latvia," *Human Rights Law Journal*, 13, 5–6, 244–49.

Mialo, Ksenia 1993. "Legko li byt' russkim v Rige?," *Novoe vremia*, 8, 10–12.

"Migracija. Galvenas tendences Latvija 1993. gada." *Latvijas vestnesis*, 16 March1994.

Minority Rights and Mechanisms Facilitating Government–Minority Dialogue 1996. Foundation for Inter-Ethnic Relations, the Netherlands, 16 May.

Misiunas, Romuldas J. and Rein Taagepera 1983. *The Baltic States: Years of Dependence 1940–1980.* London: C.Hurst.

Muiznieks, Nils 1993a. "Latvia: Origins, Evolution, and Triumph," in Ian Bremmer and Ray Taras (eds.), *Nation and Politics in the Soviet Successor States.* Cambridge: Cambridge University Press, 182-205.

Muiznieks, Nils 1993b. Unpublished data from the State Language Center, Riga.

Muizneks, Nils R. 1994. "Latvia's Changing System of Ethnic Stratification." Paper presented at the conference "Democracy and Ethnopolitics," March 9–11 1994, Riga.

Muiznieks, Nils R. 1995. "Etniska stratifikacija Latvija: padomju laika un tagad," in *Nacionala politika Baltijas valstis.* Riga: Zinatne.

My v Latvii 1989. Sbornik statei. Compiler. L.Kovtun. Riga: Zvaigzne.

Narodnoe khoziaistvo Latvii v 1989 godu: Statisticheskii ezhegodnik. Riga 1990.

Natsional'nye i etnicheskie gruppy Latvii/National and Ethnic groups in Latvia, 1996. Riga: Ministry of Justice of the Republic of Latvia.

"Noteikumi par Latvijas pilsonu pasem," Noteikumi no. 310, 24 October 1995. *Saiema un Ministru kabineta* 15 November 1995.

Nørgaard, Ole et al. 1996. *The Baltic States after Independence.* Cheltenham: Edward Edgar.

On naturalization in Latvia. 1997. Riga: The Naturalization Board of Latvia.

Opalski, M., B.Tsilevich and P. Dutkiewicz 1994. *Ethnic Conflict in the Baltic States: The Case of Latvia.* Kingston, Ontario: the Kashtan Press.

Ozolins, Uldis 1994. "Upwardly mobile languages: The politics of language in the Baltic states," *Journal of Multilingual & multicultural development*, 15, 2–3, 161–169.

Par bezdarbu valsti 1996. Pielikums Latvijas statistikas ikmenesa biletenam, no. 9.

"Par Latvijas Republikas cilvekiem 1995," *Latvijas vestnesis*, 22 March.

Pervaia vseobshchaia perepis' naseleniia Rossiiskoi imperii, 1897. 1905 vol. 11 – Lifliandskaia guberniia, and vol. 19 – Kurliandskaia guberniia.

Pettai, Vello 1993. "Contemporary International Influences on Post-Soviet Nationalism: The Cases of Estonia and Latvia." Paper presented at the American Association for the Advancement of Slavic Studies 25th National Convention, November, Honolulu.

Pettai, Vello 1996. "The Games of Ethnopolitics in Latvia," *Post-Soviet Affairs*, 12, 1 (January–March), 40–50.

Pettai, Vello 1997. "Political Stability Through Disenfranchisement," *Transition*, 3, 6 (4 April), 21–23.

Pettai, Vello 1998. "Emerging Ethnic Democracy in Estonia and Latvia" in Magda Opalski (ed.), *Managing Diversity in Plural Societies. Minorities, Migration and Nation-building in Post-Communist Europe.* Nepean, Ontario: Forum Eastern Europe, 15–32.

Plakans, Andrejs 1993. "From regional vernacular to the language of a state: The case of Latvian," *International Journal of the Sociology of Language* 100/101, 203–219.

Poulsen, J.J. 1994. "Nationalism, Democracy and Ethnocracy in the Baltic Countries," in Jan Åke Dellenbrant and Ole Nørgaard (eds.) *The Problems of Transition in the Baltic States.* Umeå: Umeå University Research Reports, No.2.

Rose, Richard 1995. *New Baltics Barometer II: A Survey Study.* Glasgow: University of Strathclyde, Studies in Public Policy Number 251.

Rose, Richard 1997a. *New Baltic Barometer III: A Survey Study.* Glasgow: University of Strathclyde, Studies in Public Policy Number 284.

Rose, Richard 1997b. "Rights and Obligations of Individuals in the Baltic States," *East European Constitutional review*, Winter, 35–43.

Rose, Richard and William Maley 1994. *Nationalities in the Baltic States. A Survey Study.* Glasgow: University of Strathclyde, Studies in Public Policy Number 222.

Russkie v Latvii, Istoriia i sovremennost 1992. Riga: Lad.

"Russkoiazychnye" 1991. *Lad'ia* (Riga), no 9.

Rutkis, J. 1960. *Latvijas geografija.* Stockholm.

Savdona A. 1994. "Dzivestasts un rakstnieciba," *LZA Vestis*, 4, 25–30.

Shneidere, I.R. 1983. *Sotsialisticheskaia industrializatsiia v Latvii. Khod, itogi, problemy.* Riga: Zinatne.

Skujenieks, M. 1930. *Latviesi svesuma un citas tautas Latvija.* Riga.

Skuland, Brita and Torunn Hasler 1994. "Nasjonsbygging og integrasjon i Latvia," *Internasjonal politikk*, 52, 183–97.

Smekhov E. 1991. *O neobkhodimosti sozdaniia Russkoi obshchiny Latvii.* Riga: unpublished manuscript.

Smith, Graham 1996. "The Ethnic Democracy Thesis and the Citizenship Question in Estonia and Latvia," *Nationalities Papers*, 24, 2, 199–216.

Smith, Graham, Aadne Aasland, and Richard Mole 1994. "Statehood, Ethnic Relations and Citizenship," in Graham Smith (ed.), *The Baltic States: The National Self-Determination of Estonia, Latvia and Lithuania*. London: Macmillan, 181–205.

Sovetskaia Latviia. Entsiklopedicheskii spravochnik 1985. Riga: Liesma.

Steen, Anton 1997a. "The New Elites in the Baltic States: Recirculation and Change," *Scandinavian Political Studies*, 20, 1, 91–112.

Steen, Anton 1997b. *Between the past and the future: Elites, democracy and the state in post-communist countries. A comparison of Estonia, Latvia and Lithuania*. Aldershot: Ashgate.

The Ethnic Situation in Latvia (Facts and Commentary) 1994. Riga: Ethnic Studies Center.

Tomasuns, A. 1994. "Etnisko minoritasu skolas Latvija," *Latvijas vestnesis*, 5 July.

Tsilevich, Boris 1993. *Vremia zhestkikh reshenii*. Riga: Insight.

Tsilevich, Boris 1994. "Etnopoliticheskii konflikt v post-sovetskom prostranstve: Baltiiskii variant" in E. Stepanov (ed.), *Sotsial'nye konflikty: ekspertiza, prognozirovanie, tekhnologii razresheniia*. Moscow: Tsentr konfliktologii RAN, issue 7.

Tsilevich, Boris 1995. *High Commissioner and Permanent Mission: The OSCE at Work in the Latvian(–Russian) Conflict on Citizenship and Human Rights*. Kiel, Christian-Albrechts-Universitat, PFK-texte No.34.

Tsilevich, Boris 1997. "Non-citizens and ownership in urban areas of Latvia," in *Zemes reforma Latvijas pilsetas, Zemes reformas vestnesis*. Riga: ES-PHARE Latvia.

Tsilevich, Boris and Alexander Ruchkovsky 1994. "Difference in Status and Rights between Citizens and Permanent Residents (Non-Citizens) in Latvia. Promoting Human Rights and Civil Society." *International Helsinki Federation for Human Rights Newsletters*, April.

Ukaz Prezidenta Rossiiskoi Sovetskoi Federativnoi Sotsialisticheskoi respubliki "O priznanii gosudarstvennoi nezavisimosti Latviiskoi Respubliki" 1991. N 1158, 24 August. Vedomosti s'ezda narodnykh deputatov RSFSR i Verhovnogo Soveta RSFSR N 35, 29 August 1991.

Ustinova, Mara 1991. "Causes of Inter-Ethnic Conflict in Latvia," in Kumar Rupesinghe, Peter King and Olga Vorkunova (eds.), *Ethnicity and Conflict in a Post-Communist World*. London: St. Martin's Press, 106–112.

Valsts valoda Latvija. Official state language in Latvia. Gosudarstvennii yazik v Latvii. 1992. Riga: LR Valsts valodas centrs.

van der Stoel, Max 1994. "Pis'mo Verkhovnogo Komissara SBSE po delam natsional'nykh men'shinstv ministru inostrannykh del Latvii ot 10 dek. 1993 g. Ref no 1463/93/L," *SM-Segodnia*, 10 February.

van der Stoel, Max 1996a. "Letter to V. Birkavs, Minister for Foreign Affairs of the Republic of Latvia," Ref. no. 1085/96/L, dated 28 October 1996.

van der Stoel, Max 1996b. "Letter to V. Birkavs, Minister for Foreign Affairs of the Republic of Latvia," Ref. no. 11147/96/L, dated 21 November 1996.

Vebers, Elmars 1997. *Latvijas valsts un etniskas minoritates*. Riga: Latvijas Zinatnu akademija.

Violations by the Latvian Department of Citizenship and Immigration 1993. Helsinki Watch 5, 19.

Volkovs, Vladislavs 1995. "Krievu migracija un pasapzina Latvija," in *Nacionala politika Baltijas valstis*, Riga: Zinatne, 157–173.

Zakon "O privatizatsii kooperativnykh kvartir," 1991 *VS-SM* (supplement to *Diena*), 24 December.

Zakon "O v"ezde i prebyvanii inostrannykh grazhdan i lits bez grazhdanstva v Latviiskoi Respublike" 1992. *VS-SM* (supplement to *Diena*), 31 July.

Zepa, Brigita 1992. "Sabiedriska doma parejas perioda Latvija: latviesu un cittautiesu uzskatu dinamika (1989–1992), *LZA Vestis*, 10, 20–28.

Zepa, Brigita 1995. "Valsts statusa maina un pilsoniska apzina." *LZA Vestis*, Nr.7/8, 31–44.

Zepa, Brigita 1996. "Veletaju uzvediba Saeimas un pasvaldibu velesanas. 1990–1995," in *Latvijas Sociologijas un politologijas zurnals*, 7, 11–18.

Literature on Kazakstan

Abdil'din, S. 1993. *Parlament Kazakhstana. Ot soiuza k gosudarstvennosti.* Almaty: Kazakhstan.

Abdrakhmanov, S. 1997: "Chto v imeni tvoem? K voprosu o toponimicheskoi politike v Kazakhstane", *Mysl'*, 3.

Abdygaliev, Berik 1995. "Russkie v Kazakhstane: Problemy, mify i real'nost" *Kazakhstan i mirovoe soobshchestvo*, 1 (2), 73–80.

Abdygaliev, Berik 1996a. "Iazykovaia politika v Kazakhstane: sostoianie i perspektivy," *Saiasat*, 5 (12), 31–38.

Abdygaliev, Berik 1996b. "Gosudarstvennaia identichnost' kazakhstantsev," *Mysl'* 7, 30–33.

Absattarov, Marat 1995. "Kazakhskii etnos: na perekrestke istorii," *Evraziiskoe soobshchestvo*, 11–12, 11–22.

Absattarov, R. 1995. "Etnopoliticheskaia obshchnost' i natsii," *Mysl'*, 46–49.

Aiaganov, B.G., A.U. Kuandykov and S.Z. Baimagambetov 1995. "Etnopoliticheskaia situatsiia v Kazakhstane: regional'nyi opyt," *Saiasat*, 1, 30–42.

Aiaganov, Berkutbai 1995. "Tendentsii i dinamika izmenenii natsional'nogo sostava Kazakhstana," *Evraziiskoe soobshchestvo*, 9–10, 3–21.

Akhmedzhanov, Askar and Alma Sultangalieva 1995. "Ideia evraziiskogo soiuza dlia SNG i Kazakhstana (popytka reintegratsii postsovetskogo prostranstva na printsipakh partnerstva (1)," *Kazakhstan i mirovoe soobshchestvo*, 1, 2, 26–39.

Akiner, Shirin 1995. *The Formation of Kazakh Identity. From Tribe to Nation-State.* London: Royal Institute of International Affairs.

Akiner, Shirin 1997. "Melting pot, salad bowl – cauldron? Manipulation and mobilization of ethnic and religious identities in Central Asia," *Ethnic and Racial Studies*, 20, 2 (April), 362–98.

Allworth, Edward (ed.) 1989. *Central Asia. 120 Years of Russian Rule.* Durham: Duke University Press.

Amrekulov, Nurlan 1995. "Reformatsionnyi potentsial intelligentsii," *Mysl'*, 6, 67–75.

Amrekulov, Nurlan and Nurbulat Masanov 1994. *Kazakhstan – mezhdu proshlym i budushchim.* Almaty: MGP Beren.

Arenov, Murat 1996. "Etnosotsial'nye otnosheniia cherez prizmu obshchestvennogo mneniia," *Kazakhstanskaia pravda*, 29 November.

Arenov, Murat and Sergei Kalmykov 1995a. "Sotsiologicheskie zametki o iazykovoi situatsii v respublike," *Mysl'*, 3, 49–53.

Arenov, Murat and Sergei Kalmykov 1995b. "O sytuacji jezykowej w Kazachstanie (uwagi socjologiczne)," *Eurazja* (Warszawa) 2, 3, 38–42.

Arenov, Murat and Sergei Kalmykov 1995c. "Sovremennaia iazykovaia situatsiia v Respublike Kazakhstan (analiz rezul'tatov sotsiologicheskogo issledovaniia)," *Saiasat*, 1, 43–52.

Arenov, M.M. and Kalmykov, S.K 1997a: "Sovremenaia iazykovaia situatsiia v Respublike Kazakhstan", *Saiasat*, 1, 21-30.

Arenov, M.M. and Kalmykov, S.K 1997b: "Sovremennaia iazykovaia situatsiia v Respublike Kazakhstan - okonchanie", *Saiasat*, 2, 29-34.

Arenov, M.M and Kalmykov, S.K. 1997c: "Tendentsii razvitiia sovremennykh etnonatsionalínykh otnoshenii v Kazakstane", *Saiasat*, 6, 40-48.

Averin, I.A. 1995. "Ural'skoe kazachestvo v Kazakhstane: Istoriia i sovremennaia etnopoliticheskaia situatsiia," in Gennadii Bordiugov, Paul Goble and Valerii Tishkov (eds.), *Sreda i kul'tura v usloviiakh obshchestvennykh transformatsii.* Moscow: AIRO-XX, 159–66.

Avtonomov, A.S. 1995. "Process stanovleniia parlamentarizma v Kazakhstane," *Predstavital'naia vlast"* (Moscow), 2, 4, 22–37.

Azimov, Sergei 1995. "Kozykorpesh Esenberlin: My prizyvaem narody Kazakhstana oshchutit" sebia edinym etnosom – kazakhstanstami," *Panorama*, 25, (24 June).

Babakumarov, B., Ju. Buluktaev and K. Kusherbaev 1995. *Kazakhstan segodnia: Mir politicheskikh partii.* Almaty: Institut Razvitiia Kazakhstana.

Baikhmanov, M.T., L.M. Vaisberg and A.K. Kotov, 1994. *Stanovleniia suvereniteta respubliki Kazakhstan.* Almaty: Natsional'naia Akademiia Nauk Respubliki Kazakhstan – Institut Gosudarstva i Prava.

Baitenova, N.D. 1995a. "Mezhetnicheskaia integratsiia v Kazakhstane: Sostoianie i perspektivy," *Saiasat*, (Almaty) 3, 27–33.

Baitenova, N.D. 1995b. "Radi mira i soglasiia," *Mysl'*, 9 (September), 42–46.

Bakaev, Leonid 1995. "Voennoe sotrudnichestvo Rossii i Kazakhstana: Sostoianie, problemy i perspektivy," *Kazakhstan i mirovoe soobshchestvo*, 2, 2, 46–53.

Bennigsen, Alexandre and S. Enders Wimbush 1985. *Muslims of the Soviet Empire.* London: C.Hurst.

Borzykh, N.P. 1972–73. "The prevalence of ethnically mixed marriages in the Central Asian republics and Kazakhstan in the 1930s," *Soviet Sociology*, (Winter–Spring) 394–411.

Bremmer, Ian 1994. "Nazarbaev and the north – state-building and ethnic relations in Kazakhstan," *Ethnic and Racial Studies*, 17, 4, 619–35.

Bremmer, Ian and Cory Welt 1995. "Kazakhstan's quandary," *Journal of Democracy*, 6, 3 (July), 139–154.

Bremmer, Ian and Cory Welt 1996. "The trouble with democracy in Kazakhstan," *Central Asian Survey*, 15, 2, 179–200.

Brusina, Olga 1996. "Natsional'naia gosudarstvennost i "russkii vopros" v Kazakhstane," in *Etnicheskii faktor v sovremennom sotsial'no-politicheskom razvitii Kazakhstana*, Issledovaniia po prikladnoi i neotlozhnoi etnologii no. 94, Moscow: Institut etnologii i antropologii RAN, 3–14.

"CSCE gives thumbs down for Kazakh election" 1994. *Central Asian Quarterly Labyrinth*, 1, 2, p. 3.

Conflict in the Soviet Union. The Untold Story of the Clashes in Kazakhstan 1990. New York: Helsinki Watch.

Conway, Patrick 1994. "Kazakhstan: Land of Opportunity," *Current History*, 93, (April), 164–68.

Critchlow, James. 1992a. "Kazakhstan and Nazarbaev: Political Prospects," *RFE/RL Research Report*, 1, 3 (17 January), 31–4.

Critchlow, James. 1992b. "Kazakhstan: The Outlook for Ethnic Relations." *RFE/RL Research Report*, 1, 5 (31 January), 34–9.

Dave, Bhavna 1995. "Cracks Emerge in Kazakhstan's Government Monopoly," *Transition*, 1, 18 (6 October), 73–75.

Dave, Bhavna 1996a. "National Revival in Kazakhstan: Language Shift and Identity Change," *Post-Soviet Affairs*, 12, 1 (January–March), 51–72.

Dave, Bhavna 1996b. "A New Parliament Consolidates Presidential Authority," *Transition*, 2, 6 (22 March 1996), 33–37.

Dixon, Adam 1996: "Kazakhstan: Political Reform and Economic Development," in Allison Roy (ed.), *Challenges for the Former Soviet South*. New York/London: Brookings Institution Press for The Royal Institute of International Affairs.

Dokuchaeva, Aleksandra 1994a. "'Eshche raz o iazyke, i ne tolko o nem,' *Vedi. Respublika Kazakhstan*, (1–31 December).

Dokuchaeva, Aleksandra 1994b. "Lad" information leaflet 25 December.

Dokuchaeva, Aleksandra 1995. "Kakie vetry goniat liudei iz Kazakhstana," *Pravda* (Moscow) 31 May.

Dzhunusova, Zh. Kh. 1996. *Respublika Kazakhstan: Prezident. Instituty Demokratii.* Almaty: Zheti Zhargy.

Elagin, A.S., 1993. *Kazachestvo i kazach'i voiska v Kazakhstane.* Almaty: Kazakhstan.

Eschment, Beate 1996. "Das 'Chanat Nazarbaevs' Innenpolitische Entwicklungen 1995 in Kazachstan," *Osteuropa*, 46, 9, 876–899.

Eschment, Beate 1998. *Hat Kazachstan ein "Russisches Problem?" Revision eines Katastrophenbildes.* Cologne: Bundesinstitut für ostwissenschaftliche und internationale Studien.

Esenova, Saulesh 1996. "The Outflow of Minorities from the Post-Soviet state: The case of Kazakhstan," *Nationalities Papers*, 24, 4 (December), 691–707.

Etnopoliticheskii monitoring v Kazakhstane zima 95–96 1996. Vypusk 2. Almaty: Tsentr monitoringa mezhetnicheskikh otnoshenii v Kazakhstane.

Feoktistov, A. 1992. *Russkie, kazakhi i Altai.* Ust-Kamenogorsk: Alfa i Omega.

Fierman, William 1998. "Language and Identity in Kazakhstan. Formulations in Policy Documents 1987–1997," *Communist and Post-Communist Studies*, 31, 2, 171–186.

Galiev, A.B., E. Babakumarov, Zh. Zhansugurova and A. Peruashev 1994. *Mezhnatsional'nye otnosheniia v Kazakhstane. Etnicheskii aspekt kadrovoi politiki.* Almaty: Institut razvitiia Kazakhstana.

Gawecki, Marek 1994. "Charakter zmian zbiorowosci polskiej w strukturze etnicznej współczesnego Kazakhstanu," *Przeglad Wschodni*, 3, 10, 165–199.

Giller, Boris and Viktor Shatskikh 1993. "Russkoiazychnye v Kazakhstane: Opredelenie berega," *Karavan*, Almaty, 24 December.

Gosudarstvennyi komitet respubliki Kazakhstan po statistike i analizu 1996: *Vysshie uchebnye zavedeniya v respublike Kazakhstan v 1995/1996 uchebnom godu*, Almaty.

Holm-Hansen, Jørn 1996. "Local, regional and cultural self-government in a divided nation-building state: The case of Kazakhstan," Paper presented at the Nordic political science congress NOPSA '96, 15–17 August, Helsinki.

Holm-Hansen, Jørn 1997. "Territorial and ethno-cultural self-government in nation-building Kazakhstan," Oslo: Norwegian Institute for Urban and Regional Research, *Report* 1997:7.

"Iazykovaia situatsiia v respublike Kazakhstan" 1997. Almaty: Departament koordinatsii iazykovoi politiki, Ministerstvo Obrazovaniia i Kul'tury Respubliki Kazakhstan.

Irgaliev, E. 1995. "'Novye Kazakhi' ili modernizatsiia etnosa," *Mysl'*, 2, 24–28.

Isabekov, Zeinesh 1996. "'Imet' pri sebe pasport...' " *Kazakhstanskaia pravda*, 4 April.

Istoriia Kazakhstana s drevneishikh vremen do nashikh dnei (ocherk) 1993. Almaty: Dayir.

Ivanov, Nikolai 1994. "Kazakhstan: sluzhenie khimere," *Moskva*, 12, 135–150.

Janabel, Jiger 1996. "When National Ambition Conflicts With Reality: Studies on Kazakhstan's ethnic relations," *Central Asian Survey*, 15, 1, 5–22.

Kaidarov, A. 1992. "Esli ischeznet iazyk ...," *Kazakhstanskaia pravda*, 15 October.

Kaiser, Robert and Jeff Chinn 1995. "Russian–Kazakh Relations in Kazakhstan," *Post-Soviet Geography*, 36, 5, 257–273.

Karsakov, I. 1995. *Prognoznye otsenki izbiratel'noi kampanii v parlament respubliki Kazakhstan (analiticheskii doklad) Chast" III*. Almaty: Institut Razvitiia Kazakhstana.

Kazakh tribalism today, its characteristics and possible solutions (analytical report) 1996. Almaty: Institute for development of Kazakhstan.

"Kazakhstan: Nazarbayev's solution to the Zhuz question: A new capital," 1994. *Central Asia Quarterly labyrinth*, 1, 3 (autumn), 1–2.

Kobets, Aleksandr 1993. "Belaia mogila – ne dlia zhuza," *Rossiiskie vesti*, 23(447) 10 February, p. 3.

Kolstø, Pål 1998. "Anticipating Demographic Superiority. Kazakh Thinking on Integration and Nation-building," *Europe-Asia Studies*, 50, 1, 51–69.

Kolstø, Pål and Irina Malkova 1997. "Is Kazakhstan being Kazakhified?," *Analysis of Current Events*, 9, 11 (November), 1 and 3–4.

"Konstitutsiia Respubliki Kazakhstan" 1995. *Mysl'* (Almaty), 10, 3–22.

"Kontseptsiia etnokul'turnogo obrazovaniia v respublike Kazakhstan," *Kazakhstanskaia Pravda*, 7 August 1996.

Kontseptsiia formirovaniia gosudarstvennoi identichnosti respubliki Kazakhstan 1996. Almaty: "Kazakhstan."

Kontseptsiia stanovleniia istoricheskogo soznaniia v Respublike Kazakhstan, Natsional'nyi sovet po gosudarstvennoi politike pri Prezidente Respubliki Kazakhstan, Almaty, 1995.

Kotov, A.K. 1995. "Iedinoe grazhdanstvo – konstitutsionnaia osnova ravnopraviia v Respublike Kazakhstan," *Saiasat*, (Almaty) 3, 21–25.

Kuandykov, Alibek and Burkut Aiaganov 1995. "Kazakhi v Kazakhstane: Integratsiia i sovremennost," *Kazakhstan i mirovoe soobshchestvo*, 1, 2, 64–70.

Kumarova, A. 1995. "Problemy formirovaniia kazakhskoi iazykovoi sredy," *Mysl'*, 10, 83–84.

Loginova, Natal'ia 1995. "Sotsial'no-psikhologicheskaia adaptatsiia russkikh v suverennnom Kazakhstane," *Mysl'*, 7 (July), 37–42.

Masanov, Nurbulat 1995. "Natsional'no-gosudarstvennoe stroitel'stvo v Kazakhstane: analiz i prognoz," *Vestnik Evrazii*, 1, 117–128.

Masanov, Nurbulat 1996. "Kazakhskaia politicheskaia i intellektual'naia elita: Klanovaia prinadlezhnost" i vnutrietnicheskoe sopernichestvo," *Vestnik Evrazii*, 1, 2, 46–61.

Mashanov, M. 1995. *Izbiratel'naia sistema Respubliki Kazakhstan i ee vlianie na kharakter politicheskogo protsessa*. Almaty: Institut Razvitiia Kazakhstana.

Melvin, Neil 1993. "Russia and the ethno-politics of Kazakhstan," *The World Today*, 49, 11, 208–210.

Mendikolova, Gul'nara 1995. "Kazakhskaia irredenta v Rossii (istoriia i sovremennost')," *Evraziiskoe soobshchestvo*, 8, 70–79.

Moroni, Federica 1994. "A State in Transition. Security Issues in Kazakhstan," *The international spectator* 29, 4, 29–53.

Nauryzbaev, Zh., and V. Primin 1994. "Put' k mezhnatsional'noi garmonii. Politiko-pravovye aspekty statusa etnicheskikh men'shinstv," *Mysl'* (Almaty), 4, 40–44.

Nazarbaev, Nursultan 1993. *Ideinaia konsolidatsiia obshchestva – kak usloviia progressa Kazakhstana*. Almaty: "Kazakhstan-XXI vek."

Nazarbaev, Nursultan 1994. *K obnovlennomu Kazakhstanu – cherez uglublenie reform, obshchenatsional'noe soglasie*. Almaty: "Kazakhstan."

Nazarbaev, Nursultan 1995. *Za mir i soglasie v nashem obshchem dome*. Almaty: "Kazakhstan."

Nazarbaev, Nursultan A. 1996. *Na poroge XXI veka*. Almaty: "Öner."

Nourzhanov, Kirill and Amin Saikal 1994. "The new Kazakhstan: Has something gone wrong?," *The World Today*, 50, 225–229.

Nysanbaev, Abdulmalik and Murat Abdirov 1996. "Zachem nuzhna doroga, esli ona ne vedet k Khramu?," *Kazakhstanskaia pravda*, 4 January.

O demograficheskoi situatsii v 1995 godu 1996. Almaty: Pravitel'stvo respubliki Kazakhstan.

"O iazykakh v Respublike Kazakhstan," Zakon Republiki Kazakhstan ot 11 iuliia 1997 goda N 151–1.

Olcott, Martha Brill 1993. "Kazakhstan: A republic of minorities," in Ian Bremmer and Ray Taras (eds.), *Nations and politics in the Soviet successor states*. Cambridge: Cambridge University Press, 313–330.

Olcott, Martha Brill 1995. *The Kazakhs*. Stanford: Hoover Institution Press. 2nd enlarged ed.

Pannier, Bruce 1995. "Kazakhstan. A step back for democracy," *Transition* 1, 11, 62–66 (30 June).

Peruashev, A.T. 1994. *Politicheskie aspekty mezhetnicheskoi konkurentsii v Kazakhstane*. Almaty: Institut razvitiia Kazakhstana.

Petrenko, V.F., O.V. Mitina and I.V. Shevchuk 1993. "Sotsial'no-politicheskoe issledovanie obshchestvennogo soznaniia zhitelei Kazakhstana i postroenie semanticheskogo prostranstva politicheskikh partii," *Psikhologicheskii zhurnal*, 14, 1, 53–88.

Politicheskie partii i obshchestvennye dvizheniia sovremmenogo Kazakhstana. Spravochnik 1994. Almaty: Ministerstvo pechati i massovoi informatsii. I–II.

Republika Kazakhstan Informatsionnyi pasport 1996. Almaty: Zheti Zhargy.

Ro'i, Yaacov 1990. "The Islamic Influence on Nationalism in Soviet Central Asia," *Problems of Communism*, 39, July–August, 49–64.

Rotar, Igor' (ed.) 1994. "Natsional'noe stroitel'stvo v Kazakhstane," *Nezavisimaia gazeta*, 8 April.

Sabikenov, S. 1994. "Natsional'nyi i narodnyi suverenitet. V chem ikh razlichie?," *Mysl'* (Almaty) 4, 9–11.

Set' i kontingent uchashchikhsia dnevnykh obshcheobrazovatel'nykh shkol, vedushchikh zaniatiiakh na raznykh iazykakh v 1995/96 uchebnom godu, 1996. Almaty: Gosudarstvennyi komitet Respubliki Kazakhstan po statistike i analizu.

Skopin, Aleksei 1995. "Migratsionnye protsessy v Kazakhstane: Proshloe, nastaiashchee, budushchee," *Evraziiskoe soobshchestvo*, 6–7, 51–59.

Smagulova, U. 1995. "Shipy i rozy postsovetskogo obshchestva," *Mysl'*, 3, 54–57.

Sovremennaia obshchestvenno-politicheskaia situatsiia v Srednei Azii i Kazakhstane, Issledovaniia po prikladnoi i neotlozhnoi etnologii no. 50, Moscow: Institut etnologii i antropologii RAN.

Shparaga, G. 1994. "Gosudarstvennaia vlast" i mestnoe samoupravlenie," *Mysl'* (Almaty), 4, 18–21.

"State Building and Population Movements" 1996. *Forced Migration Monitor,* 10, 1–3.

Subbotina, I.A. 1995. "Russkie: Migratsionnye protsessy nakanune i posle raspada Sovietskogo Soiza," in Gennadii Bordiugov, Paul Goble and Valerii Tishkov (eds.), *Sreda i kul'tura v usloviiakh obshchestvennykh transformatsii.* Moscow: AIRO-XX, 120–47.

Tanirbergenova, G. 1995. "Regional'nyi opyt realizatsii vnutrennei politiki," *Saiasat,* 5, 50–57.

Tatimov, M. 1995. "Vliianie demograficheskikh i migratsionnykh protsessov na vnutripoliticheskuiu stabil'nost' respubliki Kazakhstan," *Saiasat,* 5, 18–23.

Tolubaeva, L.T. and A.L. Syromiatnikov 1993. *Lektsii po politologii.* Semipalatinsk: Semipalatinskii tekhnologicheskii institut.

Uleev, V. 1993. ""Slavianskaia diaspora"....," *Res Publica,* Bishkek, 15 May.

Uroven' religioznosti i konfessional'nye orientatsii naseleniia Respubliki Kazakhstan 1996. Almaty: Institut razvitia Kazakhstana.

Usacheva, N. and A. Maisiuk 1996. "Mankurty ili bez viny vinovatye?," *Mysl',* 9, 42–46.

USIA 1993. *Kazakhs and Russians Close on Nationality Issues in Kazakhstan.* Washington: Opinion Research memorandum.

Zakon Kazakhskoi sovetskoi sotsialisticheskoi respubliki o iazykakh v Kazakhskoi SSR 1989. Almaty: "Kazakhstan."

"Zakon o grazhdanstve respubliki Kazakhstan" 1991. *Vedomosti Verkhovnogo Soveta Kazakhskoi SSR,* 52, 81–96.

"Zakon Respubliki Kazakhstan ob immigratsii" 1992. *Sovety Kazakhstana,* 25 August.

Zhangirov, Bek 1996. "Ukaz vstrechen s ponimaniem," *Kazakhstanskaia pravda,* 9 April.

Zhansugurova, Zh. A. 1995. "Problemy razvitiia parlamentarizma v respublike Kazakhstane", *Predstavitel'naia vlast'* (Moscow), 5, 7, 86–95.

Index

Aasland, Aadne, Norwegian political scientist, 25, 33, 137, 285, 297

Abai, 212

Abdil'din, Serikbolsyn, chairman of the Communist party of Kazakstan, 215

Abdil'din, Zhabaikhan, chairman of the committee on international affairs in the Kazakstani parliament, 170

Abdygaliev, Berik, 166, 167

Abikis, Dzintars, chairman of the Saeima commission on education, science and culture, 116

Abrene society, 104

Absattarov, Marat, 306

Absattarov, R., 306

Abyzov, Iurii, leader of the Latvian Society of Russian Culture, 26

acculturation, 48, 300, 315

Act on Education in Latvia, 1919, 121

Act on the Languages of the Latvian Republic, 1992, 11

Acton, John Emerich Edward Dahlberg, 48–49, 51

Aitmatov, Chingiz, Kyrgyz novelist, 30

akims, governors in the Kazakstani state administration, 183, 190, 193–194, 207–208, 210– 212, 220, 307

Akiner, Shirin, British researcher, 22–23, 41, 206, 299, 301

Aktol, legendary forefather of the Kazak middle horde, 216

Akuev, Nikolai, advisor to the Kazakstani president on institutional question, 194

Alash, legendary forefather of the Kazaks, 216

Alash, nationalist party in Kazakstan, 291

Alchin, legendary forefather of the Kazak small horde, 216

Aldermane, E., director of the Naturalization board in Latvia, 93

Alemsistem, business firm in Kazakstan, 217

Alternative Concept for language policy in Latvian national minority education, 126

Anderson, Barbara A., American demographer, 17

Anderson, Benedict, British researcher, 46–47

Andrejevs, Georgs, Latvian Minister of foreign affairs, 133

Antane, Aina, Latvian historian, 63, 121, 287, 297, 305–306, 308

Apine, Ilga, Latvian researcher, 100

Arenov, Murat, Director of the informational-analytical centre of the parliament of Kazakstan, 34, 163, 178, 180–181, 185, 312

Armenia, 2, 36

Arshavskaia, Tatiana , vice chairperson of the Latvian society of Russian culture, 125

Arutiunian, Iu.V., Russian anthropologist, 26

Assembly of the Peoples of Kazakstan, 164, 167, 196, 200, 211, 213, 306, 307

Association of Russia's Citizens in Latvia, 144

Astana (Akmola, Tselinograd), 38, 187, 197, 209, 217, 242, 275

Astana-Holding, business firm in Kazakstan, 217

Atmoda, Latvian national revival during perestroika, 5

Auezov, Murat, co-chairmen of Azamat, 216

August coup in Moscow 1991, 38

Austro-Marxists, 58

Averin, I.A., 26

Avotins, Viktor, Latvian Popular
    Front activist, 82
Avtonomov, A.S., 198
Azamat, opposition movement in
    Kazakstan, 216–217
Azat, nationalist party in Kazakstan ,
    216–217, 291
Azimov, Sergei, 300

Babakumarov, B., 215
Baikhmanov, M.T., 162, 168, 170–171,
    193
Baitenova, N.D., associate professor at
    the State University of Kazakstan,
    7, 301, 306–307
Baltic Assembly, 83
Baltic Constitutional Party, 104
Baltic Data House, 88, 107
Baltic Research Centre, 87–88
Baltic-Slavic Society of Cultural
    Development and Cooperation
    (BSO), 142
Baltic Times, 7
Barrington, Lowell, American
    political scientist, 291
Barry, Brian, 288
Belarusians, 23–25, 29, 33, 35–37
    in Kazakstan, 187, 212, 230, 306
    in Latvia, 64, 69–70, 85, 95, 108,
    126, 132, 238, 240, 253–254, 270,
    278
Bendix, Reinhard, American political
    scientist , 44, 62
Bennigsen, Alexandre, French
    historian, 19
Berger, Peter, L., American sociologist,
    15
Bilingualism, 11, 30, 33–34, 300
Bipolar societies, 18, 34, 301, 308
    defined, 6
Bipolarization, 7, 10, 12, 20, 38, 42,
    299, 316
Birch, Anthony, H., British political
    scientist , 51
Birckenbach, Hanne-Margret, German
    researcher, 89
Birkavs, Valdis, Latvian prime minis-
    ter , 72
Birlesu, independent labour movement
    in Kazakstan, 218, 286

"Bloody October" in Moscow in 1993,
    198
Bojars, Juris, 89
Brass, Paul, American researcher, 288
Bremmer, Ian, American political
    scientist, 38, 309, 310
Brezhnev, Leonid, 39, 57
Brichkovskii, Aleksandr , *akim* in the
    town of Issyk in Kazakstan, 183
Brubaker, Rogers, American
    sociologist, 59–61, 89
Brusina, Olga, Russian anthropologist,
    28
BSO, Baltic-Slavic Society of Cultural
    Development and Cooperation, 142,
    143
bumiputra, indigenous population of
    Malaysia, 292, 293
Burundi, 3, 289

Carrère d'Encausse, Hélène, Swiss
    historian, 57–58
Center of Russian Culture in Latvia,
    144
Central Committee of the Soviet
    Communist Party, 58
Central European University, 87
Centre of Democratic Initiatives,
    Latvia, 104
Chicherina N.G., 142
Cilinskis, Einars, leader of the
    Movement for the National
    Independence of Latvia, 83
Citizenship legislation,
    in Kazakstan, 159, 175
    in Latvia, 73–76, 79, 85, 87, 89–91,
    94, 98, 144, 303
Communist Party of Kazakstan, 169,
    173, 196, 215–217
Communist Party of Latvia, 100
Communist Party of the Soviet
    Union,146
Compatibility of group goals, 52
Connor, Walker, American political
    scientist, 45–47, 50–52
Consociationalism, model of, 284–285,
    289
Constitution,
    in Kazakstan, 175, 200, 286, 298,
    300   *(continues)*

Constitutions *(continued)*
in Fiji, 294
in Latvia, 75, 92
Constitutional Council in Kazakstan, 194
Constitutional Law on the Rights and Obligations of Individuals and Citizens in Latvia, 75
Consultative Council of Nationalities in Latvia, 79
Copenhagen meeting of the Conference on the human dimension of the CSCE, in 1990, 281
Cossacks, 26, 161, 174
Council of Europe, 84, 91–92, 133, 298
Council on Foreign and Defence Policies in the Russian Government, 148
CSCE, 90, 91, 281, 286

Dahl, Robert, A., American political scientist, 282
Daugavpils, 28, 38, 100, 114–116, 131, 143, 277, 305–306
Dave, Bhavna, British political scientist, 30, 246, 299, 302
Democracy,
and consociationalism, 285– 287
and domination, 289–295,
ethnic democracy, 6, 295–298
in Latvia, 81, 150–152
in Kazakstan, 156, 177, 215
vs. cultural diversity and stabilty, 12–13, 81, 281–284
Department of Citizenship and Immigration in Latvia, 73, 98, 144
Department of Nationalities in Latvia, 80
Deutsch, Karl, American political scientist , 44–45, 49, 50
Dimants, Ainars, Latvian journalist, 84
Dixon, Adam, 199
Dokuchaeva, Aleksandra, leader of the Slavic Lad movement in Kazakstan, 195
Dozortsev, Vladlen, deputy to the Latvian Supreme Soviet, 83
DP Saimnieks, Latvian political party, 105

Dreifelds, Juris, Canadian political scientist, 66–67, 135, 136
Dribins, Leo , Latvian ethnologist, 82, 84
Drobizheva, Leokadia, Russian anthropologist, 282, 288
Druviete, Ina, Latvian researcher, 116, 126
Dungans (Hui), 24
Dymov, Oleg , deputy head of the secretariat of the Assembly of the Peoples of Kazakstan, 213
Dzenitis, Olgerts, leader of the Latvian branch of the "Organization of Unrepresented peoples", 82
Dzhungan khanate, 212
Dzhunusova, Zh., Kh., Kazak political scientist, 188, 196, 199–201, 203, 207, 217

education,
and language in Latvia, 113–114, 116, 121–127, 129, 246, 248–250
and language in Kazakstan, 178– 179, 184, 246, 248–250
and nation-building, 283
and re-ethnification in Kazakstan , 172
as medium of integration, 11–12, 45,
ethnocultural education
in Kazakstan, 164, 167, 192
in the Soviet union, 58, 108
minority education
in Kazakstan, 195, 220–222, 225
in Latvia, 131–132
private schools in Latvia, 151
Egle, Valdis, Latvian political commentator, 84
Eide, Asbjørn, Norwegian human rights expert, 89
Elagin, A.S., 26
elections,
in Kazakstan in 1994, 199
in Kazakstan in 1995, 201–202, 295
in Latvia in 1990, 64, 86
in Latvia and Estonia after independence, 90   *(continues)*

elections *(continued)*
  in Latvia in 1993, 72, 91, 100,
    146
  in Latvia in 1995, 100, 103–107
  electoral law in Latvia, 104
endogamy, 36–37
Equal Rights Movement in Latvia, 103,
  124, 144, 146, 300
Eschment, Beate, 160–162
Esenova, Saulesh, 30
Espersen, Ole, Commissioner on
  Democratic Institutions and Human
  Rights in the Council of Baltic Sea
  States, 117
Estonia, 249, 302
Estonia, 6, 20, 36, 63, 66, 68, 80, 83, 85,
  90, 92, 98, 100, 103, 116, 145–147,
  151
Estonians, 24, 29, 33, 62, 69, 132, 151
Ethnic democracy, model of, 295–299
ethnic identity,
  and nation-building, 1
  in the Soviet Union, 15–16
  in Latvia, 28, 131, 151
  in Kazakstan, 167
  in ethnically mixed marriaged, 252
ethnic nationalism, 61, 156
ethnocentrism, 62
European Union, 148, 151

Fall, Ibrahima, 147
Farmers' Union of Latvia, 72
Fatherland and Freedom Party, Latvia,
  76, 105, 108, 291
Federation Internationale des Ligues
  des Droits de l'Homme, 144
Fehervary, Andrash, 89
Fiji, 12, 289, 294
Fleishman, Arkadii, 25, 305
Foltz, William J., 13
Forum for the Peoples of Latvia,
  80
Friedrich, Carl, J., 44, 55

Gaaga, Vladimir, 210
Galiev, A.B., Kazakh researcher, 197,
  309
Gasprinskii, Ismail, bey, (Gaspirali),
  40
Gawecki, Marek, 197

Gellner, Ernest, British
  anthropologist, 20, 27, 46, 51–52,
  283
Germans,
  in Eastern Europe, 56
  in Latvia, 20, 21, 27, 64, 66, 69, 79,
    95
  in Kazakstan, 29, 157, 160–161,
    167, 169, 172, 176–177, 187, 213,
    220, 229–230, 237, 240, 251–
    252, 258, 268–269, 277, 306
Germany, 66, 67, 74, 79, 220, 222, 226,
  240
Giller, Boris, 196, 203, 275
Glotz, Peter, 167
Goeckel, Robert, F., 19–20
Goloshchekin, Fedor, Soviet
  Communist leader, 39
Gorbachev, Mikhail, 145–146
Great Nordic war, 63
Grinblats, Maris, Minister of
  education in Latvia, 127, 129
Guboglo, Mikhail, Russian
  anthropologist, 111, 297
Gunkin, Nikolai , ataman of the
  Semirech'e Cossacks in Kazakstan,
  174
Guyana, 12–13, 289–292, 294
Gypsies, see Roma

Habsburg monarchy, 49, 56
Hallik, Klara, Estonian researcher, 62
Hanf, Theodor, 296
Hirscha, Dzintra, leader of the State
  Language Centre in Latvia, 117,
  125
Hobsbawn, Eric, British historian, 46
Hodnett, Grey, 101
Holm-Hansen, Jørn, 286, 298, 304, 306
Hooghe, Liesbet, 288
Horowitz, Donald, L., American
  politican scientist, 2–6, 13, 37, 288,
  307, 314–316
Huti, 289

ideology,
  in Guyana, 292
  in Kazakstan, 23, 146, 164, 195, 211
  in the Soviet Union, 15, 58, 138, 229,
    250, 262

immigration, 228, 308
  to Kazakstan, 28, 158–160
  to Latvia, 67, 72–75, 99
India, 3, 316
Institute for the Development of
  Kazakstan, 201, 309
Institute of Market and Social
  Research "Latvijas fakti", 88
integration, 7–10, 12, 14, 273, 274, 282,
  300–304, 308, 312, 315–316
  as buzzword, 7
  ethnic, 5, 84, 172, 179, 227, 234, 265
  European, 151
  linguistic, 249, 271, 273
  political, in Kazakstan, 191, 204–
  205, 225
  regional economic in the Baltics, 148
  social, 5, 43, 48–54, 62, 230
    in Latvia, 124–125, 129
    in Kazakstan, 153, 156, 166, 167,
    175–176
International Front of Working People
  of the Latvian SSR (Interfront),
  142–143
Irgaliev, E., 182
Israel, 74, 79, 131, 132, 222, 289, 296
Iurgen, Igor, Russian politician, 148
Ivanov, Nikolai, Russian activist in
  Kazakstan, 174

Janabel, Jiger, 25
Jews,
  in Kazakstan, 178, 220, 234
  in Latvia, 27, 33, 64, 66, 67, 69, 70,
    78, 95, 101, 132, 133, 136, 151,
    229–231, 235, 240, 253, 254, 270,
    272
  in the Soviet Union, 36, 39
  in Eastern Europe, 56
  in Western Europe, 283
  in Israel, 289

Kaidarov, A., president of the "Kazak
  tili" langauge society in Kazakstan,
  30
Kaiser, Robert, J., 17, 33, 232, 310
Kamenska, Angelita, 113, 115–116
Kappeler, Andreas, 56
Karavan, Kazakstani newspaper, 162,
  182–183, 217, 275

Kargin, Valerii, president of the Pareks
  bank in Latvia, 136
Karklins, Rasma, 16, 25, 47, 101, 138,
  309
Karsakov, I., Kazakhstani researcher,
  201
Kazak tili, Kazak language society, 30,
  182, 219
Kazakhstanskaia Pravda, 159, 169–171,
  179–181, 184, 186, 190, 193–194,
  208–210, 223
Kazakstan Independent Trade Union
  Center, 218
Kazakstani Constitution of 1995, 175
Kekilbaev, Abish, State Secretary in
  Kazakstan, 169
Kentau, mining town in Southern
  Kazakstan, 219
KGB, 58, 161
Khasanov, Bakhytzhan, director of the
  Center for the Strategy of Language
  Development in Kazakstan,189–190
Khrushchev, 28, 230
Kobets, Aleksandr, 23
Kohn, Hans, 56
Kolbin, Gennadii, Soviet politician,
  169, 209
Kolstø, Pål [Kolstoe, Paul], 15, 26, 27,
  40, 44, 57, 105 176, 227, 228, 243,
  261, 281, 297, 303
Komarova, O.D., 16, 35
Kommisrud, Arne, Norwegian political
  scientist, 56, 285
Koreans, 24, 161, 167, 172, 176, 213,
  220, 229, 230, 234, 251, 252, 268,
  269, 277
korenizatsiia, Soviet nationalities
  policy, 57
Kotov, A.K., advisor to the president of
  Kazakstan, 162, 168, 170–171, 176,
  193
Kozakhmetov, A, Kazak nationalist
  activist, 219
Kozlov, V.I., Russian anthropologist,
  34
Kozyrev, Andrei, 147
Kraslava, 28, 131, 305–306
Kunaev, Dinmukhamed, first secretary
  of the Kazak Communist party, 161,
  169

Kuper, Leo, 282, 284
Kurakina, T., 143
Kurzeme, 21, 63, 104–105, 245, 260,
    277–278
Kyrgyz, 24, 30, 36, 311

Labor Code in Latvia, 114
Lad, Slavic Movement in Kazakstan,
    161, 173–174, 176, 217, 219, 286,
    307
Laitin, David, D., American political
    scientist, 20, 24, 40, 125–126, 248–
    250, 285, 287, 290, 302
Lange, Falk, 90
Language Commission in Latvia, 111
Latgalians, 21, 28, 37–38
Latvian Association of Russian
    Societies, 144
Latvian Association of Russian-
    Language Teachers, 126
Latvian Centre of Social Research, 136
Latvian Committee for Human Rights,
    124
Latvian Human Rights Committee, 144
Latvian Popular Front, 64, 81–84, 86,
    100, 143, 145
Latvian Scientific Council, 87
Latvian society of Russian culture,
    125–126
Latvian Supreme Soviet/ Latvian
    Supreme Council, 75, 79–80, 83, 86,
    90–91, 101, 111, 146
Latvian Way Party, 86, 105, 107
Latviets, 236–237
Law on changes of names and
    nationality in Latvia, 78
Law on Citizenship, in Kazakstan,
    159, 175
Law on Citizenship, in Latvia, 91
Law on Cultural Autonomy in Latvia,
    75, 77
Law on Education, in Latvia, 122–124
Law on Elections, in Kazakstan, 202
Law on Elections, in Latvia, 113
Law on Minority Schools, in Latvia,
    121
Law on the Languages of the Kazak
    SSR, 178
Law on the Status of Former Citizens
    of the USSR who do not have

Citizenship of Latvia or of Any
    other State, 77
League of Nations, 64
Leningrad, 67
Levits, Egils, 101
Lewis, Robert, A, 59, 308
Lieven, Anatole, British journalist,
    136
Lijphart, Arend, Dutch political
    scientist, 50–51, 282, 284–286, 288–
    289
Lithuania, 20, 29, 36, 68, 92, 96, 116
Lithuanians,
    in Latvia, 24, 35, 64, 69, 70, 72, 95,
        108, 132, 229, 230, 238, 253, 270,
        278
    in the Soviet Union, 29
Livs, 24, 69, 76, 78, 92, 101, 292
LNNK (MNIL), Latvian National
    Independence Movement, 81, 83,
    105, 108, 291
Loginova, Natal'ia, deputy director of
    the Kazakstani state committee on
    nationality policies, 311
LORK, Latvian Society of Russian
    Culture , 143
Luckmann, Thomas, 15
Lustick, Ian, 288–290
Lutheranism, 19

Malaysia, 12–13, 289, 291, 293–295,
    307
mankurts, 30, 300
Masanov, Nurbulat, Kazakh
    researcher, 23, 28, 160, 183, 193,
    200, 205, 206, 223
Mashanov, M., 201, 202
maslikhats, organs of local government
    in Kazakstan, 194, 201, 207, 208,
    211, 225, 298
Mauzy, Diane, 290, 294
Mazhilis, lower house in the
    Kazakstani parliament, 200, 286
Melberg, Hans O., vii, 227
Melvin, Neil, British researcher, 23,
    25, 38, 302
Meskhetian Turks, 161, 213, 219
Mezgailis, Bruno, 66, 133
Mezs, Ilmars, Latvian demographer,
    65–66, 71, 122

migration, 22, 27, 58
  in Kazakstan, 157–162, 308– 310,
    312
  in Latvia, 68, 69, 70, 72, 73
Mill, John, Stuart, 48, 49, 51
Milne, R.S., 6, 12–13, 289–295, 307
Ministry of Education in Kazakstan,
  184
Ministry of Education in Latvia, 80,
  121, 124, 132
minorities, ethnic, 7
  and democracy, 281
  and linguistic culture, 2
  and nation-builing, 2, 45, 283
  and perceptions, 227–232
  and political representation, 9, 11
  and social integration, 48, 50, 51,
    266, 267, 271, 300, 301
  in Kazakstan, 24, 25, 195, 199, 201,
    204, 206, 214, 237, 286
  in Latvia, 33, 66, 77, 80, 81, 85, 95,
    98, 103, 116, 117, 121, 126, 132,
    141, 305
  in Malaysia, 292
minority cultures, 49, 305
Misiunas, Romuldas, J., Lithuanian
  researcher, 67
mixed marriages, ethnically mixed
  families, 16, 34, 36, 37, 77, 98, 108,
    131, 252, 300
MNIL (LNNK), Latvian National
  Independence Movement, 81, 83,
    105, 108, 291
Moldova, 6, 36
Moroni, Federica, 42
mother tongue, 23, 24, 29, 33, 248
  in Latvia, 108, 126, 131
  in Kazakstan, 182, 195, 213
Motyl, Alexander, J., American
  political scientist, 60
Movement for National Independence,
  72
Movement for the National
  Independence of Latvia, MNIL
  (LNNK), 81, 83, 105, 108, 291
Muiznieks, Nils, R., Latvian
  researcher, 101–102, 133, 141
Multicultural center in Daugavpils,
  305
multinational state, 1, 4, 51, 58, 60

Nahaylo, Bohdan, British researcher,
  58
Nairn, Tom, British historian, 46
National Congress of Kazakstan, 215
national identity, 16, 59, 76, 141, 164
NATO, 148, 298
Naturalization Authority in Latvia,
  93
Naturalization, in Latvia, 91–93
Nazarbaev, Nursultan, president of
  Kazakstan, 7, 25, 40–41, 164–167,
    170–171, 188, 198, 200– 201, 204,
    211–212, 218–221, 236, 286, 292,
    306–307, 309
Neumann, Iver B., Norwegian political
  scientist, 42
New Baltic Barometer survey, 141
New Generation (*Novoe Pokolenie*),
  political movement in Kazakstan,
    181, 189–190, 217, 300
Nikitin, Gennadii , 219
Novoe Pokolenie , see New Generation
Nørgaard, Ole, Danish political
  scientist, 103

Odnoobshchinnoe gosudarstvo (one-
  community state), 9, 83
Official registration of ethnicity,
  in the Soviet Union, 17
  in Kazakstan, 191, 301
  in Latvia, 77–79. 301
Olcott, Martha, Brill, American
  political scientist, 22, 158, 159, 209
OMON, Soviet internal ministry forces,
  90, 146
Opalski, Magda, Canadian researcher,
  98, 293
Organization of Unrepresented
  peoples, 82
Orthodoxy,
  Russian, 19, 21, 36, 42
  Jewish, 296
OSCE High Commissioner for National
  Minorities, 91, 94, 231, 298
OSCE, Organization for Security and
  Cooperation in Europe, 90, 94, 199,
    231, 298
Ospanov, Marat, speaker of the
  Mazhilis, the lower house in the

Kazakstani parliament, 182, 200, 203

Palace of Peter the Great in Riga, 149
Pantelejevs, Andrejs, Latvian politician, 86
Party of National Unity of Kazakstan, 215
Party of Russian Citizens of Latvia, 104
passport system,
in Kazakstan, 156, 191
in Latvia, 77
in the Soviet Union, 16, 17
Pavlodar television, 38
Pavlovich, Matthews, 40
Pearson, Raymond, 56
Perestroika, 5, 11, 64, 72, 108, 142, 163, 203, 297
Peruashev, A.T., Kazakstani researcher, 24–25
Peteris, Janis, ambassador of Latvia to Russia, 133
Petersone, Baiba, advisor to the Minister of Education in Latvia, 84, 125
Pettai, Vello, Estonian political scientist, 7, 90, 295
Pipes, Richard, American historian, 30, 56
Plural societies, 50, 282, 288
PNKK, National Congress of Kazakstan Party, 215, 218
Poland, 63, 131, 222
Poles,
in Latvia, 21, 64, 69, 70, 79, 95, 132, 229– 231, 253, 254, 270, 306
in Kazakstan, 24, 161, 167, 172, 176, 177, 213, 219, 220, 306
in Lithuania, 29
Politburo of the CPSU, 58
Political loyalty, 2
Political participation, 9, 10, 44, 103–108, 191–213
Political representation, 10, 99–102, 198–204, 271
Ponomarenko, Lev, Soviet politician, 39
Popular Concord Party in Latvia, 103, 105, 107

Popular Front of Latvia, 64, 81–84, 86, 100, 143, 145
Population growth, 68–74, 157–161, 312
Poulsen, J.J., 87, 150
Premdas, Ralph, R., 294
Privatization, 74, 148
Proftsentr, independent labor union in Kazakstan, 218
propiska, Soviet official residence permit, 68

Rabushka, Alvin, 18
Razukas, Romualdas , chairman of the Popular Front of Latvia, 81
Regulations on the Use of the State Language in Appellations and Information in Latvia, 112
Renan, Ernest, 59, 171
Resolution on the Restoration of the Body of Citizens and on the Main Principles of Naturalization, in Latvia, 91, 143
Rezekne, 28, 37, 38, 131
Ribbentrop-Molotov pact, 64
Ro'i, Yaacov, 19
Rokkan, Stein, Norwegian political scientist, 45, 55
ROL, The Russian Community of Latvia, 143
Roma, 24, 69, 70, 76, 95, 108, 131, 132
Romanov dynasty, 56
Rose, Richard, British political scientist, 33, 87, 136, 141, 145, 151
Rotar, Igor, 22
Rules for State Financing of Private Schools in Latvia, 123
Russia,
as "external homeland" of Russians, 7, 54, 164, 173, 238–240
and Kazakstan, 21–22, 42, 206, 315
and Latvia, 63–65, 152
migration to, 74, 150, 176, 216
religion in, 19
travel to, 93–94, 96, 177
involvement in Latvian politics, 127, 145–149, 315
business with Latvia, 133
attitudes towards 140–141, 202

(continues)

Russia, *(continued)*
Russians in Russia contrasted to
Russians in Latvia and Kazakstan,
258–261, 264–265, 272
Russian Cultural Autonomy
Association, 144
Russian Latvians, 30
Russian Parliament, 91, 147
Rutkis, J., 66–67
Rwanda, 3–4, 289

Sabikenov, S., 61
Saeima, Latvian parliament,
5th Saeima, 86, 91–92, 99, 101
6th Saeima, 75, 86, 99, 101, 103, 107,
124
Sajudis, Lithuanian popular front, 83
Sarsenov, Nurdaulet, 210
Satversme, The Latvian constitution of
1922, 75
Schermerhorn, R.A., his theory of
integration, 8, 13, 52–54, 150, 227,
274, 289, 314
Second language, 125, 126, 268
Semipalatinsk, 40, 173, 182, 186–187,
193, 197, 212, 216–217, 242– 243,
254, 256, 260, 275, 294, 307, 311
Shaikenov, Nagashbai , first deputy
prime minister in Kazakstan, 286
Shanin, Theodor, British historian, 56
Shibutani, Tamotsu, 50
Shparaga, G., 194–196
Silver, Brian, D., American
demographer, 17, 36
Simon, Gerhard, German historian, 57
Sisk, Timothy, D., 4, 5
Skujenieks, M., 65
Slavic Movement Lad in Kazakstan,
161, 173–174, 176, 217, 219, 286,
307
Slavs, 19, 35–38, 230
in Kazakstan, 24, 27, 33, 197
in Latvia, 33, 41, 64
in the Soviet Union, 58
Slezkine, Yuri, 17, 57
Smagulova, U., 159
Small Assembly of the Peoples of
Kazakstan, 211, 220
Smith, Anthony, D., British political
scientist, 15, 47, 59

Smith, Graham, British geographer, 33,
152, 297, 313
Smith, G.M., 282
Smooha, Sammy, Israeli political
scientist, 296–297
Snyder, Jack, American political
scientist, 60–61
Social cleavages, 45
Social mobilization, 49, 51
Socialist Party of Latvia, 105
Socialist Party of Kazakstan, 216
Solomin, Leonid, leader of *Birlesu*
independent labor movement in
Kazakstan, 218
Soviet Army, 67, 92
Spengler, Oswald, 309
Sri Lanka, 3, 4
stability, political, 5, 7, 13, 205, 215,
281, 282, 284, 288, 291, 295, 298,
299, 312
Stalin, Joseph, 24, 39, 58, 177
Stalinism, 82, 157, 176
starozhily, 26
State Bureau on Human Rights in
Latvia, 117
State Duma, Russia, 147
State Language Center in Latvia, 112,
115, 117
State Language Inspectorate in Latvia,
113
Steen, Anton, Norwegian political
scientist, 102, 297, 313
Stereotypes, 11, 133, 234, 264
Steshenko, Vladimir, Director of the
Department of nationalities in
Latvia, 82–83
Stolypin, Petr, Russian prime minister
28, 158
Strayer, Joseph, R., 55
Sugar, Peter F., 56
Suny, Ronald, Grigor, American
historian, 57
Supreme Council of Latvia, 145
Susokolov, A.A, Russian
anthropologist, 36
Svoik, Petr, vice-chairman of the
Socialist Party of Kazakstan, 216

Tajiks, 24
Tallinn, 146

Tanzania, 2, 316
Tatars, 19, 35, 36, 187, 220, 230, 240,
    248, 251, 259, 269, 277
Tatimov, Makash, Kazak
    demographer, 158, 162, 309, 310
Teutonic knights, 63
Tilly, Charles, Americal political
    scientistk, 44, 283
Tishkov, Valery, Russian
    anthropologist, 6
Titma, Mikk, Estonian political
    scientist, 59
Tomasuns, A., 128
Tsilevich, Boris, Latvian researcher,
    27, 63, 90, 98, 100, 105, 287, 293,
    297, 305–306, 308
Tuma, Nancy, B., 59
Türkiye Cumhuryieti, cultural society
    of Turks in Kazakstan, 177, 222
Tutsi, 289

Uighurs, 185, 202, 209, 220–221
Ukraine, 7, 16, 36–38, 74, 96, 249, 302
Ukrainians, 23–25, 29, 33, 35–37, 229–
    230, 237, 239–240, 251–252,
    253–254, 258, 268–270, 277, 278
    in Kazakstan, 164, 167, 187, 202,
    213, 306, 310
    in Latvia, 64, 69, 70, 76, 77, 85, 95,
    108, 126
    in the Soviet Union, 16
Ulmanis, Guntis, Latvian president,
    79, 92, 143
Ulmanis, Karl, Latvian president,
    66
United Nations, 147
Urbanovish, Janis, member of the
    Saeima, 84
Ust-Kamengorsk, 40, 173–174, 182,
    195, 293, 311
Ustinova, Mara, 100
Usun, legendary forefather of Great
    Horde, 216
Uzbekistan, 19–20, 206, 224

Vaivads, Janis, Latvian, minister of
    education, 124
van der Stoel, Max, The OSCE High
    Commissioner on National
    Minorities , 91, 94, 231, 298

Vasil'eva, Ol'ga, Russian researcher,
    24
Vebers, Elmars, Latvian sociologist,
    62, 82, 305, 306
Ventspils, 67, 100, 131
Vidzeme, 21, 63, 104, 129, 244, 245,
    260, 277, 278
Vilnius, 146
violence, 3– 5, 13, 150, 213, 225, 288,
    290, 310
Vitebsk, 63
Vitola, Mirdza , vice chairman of the
    Movement for the National
    Independence of Latvia, 81
Volkovs, Vladislavs, 74

Weekendavisen,   87, 150
Welt, Cory, American political
    scientist, 38, 309–310
Wiez, Union of Polish centers in
    Kazakstan, 222
World Kurultay (Congress) of Kazaks,
    170
World War I, 10, 27, 56, 65–66, 72,
    104, 176, 230, 284, 307,
World War II, 10, 27, 66, 72, 104, 176,
    230, 284, 307

Xinjiang, 206, 209, 220, 240

Yeltsin, Boris, 145–148, 173
Yugoslavia, 16

Zarins, Vilnis, Latvian philosopher, 85
Zaslavsky, Victor, 16, 57
Zepa, Brigita, Latvian sociologist, 74,
    88, 139–140
"Zero option" of citizenship legislation,
    10, 83, 85–87, 94, 175
Zheltoqsan, nationalist movement in
    Kazakstan, 216–217, 291
Zhirinovskii, Vladimir, , 147
zhuz, 21–23, 28, 37, 195, 206, 212, 299,
    311
"Zigerist's Party" (The popular
    movement Latvia), 107
Zimanov, S.Z., Soviet geographer , 171

Østerud, Øyvind, Norwegian political
    scientist, 44